# Re-Envisioning Gl Development



*Re-Envisioning Global Development* elaborates an alternative ontology and way of thinking about global development during recent centuries – one linked, not to nations and regions, but to a set of essentially transnational relations and connections. This angle of vision provides the basis for an original perspective on capitalist development from its origins to the present day.

Most approaches to understanding contemporary development assume that industrial capitalism was achieved through a process of nationally organised economic growth, and that in recent years its organisation has become increasingly trans-local or global. However, Halperin shows that nationally organised economic growth has rarely been the case – it has only recently come to characterise a few countries and for only a few decades.

Halperin argues that capitalist development has, everywhere and from the start, involved – not whole nations or societies – but only sectors or geographical areas within states. By bringing this aspect of historically 'normal' capitalist development into clearer focus, the book clarifies the specific conditions and circumstances that enabled European economies to pursue a more broad-based development following World War II, and what prevented a similar outcome in the contemporary 'third world'. It also clarifies the nature, spatial extent and circumstances of current globalising trends.

Wide-ranging and provocative, this innovative text is required reading for advanced level students and scholars in development studies, development economics and political science.

**Sandra Halperin** is Professor of International Relations and Co-Director of the Centre for Global and Transnational Politics at Royal Holloway, University of London. Her research interests include global development and the historical sociology of global relations.

# Critical Issues in Global Politics

This series engages with the most significant issues in contemporary global politics. Each text is written by a leading scholar and provides a short, accessible and stimulating overview of the issue for advanced undergraduates and graduate students of international relations and global politics. As well as providing a survey of the field, the books also contain original and groundbreaking thinking which will drive forward debates on these key issues.

1. **Global Ethics**
   Anarchy, freedom and International Relations
   *Mervyn Frost*

2. **International Statebuilding**
   The rise of post-liberal governance
   *David Chandler*

3. **Governmentality**
   Critical encounters
   *William Walters*

4. **Re-Envisioning Global Development**
   A horizontal perspective
   *Sandra Halperin*

# Re-Envisioning Global Development

## A horizontal perspective

**Sandra Halperin**

Dear Norma!
With all best
wishes –
Sandra

Routledge
Taylor & Francis Group
LONDON AND NEW YORK

First published 2013
by Routledge
2 Park Square, Milton Park, Abingdon, Oxon OX14 4RN

Simultaneously published in the USA and Canada
by Routledge
711 Third Avenue, New York, NY 10017

*Routledge is an imprint of the Taylor & Francis Group, an informa business*



*British Library Cataloguing in Publication Data*
A catalogue record for this book is available from the British Library

*Library of Congress Cataloging in Publication Data*
Halperin, Sandra.
Re-envisioning global development : a horizontal perspective /
Sandra Halperin.
pages cm. – (Critical issues in global politics ; 4)
Includes bibliographical references and index.
1. Economic history. 2. Economic development–History.
3. Capitalism–History. I. Title.
HC51.H35 2013
338.9–dc23
2012039850

ISBN: 978–0–415–46765–0 (hbk)
ISBN: 978–0–415–46766–7 (pbk)
ISBN: 978–0–203–62903–1 (ebk)

Typeset in Times New Roman
by Swales & Willis Ltd, Exeter, Devon

MIX
Paper from
responsible sources
FSC® C018575
FSC
www.fsc.org

Printed and bound in Great Britain by MPG Printgroup

**For Bill**

# Contents

# Tables and figures

## Tables

## Figures

# Preface

This book emerged from an exploration into structures of social power and their reproduction in different regions of the world: since the frames that localize human interactions are constantly 'erased by networks going over in all directions' (Latour 1996: 238), an exploration of social power, if pursued long enough, is bound to lead to reflection on the nature and history of global development.

The book begins by setting aside the notion of a world 'vertically' divided by bounded national entities and binary divisions of the globe. Instead, it treats these as secondary phenomena arising from the properties of trans-local/cross-regional structures and relations that have underpinned global development continuously for many centuries. Adopting this 'horizontal' angle of vision forces us to read history 'against the grain' of dominant historiographic conventions; and the re-envisioning of global development, or 'gestalt shift', that this produces enables us to place issues of structural consequence in a new light.

The book traces key periods of transition and supposed disjuncture that were shaped by, and that worked to extend and reproduce, trans-local/cross-regional structures of power. While the general terrain it traverses will be familiar to students of world history, the angle of vision it adopts makes visible features that existing accounts tend to obscure. So, for instance, it places globalization at the beginning, rather than near the end, of the story of the development and expansion of capitalism. Studies of globalization describe global capitalism and transnational class formation as relatively recent phenomena. But capitalism has been essentially transnational from the start. It has been characterized, not by processes centred on empires and nation states, but by trans-local structures of social power; and by interactions and connections involving, not whole societies, but interdependent centres of elite accumulation across the world. It is not nation states, but cities and urban-based export centres that fuelled the expansion, and became integrated into the domain, of capital; nation states and national markets emerged only after World War II and only, briefly, in a few countries.

The story of the 'rise' of Europe that this book tells emphasizes the gradual integration of Europeans into a prosperous, sophisticated and already expanding Afro-Eurasian system of trade and intercultural exchange. The rise to power of Europe within this system is slower and more difficult, and remains far less complete, than is usually assumed. Typically, accounts emphasize Europe's discovery of a backward 'new' world to its west; and either they overlook its discovery of the wondrous achievements of the afro-Eurasian system, or they airbrush them out of history with the preposterous claim that Europe discovered a stagnant and dissolute world to its east.

As capitalism expands it is characterized, not by the formation of a global core and periphery, but by the interdependent and synchronous growth of sites of elite accumulation across Afro-Eurasia and the Americas. In the nineteenth century this regime of accumulation was consolidated and maintained by an imperial order that was far more cooperative, and distributed its benefits far more widely, than many scholars recognize or have been willing to acknowledge. The imperial order never destroyed or displaced the wealth and the power of the east; these continued to grow and local elites continued to prosper. Airbrushing *this* out of the story of global development makes it difficult to understand the structures of power that today reproduce so-called 'underdevelopment' in the contemporary 'third world'. The nineteenth century regime of accumulation survived decolonization and the nationalization of capital in the 'first' and 'second' worlds after World War II. Evidence of its durability is provided by the 'new' transnational capitalist class that increasing numbers of scholars are wrongly depicting as newly emerging.

The account that this book presents emphasizes the existence of a transnational elite that straddles international frontiers, rather than a vertical view of whole nation states in interaction with each other.

Its aim is to show how existing research and writing on world history and development readily produces a 'gestalt shift'. The accounts which structure our thoughts and perceptions cause us to see one pattern rather than another. But, if we set aside the conventional structure of assumptions and stress different elements than are usually stressed, parts of the standard picture will form a different pattern, and so produce a different picture, than the one we usually see. By stressing transnational/cross-regional networks and structures our analytic focus on whole nations or regions dissolves and shifts, instead, to a horizontal set of connections, relations and processes. The aim is not to ignore national boundaries and binary divisions of the globe, but to contextualize them.

This is a work of aggregation and synthesis. It draws together insights from a variety of perspectives in order to facilitate explorations already under way. The aim is to pose questions, rather than to assert answers, to invite a dialectical engagement between the specialized knowledges produced within regional studies and the general propositions that are here being advanced.

Thus, I dispense with the usual list of acknowledgments, as the debt of gratitude I owe is to the many scholars whose work inspired, and is cited throughout, what follows. I must, however, single out Philip McMichael for special thanks; for without his encouragement and great generosity this book might never have been written, though I, of course, retain sole responsibility for its shortcomings.

It is with great thanks for sharing the journey that I dedicate this book to William Gray.

# 1 Global development

## Introduction: The 'Victorian Edifice' of conventional European historiography

This is an inquiry into the nature and causes of 'global development'. 'Global development' refers to social changes across large areas of the world which appear to be linked to interactions and connections among different regions of the globe and to follow rhythms and flow from broadly similar causal foundations. This book describes its nature as reflecting a *horizontal* set of connections, relations and processes among elites and wealth-owners around the world; it explains its causation as located in a recurring social logic of elite reproduction.

The study of global change is not new. A global vision is evident in the work of Herodotus. It can be seen throughout the centuries in the striving of scholars to identify broad patterns of human development across cultures and within the whole record of human achievements. However, there was a critical point in the more recent past at which 'we seem to have taken a wrong turn' in our understanding of global development. That point, as Eric Wolf has noted, is identifiable: it occurred in the middle of the nineteenth century, when the varieties of human experience were conceptualized as taking place within 'separate, narrowly-conceived spheres of social action' (Wolf 1982: 7), and in a world divided into separate, culturally distinctive, nationally bounded societies.[1]

While nineteenth-century social scientists were developing these analytic conventions (which became, in the twentieth century, the basis for social science disciplines and inquiry), they were also at work producing what the historian William McNeill calls the 'Victorian Edifice' of conventional European historiography (McNeill 1974: 3).[2] This involved a writing project whose purpose, it would seem, was to refashion then-popular ideologies of Western superiority and progress in Europe into a durable and imposing historiographic tradition. The historiographic edifice that emerged was structured around a central theme: how the rise of Europe and the birth of modernity defined a radical disjuncture and discontinuity in world history.

As McNeill notes, the inspiring tale of European modernity and human progress that it told ceased to be convincing after the horrors of World War I. However, beginning in the 1950s, theorists of 'development' in the United States, working within its basic structures but with new techniques and generous funding from the United States government (see Chapter 7), refurbished the edifice to highlight capitalism and nation states as key features of western modernity and the goal towards which all humankind was moving.[3]

Before the Victorian Edifice came to dominate historical thinking, European observers had written prolifically about what they had considered to be the most characteristic aspects of their time: domination, exploitation, uneven development, inequality, political instability, and authoritarianism. These had been the principal foci of the narratives and analyses of countless social scientists and reformers; the speeches, official documents and reports, and other writings of European statesmen; and the work of Europe's greatest literary figures.

Processes of capitalist development and the consolidation of nation states had cast large numbers of Europeans and other populations into an 'abyss of human degradation', as Karl Polanyi so compellingly phrased it (Polanyi 1944: 39) and as so many records of the time had convincingly shown. These processes had culminated in two global wars and, in a further extension of industrial technology, the extermination of millions of people in a truly modern, European 'holocaust'. But in the historical accounts that became the basis of theories of development, all these aspects of Europe's development, all the elements that for European observers had revealed its intrinsic costs and engendered pessimism and doubt about capitalism and industrialization,[4] recede into the background. Instead, industrial capitalism is depicted as steadily diffusing wealth, and gradually, but inevitably, spreading equality and liberty into increasingly wider domains. It is a reassuring tale of progress unimpeded by power and privilege, suffering, division, and struggle.[5]

Refurbished to serve as housing for the story of capitalist development, the Edifice survived. It was still standing in 1974 when, with a touch of incredulity, William McNeill noted that, despite its 'leaky' roof and 'deplorable' plumbing it continued to give shape to what we chose to emphasize 'amidst all the buzzing confusion' of the past.[6] Some 40 years after McNeill wrote those words and despite the growing number of scholars who reject its euro-centrism and themes of disjuncture and discontinuity, and who seek to re-centre global history on interactions and encounters in which humanity as a whole participated, the Edifice still stands.[7] Recent decades have produced an array of neo-Marxist and world systems, post-colonial and subaltern perspectives on global development; and rich histories of the world and of its different regions explored in a global context. But the Edifice still stands, obstructing our vision of the global terrain and distorting our apprehension of its basic contours. McNeill suggests that the Edifice endures because of 'the absence of any alternative housing'. Perhaps this is why, despite abundant evidence of its defects, we continue to toil away beneath its leaky roof. If so, what is needed is to break decisively with its assumptions and habits of thought, relocate to a different plot, and build on new foundations.

Much research and writing is concerned to do just this. But, because the national frame and other elements of the Victorian historiographic tradition have so significantly shaped existing sources, it is difficult to find in them the materials from which to develop an alternative ontology and history of the world. What we need, then, is a strategy that will enable us to do two things: to transcend this historiographic tradition and to develop a non-national ontology sturdy enough to support a global analysis of modern development.

This chapter suggests how elements drawn from existing development theories and recent research and writing on global history can be combined to produce a 'gestalt shift'. What this shift enables us to see is a world in which the interactions of interdependent cities are ontologically primary, and national societies appear as secondary phenomena arising from and reflecting their properties.[8] The modern world history it enables us to construct focuses not on Europe and highlights of 'European history', but on the emergence of dynamic focal points of growth throughout the world as a result of Afro-Eurasian and, eventually, global processes of interaction and expansion, and the urban-based system of networks that these produced and through which capitalism and processes of industrial production develop.

This chapter first highlights some weaknesses of the Victorian edifice – the 'leaky roof', the 'deplorable plumbing' (Section I). It then discusses efforts to repair these (Section II). Finally, it suggests how, rather than filing in gaps and repairing faults, we might build on new foundations (Section III).

## I. Global development as western modernity: Foundation myths

Histories of the world written by nineteenth-century Europeans defined a radical contrast between Europe (the 'West') and Asia (the 'East'),[9] and characterized the rise of the 'West' as representing a disjuncture and discontinuity in world history. They described a Europe radically cut off from other cultures, and explained its rise as the result of dynamic developments within Europe itself: world-historical 'revolutions' in science and technology, agricultural and commercial practices, intellectual life, and social and political institutions. These advances enabled Europeans to navigate the oceans and, inspired by a spirit of discovery, to embark on a series of voyages that revealed a primitive and backward 'new' world (the Americas) to their west; and a now stagnant and dissolute 'old' one to their East. Europeans had found that when – as a result of – revolutions and discoveries – the 'lights went on' again in Europe (following what thereafter was to be called 'the dark ages'), they had yet to come on in the lands to its west, and had long gone out in the world to its east.

This is a startlingly audacious fiction. When the 'lights went on' in Europe, they were, and had long been, shining brightly throughout the vast, prosperous Asian-based system of economic and cultural interconnection and exchange that, at that time, stretched from western and southern Europe through the Middle East to China; a system to which Europe was a mere 'appendage', struggling to find something to trade for the Moslem, Indian, and Chinese silks and other textiles, spices and aromatics, timber, metals, and ceramics that it coveted. In the sixteenth century, Europe's exploits in the Americas gave it, for the first time, a range of goods for export to the east. With precious metals of the New World and ocean-going ships originally developed for their own coastal trade (and later used to search for a quicker, westward route to the riches of the East) Western Europeans began to seize control of the great highways of international exchange that linked this system together – analogous, as Gunder Frank pointed out, to the seizure by the Mongol hordes of the trade routes of the Silk Road in the thirteenth century (Frank 1998: 256).

Processes of global diffusion and integration moved, not from west to east, but from east to west. The West was born from within the East and long remained its child. Even after Europeans seized the prosperous trade routes, markets, and industries of the East, European developments – modes of production, urbanization, class structures, and systems of spatial exchange – continued to reflect developments elsewhere in the world. Europe's coercive entry and eventual integration into Afro-Eurasian networks changed the scale and geography of exchange networks, but they did not destroy or displace them. Until well into the nineteenth century, the volume of exchanges continued to remain greatest in East Asia, with trade flows between Chinese, Indians, Japanese, Siamese, Javanese and Arabs remaining much greater than those within Europe, and Europe and the Americas playing a minor role overall, centred mainly on the triangular transatlantic trade.

### *European expansion*

The rise of Europe was accompanied by the most destructive military expansion in human history. It continued the brutal and bloody expansion that had taken place in Europe itself during the eleventh, twelfth, and thirteenth centuries, when a conquering military aristocracy from Western Europe established conquest states and colonial societies throughout the region. The establishment of these states and colonies, in Greece, Andalusia, Ulster, and Prussia, had been mythologized 'as a founding moment and a defining breach in time' between pre-conquest barbarism and post-conquest progress

(Bartlett 1993: 92). This mythology of disjuncture and difference was used by those who settled in the newly conquered and colonized parts of Europe to invalidate pre-conquest legal and other claims to possessions and privileges, and to authorise a new definition of property rights in the conquered areas.

In the eleventh century, conquering Western European elites began to establish colonial bridgeheads and bastions outside of Europe. From the beginning of this European expansion, observers noted the conquerors' appetite for domination and for 'a new cruelty, brutality and bloodthirstiness' (Bartlett 1993: 86).[10] By the latter half of the eleventh century, a dense network of Italian trading and settlement was being developed by 'aggressive merchants-cum-pirates-cum-crusaders' trading in large ports (e.g., Constantinople and Alexandria), plundering (e.g. in al-Mahdiyyah in North Africa) or trying to establish crusading principalities (e.g., in Antioch and Lattakieh) (Bartlett 1993: 183).

By the sixteenth century, changes in the conduct of warfare and advances in military technology had enabled the European military expansion to extend into the lucrative Asian trade system. Europeans, using armed ships and through predatory acquisitions, established domination over societies that were more developed, technologically and institutionally, and more prosperous and 'civilized' than their own (Abu-Lughod 1989: 5). Portuguese men-of-war operated in the heartland of the Asian system, burning or boarding ships and confiscating the cargoes of indigenous and unarmed merchant fleets. Using the precious metals of the New World to invest in military organization, supplies, and shipping, Europe achieved by the end of the sixteenth century a worldwide military lead based on naval superiority.[11] As with European conquests in Europe itself, European conquests everywhere were mythologized as defining a disjuncture between pre-conquest darkness and emptiness and post-conquest enlightenment and progress (Bartlett 1993: 86).[12] Europe had expanded into parts of the world that, in every area other than naval weaponry and brutality, were superior to itself. Its domination rested on military advantages rather than on deep structural differences. However, ideas of European cultural and intellectual superiority propounded to provide ideological support for this campaign of conquest and domination would eventually produce a profoundly erroneous representation of these encounters. A key element in this representation was the notion that European discoveries and revolutions had enabled Europeans to move to the centre of global development and to lay the foundations of its future progress.

### *The European discoveries*

In order to maintain the notion that European domination was based, not on brutal conquest but on intellectual, cultural, and scientific superiority, the fiction developed that Europe had established domination over a dark and stagnant world. But what Europeans had actually discovered to their east were societies far in advance of the ones back home. They discovered in Islamic Andalusia a multiethnic, multilingual, religiously pluralistic state that fostered a culture of tolerance; and major centres both of commerce and culture in the Islamic cities of Constantinople, Alexandria, Cordoba, and Baghdad. These, at the time, were the largest cities in the world (along with Kaifeng, in China). They had paved streets, street lamps, sewage systems, freshwater systems provided by aqueducts, and businesses and stores that stayed open 24 hours a day (Menocal 2002). They discovered China, the world leader in technology, industry, and commerce, with thriving coal, steel, and armaments industries, and a market-regulated commerce carried out with massive sailing vessels (capable of carrying 1000 people) with pivoting sails and watertight compartments.

But these discoveries are not what the term 'European discoveries' alludes to in conventional European historiography. The term refers only to the 'barbaric' peoples to the west. Missing entirely is Europe's discovery of the prosperous, sophisticated East.

European voyages of discovery occurred in 'an age of travel, discovery, of geographical redefinition' throughout Eurasia (Subrahmanyam 1997: 737). They were part of a broader Eurasian expansionism that included 'the consolidation of Ming absolutism, the emergence of a new world power in the Ottoman Empire, the reunion of Iran under the Safavids, the rapid expansion of Islam into South East Asia, and the creation of a vast new Islamic Empire in North India (Darwins 2007:51). European historiography treats Europe's discovery of a 'New World' to the west as 'signalling the Birth of Modernity and the beginnings of a truly universal sensibility' (Subrahmanyam

1997: 749). But it was the advances in navigational techniques and geographical knowledge of the East – the achievements of generations of Chinese, South Asian, and Muslim seafarers, geographers, astronomers, and cartographers – that made them possible.[13] And it was not modernity that motivated Columbus on his westward voyage, but millenarianism, 'a view of the world which had as much in common with Franciscan apocalyptic thought of the medieval period as with Copernicus' (Subrahmanyam 1997: 749). The dynamism said to have led to the European discovery of the Americas, is also said to have driven the global networks of trade that linked up the world for the first time. However, the emergence of global trade was based, not on European initiatives, but on a worldwide silver trade driven by Chinese demand.

### *The European revolutions*

According to conventional European historiography, the foundations of modernity were laid by revolutionary transformations in Europe that occurred as a result of a series of advances – scientific, military, intellectual, commercial, agricultural, political, industrial, and technological – beginning in the seventeenth century. A sixteenth and seventeenth century 'secular revolution' was followed by a political revolution (in England) and the beginning of scientific, commercial, and military revolutions, which, together, helped to launch the eighteenth century intellectual revolution known as 'the Enlightenment'. The Enlightenment set in motion trends of thought that culminated in the eighteenth-century American and French revolutions and, coinciding with these, the beginning of the industrial revolution.

The European Enlightenment appears, in this account, as the product of endogenous cultural and intellectual developments. But it was influenced by Stoic ideas associated with the Hellenic world that had been influential for some 2000 years. Hellenic culture was a heritage shared by both Islamic and Christian civilizations, but it was Islamic empires, and not Europe, that rejuvenated it. Beginning in the eighth century, the Islamic Caliphate in Baghdad undertook a 'massive and systematic' translation into Arabic of ancient Greek scientific and philosophical texts. This was not a 'mechanical or curatorial effort to "preserve" the Greeks for posterity', but an effort to reintegrate the Hellenistic intellectual universe 'back into a living culture' (Menocal 2002: 205). Europeans later 'discovered' this legacy by translating it from Arabic into European languages.[14] European thinkers of the 'European Enlightenment' characterized this discovery as the rebirth (*renaissance*) of a specifically European intellectual tradition and legacy, one that had 'originated' from and then 'returned to' Europe (Subrahmanyam 1997: 737). In this formulation, the development of modern thought proceeded through a European trajectory running from Greece through classical Rome, the Middle Ages, and the Renaissance. But the cultural and intellectual materials that transformed European thought travelled to Europe via the world of Islam. Without the libraries of Islamic Spain, and centres of learning elsewhere in the Islamic world, Europe's *renaissance* would not have been possible (Chanda 2007: 205). What we call 'European Revolutions' represent the diffusion into northwest Europe of scientific, intellectual, technological, and industrial developments which originated in other areas of the world and to which Europeans appended modest changes. Along with Europe's voyages of discovery, these revolutions were characterized as defining a breach in time, a turning point in human history.

The advance of modernity is assumed to have taken another major step forward with the social revolutionary transformation said to have taken place as a result of Europe's industrial and French revolutions. There is a huge scholarly investment in the view that these revolutions changed everything. Subsequent chapters will argue that the French Revolution did not inaugurate the significant political and economic changes that are usually attributed to it; that, rather than representing a revolutionary break with the past, it marked the beginning of processes that were slow, bloody, and finally culminated in two world wars. Perhaps its most significant outcome was to instil such a horror of revolution into the hearts and minds of elites everywhere that even those who adopted industrial technologies used them throughout the next two centuries to engineer 'the slowest possible pace of change' (Wallerstein 1990: 125; more on this in Chapter 3, below).

As for the Industrial Revolution, historians have challenged the notion that the period to which we apply this term represented a radical break with the past (Cameron 1981, 1985; Fores 1981;

North 1981: 162). In 1914, on the eve of another 'Great War', Europe was still 'pre-eminently pre-industrial' (Mayer 1981: 187). Britain had actually experienced only gradual industrialization (Crafts 1985; Harley 1982) while in Europe as a whole agriculture was still the single largest and weightiest economic sector. Central Europe had not yet begun its industrial take-off; Eastern and Southern Europe had neither developed industrially nor moved significantly into agricultural exports. In 1914, most of Europe was still rural, and most of rural Europe had not changed substantially since the Middle Ages. In fact, on the eve of World War I, Europe as a whole had achieved a level of economic wellbeing about equal with that of Latin America (Halperin 2004, 1997).

A key aim of the historiographic edifice constructed in nineteenth-century Europe was to define a radical contrast between Europe and the rest of the world; to convert the history of Europe's five centuries of militarized expansion, conquest, and control into a story of the European origins of 'modernity' and the advance of progress and freedom, first in Europe and then, under European influence, in other portions of the globe. The story it tells is that, by the late eighteenth century, as a result of technological, scientific, and intellectual developments, Europe had achieved a level of civilization that made possible world-historical democratic and industrial revolutions. After World War II, the sharp division that opened up at that time between what came to be called the 'advanced industrial world' and the 'third world', would be characterized by theorists of 'development' as a further evolution of this process. But neither the expansion nor the discoveries of Europe, nor its intellectual, political or industrial revolutions, had caused European development to diverge significantly from what was occuring in other parts of the world. The notion of a division between a developed and a developing world emerged after 1945 precisely because it was only *then* that this developmental divergence occurred. Placing Europe's decisive advance a century and a half earlier than it actually happened airbrushes out of *history* the social revolution that transformed Europe and out of *theory* the importance of social revolution for the achievement of broad-based prosperity and democracy.

## II. Post-World War II 'development' theory: variations on the themes of western modernity and national development

'Development' is a relatively new notion. It emerged in the United States after 1945 to refer to national economic growth and in association with a key American foreign-policy concern: how to shape the future of the newly 'independent' states in ways that would ensure they would not be drawn into the Soviet communist bloc. It was this concern that motivated the United States government to enlist its social scientists to study capitalist economic development and political stability and devise ways to promote these in what was termed the 'developing world' (see Chapter 7).

'Development theory' refers to the research and writing that resulted from this effort. It engaged the theme of disjuncture and modernity elaborated in the writings of nineteenth-century European political theorists and historians and amplified it with a view of a world divided between a set of advanced industrial capitalist countries, and a far larger set of 'developing' societies that had not yet achieved this modernity. As is often noted, the basic blueprint for early development theories was Walter Rostow's book, *The Stages of Economic Growth: A Non-Communist Manifesto* (1960), which defined development (the conditions of life that had been achieved in 'the West'), not as a revolutionary social transformation (such as had occurred in advanced capitalist countries), but as a process involving a sequence of stages through which all societies must pass.

The study of development converged on a common set of analytic conventions and general themes. One was to conceive of 'development' as *national* growth,[15] and focus study on how whole, internally undifferentiated societies or states move from backwardness to modernity.[16] A second convention was to conceive of 'development' as specifically capitalist, but to have this remain an unspoken assumption. As Colin Leys observes, 'It was implicit that the development that was being discussed was not socialist'; but its capitalist character went unacknowledged: capitalist development was simply 'development' (Leys 1996: 11). Certainly, development theory neither drew on nor related itself to 'the existing body of theory about development that had been prompted by the original advent of capitalism', or the highly influential critiques of capitalism (like Marx's) that had emerged during the nineteenth century.[17] However, Walter Rostow did make this elision explicit in the subtitle of his book, *The Stages of Economic Growth: A Non-Communist Manifesto.* The book equated modernization with the standards of living of Western Europe and the United States. Analyses of capitalist development (a historical process) and the theorization of development outcomes contributed to the same examination of how these conditions were achieved. But 'development' need not be conceived of as capitalist development.

Rostow asserted that the path that had been traversed by today's advanced countries was one that must be followed by all countries seeking development. But the model he and others offered as a guide to 'developing' states was based on a highly ideological, profoundly erroneous account of European (and global) history. Among other things, this historical account ignored the more-or-less similar global development that had taken place up until the world wars of the twentieth century. It also ignored the social revolutionary changes that had occurred as a result of these wars and that had defined a division between 'advanced' and 'developing' countries.

## *Core and periphery*

Modernization theory claimed that, once developing societies come into contact with those of Western Europe and North America they would be impelled toward modernization and, after passing through a sequence of prescribed stages, would eventually achieve the economic, political, and social features characteristic of developed societies. However, by the 1960s it was apparent that the 'third world' was not passing through a stage of underdevelopment but was remaining underdeveloped. To explain this lack of progress, a 'structuralist' approach, developed by intellectuals brought together by the United Nations Economic Commission for Latin America (ECLA; today known as Economic Commission for Latin America and the Caribbean, ECLAC), advanced a counterclaim: that former colonies and non-industrialized nations were structurally different from industrialized countries, and, therefore, would need to develop along different lines. The basic argument was that colonization had restructured former colonies' economies so that they specialized in producing raw materials for export at low prices to the colonizers' home countries. These structures created a dynamic that was continuing to impoverish the former colonies and to thwart their modernization. ECLA argued that the international division of labour created by colonization had separated the international economy into a centre, consisting of the industrialized countries, and a periphery that included all other countries outside of the socialist camp. Because the prices of manufactured goods bought by the periphery were rising faster than those of the commodities – raw materials, cash crops and foodstuffs – sold by the periphery to the centre, international trade ensured the persistence of an unbalanced process of development. Thus, in contrast to modernization theory, which emphasized the benefits of free trade, foreign investment, and foreign aid, these theorists argued that free trade and international market relations occur in a framework of uneven relations between developed and underdeveloped countries and work to reinforce and reproduce these relations. This perspective formed the basis of what came to be known as 'dependency theory'.

Andre Gunder Frank articulated its main tenet: that colonialism created fundamental and interrelated structural distortions in the economies of third-world countries and that these were continuing to thwart development.[18] A key structural distortion and difference between 'Western' and contemporary third-world development is the coexistence of an advanced or modern sector with a backward or traditional sector (Amin 1976a; Cardoso & Falleto 1973; Dos Santos 1970; Frank 1972; Sunkel 1973). 'Dependency' describes a situation in which development is oriented to a restricted, limited elite-oriented type of market and society (Cardoso 1973), in which capital cannot find its essential dynamic component inside the system (Cardoso & Falletto 1979: xx). The foreign-oriented 'corporate' sector encompasses all capital-intensive enterprise, whether in industry or agriculture, as well as utilities, transport, and the civil service; but there is no investment beyond the enclave: profits are either reinvested there or exported, and improvements in technology do not diffuse outward to agriculture or to cottage industry. Thus, the economy as a whole is characterized by a lack of internal structural integration; the coexistence of an advanced or modern sector with a backward or traditional sector, the concomitant coexistence of pre-capitalist and capitalist relations of production, and dependency on outside capital, labour, and markets.

Dependency theorists drew an historical contrast between the foreign-oriented export sectors of colonial countries and the leading sectors in the industrializing countries in the West. In the West, leading sectors had been essentially indigenous and closely interwoven with the other sectors of the economy (e.g., cotton textiles in Britain's 'take-off' from 1783 to 1803, railroads in France from 1830 to 1860). Those of contemporary developing countries were imposed by external agents acting on behalf of the reproductive requirements of advanced capitalist economies and, consequently, remained largely alien to the other sectors and produced a sectorally uneven capitalist development that restricted the growth of the domestic economy.

But, in fact, the dualistic development that is found, with variations and in varying degrees, throughout the contemporary 'third world', was also characteristic of the development of today's advanced industrial countries until the twentieth century. Most European economies were dualistic before 1945. Development was organized, not to expand and integrate national societies and economies, but to link export sectors to each other along networks of elite exchange. Everywhere, modern industrial sectors oriented to and dependent on international markets formed enclaves within non-industrial mainly agricultural hinterlands. Great Britain, France, Italy, Germany, Spain, Portugal, the Austro-Hungarian Empire, Russia, Belgium, and much of the Balkans had a dynamic, foreign-oriented economic sector which failed to transform the rest of society. Most European countries adopted from abroad an already developed technology while retaining their 'traditional' social structure. All were dependent on foreign capital to finance growth: British capital in France and Belgium; British and French capital in Germany; French and German capital in Austria; and German capital in Sweden and other Scandinavian countries. Many countries in Europe, both in the east and in the west, were unable to diversify their exports or trading partners until well into the twentieth century. Nowhere in nineteenth-century Europe was a strong, independent, indigenous industrial capitalist bourgeoisie to be found. Development was financed by the state, by banks, and by foreign investment. As in the contemporary 'third world', in Europe alliances were forged between business and landed interests, for similar purposes, and with similar consequences for class structure and for national development. These alliances were so successful in preserving and reinforcing pre-industrial civil society that, on the eve of World War I, Europe was still largely 'agrarian, nobilitarian, and monarchic' (Mayer, 1981: 129).

The model constructed to describe and explain what is assumed to be an idiosyncratic dependent, dualistic development in three-quarters of the world (the 'third world') following World War II was, in fact, the 'European model'. It was a model developed in and for Europe and then adopted by elites in other areas of the world, who collaborated with Europeans to create another version of these same dualistic and oligarchic societies.

In Europe, the two world wars and their social revolutionary outcome brought to an end, for a time, the dualism that had characterized societies there since the eighteenth century. As already noted, most traditional accounts place Europe's post-1945 social revolutionary transformation a century and a half earlier than it actually occurred: in the French and industrial revolutions. Europe's dualistic system was not gradually displaced by the rise of the middle classes, urbanization and de-peasantization, and working-class opposition. It was destroyed within a short period of time and as a result of much violence and destruction. European economic history diverged decisively from that of the rest of the world only after 1945.

### *World systems theory*

During the 1970s, there emerged a theoretical enterprise known as 'world systems theory'. Its founding text was *The Modern World System,* published in 1974 by the American sociologist Immanuel Wallerstein. Based on a conception of capitalism advanced by the French historian, Fernand Braudel,[19] Wallerstein treats the entire world since the sixteenth century as a single capitalist world economy characterized by an international division of labour among a core (that developed originally in northwestern Europe); a periphery, and a semi-periphery (core regions in decline, e.g., Portugal and Spain, or peripheries attempting to improve their relative position in the world economy, e.g., Italy). The division of labour among these regions determines their type of labour conditions and political system: strong states and the predominance of wage labour characterize the core; weak states and coerced labour are found in the periphery;

and predominantly semi-coerced labour (sharecropping) in the semi-periphery.

The conceptualization of capitalism as a system based on a single, trade-induced, worldwide division of labour has generated much debate. One debate concerns the emphasis Wallerstein places on exchange (trade) relations as driving the development of capitalism, rather than, as in the classical Marxist view, production (class) relations. Based on this latter view, Robert Brenner argues that capitalism involves developing the forces of production through innovation; and since innovation results, not from production for profit on a market, but from processes at the local level that revolutionize social relations of production, that is where an analysis of capitalist development must begin (Brenner 1976, 1977).

These positions have been elaborated by a 'circulationist' school, which emphasizes markets as the critical dynamic in capitalist development; and a 'productionist' school, which upholds the importance of relations of production at the local level. Chapter 2 will argue that the productionist/circulationist debate dissolves when we recognize that maintaining capitalist social relations depends on patterns of consumption and exchange that reproduce hierarchy; and that producing for external markets helps to do this by obviating the need to provide workers with the means to consume what they produce, something which would lead to social levelling. If the goods that workers produce are destined for foreign markets, their wages can be suppressed – and they can be further suppressed if articles of their daily consumption are produced abroad by still cheaper labour.

Debate has also focused on Wallerstein's notion that developmental outcomes are set by a global division of labour and a process of synchronous regional differentiation. Much criticism has focused on the emphasis this gives to the agency and 'needs' of the core to explain how each region functions, rather than the local class configurations and struggles which many see as having been important factors in how different regions of the world were articulated with the world economy (for a review see Aston & Philpin 1985).

The notion has also been challenged on empirical grounds. A key outcome of regional differentiation, according to Wallerstein, is relatively strong state structures in the core areas and relatively weak ones in the periphery. But a number of scholars have shown that, empirically, these characteristics do not appear to correlate with core/periphery placement in the world economy (for a useful discussion see Benton 1996). Peter Gourevitch (1978) proposed a test of the argument by selecting two points in time within the period of Wallerstein's study,[20] then identifying those countries or areas whose economies place them in the core of the world system and which could also be considered strong states. What he finds (Table 1.1) is that there were more strong states than core economies: some strong states were located in the periphery (Prussia, Austria, Sweden); and some weak states were found in the core (Netherlands) (Gourevitch 1978: 423–424):

Scholars argue that, not only forms of state, but forms of labour (wage, coerced, and semi-coerced) also fail to correlate with the regions (core, periphery, and semi-periphery) where, according to Wallerstein, we should expect to find them. They show that, in the core, forms of labour appropriation persist that are not associated with 'classic' capitalism (Portes *et al.* 1989; Sassen 1991, 1994; Stern 1988).

An important debate generated by Wallerstein's world-systems perspective concerns the place of Europe in the world economy and, related to this, the issue of determining continuity and discontinuity in world history. A number of scholars have argued that analyses of the modern world that begin, as Wallerstein's does, with the 'rise of Europe', neglect the broader system to which Europe was connected; that the rise of Wallerstein's Europe-centred capitalist world economy in the sixteenth century cannot be understood in isolation from the world system that preceded it. Janet Abu-Lughod elaborated this argument in her 1989 book, *Before European Hegemony: The World System A.D. 1250–1350*. She argued that, though it was

*Table 1.1* Core economies and strong states

| | *Core Economies* | *Strong States* |
|---|---|---|
| **1550** | Netherlands, Northern Italy, southeast England, parts of Spain, parts of southern Germany, Portugal | Spain, England, France, Portugal |
| **1770** | Britain, France, Netherlands | Britain, France, Prussia, Austria, Sweden |

not yet global (the Americas had not yet been linked to it), the system that preceded Europe's rise was 'substantially larger', and 'more complex in organization, greater in volume, and more sophisticated in execution', than anything the world had previously known (Abu-Lughod 1989: 353).[21] By 1350 this system was disintegrating due to the rupture of trade links between the eastern Mediterranean and the Orient, and the deepening trade relations between the Mediterranean and northwest Europe, and it was this decline that opened the way for a European-dominated world system.

But for Wallerstein, the modern capitalist world-system that developed with the expansion of European commerce in the sixteenth century cannot be seen as emerging within a pre-existing world economy, because it was qualitatively different from this earlier system. Eurasia's long-distance trade had been based on the production and exchange of preciosities, and these, Wallerstein maintains, did not produce important impacts (Wallerstein 1974: 41–42). They could not have driven the expansion of the Atlantic economy and sustained the formation of a capitalist world economy as did the trade in bulk goods that developed with the expansion of European commerce. However, a number of scholars argue that the qualitative difference between the European-dominated system and the previous one cannot be established on these grounds. Flows of luxury commodities *did* generate systemic effects. The production of industrial goods for the luxury market – textiles, food – not only provided local elites with important sources of power and stability,[22] it was a key element in driving the expansion of trade over longer distances and in developing the complex long-distance trade relationships that connected the Afro-Eurasian system.[23]

Others argue that, while Wallerstein dates the emergence of a European-led capitalist world-system from the sixteenth century, it was not until the advent of industrial labour and commodification on a world scale in the eighteenth century that a European-dominated core–periphery pattern of exchange, and a capitalist world system, emerged (Dodgson 1977; Nell 1977; Wolf 1982). Andre Gunder Frank and Barry Gills have argued that it was not until 1800 that the European-based system became qualitatively different from the Asian-based Eurasian world economy of which it was a part, the continuous development of which can be traced over at least the last 5000 years (Frank 1990a, 1990b; see also Frank & Gills 1993).[24] They place the origins of modern global development, not in the autonomous 'rise of Europe' in the sixteenth century, but in a vast and sophisticated Asian-centred system that remained the heartland of global exchange into the nineteenth century.

Much productive reflection and debate has been generated by Wallerstein's attempt to develop a non-national ontology for understanding the development and operation of capitalism. But, as Neil Brenner points out, though Wallerstein 'maintains that the division of labor within the world-system transcends the territorial boundaries of each national state . . . he consistently describes the historical dynamics of the world economy in terms of the differential positions of national states within its stratified core–periphery structure, rather than, for instance, with reference to firms, industries, circuits of capital, urban systems, or spatial divisions of labor' (Brenner 2004: 51).

Despite defining three supra-state zones created by a global division of labour, the world system's 'most elemental geographical units are nevertheless national states, or more precisely, the bounded territories over which national states attempt to exercise sovereignty' (Brenner 2004: 51). Moreover, Wallerstein's analysis not only fails to break with the national frame, it also fails to explain outcomes with reference to a unit of analysis at the supra-state level. The explanation it offers ultimately gives greatest weight to the functionally specific ways that states act as a result of their location in the international system.

### *Post-colonial theories and subaltern studies*

Dependency and world systems approaches both place Europe at the centre of analysis of the global system and its different developmental outcomes. In the 1970s and 1980s two perspectives emerged as a critique of Eurocentrism, as well as of binarisms and of the national frame, in analyses of development. Both perspectives – post-colonial theory and subaltern studies – are concerned to highlight the tension between universal theories and a diverse developing world, and to show how the colonial experience and the 'contrapuntality' created by subaltern voices can provide material for alternative narratives or histories, and deepen and expand our understanding of both history and the contemporary world.

Post-colonial theory investigates how Western knowledge systems are related to the exercise of Western power: how knowledge of colonized people has served the interests of colonizers; how 'Western' canonical traditions and universalisms, as well as the colonial relationship itself, represses, excludes, marginalizes, and objectifies the 'other'.[25] It focuses, in particular, on the legacies of nineteenth-century British and French colonial rule for its subject people as, for instance, the difficulties faced by former colonial peoples in developing national identity. The Subaltern Studies project emerged from within this general perspective beginning in the 1980s.[26] Its key concern was to recover history from 'the bottom up' – to bring to light and assert the value of alternative experiences and ways of knowing and, in this way, illuminate the history, agency, and autonomy of the common people. According to the Subaltern Studies perspective, elite-centred colonialist (Liberal), nationalist and Marxist narratives are incapable of representing the history of the masses in the third world. They are forms of Western teleology, ideologies of modernity and progress, meta-narratives of the advance of capitalism and the triumph of the nation state, that reproduce knowledges and practices grounded in European history, and that seek either to endorse or to universalize Europe's historical experience.[27]

Post-colonial and subaltern studies are animated by a similar critique and share similar goals. They also share a number of interrelated weaknesses. While the Subaltern Studies project has been pre-eminently concerned to 'liberate "history" from the meta-narrative of the nation-state' (Chakrabarty 1992: 19), much of its scholarship has tended to assume and reinforce the nation as a concept and as a boundary. By treating the victims of colonialism as whole, internally undifferentiated national societies, post-colonial studies tend to work within the national frame, as well. Both perspectives also share the tendency to essentialize the colonial experience. Despite their insistence on the historical specificity of third-world societies, they tend to ignore the geographical and historical specificity of the colonial experience in different parts of the world and to impose universal conceptual frameworks on 'different degrees, forms and histories of colonialism' and post-coloniality (Moore-Gilbert 1997: 12; see, also, Ahmad 1992; Mohanty 1995; Mohanty, Russo, & Torres, 1991; Parry 2004). European colonialism involved a variety of forms of settlement, acts of political domination, and circumstances of economic dependency (de Alva & Jorge 1995: 254). Large areas of the 'third world' were never formally colonized by Europeans; and in those parts of the world that were, many were colonized for only a short time. Moreover, parts of the 'third world' were victimized, and perhaps more so, by *non-European* colonialism and imperialism; some for a much longer time than by European colonizers.

One of the most characteristic features of these approaches is their insistence on the primacy of race, rather than class, as relevant to an understanding of the subject positions of colonized people and of developmental outcomes in the third world. Class analysis is seen as inapplicable to 'backward capitalism': applied to a colonial context it operates as a 'Marxist teleology', reproducing knowledges and practices grounded in European history, and emptying subaltern movements of 'their specific types of consciousness and experience' (O'Hanlon 1988: 191).[28] Though workers might have multiple oppressors, imperial oppression is the dominant condition. Why this should be the case is not entirely clear. Why should the impact of European imperialism be to render the experience of miners, railwaymen, weavers, and artisans in, say, Anatolia, Damascus, or Egypt fundamentally different from those in Europe? Why should it be assumed that the conditions of their life were shaped more by European imperialism than by the relations of power that shaped working-class experience elsewhere?

The concept of 'class' is meant to capture a relationship of inequality and exploitation that gives rise to conflicts over the distribution of wealth, income, and power.' Wherever the production of a surplus beyond the bare necessities of life is appropriated by a small minority, it provides a means of collectively expressing the fact of this exploitation 'and the ways in which it is embodied in a social structure' (de Ste. Croix 1981:43). As Ahmad Aijaz argues, 'societies in formations of backward capitalism are as much constituted by the division of classes as are societies in the advanced capitalist countries' (1992: 99–100, 102–103).

The distinction defined in post-colonial theory and subaltern studies between class and race ignores the ways in which relations of inequality and exploitation may overlap with a variety of identities. Class struggles often are embedded in, or intersect with, ethnic, national, and other communities and identities; and both within and outside of Europe, class struggles often merged with and were interpreted as nationalism.[29] The fact that workers do not express their identity or articulate their grievances in the way that classical Marxism defines as 'proletarian', but rather through nationalist, religious, and other discourses, 'only strengthens the argument that one can speak of class in this context; for precisely the same is true in the most developed capitalist countries that are usually held up as the norm' (Lockman 1994: xxix). Capitalist development every where produced a basic antagonism between monopolists (large plantations, trading companies, and transnational corporations) and working populations seeking to reclaim more of the surplus value they create. The notion that the surplus produced in the 'third world' is appropriated by the 'West' to serve the requirements of 'Western' expansion is misleading. Local elites everywhere ('East' and 'West') collaborate with foreign states and groups in extracting surplus; and societies that have never been colonized or that are fully independent from foreign control distribute their gains no more equitably or use them any more productively than do states which are or were under colonial or imperial rule.[30] The point is not to deny the centrality and importance of race and racism in relations between different areas of the world, but to highlight the extent to which an emphasis on racialized relations between 'the West' and 'the rest' obscures important aspects of the imperial and colonial relation (more on this in Chapter 5, below).

Finally, post-colonial and subaltern studies tend to accept the West's account of itself. In common with conventional European historiography, they assume, wrongly, that the theories and practices universalized by Europeans originated in Europe and were actually employed there; and they airbrush out of history the subject positions of European workers, ethnic minorities, and others, and their role in achieving welfare states and the democratization of national politics in Europe. They emphasize the 'radical heterogeneity' and variegated forms of power and domination found in the third world, but tend to treat the European experience as singular and unified. They reject development thinking that essentializes the 'third world' and its inhabitants as homogeneous entities, but then homogenize and essentialize 'the west'. By reproducing the essentialist categories or binarisms (West/rest, core/periphery, colonizer/colonized) of the approaches that they reject, they fail to escape their own critique and obscure key aspects, not only of Western imperialism, but of global development.

Perspectives that emerged as critiques of mainstream development theory have helped to 'bring the rest of the world in'. They have illuminated the broad historical terrain of imperialism and its relation to processes of capital accumulation. They have elucidated European representations of non-European 'others' and confronted them with the 'contrapuntality' created by the colonial experience and by subaltern voices. But the dynamism of their analyses continually comes up against, and is undermined by, myths popularized by conventional European historiography. Consequently, they fail to fully 'de-centre' and properly resituate Europe in global development. By treating nationally bounded societies as the unit of analysis and conceiving of 'development' as national growth, they leave intact the ontological basis of conventional development thinking. Their attempt to re-envision global development consequently remains partial and limited in its impact.

## III. Re-envisioning global development

Despite their claims and aspirations, existing perspectives on global development have been unable to produce analyses that remain consistent with a non-national ontology or to produce, from post-colonial perspectives and subaltern voices, a non-national history. They have been unable to escape the snares of national historiography and are continually subverted or assimilated by it. The problem is that analyses that begin by envisioning the totality of supra-local flows and interactions already disassembled and separated into bounded 'national' units will, irrespective of what non-national phenomena are its focus, likely continue to treat these bounded bits as the ontologically primary locus of social relations.[31] The solution that this book suggests is explained below.

As previously noted, the influence on existing sources of the national frame and other elements of the Victorian historiographic tradition makes it difficult to find in them the materials from which to develop an alternative ontology and history of the world. Existing sources *do* contain these materials, but to see how they combine to produce an alternative view of the world requires a 'gestalt shift'. What the term 'gestalt shift' implies can be illustrated with reference to the famous face-goblet sketch devised by Edgar Rubin (1915) to demonstrate figure–ground reversibility (Figure 1.1). For many people, the figure appears at first glance to be that of a vase. But by drawing attention to how the picture's contours might be viewed differently, figure and ground reverse and the picture reconstitutes itself as a pair of facial profiles. No new data (lines) are added to produce the alternative view. Both pictures emerge from the same 'data'. But once it is pointed out that elements of the goblet picture can be interpreted differently, the goblet dissolves and a picture of two faces comes into focus. It does so because a reinterpretation of certain of its elements confront it with an unassimilable difference, one that cannot be rendered compatible with or incorporated into it but that, if accepted, makes it impossible to retain.

It is possible to produce a similar 'gestalt shift' by weaving together insights from development theories (e.g. aspects of the work of Wallerstein, Cardoso & Faletto, Sunkel, Senghaas, Galtung, and Frank) and recent research and writing by regional specialists and world historians

*Figure 1.1* Gestalt shift

(e.g., O'Brien, Chaudhuri, Bayley, Subrahmanyam, Pomerantz, Goldstone, Sugihara, and Washbrook). These literatures provide abundant evidence of cross-setting similarities in processes and outcomes of growth in world history that, when added together, undermines conventional distinctions between 'Western' and 'non-Western' historical development, and 'developed' and 'developing' worlds. Empirical anomalies for core/periphery perspectives and 'surprising resemblances' across different regions of the world can be combined to illuminate aspects of past centuries that conventional binary divisions tend to obscure: the role of elites in the exploitation of their own societies, and the existence of colonialism, exploitation, and subalternity in Europe. All of this brings into focus a 'horizontal' division of the world of domination and subalternity, and analytically shifts the axis of view from the vertical (states, regions) to the horizontal (classes, networks).

By foregrounding different elements than are usually stressed in the standard picture of global development, parts of it form a different pattern, a different picture, than the one we usually see. What comes into focus is a structure of trans-local social power that over many centuries underpinned the development, not of whole nationally bounded societies, but of sectors or regions within them. The data on which this picture is based are there for anyone to notice, except that a pre-existing pattern of expectations causes us to filter out certain facts as irrelevancies and to keep most clearly in view those which support the standard interpretation. If we start with a different set of expectations, a different picture emerges. It is comprised not of anything *new*, but of evidence explicitly discussed by scholars investigating the development of different regions of the world and their integration into a world economy.

Placing supra-local dynamics, processes, and relations in the foreground of the story of global development dissolves the various binary divisions of the globe that are usually pictured (core/periphery, colonizer/colonized, West/rest, modern/traditional), as well as the vertical divisions that define a multiplicity of bounded whole nations locked into antagonistic relations with each other. What then becomes possible to see is a world horizontally divided into a single trans-local elite and a multiplicity of partially bounded local domains: not the fictive systems created by national historiography and national accounting, but local domains that are transected by an interrelated, interdependent elite based in, and situated across, their 'open tops'. Once our analytic focus shifts to this horizontal division of the world, many hitherto invisible processes and structures become discernible, enabling different questions to be asked and different accounts to be told.

To start, it enables us to envision global development as proceeding neither through the common phases or stages described by early theoretical models of development, nor by the diffusion or contagion processes favoured by core–periphery perspectives. Instead, a process which Andrew Sherratt (2000) has suggested, and that, in some ways, combines these two, seems more apt: this is a process in which long-lasting structures grow upwards through time and outwards in space. Sherratt invokes the image of a calyx to describe this process: one in which many different impulses interact to produce change on a global scale (Figure 1.2). Global development, as Sherratt observes, tends to be characterized by a multi-centric pattern in which several regions that are interconnected by networks of trade and exchange stand out as the foci of fast-spreading contagious processes. This seems to fit conceptually with the polycentric world economy described by recent research and writing on world history.

### *The transnational elite*

Historically, dominant classes of the world unite (not, as Marx assumed, proletariats). Relatively few in number, they ensure their

*Figure 1.2* A calyx

reproduction by developing collective solutions to their common vulnerability. For instance, as Chapter 3, 4, and 5 will endeavour to show, when elites throughout the world sought to set masses of labour to work for industrial capitalist expansion, they developed a common set of solutions to the broadly similar problems of mobilizing labour and maintaining its subordination to capital.

*Elites* are groups that command certain resources (political support, economic power, communication, knowledge) that give them the ability to affect the behaviour and beliefs of others. They inhabit organizational apparatuses that enable them to extract resources from non-elites 'and to protect themselves from encroachments by other elites' (Lachmann 1990: 406). Multiple elites may coexist when different groups develop the capacity to extract resources from non-elites. In this case, the capacity of an elite to exploit the producing class will derive primarily from its relations with other, coexisting elites. Different groups of elites must cooperate, or at least tolerate each other, in order to preserve their own access to non-elite resources (Lachmann 1990: 401). However, when a single elite exists, its capacity to exploit the producing class will derive solely from interclass relations of production. Unconstrained by other elites, that elite's fundamental interest will be to reproduce its exploitative relation vis-à-vis the producing class, and its capacities and interests will be directed solely against the subordinate classes. In that case, its position and interests can be analysed in terms of class and of relations of production (Lachmann 1990: 411).

Class is a social category used to analyse a structure of antagonistic socio-economic interests. A class is 'a group of people who share a common relationship to the process of social production and reproduction, constituted relationally on the basis of social power struggles' (Robinson & Harris 2000:16). Individuals form a class only insofar as they are engaged in a common struggle with another class. Class does not claim all of its members' identity, and neither does nationality or religion. However, at certain times and places, more of a person's identity is bound up with one or another of these; and it thus becomes relevant to distinguish individuals according to that one.

Through trans-local circuits of capital and commodities, institutions and forms of accumulation, elites build and maintain fortunes; and these fortunes, and the ways of life that they make possible, are the basis of an encompassing and bounded *transnational* identity. Members of a transnational elite have a subjective self-awareness, organization, and agency distinct from that of established national elites pursuing narrow self-interests.

Within the transnational elite, groups of 'national' elites are not 'taxonomic groups', i.e., groups 'whose members show similar (formal) attributes but which need not actually connect or interact with one another' (e.g., the clergy). Relations among taxonomic groups are relations of similarity, but not necessarily of connection. Their similarity, therefore, does not explain why and how – through what connections – they might act similarly. However, if groups whose members 'relate to each other structurally or causally' (Sayer 1992: 244) act similarly, it is because the relations *themselves* are relations of connection. They constitute, *not* separate but similar groups, but a supra-local elite with broadly similar interests, capabilities, and policies, constituted and reproduced through interaction and interdependence. Groups of 'national' elites are individuated and move in a *horizontally* differentiated system. They are internally differentiated based on different forms of power – coercive, financial, etc.,[32] and these forms produce 'complex gradations' such as are found among the officer corps within the 'military class' (Gramsci 1971: 13).

While the transnational elite is united by a fundamental and long-term unity of interests and purpose, this does not mean that there are not shorter term conflicts of interest. The primary interest of elites is to maintain class power. But they also must maintain autonomy against rival elites (Lachmann 1990: 412). This is where intra-elite conflict emerges.

During the centuries that are the focus of this book, the opening up of new sources of wealth and new ways of creating it gave rise to sharply antagonistic interests and rivalries. But these quickly became submerged by a common interest in maintaining the subordination of labour and staving off revolution. Pressures from below can intensify rivalries among elites. Pressed from below, elites struggle for a greater share of the surplus appropriated from producing classes, and for a division or redivision of territory among themselves. At times, elites mobilize their local population in order to prevail in these struggles. However, they usually do not want to wholly destroy another elite, but only to gain a portion or larger share of what the rival elite appropriates from the producing classes. 'International' conflicts organized by elites against other elites may present opportunities for non-elites to better their position locally by allying with foreign elites against their 'own' elites, or by demanding concessions from them in exchange for their support.

Through collaboration, emulation, learning, and the adoption of best practice, transnational elites develop a system of social institutions, relationships, and norms. They own a disproportionate amount of the world's yearly income, and dominate the policy-forming process of international bodies and decision-making groups through a variety of means. These organizational elements and capacities provide them with the ability to work in concert. Motivated by their common vulnerabilities to seek collective solutions, they are more closely tied by culture and concrete interests to elites elsewhere than to the classes below them.

These statements might be seen as consistent with the Liberal idea that 'Great Britain was merely another atom in the universe of trade and ranked precisely on the same footing as Guatemala' (Bayly 2007: 344). This is *not* the argument being advanced here. The world is *not* 'flat' (*contra* Friedman 2005): only the world of elites is flat.[33]

## *The organization of the study*

The following chapters present a series of interlinked arguments. The first is that capitalism was monopolistic, anti-market, and global from the start. It developed through the formation of monopolies and trans-local/cross-regional networks (Chapter 2).What we call the 'Industrial Revolution' was principally a reorganization of production that was designed to accelerate the globalization of capital. This reorganization provided the basis for an externally oriented, dualistic system of industrial expansion that enabled elites to monopolize gains from expanded production while leaving intact, as much as possible, the traditional bases of their social and political power. Consequently, before 1945, the extent of industrialization, even in Britain – 'the first industrial nation' – was actually quite limited. The changes associated with Britain's 'industrial revolution' primarily involved, not mechanization and industrial production, but the globalization of capital and the deregulation and reorganization of economic relationships (Chapter 3).

Monopolistic, anti-market accumulation expanded the wealth and power, not of nations, but of cities. The de-industrialization of rural areas and concentration of production in cities, and alliances between urban notabilities and rural landowners, ensured that the power of cities increased and remained greater relative to that of the surrounding areas. The consolidation of larger territorial domains consequently produced a form of state that more closely resembled the city-state systems of the past 5000 years than the nationally integrated state form of national cultural imaginaries and nation-state ideology. And it was largely the city-state form that European imperial powers maintained or created abroad (Chapter 4).

Chapters 2, 3, and 4 focus largely on developments in Europe, because of their central role, not in global development, but in historical narratives and theories that this book is concerned to challenge. With Chapter 5, the discussion moves onto a broader terrain, arguing that industrial production throughout the world expanded through producing largely for export to elites and ruling groups. As a result of the trans-local relations, and the similarities and interdependencies that this created, a global social order emerged that was constituted by horizontal solidarities among groups of elites in different parts of the world. This was the basis for an essentially collaborative imperial project that, everywhere, worked to appropriate resources with the active collusion of local elites. However, as more and more areas of the world began to enter into this system of externally oriented expansion, imperialist rivalries became endemic and eventually culminated in a two-phased global conflict. Because the war was fought largely in Europe, governments and ruling elites there were forced to do precisely what a century of external expansion had enabled them to avoid: mobilize (feed, clothe, organize, train, politicize and, in other ways, empower) the masses. As a number of scholars have shown, mass mobilization for war often produces social levelling and revolution. In the course of the world wars this is, in fact, what happened in Europe (Chapter 6).

The crisis of the world wars and the great depression brought about an important social, economic, and political transformation in Europe. For a time, European states resumed the welfare and regulatory functions that they had relinquished at the end of the eighteenth century, and pursued policies designed to increase domestic investment, produce a more equitable distribution of income, and expand domestic markets. A similar change took place in Japan and in the Asian 'tigers' as a result of externally imposed reforms following World War II; and in the Soviet Union as a result of the 1917 Revolution. These changes brought the social structures of these areas into greater conformity with those that existed in 'areas of new settlement': the United States, Canada, Australia, and New Zealand. These became the 'developed world' or the 'first' and 'second' worlds. In other areas, social structures remained similar to those that had predominated both here and in Europe before 1945. These regions of the world, today, are what we call the 'developing' or 'third' world (Chapter 7). But, while the binary and tripartite schemes that have been applied, wrongly, to the pre-war epoch, became relevant following World War II, the existence of these different 'worlds', was brief. In the late 1970s, 'first world' countries began to roll back the restrictions on capital mobility and to eliminate regulatory agencies and social welfare programs that, after World War II, had produced the conditions of life associated with 'first world' development. At the end of the 1980s, the 'second world' (the Communist world) adopted similar measures. These changes are the basis of what we call 'globalization' (Chapter 8).

# 2 The origins and development of capitalism

There is no single definition of capitalism. Scholars have identified a set of features that are associated with capitalism, but they don't agree about which of them are essential to it; and the features that different definitions emphasize are, in most cases, found in systems that pre-dated capitalism. Most definitions are based on the writings of the classical political economists (Smith, Say, Ricardo, Malthus, J. S. Mill), all of whom assumed that capitalism was born in Europe, and who were writing in the context of, and as a contribution to, political and ideological battles being fought in Europe during the eighteenth and nineteenth centuries. Those who follow in this tradition emphasize markets and how the competition of *free markets* stimulates entrepreneurship, technical experimentation, and efficiency.[1]

Scholars who work from a Marxist perspective point out that these existed in ancient Rome and at various other times and places throughout history. They emphasize that capitalism, unlike other systems, is a system of *general commodity production* in which *all* goods and services, including the most basic necessities of life, are produced for profitable exchange in a market. In this system, all inputs and outputs of production are totally commodified, including labour power, land, and other means of production. For Marx, it is the commodification of labour and, specifically, the replacement of servile labour with *free wage labour* that is unique to capitalism and is its defining characteristic. 'Free' wage labour is different from other forms of labour commodification in that the mass of the population is 'freed' from direct access to the means of production and must sell their labour power to produce surplus value for a small minority in order to survive. It is this unique feature of capitalism which led to technological advance and progress in production.

Like other features that are thought to define capitalism, wage labour also pre-dates capitalism.[2] But what Marx argued was that, in capitalism, wage labour becomes increasingly the predominant form of labour commodification. Both the classical and Marxist traditions assume that the dependence of all economic actors on the market means that *competition is the fundamental rule of life* and that it drives the *development of the forces of production and improvement in the productivity of labour by technical means*.[3]

While scholars disagree about what features are essential to capitalism, they broadly agree that capitalism emerged when a 'crisis' led to the dissolution of feudal society in early modern Europe. A consideration of the nature of that crisis should give us a clearer sense of what sort of system was developed to resolve it and how and why (and if) it differed from other systems.

## I. Origins

It has often been observed that the history of wars is written by the winners. The same might be said of political and ideological conflicts, such as those that characterized the development of capitalism. Capitalism emerged as a result of recurring battles over rights and the distribution of valued goods, and all accounts of these battles from all perspectives, including those most recently produced and even those written by its most passionate critics (from Marx to Polanyi), adopt assumptions and judgements, even the idiom, of those who won the battles.

Consider, for instance, that until fairly recently nearly all accounts of the birth of capitalism began with the 'crisis of feudalism' that arose in early modern Europe. In common usage, the term 'crisis' describes a general calamitous situation that occurs at a particular time and place. However, what historians call the 'crisis of feudalism' was *not* a general crisis, but a crisis only for aristocratic landowners. The dissolution of feudalism made possible, for most people, increased freedom and a better standard of living. For the great mass of the population, what we call a 'crisis' was a period of great opportunity and prosperity. It followed the demographic collapse caused by the Black Death, and the social levelling that occurred as a result of it. This undermined feudal mechanisms of economic exploitation and threw lords and nobles into crisis. 'Capitalism' is the system that emerged from their efforts to reverse the social levelling that had taken place and resolve the crisis. It developed through a series of conflicts, first, to privatize land, later to privatize state assets, and dismantle regulations against monopoly and capital flight, as well as those establishing labour protections and government-sponsored welfare systems. By the end of the eighteenth century, these battles had succeeded in reversing the social levelling that had occurred in Europe and had developed a system that sharpened inequalities and worked to reproduce them.

## *Feudal 'crisis' and transition*

Most accounts of the crisis of feudalism and the emergence of capitalism begin with the breakdown of agrarian society in northern Europe beginning in the thirteenth century. The most prominent explanations of this breakdown and ensuing crisis focus on tendencies within feudal society that produced population shifts and falling seigneurial rents, and on class conflict, and commercialization. While all of these factors contributed to the crisis of feudalism and are related to the same overall story, debate continues about which of these factors should be treated as ultimately most determinative, both of the crisis that began in the thirteenth century, and the emergence, by the sixteenth century, of capitalism.

Most accounts start at the end of a long period of expansion in Europe and the beginning of a contraction by around the middle of the thirteenth century. Some explanations assume that feudal society ceased to expand when the 'limits' of feudal production were reached, either because of an inability to raise agricultural productivity, or the emergence of structural contradictions between small-scale production and large-scale property. Explanations that focus on population expansion and decline[4] argue that the dissolution of feudalism came about when population growth outstripped the supply of the means of subsistence; and that this occurred due to a combination of the natural tendency of population to increase on a limited supply of land, and the inability of medieval agrarian production to raise agricultural productivity. Famine, plague, and war brought the population back to its 'proper' relationship with resources (as well as rising wages and falling food prices and rents). But a population upswing in the sixteenth century caused a breakthrough in agriculture by stimulating demand for food. Claudio Katz argues that 'the prevailing mechanisms of surplus extraction contained their own internal barrier' and that, sometime during the opening decades of the fourteenth century, this barrier was reached when the lords' exactions produced a general exhaustion of the soil and crippled the capacity of the peasant economy to reproduce material life. 'The medieval economy entered upon a precipitous decline', which took the form of 'repeated harvest failures and demographic collapse' (Katz 1993: 371).

Other accounts emphasizing natural tendencies within the feudal system that halted its expansion focus on the tendency of the rate of seigneurial levies to fall. According to this view, the rate of seigneurial levies had a tendency to fall in the feudal system because of the structural contradiction between small-scale production and large-scale property. With the general expansion of cultivation, which was going on until the middle of the thirteenth century, the fall in rents (due to the increase in land) was offset by an increase in new tenures (and rents). When economic expansion drew to an end, the fall in the rate of levy was no longer offset by the establishment of new tenures. Feudalism had come up against a ceiling of growth. Seigneurial income decreased and, because of the very low level of the various rents levied on their holdings, the seigneurial class radically reorganized production relationships by increasing their accumulation of landed property and hiring labour (Bois 1985: 111).

Marxist accounts generally emphasize class relations as the motor of social change in the transition from feudalism to capitalism. In *Studies in the Development of Capitalism* (1963; orig. 1947), Maurice Dobb argued that a class struggle between landlords and peasants had driven nobles into a game of spiralling status emulation that required greater and greater levels of surplus extraction from the peasantry. Intensified exploitation by landlords provoked peasant flight from the land, and led to a decline of feudalism and a transition to a capitalist mode of production. But some Marxist accounts, and most notably that by Paul Sweezy (1970 [1942], 1976), emphasize the revival, from about the eleventh century, of long-distance trade between Europe and other world regions, of commodity production in Europe, and of trade and town life. Non-Marxist accounts also emphasize the growing commercialization of European society in the sixteenth century and, in particular, the effects of urbanization and the growth of trade as bringing about the decline of serfdom and, with it, the rise of capitalist agriculture. But Sweezy (1970 [1942], 1976) argues that capitalism emerged as a result of forces exogeneous to feudal society. It arose in an urban, market sector outside the control of feudal lords and eventually became a challenge to feudal society; that production for the market was inherently more profitable than realizing a surplus through feudal appropriation; and that the more efficient market sector was able to outbid feudal rivals for the inputs of land, labour, and capital. Building on Henri Pirenne's thesis (1958, 1969), Sweezy argued that Islamic invaders in the seventh and eighth centuries cut the Mediterranean trade routes so that both international and local trade in Europe dried up. As a result, there emerged in Europe a system of production for immediate consumption. The restoration of international trade between the western and eastern ends of the Mediterranean stimulated a revival of commodity production in Europe and of trade and town life. It was this that was the impetus for the development of capitalism.

Sweezy argued that the transition from feudalism to capitalism occurs at the point at which production for exchange replaces production for use. Feudalism was a mode in which all production was for use, not for exchange. It was static and self-perpetuating. Its dissolution and the subsequent emergence of capitalism could only have resulted from a force exogenous to feudal society – the expansion of trade. Long-distance trade was a creative force in resolving the problem of the feudal ruling class's need for increased revenue in the later Middle Ages. The very existence of exchange value as a massive economic fact tended to transform the attitude of producers and to develop new tastes for consumption on the part of the feudal ruling class. Manors were fundamentally inefficient and unsuited to production for the market; and the growth of towns as alternative centres of employment impelled the lords to grant concessions marking the elimination of serfdom.

A debate initiated by Maurice Dobb and Paul Sweezy in the early 1950s (the 'transition debate'; see Sweezy *et al.* 1976) turned on the correct Marxist explanation of the transition from feudalism to capitalism in the light of the European experience. Marx saw the transition from feudalism to capitalism as a transition from a primarily agrarian society of petty producers, whose most important social classes were the landlords and unfree tenants, to a society whose principal classes were capital-owning entrepreneurs and propertyless wage earners producing commodities for exchange on the market (Marx 1990: Vol. III, Chs. 20, 36, 47). The change thus involved both (1) a change in relations of production and (2) an expansion of trade and commodity production. Which came first? The expansion of trade, or the transformation of relations of production?

This debate was renewed and elaborated in the 1970s by Immanuel Wallerstein and Robert Brenner. Wallerstein argued, as had others, that the feudal system had been expanding between 1150 and 1300 but had reached a point beyond which it could no longer go, and a contraction then set in.[5] The declining ability of feudalism to create wealth necessitated the shift to a new mode of production, and this entailed creating, through geographical expansion into areas outside Europe, a capitalist world-economy based on the world market. Wallerstein contends that, in the 'long sixteenth century', and despite the persistence of feudal relations of production, the European feudal aristocracy became a capitalist landed aristocracy, and that they were capitalist because they got their revenues by producing commodities for sale on a market. For Wallerstein, the defining element of capitalism (conceptualized as a world system) is 'production for sale in a market for which the object is to realize the maximum profit' (1974: 398).

Robert Brenner (1977) has argued that capitalism involves innovation in the production process; and since production for profit on a market does not necessarily lead to innovation, it must have been processes that revolutionized social relations of production at the local level which led to innovation in the production process and, thus, to capitalism. Brenner argued that explanations that focus on demographic and commercial trends have a fatal flow because, as Brenner points out, 'precisely the same demographic and commercial trends yielded widely divergent results'(Brenner 1982: 16–17).[6] The factors taken to be of causal significance in these explanations led to the decline of serfdom (in the West) and, contrarily, to its intensification in the East. Sweezy explained these different outcomes in terms of geography – the distance of these countries from the centre of the new exchange economy. But Brenner argued that only class relations can account for these different outcomes; that it was different property structures and balances of class forces that produced the different historical experiences of Eastern and Western Europe.

While adherents of these various accounts frequently insist on the significance and importance of their differences and counsel against minimizing them, they are not true alternatives. All agree that (1) capitalism emerged in Europe, and (2) as a result of changes that were unique to Europe. While Sweezy emphasized the impact of expanding trade as determined by attributes of that trade (the volume and type of goods being traded), Dobb emphasized existing social structures. But no one need deny either that large-scale economic forces impacted Europe, or that class and property determined the local effect of them.[7] Rodney Hilton (1969) argued that feudal rulers strove to increase feudal rent in order to maintain and improve their position as rulers against their many rivals as well as against their underlings. As Hilton pointed out, rent had to be maximized in order to maintain class power in existing hands, and this struggle both promoted and was intensified by the expansion of trade. No one would dispute that, with the revival of trade, towns grew in size and importance; that serfs were attracted to them and fled the land in large numbers; that richer peasants expanded their holdings, employed wage labour, and became capitalists (Dobb); or that the feudal lords, attracted to the growing trade of the towns and the possibilities inherent in the market economy for the generation of large fortunes, also transformed themselves from feudal lords to capitalist landowners (Brenner, Wallerstein, and Sweezy). Figure 2.1 shows how the perspective that this chapter advances stands in relation to all of these.

The demographic collapse in Europe caused by the Black Death shifted the balance of social forces. It exacted heavy casualties among the nobility, generated a severe labour shortage, weakened the feudal power of the nobles, caused a dramatic fall in the incomes of the landlord class, and shifted the balance of class power in the direction of the peasantry.[8] Peasant resistance in the context of the acute labour shortage forced landlords to remove virtually all feudal controls on peasant agriculture. This gave rise to an economy of petty commodity production. The peasants' liberty to move and to buy, sell, or let land enabled the direct producers to make substan-

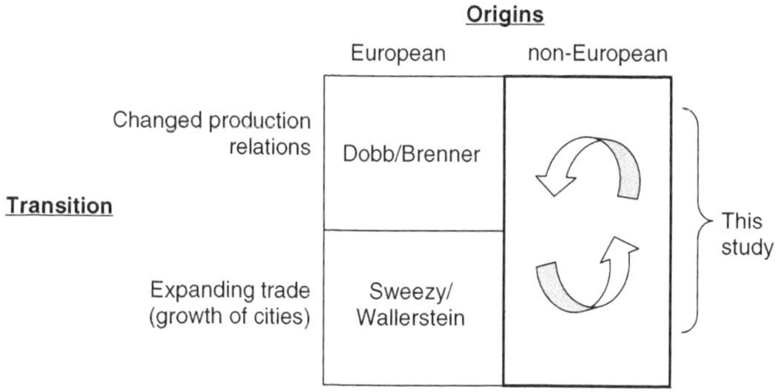


*Figure 2.1* The transition from feudalism to capitalism

tial gains in their material conditions of life. English lords were no longer able to appropriate an economic surplus by reasserting feudal controls over the peasantry; 'villeinage had melted away' (Katz 1993: 377). This great 'leap forward' in the standards of life of the mass of Europe's population was accompanied by a fall in landlord incomes. This fall, which reached its nadir in the mid-fifteenth century, was experienced by English lords, and was recorded by historians, as a 'crisis'.[9]

The Black Death did not hit Poland, Lithuania, and other areas of northeastern Europe that were relatively less densely populated and urbanized. Whatever the consequences of this for its subsequent development, the East is generally thought to have developed differently from the West because of the deterioration of the status of free peasant tenants in the east beginning in the fifteenth century (the so-called 'second serfdom'). However, the status of free peasant tenants also deteriorated in Western Europe, not with the imposition or reimposition of serfdom, but with the expansion of absolute surplus value extraction.

## II. Agrarian revolution (the 'Brenner Thesis')?

How the crisis caused by the dramatic fall in landlord incomes was resolved was through the development of an alternative system of surplus extraction, capitalism. But since, through this discussion of its origins, we are inquiring into the nature of capitalism, we need to examine whether cities were the site of these changes or whether it was changes in European rural society that were determinative.

The notion that capitalism had its origins in an agrarian revolution in England during the 'long sixteenth century' is associated most notably with the view, elaborated by Robert Brenner, that it was the uniquely capitalist and uniquely productive character of British agriculture from the fifteenth century onwards that gave birth to capitalism.

For Brenner, capitalism is a system based on free labour and technological innovation driven by competition. So any account of the emergence of capitalism must focus on processes that revolutionized social relations of production at the local level which led to innovation in the production process. According to Brenner, these processes included the consolidation of larger farms, the use of free labour, and the adoption of new technologies to increase labour productivity (relative surplus value production). Brenner's thesis is shown in Figure 2.2.

In Brenner's account, population decline enabled the peasantry to win their freedom, since conditions of labour scarcity impelled the lords to offer better terms to them.[10] The feudal class had appropriated part of peasant production by juridical and political power, backed by force. But with the weakening of that power as a result of population decline, conditions of labour scarcity, and successful peasant resistance, the feudal class shifted from claims to power over people to claims to power over land (enclosures). Brenner argued that a number of changes flowed from the enclosures. Let us explore this argument.

Social relations of production in agriculture were revolutionized when **enclosures** produced

(1) → **larger farm size and** use of landless, **'free' labour**

(2) → **adoption of new technologies to increase labour productivity**
(relative surplus value production)

(3) → **greater yields, which supported industrialization**

*Figure 2.2* Agrarian revolution and the 'Brenner thesis'

### *1. Large farms and 'free labour'*

With the enclosure of open-field villages and common land and the consolidation of smaller holdings into larger farms, landlords leased large parcels of land to free, market-dependent commercial tenants, who increasingly hired landless peasants as wage labourers (Brenner 1993: 642, 649–651). Land was cultivated not for subsistence but for the market, by means of wage labour. By the early nineteenth century, 'most of England's farmland had passed from family farms to large-scale capitalist tenants' (Allen 1992: 265).

Brenner argued that small-scale production was, by its nature, incapable of technological innovation; that large farms were more efficient because they used labour more efficiently and produced more food per acre than small, family-owned farms; that they had more capital to invest in improvements and were more likely to adopt new methods and techniques. But that does not appear to have been the case. Smaller farms in England also adopted new methods and techniques. Manuring and new crops were innovated on smaller farms, and smaller farms also got into convertible husbandry.[11] But, in 1830, two-thirds of English tenant farms, the supposed sparkplug of capitalist growth, were under 100 acres (Clarkson 1971: 66). An 1878 study of land distribution in Great Britain shows that 70 per cent of tenant farms were less than 50 acres – by any definition a small farm; only 18 per cent were larger than 100 acres (cited in Albritton 1993: 431).[12]

For Brenner, fully commodified labour power (wage labour) is an indispensable prerequisite of agrarian capitalism. Without the availability of 'free' labour – labour free from feudal ties to the land so that capitalists can exploit it – there is no capitalism. However, large farms were not necessarily worked with wage labour. According to G. E. Mingay (1994), half of all farms in Great Britain in 1831 employed no labour outside members of the immediate family.[13] Commodified labour power means that labour is coerced by the market rather than by the 'extra-economic' forces of feudalism. But, according to Robert Albritten, there is little evidence that an agrarian proletariat existed in England until the nineteenth century (Albritton 1993: 424).[14]

It is assumed that, unlike slaves, wage labourers are endowed with freedom of contract and can decide whether they work and for whom;

that unlike serfs, they can move freely and seek work wherever they choose. But freedom of contract can be effective only if it is accompanied by rights of association, speech, assembly, thought, ownership, etc. These freedoms were not secured by workers in the supposed birthplace of capitalism until the twentieth century. But, even then, to survive in a capitalist society without paid work is difficult, and the choice of work or employer is often too limited to allow us to say that workers can 'move freely and seek work wherever they choose'.

## *2. Relative versus absolute surplus value production*

Brenner argues that the adoption by large landowners of new technologies to increase labour productivity revolutionized social relations of production.

Marx defined two forms of capital accumulation (in Marx 1990: Vol. I): absolute surplus value production and relative surplus value production. The first involves extensive gains – a simple multiplication of the capacity at a given moment, e.g., through lengthening of the work day;[15] the latter involves intensive gains – an improvement in production techniques (more discussion of this can be found on page 69).

Brenner argues that in pre-capitalist societies social relations of production are 'in large part' confined to 'the realization of surplus labour through the use of 'methods of extending *absolute* labour' (Brenner 1977: 32); what occurred in the English countryside in the fifteenth century was the production of *relative* surplus value, which produced a social system in which labour had become commodified.

But Kenneth Pomerantz argues that there is abundant evidence that the expansion of output that occurred between 1500 and 1800 in Western Europe resulted 'largely from the application of much larger amounts of labour (i.e., methods of absolute surplus value production), 'rather than any breakthrough in productivity' (i.e., the use of relative surplus value production) (Pomerantz 2000: 91).

Owners of large farms were primarily concerned, not with increasing yields per acre, but with preserving the long-term value of their land and making money. This 'often involved forms of estate management which did not maximize food production at all' (Williamson 2002: 19). They were just as likely to use this land for 'the mere exploitation of short-term market scarcities or the formation of convenient country seats for the enhancement of status' (Reddy 1987: 9). When landowners were inclined to increase yields per acre, they did not necessarily care to invest in new agricultural techniques in order to do so. They were more likely to increase production through using the methods of absolute surplus value production. Why invest in new technology, why undertake new expenditure on fixed capital and pay for harvesters or tractors and the skilled labourers to operate them when you can lower wages by spreading the same amount paid for wages over a longer workday or a larger number of workers (whole families working to provision the household rather than just a single 'breadwinner')? Employers wish to reduce the number of labourers employed in order to reduce labour costs and to maintain a reserve army of workers in order to keep wage levels down. But if a worker's wife and children are pulled into the workforce, and the wage paid to him alone is reduced so that the employer gains a larger workforce for the same amount of wages, then these theoretical incentives for increasing relative surplus value disappear.[16] Moreover, increasing absolute, rather than relative, surplus value production was preferable in that it did not require a transformation of class relations.

English agriculture was not mechanized, but remained, instead, dependent on methods of absolute surplus value production. The majority of farms in England and Wales did not possess either a tractor or a milking machine until World War II. Despite their having been available for some 30 years or more, their usage remained relatively limited and investment in them relatively low.[17] When blockade and the shortage of shipping during World War II made it necessary to expand domestic food production, within five years 'British agriculture changed from one of the least to one of the most mechanized of farming systems in advanced countries'. Arable acreage increased by 50 per cent and the number of tractors and combine harvesters on British farms multiplied almost fourfold. Food imports decreased by half, and home output almost doubled, with only about a ten per cent increase in the workforce (Hobsbawm 1968: 204–5).

Labour costs can be reduced by lowering the costs of food. But the acquisition of the New World made it unnecessary for Europe to use its own land in a much more intensive and productive way.

American agricultural productivity in the 1830s was 50 per cent greater than Britain's and three times greater than continental Europe's (Darwin 2007: 241). There was a 50 per cent increase in world crop cultivation between 1840 and 1880, half of it from the United States, Australia, and Canada (Hobsbawm 1975: 179). A growing world trade in agricultural produce and raw materials meant that manufactured goods created without much use of British land could be exchanged for ever-increasing amounts of land-intensive food and fibre at reasonable prices (Pomerantz 2000: 269). Later, of course, 'the New World supplied land-intensive cheap commodities, especially cotton and wheat and then also meat, while also absorbing 60 million of Europe's surplus population' (Frank 2001: 180). 'The import of virtually free calories from the sugar/slave plantations . . . obviated their production in Europe' (Frank 2001: 181). The increase in agricultural productivity, measured in calories per acre, was due not to new relations of production, but to new products from the Americas, such as the potato (Komlos 1998).

Wheat yields did not increase as a result of relative surplus value production. Greater yields per acre does not mean more wheat is being produced. The adoption of a four-course rotation – not greater productivity – yielded more wheat. As Williamson explains, farmers practiced a three-course rotation in many parts of England in the seventeenth century and, by the 1830s, had adopted a four-course rotation. While wheat yields increased, less land was sown with wheat; so 'the actual increases in *production*' were not as great as the raw yield figures suggest (Williamson 2002: 18).

### *3. Increased labour productivity and industrialization*

According to the overall argument being considered here, improvements in agriculture and increasing agricultural productivity provided the basis for England's industrial take-off by releasing workers for, and supporting them in, industrial jobs in the city. The fact that urban population of England doubled between 1500 and 1700 confirms, for Ellen Meiksins Wood, the highly productive character of British capitalist agriculture. It was because fewer people were required to produce foodstuffs, she maintains, that workers were freed up to work in the cities in burgeoning industrial enterprises (Wood 1999: 97).

But Charles Tilly has shown that workers for urban industrial centres more often came, not from agriculture, but from 'de-industrializing towns and villages of the hinterlands' (Tilly 1983: 138–39). 'Various forms of proto-industrial production – including cloth making, metalworking, and mining industries – had developed in many rural regions during the sixteenth and early seventeenth centuries and had formerly constituted a major part of the economy' (Williamson 2002: 169). The second half of the eighteenth century saw the progressive deindustrialization of these regions. This led to 'an exodus of wage-workers from rural areas' followed by smallholders, sharecroppers, and petty tenants. 'The result was to leave behind the larger farmers, both owners and leaseholders'. It was often to make farms less dependent on hired labour, and more dependent on family labour than they had been for centuries (Tilly 1983: 133, 136).

The profit-driven reorganization of agriculture in the sixteenth century was not based on relative surplus value production. The key element in increased agrarian production was labour intensification and crop specialization rather than class relations or farm size.

This produced neither prosperity and a well-fed population in the countryside, nor industrialization in the towns and cities. In 1851, 'agricultural units of production, tenurial arrangements and techniques of cultivation had hardly changed since the Restoration (1660)' (O'Brien 2000: 124–125). In the eighteenth century, 400 landowners controlled over 20 per cent of the cultivated land of England and Wales. At the end of the eighteenth century, these landowners and the wealthy gentry (comprising around 700 or 800 families) and the lesser gentry (3000 or 4000 families) together controlled about 75 per cent of the cultivated land of England and Wales (Tribe 1981: 42). At the end of nineteenth century, 175,000 people owned ten-elevenths of the land of England, and 40 million people the remaining one-eleventh (Romein 1978: 195). The landless rural population subsisted on low wages, the rest on small plots of land which produced few crops for export or sale to industry, as most farmers had no access to loan capital for the purchase of tractors, metal ploughs, or chemical fertilizer. On the eve of World War I, more than 60 per cent of the adult agricultural labourers of the Kingdom received less than the amount necessary for the maintenance of a labourer and his family on workhouse fare (Ogg 1930: 174).

## III. The integration of Europe into the Asian-centred trading system

We can draw together different strands from various accounts to form a single narrative, starting with (1) the Black Death, which shifted the balance of class power in Europe; (2) the weakening of juridical and political power as a result of continued peasant resistance and its re-establishment in the absolutist state (missing from Brenner's account); (3) the revival of trade and growth of cities, which made it possible to get value from land, not from agriculture but by producing for export industries; and (4) the shift, by the feudal class, from claims to power over people to claims to power over land (enclosures).

Changes within late feudalism in Europe occurred within the context of an expanding world economic market – a major new phase of world commercialization that had developed after AD 1000 (Mann 1986). The rise of a massive market economy in China during the eleventh century was, as William McNeill describes it,

> a tipping point which may have 'sufficed to change the world balance between command and market behavior in a critically significant way. . . . and as Chinese technical secrets spread abroad, new possibilities opened in other parts of the Old World, most conspicuously in western Europe
>
> (McNeill 1982: 50–54)

It was the scale on which this kind of behaviour began to affect human lives that was new. 'New wealth arising among a hundred million Chinese began to flow out across the seas (and significantly along caravan routes as well) and added new vigour and scope to market-related activity' (McNeill 1982: 53). Within the Sea of Japan and the South China Sea, the Indonesian Archipelago and the Indian Ocean, and in the Mediterranean, an upsurge of commercial activity took place over the next 300 years.

Trade routes across the Mediterranean reopened from about the eleventh century, for the first time since the Islamic conquest of the Mediterranean region had cut Europe off from them in the eighth century, and this led to a revival of long-distance trade between Europe and other world regions. Consequently, the kind of trade and commerce that had been pursued elsewhere for centuries now developed in Europe. As Stephan Sanderson notes, 'European seamen and traders made the Mediterranean a miniature replica' of the commercial activities occurring simultaneously in the southern oceans. In the fourteenth century, these separate sea networks were 'combined into one single interacting whole' (1995: 266).

Beginning in the fourteenth century, this westward extension of the Asian system was marked, in Europe, by repeated waves of major epidemic diseases. The plague called the 'Black Death' originated near China and spread along the Silk Road, finally reaching Europe in 1348. By 1400, 70 to 80 per cent of the population of some cities and villages in England had died. By 1420, the Black Death and its related ailments had killed between 30 and 60 per cent of Europe's population (Herlihy 1997: 17). It took 150 years for Europe's population to recover. The demographic devastation in Europe shifted the feudal social structure towards a system of relatively equal small-scale peasant producers and decentralized political structures. This undermined traditional bases of social power and aristocratic incomes and threw the landed aristocracy into 'crisis'. The crisis was further exacerbated when, after the fall of Constantinople to the Ottoman Turks in 1453, the refusal of Muslims to trade with the Venetians and other Westerners disrupted the flow of status goods – spices, silks, and other luxury items – to Western Europe.

The inability to maintain the economic basis of their hegemony led to a crisis for aristocratic landowners in Europe. It is reasonable to assume that they would seek, as in fact they did during the 'long sixteenth century' (1450–1600), to resolve the crisis in ways which would enable class power to remain in existing hands; through (1) the centralization of feudal mechanisms of economic exploitation in the absolutist state; (2) the use of armed ships to search for an alternative route to the East and the status goods on which they depended; and (3) the attempt to secure, through enclosures, the dominance of a new form of property in the means of production that shifted the balance of social power decisively in their favour.

### *The long sixteenth century (1450–1600)*

The crisis that threatened to destroy serfdom led coalitions of feudal lords to reorganize the feudal framework by combining feudal seigneuries in the hands of the Absolutist state.[18] These states operated to reproduce, on a national scale, the feudal mode of extracting profit: the monarch lived largely on the taxes of peasants; the nobility was exempted almost entirely. Although the aristocracy lost some of its political powers, it continued to own the bulk of the fundamental means of production in the economy. Under feudalism, the authority to wage war, to tax, to administer and enforce the law had been privately owned as legal, hereditary rights by members of a military landed aristocracy. Under Absolutism, the King's great vassals continued to own important elements of public power as hereditary and legally recognized property rights. From the beginning to the end of the history of absolutism, the feudal nobility was never dislodged from its command of political power (Anderson 1974: 40).

In addition to securing the feudal mode of extracting surplus, states supported a search for an alternative route to the Asian luxury (status) goods needed to maintain traditional hierarchies.[19] Using the ocean-going craft that had developed to carry Europe's Atlantic coastal trade, sea voyages were launched to the East (around Africa) and West (across the Atlantic). These were followed by warrior merchants whose state-backed war fleets were used to plunder resources from the Americas and to muscle into and capture the trade routes, industry, and markets of Asia.

Ocean-worthy ships had been developed in Europe's port cities to carry the coastal trade linking the Baltic[20] with the Mediterranean. After Muslims refused to trade with Westerners following the fall of Constantinople in 1453, these ocean-going ships set out to find a means to reinstate the flow of luxury goods from the East. This search led to the discovery of the Atlantic islands (Canaries, Madeiras, and Azores), a sea route around Africa to the Indian Ocean, and the great clockwise wind systems of the northern and southern Atlantic, and the Americas. These state-financed discoveries were followed by the launching of state-supported war fleets to find and capture wealth. It was the exploitation of overseas riches that, in addition to the changes they forced in property and production relations at home, enabled elites to reverse the social levelling that had undermined feudal structures and mechanisms of surplus extraction in Europe.

With armed ships, maritime powers along Europe's Atlantic coast – first the Portuguese, then the Spaniards, Dutch, French, and

English – gained access to Asia's flourishing trade. With government backing, Portuguese traders were able to acquire gold from west Africa, fund sea voyages to and beyond the Cape, and then 'fight or buy their way into the rich trade networks of Asia' (Christian 2004: 394). The Portuguese 'were able to enforce their naval supremacy in the Indian Ocean' with fleets carrying thunderbolt weapons that were able to overawe the smaller, more lightly armed vessels they encountered in the Indian Ocean. These weapons were 'more powerful, accurate, and psychologically devastating than any firearms hitherto available' there, and could only be defended against by building massive, and massively expensive, fortifications (Lieberman 1993a: 493).

Using its monopoly over some 80 per cent of the world's supply of silver (Darwin 2007: 97), Spain funded armed ships to wrest control of various trades from Asian competitors in the Moluccas ('Spice Islands'), Sri Lanka, the Straits of Melaka, Hormuz, and the Red Sea. Government-backed fleets of Dutch and British warrior merchants followed with a ruthless pursuit of trade monopolies by the Dutch East India Company and the British East India Company. During the sixteenth century, Amsterdam gained control of the trade in the Baltic, the North Sea, and along the Atlantic coast; and, towards the end of the century, held a quasi-monopoly over the trade of bulk commodities in Europe's coastal commerce, including grain, timber, iron ore, and copper, which were exchanged for salt and herring (Kriedte 1983 15). In 1602, the Dutch government sponsored the formation of an East Indies Company, which granted its merchants the right both to the spice-trade monopoly in East Asia, and to build forts, maintain armies, and conclude treaties with Asian rulers. Around the same time (1600), the British East India Company was granted a monopoly on trade with all countries east of the Cape of Good Hope and west of the Straits of Magellan.

Intense competition among Dutch, Portuguese, and British warrior merchants during the sixteenth century accelerated the militarization of Indian Ocean routes and sites. Charles I of England (1600–1649) launched a major programme of warship building and created a fleet of powerful ships. The British navy established military control of the oceans and the trading routes to the Americas and the East by constructing strategic bases at Gibraltar, Singapore, the Cape of Good Hope, Malta, Alexandria, Vancouver Island, and, later, Aden and Hong Kong.

### *Capitalism and mercantilism*

A useful starting point for elaborating the system that resolved the crisis of feudalism is Fernand Braudel's understanding of capitalism.

According to Marx, capitalism developed through three phases, dominated respectively by merchant (commercial), industrial (productive), and financial (money) capital. Capitalism, in the stage of *merchant capitalism* (referred to as 'mercantilism') revolves around trade, and is a form in which merchants mediate between the producer and the consumer in order to make a profit. *Industrial capitalism* revolves around production. Here, profit is sought through organizing the production and selling of manufactured goods. *Finance capitalism* is a form which makes profit from purchasing, selling, and investing in currencies and financial products (e.g., stocks and bonds), making more money from money without having to produce anything.

Braudel challenges the notion that capitalism developed 'in a series of stages or leaps from mercantile capitalism to industrial capitalism to finance capitalism', and that true capitalism appears 'only at the stage when it took over production' (Braudel 1984: 621). He points out that, because the goal of capitalism is to maximize capital accumulation, capitalists are 'inherently generalist in nature: they are neither financial, nor merchant, nor industrial, but any and all, depending on the size of the profits available' (Taylor 2000: 7). The 'whole panoply of forms of capitalism – commercial, industrial, banking – was already employed in thirteenth-century Florence, in seventeenth-century Amsterdam, in London before the eighteenth century', and all were used simultaneously to maximize profit. Great 'merchants' were involved 'simultaneously or successively in trade, banking, finance, speculation on the Stock Exchange, and "industrial" production, whether under the putting-out system or more rarely in manufactories' (Braudel 1984: 621). The landowning aristocracy and the urban commercial bourgeoisie were closely connected; and agriculture, financial, and industrial interests were often found in the same economic groups, firms, or families. Landowners were often owners of or investors in urban enterprises. Colonial merchants supplied investment funds for plantation development in the Americas, and so were involved in production as well as exchange.

### *The domain of capitalism*

Capitalist development is usually seen as beginning with growth within national borders, and then continuing, through cross-border expansion. The general view is that domestic economies reach a point of 'saturation' and so expansion abroad becomes necessary as a means of securing markets for surplus goods and capital. But capitalism was 'born global':[21] it developed from the start across international frontiers rather than within them. This is the view that Fernand Braudel advanced.

Braudel understands material life as existing on three levels.[22] The first level is the world of daily ordinary economic life, of village barter and production for local consumption. The *second* or 'national' level is the level of towns and trade, of markets, currencies, and transport systems. Economic life within political units 'took place in *micro-economies* centred in market towns surrounded by an agricultural hinterland of about twenty miles' (Schwartz 1994: 13). These did not trade with other towns until well into the era of inland waterways (canals) and railroads. An international economy – a complex division of labour linking economic areas located in different political units – existed long before then (Schwartz 1994: 13); and when micro-economies became linked together it was for the purpose, not of expanding and integrating local, national economies, but for international trade. We might think of Braudel's *second and third levels as together constituting his third, supra-local domain:* an arena above that of local and national markets, in which 'regular transactions are possible for only a subset of the population'.[23] It is on this third, *supra-local level where we find the domain of capitalism.*

As Braudel emphasized, material progress generally delivers advantages only to a narrow elite; and the expansion of capitalism was, from the start, no exception. The basic objective of capitalism is, not to produce goods and services, but to maximize capital accumulation (create and concentrate wealth). Since the best way to secure large profits is not through engaging in competition with others in open, free markets, but through establishing monopolies, capitalism was, from the start, anti-market and dominated by monopoly.

Capitalists pursue monopoly not only to maximize capital accumulation, but to maintain the subordination of labour. The production of surplus value depends on maintaining the unequal factor endowment between owners of capital and sellers of labour. It requires a strategy for how value is both to be realized (trade patterns) and allocated (investment patterns) (Lefebvre 2003: 93). Expanding long-distance exchange avoids the social levelling that the expansion of domestic markets might generate and helps provide resources for maintaining the subordination of local labour, creating connective relations and capacities among elites within and across national territories.

### *Monopoly versus markets*

Capitalism, for Braudel, is dominated by monopoly and relies, not on markets, but on political relations and military power. Capitalists are not interested in maintaining general, fair, and free access to resources. Accumulation, whether capitalist or non-capitalist, is based on exclusion. The great trading cities of the fifteenth and sixteenth centuries, such as Venice and Genoa, 'were in search of an international monopoly' (Braudel 1982: 420); all the big businesses in seventeenth-century Amsterdam were built up on monopolies (Braudel 1982: 422); and state-supported monopolies dominated in England – the South Sea Company, the Hudson's Bay Company; and the English East India Company, which had a monopoly on the sale of all commodities imported into England from the 'East Indies' (all the land east of Lebanon).

In the nineteenth century and early twentieth century, monopoly continued to dominate in the large plantations, large trading companies, transnational corporations, and state enterprises that formed the basis of networks of transnational, cross-regional exchange. Even in Britain, the supposed home of the free market, the agricultural, financial, and industrial sectors were bound by monopoly and restriction. Monopolies (trusts, cartels, syndicates) dominated industry right into the twentieth century. These eliminated competition, fixed prices, shared out supplies, bought raw materials *en bloc*, cut out middlemen, led to a hyperconcentration of capital, and enabled employers to unite more effectively against labour. Braudel observes that capitalism in the nineteenth century 'has been described, even by Marx, even by Lenin, as eminently, indeed healthily competitive'. We may well ask, as he does, whether such observers were 'influenced by illusions, inherited assumptions, ancient errors of judgement?' (Braudel 1984: 628).[24] Lenin believed, wrongly, that 'monopoly capitalism' was a new, late stage of capitalism. What he was observing was a diversification of the forms of monopoly.

For both Weber and Lenin, genuine capitalism is associated with competitive markets, and monopoly with nineteenth century imperialism. For Weber, imperialism was a monopolistic system of control pursued by groups who sought monopoly profits. Lenin argued that free competition began to be replaced by 'monopoly capitalism' at the end of the nineteenth and the beginning of the twentieth century as a result of the internationalization of capital and vast increase in large-scale production (Lenin 1973: 11). But there is no evidence that there was a stage of competitive capitalism that predated the emergence of imperialism or 'monopoly capitalism'. Monopoly, not competition, became central to the normal operation of capitalism from the start – not as an exception (as Weber thought), or as a late stage in its development (as Lenin would have it).

### *The last frontier: freeing capital from local economies*

In Western Europe, the Ottoman lands, China, and Japan a 'general crisis' seems to have occurred in the first half of the seventeenth century. Falling prices, depleted stocks of precious metals, and dramatic climatic shifts caused fiscal crises for the absolutist agrarian states characteristic of Eurasia (Richards 1990: 625; see also Atwell 1986, 1990; Goldstone 1988). Throughout Eurasia this was a period of political instability and war. China and Japan 'experienced severe economic problems that were at once interrelated and strikingly similar to those that were occurring in other parts of the world at the same time' (Reid 1990: 639). In Europe, this was 'the darkest era . . . since the catastrophe of the fourteenth century' (Fischer 1996: 91). Everywhere, economic contraction was accompanied by social upheaval. There were major political crises in Brazil, Morocco, India, China, and the Ottoman Empire. Within Europe, there were crises in Bohemia, Germania, Catalonia, Portugal, Ireland, England, Scotland, Holland, Sweden, Italy, the Ukraine, and Muscovy. The Thirty Years' War (1618–1648) – one of the most destructive conflicts in European history – was followed by civil conflicts in England, France, Spain, Portugal, and Italy, and the First Russo-Turkish War (1677–1681), the Austro-Turkish War, the fall of Vienna in 1683, and the European Nine Years' War (1689–1697), which became a worldwide event.

By 1700, political upheavals and wars in Europe had come to an end, leaving in their wake falling grain prices, rents, and interest, and rising wages. As in the aftermath of the Black Death, the distribution of wealth became a little more equal (Fischer 1996: 103–104). This had made European societies more egalitarian. However, this 'age of improvement' for artisans and labourers and the great majority of Europe's population, during which wealth became more broadly distributed, was experienced by lords ('and the historians that read their letters and shared their perspective') as a depression (Fischer 1996: 108).

In England, the expansion of trade had led to a growing interest on the part of local elites in enclosures, something which, prior to the English Civil War (1642–1651), the monarchy had resisted. Enclosures had continued mainly by 'individual acts of violence against which legislation, for a hundred and fifty years, fought in vain' (Marx 1990: Vol. I, 677; in Katz 1993: 379). However, after 1660, parliamentary leaders 'converted all lands that were formerly held of the king by feudal tenure into absolute ownership'; and by the late seventeenth century, enclosures had given the gentry ownership of 60–70 per cent of the land: 25–33 per cent was owned by the yeomanry, and 5–10 per cent by the Church and the Crown (Lie 1993: 292). The enclosure movement in England 'experienced a veritable boom' during the eighteenth century, 'reaching its climax during the Napoleonic Wars' (Katz 1993: 379); and, with it, came 'the destruction of the peasantry, the rise of agrarian wage labourers, and the growing spectacle of the rural poor' (Lie 1993: 292).

The expansion of Eurasian markets, which drew feudal lords in like a magnet, accelerated the enclosure movement. The ability of elites to privatize gains from foreign trade shifted the balance of power locally, and reinstated and worked to reproduce social hierarchies. All over the world elites faced with opportunities to accumulate wealth dispossessed peasants and turned them into serfs or wage slaves. In Western Europe, nobles expropriated the peasantry from the land and turned their estates over to the raising of sheep in order to sell their wool on the market. In other parts of the region, elites took advantage of these opportunities by maintaining, and even strengthening, the traditional mechanisms of economic exploitation.

Enclosures shifted the balance of power in the English economy away from cottagers and yeoman farmers and towards the rural gentry and the traditional landowning aristocracy. The developing commercial interests of these elements eventually drew them together and into an alliance with the rich and powerful merchant elite of London (Lie 1993: 292).

By the middle of the eighteenth century, the increase in rural population and the pressure of aggregate demand had pushed up prices everywhere in Europe, particularly for staple items purchased by the poor. With prices rising, pressure mounted for monetary expansion. As governments responded to the price revolution, public spending tended to exceed income. Rents increased sharply, making the mid-eighteenth century a golden age for country gentry and landowning elites, as well as for commercial capital.

With wages falling behind inflation, income differentials, once again, began to widen. The concentration of wealth and growth of inequality was evident throughout Europe (Fischer 1996: 138). Sharp rises in the cost of living in Britain in 1740–1741, 1757, and 1767 were accompanied by rioting over large parts of the country. In Prussia recurring peasant revolts broke out beginning in the 1770s. In France, a grain crisis and an industrial depression in the 1770s raised the price of grain by 56 per cent, but increased wages by only 12 per cent to offset it (Hufton 1974: 16). There were interstate wars (1740–1748, 1754–1763), and colonial movements for autonomy and secession (in the United States, 1776–1783; Ireland, 1782–1784; Belgium and Liège, 1787–1790; and Holland, 1783–1787), and a global war (1754–1763) involving heavy fighting in the Americas, Asia, and central Europe.[25]

A world depression in commerce and industry began in 1782 and, by 1789, had cut the output of France's textile industry by 50 per cent (Fischer 1996: 44). Unemployment rose sharply, wages fell, and the price of food shot up. This shifted the balance of social power throughout Europe still further towards the wealthy elite, thus enabling them to dismantle the moral economy of the eighteenth century.

### *The end of the 'moral economy'*

The term 'mercantilism' was coined during the nineteenth century. Adam Smith (1976) used the term 'mercantile system' to describe the system of political economy that dominated Western European economic thought and policies from the sixteenth to the late eighteenth century. The term is usually used to refer to a political order characterized by strong central government, and a set of policies, regulations, and laws, developed over the sixteenth to eighteen centuries, that subordinated private economic behaviour to national purposes (Heckscher 1955).

Mercantilist policies promoted merchants and trade. But, by the eighteenth century, absolutist rulers regarded the aim of trade to be the accruing of benefits to one's country. They favoured state overview, regulation, and subsidy to promote the broader interests of the nation over the private interests of merchants, and to align the merchants' interests with the nation's. They offered subsidies and privileges as a way of orienting production, and regulated both foreign and internal trade. Mercantilist policies promoting overseas trade provided governments with a source of tax revenues and loan capital that enabled them to gain a certain degree of autonomy from the local nobility. Overseas trade could be taxed to the benefit of central government more efficiently and with fewer negative domestic consequences than any other activity.

In Europe, states eventually obtained outside sources of revenue by allowing a high degree of foreign ownership of industry and a variety of credit, ownership, technological, and marketing dependency relationships with international capital. In Portugal and Spain, the Netherlands, England, and France, central governments adopted mercantilist policies and profited from taxes on trade, and also through borrowing from the very merchants whose trade they promoted. Strong central governments could more powerfully protect businesses that improved societies by buying and selling the produce of the land and putting workers to work.

While originally the 'Absolutist' state was an instrument of feudalism, eventually it competed with and encroached upon direct seigneurial extraction. By the eighteenth century, European monarchs had been able to gain sufficient autonomy to establish what later came to be characterized as a 'moral economy' – one in which states ensured that basic needs were met either through public or through private bodies but with state oversight and enforcement.[26] In Britain, France, Prussia, the Hapsburg Empire, Prussia, and elsewhere, governments established equality before the law, the free circulation of property and goods, and religious toleration, and confiscated church lands and removed occupational barriers. Louis XV (1715–1774) attempted to abolish feudal rights and guild restrictions, and to introduce a general property tax, a tax on aristocratic incomes, and abolition of numerous feudal burdens of the peasantry. In the Hapsburg Empire, Joseph II (1765–1790) decreed the abolition of serfdom and the guilds, and toleration for the denominations. Frederick William I of Prussia (1688–1740) instituted far-reaching educational, fiscal, and military reforms. Frederick II (1740–1786) introduced legal reforms and sought to extend freedom of religion to all his subjects.

Absolutist governments in England,[27] France, and elsewhere in Western Europe regulated local markets, controlled employment and settlement, and were active in providing welfare.

In England, marketing, licensing, and forestalling measures set maximum prices on staple foods such as meat and grain, prevented middlemen merchants from bypassing or cornering the market, and ensured quality control, a 'just price', and an adequate domestic supply of goods (Lie 1993: 282). Magistrates surveyed corn stocks in barns and granaries, ordered quantities to be sent to market, and attended the market to ensure that sellers adhered to regulations and statutes governing quality and price. Legislative controls were placed on the export of grain when prices were high. Municipal governments made bulk purchases of corn and sold them to the poor, sometimes below the prevailing market price. 'Whether hidden or open, real transfer payments were made when food was provided for the urban poor in the sixteenth and seventeenth centuries'. When town councils incurred losses as a result, these were often made up by corporation or charitable funds, from councillors' own pockets, from benevolences from city companies, or from rates levied for the purpose (Slack 1988: 146). German towns 'applied price controls to protect the consumer from attempts by the guilds to form cartels and also fixed minimum and maximum daily rates for labourers and craftsmen'. Munich set wage rates for weavers that would see them through times when demand for their labour fell off. The Nuremberg Council set a maximum profit for bakers when their earnings seemed too high (Kellenbenz 1976: 36).

Absolutist governments also recognized it as the responsibility of the state to provide maintenance. The state role in the provision of welfare was a Europe-wide phenomenon. The growth of urban areas in Europe in the later Middle Ages generated new problems and legislation by city governments to protect individual welfare through consumer protections and with legislation with respect to poverty. Legislation introduced by more-or-less autonomous city governments became the basis of national welfare systems.[28] Territorial states 'eventually took over the legislative and regulative functions performed by the cities', and then 'expanded the perimeters of welfare to include public education, public security in all forms, and social welfare' (Dorwart 1971: 3).

Tudor and Stuart governments in Britain introduced legislation making the state responsible for social welfare, and began to put in place 'a complex apparatus through which to realize it' (Slack 1988: 1). Legislation was introduced to set up new institutions for poor relief, and to establish a system of hospitals to provide medical care for paupers. By 1700, England had a national welfare system.[29] By the eighteenth century, France had established a nationwide welfare system.[30] By 1770, Prussia had introduced measures establishing a cradle-to-grave welfare system guaranteeing every Prussian subject adequate food, sanitation, and police protection.[31] In 1776, miners were guaranteed a fixed income and the right to work, a workday restricted to eight hours, and a prohibition against female and child labour and Sunday shifts. A benefits scheme (*Knappschaftswesen*) provided free medical treatment in case of illness or accident, sick payments during the whole period of illness, and invalid payments in case of permanent disablement (Tampke 1981: 72–73).

In sum, Europe's eighteenth century 'moral economy' was the product of government regulation that enabled workers to exercise power both as labourers and consumers. Governments regulated markets on behalf of local people, instituted price and wage controls and other labour protections, and were active in providing welfare. In order to escape these and other aspects of the 'moral' economic order, locally powerful groups sought to expand production for export and increase long-distance trade. Seeking to enlarge profits by expanding production for export, they pressed increasingly for a reorganization of economic relations and freedom of market relationships from legal control (textile manufacturers were opposed to regulations, taxes, and the welfare system; commercial banks wanted an end to restrictions on the free movement of capital). Their aim was to preserve their privileges and prerogatives, to privatise new sources and means of producing wealth, to dismantle much of what today we would consider socially enlightened about 'liberal absolutism', and retain much of what was not in a new guise. Governments ultimately bowed to these pressures and, having previously allowed changes in the institutions of property and the relationships of production, enclosures of land, and the concentration of capital and landownership, ended their limitations on exploitation for personal profit, protections for labour, including apprenticeship and wage regulations, and the provision of welfare. By the end of the century, a broad campaign to dismantle regulations tying production and investment to local economies succeeded in 'disembedding' capitalist development and accelerating the globalization of capital. The outcome of this campaign will be the focus of Chapter 3.

## Conclusions

In contrast to the theme of disjuncture emphasized in standard accounts, this chapter has emphasized how a changed domain of global interaction combined with fundamental structural continuities to produce roughly contemporaneous similar developments in cities across the world. The transition from feudalism to capitalism in Europe did not entail a leap forward to a radically new form of social organization, as Table 2.1 shows.

Conventional accounts of the 'crisis of feudalism' and the emergence of capitalism tell the story of an outmoded system that had reached its limits and was forced to give way to a new world. This chapter has argued that the 'crisis of feudalism' was not a general

*Table 2.1* Co-existence of capitalism and non-capitalism
(**Boldface** indicates characteristics which predominated throughout the century)

| Capitalist | Pre-capitalist[32] |
|---|---|
| • **Labour is:**<br>(1) 'free' of feudal obligations<br>(2) **dispossessed (separated from the means of production)** | • **Labour is:**<br>(1) **bound by feudal obligations**<br>(2) in possession of means of production |
| • Surplus extracted from the dispossessed producer by economic 'coercion' | • **Surplus extracted from the dispossessed producer by extra-economic compulsion** |
| • Generalized commodity production (production primarily for sale; labour power itself a commodity)* | • **Self-sufficient localized economy supplemented by simple circulation of commodities** |
| • Extended reproduction of capital and rise of organic composition of capital* | • **Simple reproduction where surplus is largely consumed** |

* Found only in industrial sectors producing for export, as will be discussed in Chapter 3.

crisis, but a crisis for the wealthy elite. It involved a flattening of traditional hierarchies that undermined the system of accumulation and those it privileged by redistributing wealth and reducing aristocratic incomes. Elites sought to resolve the crisis by finding ways to reinstate and reproduce those hierarchies. This did not entail a leap forward to a structurally new form of social organization, but Europe's integration into an expanding Eurasian mercantilist trading system. Europe's entry into this system did not bring about a radical disjuncture or difference in it. Born within this system and, even while contributing to its ongoing development, Europe long remained its child.

# 3 Industrialization and the expansion of capital

## Core and periphery redefined

The development of capitalism, according to most accounts, involved sweeping changes, first in agriculture and then, in its second and most vital stage, in industry. The previous chapter challenged conventional assumptions about the *agricultural revolution* which, it is generally thought, laid the basis for England's industrial 'take-off'. This chapter challenges widely held assumptions about the *industrial revolution.*

We can begin with the term 'industrial revolution' itself. As historians have long argued, the use of the term 'industrial revolution' to describe the changes that took place in Europe during the latter half of the eighteenth century is misleading (Clark 1957: 652).[1] The term suggests that there occurred at that time a revolution in technology that transformed the means of production. But there was no technological revolution, no transformation in means of production during the period of what we call the 'industrial revolution'. Large-scale mechanized manufacturing had existed, in Europe as elsewhere, for at least a century (more likely several); and while Europe at that time saw an increase in the scale of industrial production, involving a massive mobilization of human and material resources and a reorganization of production processes, this revolution of scale, as it might be called, involved neither a revolution in technology nor a transformation either of means or relations of production.

What, then, is meant by the term 'industrial revolution'? The previous chapter ended by noting that, in the eighteenth century, powerful groups in Europe had launched a broad campaign to dismantle regulations tying production and investment to local economies. As this chapter will recount, by the end of that century, these efforts had succeeded in bringing about changes designed to 'disembed' local economies and accelerate the globalization of capital.[2] Conventional historiography would lead us to assume that these developments, along with other changes at the time, were a result of the 'industrial revolution'. But this chapter will argue that it was precisely these changes – the disembedding of local economies and the globalization of capital – that came to be called, misleadingly, the 'industrial revolution'. Wherever industrial production expanded, whether of manufactured or agricultural or mineral goods, it was in order to increase exports. In Britain ('the first industrial nation'), the capture of overseas markets through military means, and the successful struggle by aristocrats and wealthy merchants to free capital from state regulation, provided opportunities for these groups to profit from increasing overseas sales. It was only *then* that existing technologies were used to expand industrial production; and this expansion was designed, from the start, to produce goods, not for local and national economies, but for export, principally, to elites, ruling groups, and governments abroad.

## I. The 'Industrial Revolution'

'Industrialization' refers to the application of non-human energy and the factory system to the production of goods. But there was no significant change in technology in the mid-eighteenth century (that came in the mid-sixteenth century). The first manufacture to be industrialized, cotton, used 'fairly simple' technology that 'required little scientific knowledge or technical skill beyond the scope of a practical mechanic of the early eighteenth century' (Hobsbawm 1968: 59). Mechanized large-scale production existed in Europe before the so-called 'industrial revolution', and 'factories' in previous centuries ('i.e. large scale firms, partly mechanized and with considerable fixed capital investments'), as for instance, silk filiatures, 'bore similarities to their eighteenth-century counterparts producing cotton yarn' (Komlos 2000: 317).

Before the 'industrial revolution' there were huge iron combines (multi-plant firms) in operation, and large-scale copper smelters, chemical works, and engineering shops. In the early part of the eighteenth century, there were 'bleacheries, dye works, glass works, blast furnaces, paper works, and textile printing firms' that employed 'hundreds, often thousands, of workers, and used some machines in the process of production' (Komlos 2000: 317). The 'first modern British textile factory', a large water-powered silk throwing mill, was put into operation in Derby in 1721 (Komlos 2000: 316).

Industrial production in Britain was undertaken in order to expand exports; but even in its export industries – textiles, coal, iron, steel, railways, and shipbuilding – Britain was slow to adopt new techniques or improvements. Britain's industrial 'breakthrough' began in the 1780s and 1790s with the mechanization of one branch (spinning) of one industry: cotton. The other branch, weaving, remained unmechanized for 40 years. The introduction of the factory system in spinning actually increased the number of *domestic* weavers (to handle the expanded production in yarn). Between 1806 and 1830 the number of factory workers in textiles rose from 90,000 to 185,000, while the number of domestic weavers increased to almost 240,000 (Gillis 1983: 41). Traditional manufacturing organized around the putting-out system continued to make profits of as much as 1000 per cent (Gillis 1983: 159) and, as long as it did, there was little incentive to introduce new techniques.[3]

In major industries, such as glass, bricks, mining, furniture, shipbuilding, food processing, finished metallurgy, and clothing, 'ratios of capital to labour' and 'the tools and techniques used to perform manual and skilled work were the same in 1851 as they had been in 1700'. There was a slow diffusion of steam power; but the use of traditional forms of energy – provided by wind, water, animals, and human toil – predominated, as did small-scale units of production. Factories and corporations 'were untypical, not modal forms of organization' (O'Brien 2000: 124–125). By 1850, the total number of factory workers in England amounted to not much more than 5 per cent of the work force (Lis & Soly 1979: 159).

Industries producing goods for domestic household consumption were not mechanized. These industries, 'hosiery production, clothing, leather trades, coach making, building industry, food stuffs, and scores of others were produced using traditional methods well into the century' (Komlos 2000: 320). Those that made buttons, locks, nails, cutlery, and tools continued to turn out their products in small forges with moulds and hand tools. They 'were not transformed before the latter part of the nineteenth century', and then often by adopting techniques from abroad (Davis 1979: 64). Despite the British origins of the machines and machine tools industry, it was not until the 1890s that automatic machine-tools production was introduced in Britain under the impetus of the United States, and the desire on the part of employers 'to break down the hold of the skilled craftsmen in the industry'. Gas manufacture was mechanized late, and as a result of pressure from trade unions (Hobsbawm 1968: 181).

### *What was the Industrial Revolution?*

What we call the 'industrial revolution' was essentially a *reorganization* of production involving the deregulation of markets and capital, the concentration of production, and the introduction of new forms of dominating and putting to work the lower classes. Having succeeded in circumscribing the power of 'absolute' monarchs, alliances of urban-based merchants and rural elites in Europe dismantled state regulatory and welfare systems that required capital to serve the needs of local communities; they then introduced measures that eradicated the remaining vestiges of Europe's 'moral economies'. This reorganization of economic life was undertaken to prepare the way for a brutal expansion of production-for-export that became a model for elites and ruling groups throughout the world. It is this disembedding of local economies and expansion of production for export that we call the 'industrial revolution'.

### *The deregulation of markets*

By the eighteenth century, the occupation of the North American interior by Europeans and their slaves had brought about 'a colossal extension of the European economy' (Darwin 2007: 211).

In the seventeenth century, societies across Eurasia had been wracked by crises. In response, European monarchs ('Absolutist' rulers) attempted to promote economic expansion by ending internal customs dues, breaking up entailed estates, and eliminating complex feudal regulations and customs. In the eighteenth century, fiscal crises increased pressures to expand agricultural productivity and urban commerce, especially after the world war of 1756–1763 (the 'Seven Years' War'), which left all the major European countries with large new debts. Throughout Europe, monarchs sought to introduce economic, fiscal, political, and social reforms aimed at improving agriculture, encouraging freer trade within their realms, eliminating the privileges of religious orders, setting up independent judiciaries, substituting salaried officials for hereditary office holders, and improving the status of peasants. Throughout these centuries, Europe's wealthy classes struggled against monarchical reforms that threatened to curtail their privileges and reduce their fortunes. After the mid-eighteenth century, alliances of urban-based merchants and rural elites in Europe increasingly sought to encroach upon the power of 'absolutist' states and to use that power to 'free' economic life from state control.

It is worth briefly reviewing this struggle, as it bears on assumptions, to be discussed further along, concerning the class structures that developed in the 'core' of the world economy.

Absolutist states emerged when a crisis threatened to destroy serfdom and undermine the feudal mode of production (see Chapter 2). The Absolutist state was, 'first and foremost' an instrument for 'the maintenance of noble domination over the rural masses': 'a redeployed apparatus of feudal domination', a 'new political carapace of a threatened nobility' (Anderson 1974: 18, 20).[4] Established at the behest of the landed aristocracy, it combined feudal *seigneuries* in the hands of a single seigneur (the monarch) in order to protect aristocratic property and privileges. Monarchs, who themselves belonged to the hierarchy of landed nobles and depended largely on their support, did not bring about any far-reaching changes in aristocratic social and economic domination. The landed nobility was exempted almost entirely from taxes (absolute monarchies lived largely on the taxes of peasants), continued to own the bulk of the fundamental means of production in the economy, and to occupy the great majority of positions within the total apparatus of political power (Anderson 1974: 18).

However, after the sixteenth century, European monarchs introduced reforms in response to fiscal crises which encroached on aristocratic privileges. The struggle that this precipitated has often been characterized as culminating in a revolt against the mercantilist systems of 'Absolutist' states. But, once in control of state power, aristocratic landholding and financial interests only selectively dismantled these systems.[5] The social logics, structural forms, and cultural themes of those economic systems endured. In Britain, as in most European countries, mercantile policies and doctrines predominated until the middle of the twentieth century, particularly those that promoted overseas commerce, restricted the domestic market, and established monopolistic enterprises allied with state power (but with the privatization of their returns).[6]

Conventional accounts of this history assume that opposition to absolutism was principally concerned with a variety of 'freedoms'.[7] But the freedom that was being sought was freedom from a regulatory apparatus that ensured transparent, competitive markets, adequate provisioning of local communities, fair practice, and protection against monopoly and speculation, shortages and high prices.[8] Proponents of the 'free' market railed against the 'inefficiencies' of this apparatus; but their chief concern was to secure freedom from 'the requirement to trade inside open markets, by means of open transactions, and according to the rules and regulations which ensured fair practices and prices' (Lie 1993: 283).

In Britain, government rules and restrictions on economic activity were 'swept out of the statute books' (Deane 1979: 220), ending restrictions on capital, and dismantling the regulatory infrastructure of the moral economy that had developed over the course of the previous century. Restrictions on exports were lifted, import taxes imposed, and measures against engrossing and forestalling abolished (Lie 1993: 293). With these acts, the 'very authority whose responsibility it was to ensure the open market became the force which undermined it' (Lie 1993: 294).

### *Industrial concentration and production for export*

It is generally assumed that differentiation was the master process in nineteenth-century European industrialization. It was not. Instead, rural areas were deindustrialized and this led increasingly to the concentration of production in urban centres.

For several centuries industry was found mainly in small towns and rural areas, much of it owned by aristocrats, who played a major role as both entrepreneurs and investors of capital (Lieven 1992: 119).[9] Feudal landlords, drawing solely on the labour of serfs, dominated textile and mining industries and funded canal building and other improvements in transport in order to exploit the mineral deposits on their lands. The large increase in manufacturing in the seventeenth century, which produced workshops all over Europe and in all branches of production, came mostly from the proliferation of semi-independent producers in households and small shops. Capitalists multiplied as well, acting mainly as merchants rather than direct supervisors of manufacturing.[10]

But as capitalists began to take direct hold over the processes of production there was 'a great movement of capital concentration'. Production became concentrated into 'a few intensely industrial regions and, as capital, labour, and trade drained from the rest of the continent' (Tilly 1984: 48), many previously industrial areas were deindustrialized (Tilly 1983: 134), 'proletarians departed from the countryside and withdrew from agriculture, net rural–urban migration accelerated, cities increased rapidly, and differences between country and city accentuated' (Tilly 1984: 7–8).

The concentration of production in cities during the eighteenth century swelled the urban population, leading to the development of large-scale shoemaking and clothing industries and a great boom in the building industries. This boom required stonemasons, carpenters, and joiners, and led to a corresponding boom in the furniture, paperhanging, and artistic trades. Butchers, bakers, and metalworkers were needed to provision workers with food, cooking pots, cutlery, and other products. There was also demand for pottery, glass, and cotton manufacture on the part of a growing middle-income group of professional men, independent craftsmen, merchants and shopkeepers, small rentiers, and farmers, both in Britain and in the American colonies (Davis 1979: 64).

This expanding domestic economy provided the means for Britain's industrial 'take-off'. But, long before it had been exhausted as a market for goods and capital it ceased to expand. Instead, in Britain, as everywhere, industrialization led, not to the growth of a national market, but to the expansion and cross-national integration of export sectors. The output of Britain's industrial production consisted largely of transport and communication infrastructure for purchase by foreign governments and ruling groups. Its export industries expanded 'much more, and more rapidly' than its home markets in the first half of the eighteenth century;[11] and they expanded faster than the economy as a whole throughout the nineteenth century.

A comparison of British industries that remained overwhelmingly dependent on home consumption[12] and those that relied mainly on export markets between 1781 and 1913 is given in Table 3.1.

### *The increased exploitation of labour*

As they took control of the industrial production that had grown up in Europe over several centuries and encroached upon the power of the state, landowners and their merchant allies in Europe turned the state back into an 'apparatus' of aristocratic domination.[13] Governments abdicated from previously held responsibilities and commitments, ended governmental limitations on exploitation for personal profit, and changed the nature and scope of exploitation.[14] New forms of dominating and putting to work the lower classes emerged, based, not on a revolutionary transformation of means of production (and an increase in relative surplus value production), but on an increase in *absolute* surplus value production.

*Table 3.1* Mean coefficient of growth of selected UK industries, 1781–1913

| *Industries producing largely:* | | | |
|---|---|---|---|
| *For export* | | *For the home market* | |
| Iron and steel products | 4.2 | Sugar | 2.1 |
| Pig iron | 4.2 | Bread and pastry | 1.1 |
| Coal | 3.1 | Flour | 0.8 |
| Cotton fabrics | 3.0 | Meat products* | 0.8 |
| Cotton yarn | 2.8 | Leather | 0.1 |
| Woollen fabrics | 1.8 | | |
| **Total** | **3.2** | | **1.0** |

Source: Hoffman (1955: 83, 85).

* Figure is for 1855–1913.

Profit is increased by reducing the cost of labour, either by (1) using machines to reduce the number of workers used to produce the same amount of articles (i.e., increasing *relative surplus value production*), or (2) increasing the amount of labour at no additional cost by, for instance, applying large quantities of unskilled or semi-skilled labour to production, or increasing the duration or the normal intensity of labour (i.e., increasing *absolute surplus value production*). The *first* of these raises the amount of capital devoted to technological inputs, and so lowers the relative contribution of capital invested in labour power in the total mix of capital inputs. While this might raise the amount of surplus, the *rate of surplus production* – and, thus, the rate of profit – would decline.[15] If machines are used to increase productivity in food and other wage goods sectors, this would reduce the cost of labour (the cost of reproducing labour physically) and so increase surplus labour time (unpaid labour) and, thus, the rate of surplus production. But this requires reform of land tenure and agricultural systems, and also increases the value of agricultural workers. The *second* way to reduce the cost of labour, increasing absolute surplus value production, reduces the cost of labour by getting workers to work longer or faster, by reducing the periods of the working day when they are not actually working; or by putting to work whole families (women and children) to earn, together, the same wage once paid to a single 'head of household'. Here, the employer gets more surplus labour time for no additional cost.

Britain's industrial expansion was based, not on increasing relative surplus value production, but on methods of absolute value production; not on a 'sharp rise in overall productivity', but on a 'massive enlargement' of the workforce (Darwin 2007: 195). Even where new machinery was introduced, the tendency was to increase absolute surplus value production in order to keep new machinery working and, thus, to pay back its cost (Marx 1990: Vol. I, 526, 530–531). The supply of coal increased, not by the introduction of labour-saving techniques, but by increasing the numbers of coal miners.[16] In the 1930s, 'more than 40% of British coal was cut, and practically 50% conveyed, without the aid of machinery' (Benson 1989: 16). Although British industrialization was based on the expansion of capital goods production for railway building, even here, rapid technical advances came, finally, only when compelled by military competition and the modernizing armaments industry (Mathias 1983: 373–93). The growth of Britain's metal industries, driven by expanding markets for copper for sheathing ships' bottoms, and for tin and lead, was based, not on any revolution in production techniques, but on large amounts of non-factory labour 'making little or no use of mechanical power' (Davis 1979: 26).[17] Although Britain was pre-eminent in steel production and had pioneered major innovations in its manufacture, with the exception of the Bessemer converter (1856) it was slow to apply the new methods and failed to keep up with subsequent improvements; by the early 1890s, its steel production had fallen behind that of Germany and the United States.[18] Britain had also pioneered electro-technics; but by 1913 the output of its electrical industry was little more than a third of Germany's (Hobsbawm 1968: 180). The building industries grew by expanding employment, rather than by introducing innovations either in organization or technology. New techniques were introduced 'slowly and with considerable reluctance'. In the 1930s, half the industry's workforce still practiced 'their traditional handicrafts, especially in house-building' (Benson 1989: 20). A majority of those engaged in transport worked for small employers or were self-employed; in 1931, only 28 per cent of those employed in the sector were employed by the railways (Benson 1989: 22–23).

Methods of increasing absolute surplus value production were preferred because they increase the magnitude of surplus value irrespective of whether the products of the industries affected are articles habitually consumed by workers.[19] They also offer a means of expanding production and increasing profits without additional cost either in skilled labour or machinery. New machinery requires not only an outlay of capital, but an investment in workers' training which, in turn, converts workers into a 'quasi-fixed factor' of production (Becker 1969). These costs can be avoided by applying methods of absolute surplus value production,[20] and reducing the value of labour (the cost of reproducing it) by importing cheap food from abroad.[21] Securing cheaper food and other wage goods in exchange for exported manufactured goods cheapened labour and decreased pressure on landlords to lower agricultural prices through the rationalization of agriculture. But the mass of the labour force gained nothing; food costs decreased, but so too did wages.

Workers were gathered together in common locales on coordinated work schedules, placed under continuous surveillance and standard discipline, and transformed into mere instruments of production, 'hands'. This was a radical and often brutal process, and it was affected through political and military, in addition to economic, means.[22] Between the onset of war in 1793 and 1820, Britain passed more than 60 acts concerned with repressing working-class collective action. The anti-Combination Acts of 1799 and 1801 marked the 'abdication of the State from its role as neutral arbitrator in industrial conflict' (Randall & Charlesworth 2000: 4); by 1834, 'virtually every form of working-class association or collective action' in Britain was made 'illegal or licensable by the justices of the peace' (Munger 1981: 93).[23]

Thousands of troops were deployed to keep the 'peace' in industrial towns. By the late 1830s over thirty thousand troops were on permanent garrison duty in working-class areas of industrial towns in England. In the 1840s, local barracks and a state-controlled system of paramilitary and police forces were established as part of an organization headed by the Home Office, the local military command and the local Home Office intelligence network (see Foster 1974: Chs. 3 and 4).

Along with demands to eliminate the price and wage controls and labour protections of the Absolutist state came a clamour to eliminate the remaining vestiges of the national welfare systems that, in Britain, France, and elsewhere, had developed by the eighteenth century.[24] That these pressures were linked to the demand of manufacturers for an extensive, cheap, and docile labour force[25] was clearly reflected in the New Poor Law of 1834. The Law centred poor relief on workhouses, which locked workers into a choice between 'the iron-discipline' of either the factory or the workhouse (Lis & Soly 1979: 201). Public support would not go to individuals whose situation was in any way better than 'the independent labourer in the lowest class' (from report to Parliament, quoted in Lis & Soly 1979: 200), and would provide a standard of living below that of the lowest independent producer. To force the destitute to accept any job in any place for any wage, workhouses were designed to be as much as possible like prisons (Lis & Soly 1979: 202); an able-bodied man would receive no support unless he worked. As the safety net was dismantled, women, children, and the inmates of poorhouses, workhouses, and penitentiaries became suppliers of labour; the workhouses and orphanages themselves became increasingly important as factories and workshops.[26] In this way, the cost of labour was shared between wages and poor relief.[27]

## II. Industrial production and the expansion of capital

The previous section provided snapshots of the 'industrial revolution'. We must move slightly backwards in time to fill these with detail and explain the underlying logic of the outcomes they describe.

The seventeenth century had seen an enormous increase in manufacturing throughout Europe. In England, and then in Holland, France, Spain, Italy, and Germany, domestic markets had expanded to provide an outlet for this increased production and had democratized local consumption (Perrotta 1997: 296). The idea became commonplace that increasing consumption, also by the lower classes, 'would provide a vital stimulus for industriousness and the spirit of enterprise' (Perrotta 1997: 298–299).[28]

However, after the mid-eighteenth century 'feeling against the labouring poor grew' as the appearance of new luxury goods and the growth of the merchant class began 'to change patterns of consumption and to blur the lines between the classes' (Perrotta 1997: 304).[29] With the blurring of class distinctions, and concern with enforcing the industriousness of labour and increasing and cheapening its supply,[30] writers began 'to condemn consumption by labourers of goods which were not demanded by the traditional standard of the labourer's class'.[31] Many condemned the luxury of the lower classes as a social or political evil. The general argument was that increased consumption by the lower classes and 'the luxury of the rising classes' would lead to the destruction of moral values and traditions and the overthrow of the old social order.[32]

Debates about consumption, class, and social order continued throughout the remainder of the eighteenth century. But they appear to have been definitively resolved as a result of the experience of mobilizing mass armies for the French Revolutionary wars.

### *Mass mobilization for war and its implications for industrial production*

Europe emerged into its first century of industrial capitalism from the crucible of the French Revolution and the quarter century of war and revolutionary turmoil that followed. The Revolution marked 'a date in the human mind', as Lamartine said (in Hobson 1902: 9). It was 'something quite unprecedented': a political revolution that claimed to be acting on behalf of humankind and sought proselytes all over the world (de Tocqueville 1955: 110). In the world war which it triggered, French Revolutionary armies overran 'a vaster area than any body of conquerors since the Mongols' (Hobsbawm 1962: 117). This was the context within which dominant classes in Europe undertook to mobilize mass workforces for industrial production. A quarter of a century of political volatility had revealed the dangers of mobilizing – training, educating and, in other ways, empowering – masses of workers. At the time, many analogies were drawn between the trained and compact mass army of soldiers created in the Great War (1793–1815) and the mass industrial army of workers needed for industrial capitalist production.[33] Moreover, socialism had been born in the French Revolution and its focus, in particular, on eradicating private property – something dominant classes had struggled to achieve over the course of a century or more[34] – seemed, in combination with the revolutionary ferment unleashed by the war, to threaten an anti-capitalist revolt of the masses.

Wars in the eighteenth century had been fought with massive and expensive professional or mercenary armies recruited from all over Europe. The use of these armies had worked to increase the power of wealthy classes. But mass mobilization during the Napoleonic era had strengthened radical forces throughout Europe;[35] so much so that, after the wars, Europe emerged into what would be the start of a century of more-or-less continual struggle.[36] Consequently, there was a return to old-style armies of paid professionals, mercenaries, and 'gentlemen' (Silver & Slater 1999: 190).[37] Mass armies were not mobilized again, either for war or for industry, until 1914. Mass mobilization for industry (as for war) creates a compact and potentially dangerous force. Thus, to maintain control over labour, dominant classes limited the expansion of industry at home and expanded production largely for export. For centuries, landlords, confronted with the 'great fear' of mass peasant uprisings, had organized production in ways that reinforced the existing relations of power and authority. They did the same when seeking to profit from industrial production.[38]

It is generally assumed that, in the nineteenth century, capitalists in Britain and France and elsewhere in Europe were forced to seek for larger markets and more profitable fields of investment abroad because domestic markets were not yet developed enough to absorb the output of expanded production and to provide profitable investment opportunities for surplus capital. The notion that these countries had capital-saturated economies was current during the nineteenth century (and has since been embraced by a wide variety of theorists and historians).[39]

But capital exporters did not have capital-saturated domestic economies.[40] The two largest foreign investors, Britain and France, suffered from inadequate investment at home.[41] London's institutions were more highly organized to provide capital to foreign investors than to British industry.[42] Capital flowed between London and every corner of her Empire, but at home only 'a limited number of firms in a limited number of industries could get access to the London new-issues market' (railroads, shipping, steel, cotton after 1868, and banks and insurance companies). For the most part, 'the flow of savings was aimed abroad and not to domestic industries' (Kindleberger 1964: 62). The French, on the whole, also did not invest domestically in large-scale industrial enterprises. French industrial banks were mainly interested in underwriting foreign bonds rather than in lending to domestic industry (Baldy 1922, Collas 1908). The merchant banks also concentrated mainly on the sale of foreign securities, rather than on securities for domestic industry (Bigo 1947: 124).

This was not due to the 'saturation' of their domestic economies. The notion of 'saturation' only makes sense if domestic markets are assumed to consist solely of owners of capital, and if the mass of the population is assumed to be irrelevant to demand for any goods other than those necessary for their own physical reproduction. As John Hobson argued, home markets were 'capable of indefinite expansion' given 'a constantly rising standard of national comfort'; and that whatever was produced in England could be consumed in

England, had there been 'a proper distribution of 'the "income" or power to demand commodities' (Hobson 1902: 88). The 'rate of national consumption would probably have given full, constant, remunerative employment to a far larger quantity of private and public capital' than had been employed. Instead, he noted, more than a quarter of the population of British towns was living at a standard 'below bare physical efficiency' (Hobson 1902: 86).[43]

Funds used for British foreign investment could have found productive uses at home and could have 'helped to augment the stock of domestic housing and other urban social overhead projects that would have expanded the domestic market for the expanded output of the British economy' (Barratt Brown 1970: x).[44] If foreign lending had been on a smaller scale and investors had exploited opportunities at home, the technical performance of British industry would have been improved (Lewis 1972: 27–58; 1978a: 176–177; see, also, Trebilcock 1981). France, the second largest investor, was technologically backward, and clearly in need of much larger home investment.[45] French deposit banks, while furnishing capital to German producers through loans to financial intermediaries, were reluctant to provide capital for French industry. By 1914, France's total industrial potential was only about 40 per cent of Germany's (P. Kennedy 1987: 222).

Not only was investment needed at home but, Patrick O'Brien argues, there is no evidence that 'average' rates of profit 'which European capitalists derived from investment and trade with Africa, Asia, and tropical America' rose persistently 'above the rates of return which they could have earned on feasible investments at home' (O'Brien 1982: 8). According to Lance Davis and Robert Huttenback (1988), after 1880 the rates of profits on Britain's colonial investments fell *below* comparable returns from Britain itself. In addition, 'conducting business in a colony or other countries with different cultures, languages and market structures undoubtedly increased the level of risk' (Brayshay, Cleary, & Selwood 2007: 146).

Many theorists contend that, irrespective of the rate of profit it earned, colonization was crucial to the industrialization of Europe, as a means both of acquiring raw materials and of accumulating capital (see, e.g. Wallerstein 1974: 38, 51, 93–95, 237, 269, 349). But Paul Bairoch has argued that not only did 'core' countries have an abundance of the minerals of the Industrial Revolution (iron ore and coal), they were almost totally self-sufficient in raw materials and, in fact, exported energy to the Third World (Bairoch 1993: 172).[46] Bairoch argues that colonialism may actually have hampered national economic growth and development in 'core' countries. Colonial countries like Britain, France, the Netherlands, Portugal, and Spain were characterized by a slower rate of economic growth and industrialization during the nineteenth century than Belgium, Germany, Sweden, Switzerland and the United States (Bairoch 1993: 77).

## *The social logic of industrial capitalist expansion*

The inherent drive or necessity generating expansion was the need both to maintain the basic relation of capital and to resolve the tension between commercial expansion and the maintenance of rural hierarchies. Neoclassic economics treats markets as arenas in which economically rational actors trade without regard to social identity, political loyalties, or affiliations (Carruthers 1996: 162).[47] But, as Braudel noted, capitalism does 'not take up all the possibilities for investment and progress' that economic life offers (Braudel 1982: 422). The preferences of market participants concerning what to produce and for whom are shaped by social relations and by concerns relating to class, power, and status.[48]

Industrial capitalism requires foreign markets in order to maintain the basic relation of capital (the subordination of labour to capital). To maintain the basic relations of capital – to maintain a largely unskilled, uneducated, impoverished, and disenfranchised workforce that could be easily subordinated to capital – required that industrial production be geared to producing commodities for consumption *abroad*; for to industrially produce goods for home use would require that workers be paid sufficient wages to enable them to consume what they produced, and this would lead to social levelling. Thus, in the nineteenth century, there was a change in the composition of output in favour of capital goods and services for upper-class consumption (Deane 1979: 270). European producers created consumers by encouraging rapid capital accumulation and concentration in other countries. They introduced new export crops – coffee, tea, cocoa, sugar, rubber – or devised land-settlement schemes that stimulated production of traditional crops, such as rice, for export; and constructed physical infrastructure (roads, railroads, port facilities). Dominant classes everywhere pursued an externally oriented industrial expansion that limited the geographic and sectoral spread of development and the growth of organized labour.

Britain used capital exports to develop purchasing power and demand among foreign governments and elites for ships, guns and ammunition, railways, canals, and other public works and services. These enabled the development and transport of food and raw materials exports to Britain, thus creating additional foreign purchasing power and demand, while decreasing the price of food, and thereby the value of labour, at home,[49] and obviating the need for agricultural reform (thus, alleviating the tension, supposedly resolved by an earlier 'agricultural revolution', between traditional rural structures and commercial expansion).[50] Elites sought to keep labour poor and in excess of demand (in 'reserve'). They worked to destroy the market position of the skilled labourers of previous centuries who were more independent and valuable, and could therefore command higher wages and regulate their own time; and kept peasants and rural workers poor and weak. They created cartels, syndicates, tariffs, and corporatist arrangements of a discriminatory and 'asymmetrical' nature that enabled them to monopolize domestic industry and international trade. Thus on the eve of World War I, industrialization in Britain (the first 'industrial nation') was still sectorally and geographically limited;[51] carried out by atomized, low-wage, and low-skilled labour forces; based on production for export to governments, elites, and ruling groups in other states and territories; and characterized by restricted and weakly integrated domestic markets. Mechanization, skilled labour, and rising productivity and real wages were found only in sectors producing for export; and these sectors had only a limited impact on the rest of the economy. Little attempt was made to expand or mechanize industries producing goods for domestic household consumption.

Throughout the nineteenth century, Britain expanded its shipbuilding, boiler making, and gun and ammunition industries to penetrate and defend markets overseas; and built foreign railways, canals, and other public works, including banks, telegraphs, and other public services owned by or dependent upon governments. It exported rails and rolling stock for railroad building abroad, and financed its construction with loan capital. Railroads brought cheap grain and meat to the ports (also constructed with British capital), and British steamships, protected by British naval ships and armaments, brought it to Britain. The financial centre of this system was the City of London, which, like the advanced sector of a 'dependent' third-world economy, worked to build strong linkages between these British export industries and foreign economies, rather than to integrate various parts of the domestic economy (more on this below). At the same time, elites around the world, whether in colonies, former colonies, or states that had never been colonies, imported British capital and goods, developed mines and raw materials exports, and built railways and ports, in order to extend, consolidate, and maintain their power and become wealthy. While increasing blocs of territory throughout the world were covered with networks of British built and financed railroads and provisioned by British steamships and defended by British warships,[52] by the beginning of the twentieth century Britain itself was, as one scholar described it, 'the equivalent of an underdeveloped country in such a critical condition that [today] the relief agencies of the world would be mounting huge campaigns to work there' (Warner 1979: 17). One observer described England on the eve of World War I as consisting of 'small islands of luxury and ostentation surrounded by a sea of mass poverty and misery' (Joad 1951).

According to the conventional view, the separation of the direct producer from the means of production creates a home market by transforming the great mass of the rural population into freely mobile wage earners, who then migrate to the towns and factories where their labour is increasingly needed. Urban populations depend on the market to procure their needs. A rise in urbanization, therefore, leads to an expansion of the market for mass-produced goods for local consumption: food, buildings, clothing, shoes, furniture, tools, and utensils of all sorts. But domestic markets can only expand to absorb more of the output of production if the standard of consumption of the masses is being raised. However, elites were reluctant to provide the mass of the population with a standard of consumption high enough to absorb the output of expanded production through higher wages and through inward investment and development. They feared that this would lead to social levelling and undermine the social hierarchies that reproduce the elite as an elite. Consequently, labour was 'too poor to provide an intensive market for anything but the absolute essentials of subsistence: food, housing and a few elementary pieces of clothing and household goods' (Hobsbawm 1968: 135; see, also, Benson 1989: 41).

Europeans, facing poverty and economic fear, left *en masse*. More than 50 million people emigrated to Canada, the United States, Latin America, South Africa, Australia, and New Zealand. The British Isles, where people were affected first and worst by the new industrial system, were the main source of migrants until the last decades of the nineteenth century.

## III. Core and periphery redefined

The division of the world between a 'core' of states (that developed originally in northwestern Europe: England, France, and Holland), and a 'periphery' (most of the rest of the world) has become a commonplace. A key aspect of this division is thought to have been the development of different class structures in Europe (the core) and non-European (peripheral) areas of the world. The general assumption is that, in Europe a strong, independent capitalist bourgeoisie emerged in the nineteenth century and played an important role in the development of industrial capitalism; while in other regions of the world, imperialism prevented the indigenous bourgeoisie from acquiring either political or economic hegemony. If it developed there at all, it was either too weak to challenge the power of traditional elites (e.g., Chase-Dunn 1975) or was itself a vital part of the system of domination that perpetuates dependency relations.[53] Despite the centrality of this distinction in core/periphery perspectives, it is one that depends on a very selective and ideological reading of modern European history.

### *The 'class succession' thesis and the capitalist bourgeoisie*

Many scholars assume that the social structures which characterized the European societies of the 'core' during the course of their industrial development were strikingly dissimilar from those found in other areas of the world in the nineteenth century. Most assume that a strong, independent capitalist bourgeoisie emerged in western Europe as a result of 'bourgeois revolutions'. Either (1) the struggle between the capitalist bourgeoisie and the old aristocracy resulted in the victory of the capitalist class in the course of the nineteenth and early twentieth centuries (e.g. Chirot 1977), (2) a process of 'bourgeoisification' destroyed the old landed class by fusing it with or subordinating it to the new capitalist classes,[54] or (3) the European feudal landowning class became a capitalist landed aristocracy in the sixteenth century so that, by the nineteenth century, there was no feudal aristocracy because its class nature had become thoroughly transformed (e.g. Wallerstein 1974, 1991).[55] In all cases, the result was a 'bourgeois revolution' that marked the emergence of a new capitalist bourgeoisie, either through defeating, subordinating, or assimilating the old landed elite, or through the transformation of the old elite into a new class.

It is generally recognized that many states in Europe did not experience a 'bourgeois revolution' and, consequently, travelled a 'road' to industrial capitalist development that was different than the one travelled by Britain and other northwestern European societies. This second road also led to the achievement of industrial capitalism, but it was slower and took longer because the absence of a bourgeois revolution meant that a well-entrenched aristocracy remained separate from the industrial bourgeoisie and was able to resist and block industrialization.[56] What determined which of these roads characterized a society's industrial development was the nature of the relationship between the aristocracy and the Absolutist state. The first road emerged as a result of an Aristocratic–Absolutist conflict, the second as a result of an Aristocratic–Absolutist fusion. But the distinction defining these two roads – Aristocratic–Absolutist conflict versus Aristocratic–Absolutist fusion – is based on a misunderstanding of the conflict between aristocracies and Absolutist states.

As was argued in the previous section, opponents of Absolutism had limited aims: they sought, not to revolutionize production or transform societies, but to deregulate capital. Their success did not produce bourgeois revolutions and bring new classes to power: it ensured that the expansion of industrial production would reproduce existing hierarchies. Their chief concern was with state regulation of economic resources and activities.

Marxist historians once assumed that France's Aristocratic–Absolutist conflict ended in the Revolution of 1789 with the victory of a rising industrial and commercial class whose values and policies were opposed to those of a decayed 'feudal' order. However, the old feudal classes in France were not eliminated in the Revolution; and, in the 'restoration' that followed, these classes returned to their titles and much of their land, and consolidated their position as a 'governing class'.[57] The features of France that, in 1815, resembled a 'bourgeois' state, were the work, not of the Revolution, but of the *ancien regime*.[58] Marxist historians also assumed that England's revolution in 1688 established the political supremacy of the bourgeoisie (Anderson 1979: 18–19). Though views on this have changed, it is still assumed that Britain's subsequent industrial development was 'promoted and led by an independent capitalist middle class (Chirot 1977: 223).[59] However, industrial expansion in Britain, as in other European countries, was dominated by its traditional landowning elite. The old forms of medieval England 'were not shattered or swept away, but filled with new content' (Luxemburg 1976: 232); 'new wealth did not challenge old, but simply bought a landed estate. . . . At the same time, the younger sons of landowners were joining the sons of urban tradesmen and master manufacturers among the merchants and professional men, thus strengthening the social bonds between landed and other forms of economic and social power' (Morris 1979: 15).

While the European feudal landowning class may have become a capitalist landed aristocracy, there is no evidence that its class nature became thoroughly transformed, as Wallerstein maintains (1997: 105–106). They may have embraced a market philosophy, but they remained the heirs of a feudal tradition and were 'heavily influenced by pre-capitalist notions of order, authority, and status'.[60] They 'absorbed the brains from the other strata that drifted into politics' and 'continued to man the political engine, to manage the state, to govern' (Schumpeter 1976: 136–37). They held on to their power and wealth, either by directly controlling the government (as in Germany and Austria), or under either a new bourgeois governing elite (as in Spain) or an elite composed of traditional notables and newly assimilated wealthy bourgeois elements (as in many other parts of Europe). Either way, political leadership, both at the national and local levels remained in the hands of large landowners or traditional bureaucratic elites. In Britain, rising industrial and commercial interests did not dominate cabinets, governmental bureaucracies, legislatures, or local government until after World War II. The overrepresentation of the nobility in both national and provincial assemblies[61] allowed them to remain a major political force. Until 1914, non-industrial Britain could easily outvote industrial Britain (Hobsbawm 1968: 196). Despite all that had been written about industrialists replacing landowners as the dominant element in the ruling elite, as late as 1914 industrialists 'were not sufficiently organized to formulate broad policies or exert more than occasional influence over the direction of national affairs' (Boyce 1987: 8).

The continued importance of the aristocracy can be seen also in positive outcomes in struggles that had class-differentiated interests. State policies were generally consistent with the immediate interests of the landlords. In Britain, agrarian reform was not a serious item on the historical agenda until the world wars. Because of tariffs and agricultural subsidies from the government, as well as tax and pricing policies, agricultural production was not subordinated to the market until after World War II. State protection of the agricultural sector allowed agrarian producers to maintain the social *status quo* in rural areas. Landlords experienced no significant political setbacks nor suffered any erosion of their hold on agrarian labour until the world wars.[62] Labour legislation effectively prohibited the organization of agrarian labour until World War I; even after the war, organizers had limited access to the peasantry and rural labour.[63] Wages of agricultural workers were kept depressed until World War I. In 1912, more than 60 per cent of the adult agricultural labourers of England received less than the amount necessary for the maintenance of a labourer and his family. The average wages on the land were lower, the hours longer, and the housing and other conditions of living worse, than in any other large industry. Labourers could not combine. If they attempted to do so, they could be turned out of their homes.[64] A statutory minimum wage was not achieved for rural workers until 1917 (Read 1964: 217–219).

The great landowners' monopoly of most arable and irrigated land and their control of the rural population – of its vote as well as its labour power – guaranteed them a continuing base of political and economic power. Throughout the nineteenth century, the larger landowners continued to enlarge and consolidate their holdings. In 1897, 175,000 people owned ten-elevenths of the land in England, and forty million people the remaining one-eleventh (Romein 1978: 195). The landless rural population subsisted on low wages, the rest on small plots of land without access to loan capital for the purchase of tractors, metal ploughs, or chemical fertilizer. Despite their having been available for some 30 years or more, the majority of farms in England and Wales did not possess either a tractor or a milking machine until World War II. As late as 1935, 18 per cent of all agricultural holdings comprised less than five acres, and a further 45 per cent less than 50 acres (Benson 1989: 19).[65] On the eve of World War I, more than 60 per cent of the adult agricultural labourers of Britain received less than the amount necessary for the maintenance of a labourer and his family on workhouse fare.[66]

## *Dependent and independent development*

The different social structures that are assumed to have characterized the core and the periphery are thought to have been responsible for shaping their development in significantly different ways. In the core, the local independent capitalist bourgeoisie was able to obtain control over international commerce and accumulate capital surpluses from this trade. States in the periphery, which lacked independent, indigenous bourgeoisies, exported raw materials to the core, and much of the capital surplus this generated was expropriated by the core through unequal trade relations. Instead of undergoing an independent process of capitalist development, regions in the periphery 'found themselves incorporated into the emerging Europe-centred capitalist system as colonies, dependencies, or clients of one sort or another' (Sweezy 1982: 211). The term 'dependent development' is meant to describe the characteristics of peripheral development. Chief among these are dualism and monopoly, a lack of internal structural integration, and dependency on outside capital, labour, and markets. What this produced was not the viable, diversified modern economic system that developed in the countries of the 'core', but rather a few islands of economic modernity separated from the rest of the local economy and tied to Europe' (Borthwick 1980: 52).

But all of the elements associated with dependent development were also characteristic of development in Europe before 1945. These elements were not just present in some European regions at some points in time: they were found everywhere in Europe and throughout the nineteenth century, and were characteristic of and integral to long-term processes of growth.[67]

In *The European Experience* (1985), Dieter Senghaas pointed out that typical enclave economies had formed in parts of Europe in the nineteenth century (e.g., in southern, southeastern, and eastern Europe, and in Ireland). In Denmark, Norway, Sweden, Finland, Ireland, Portugal, Spain, and Romania development was characterized by the export-oriented production of foodstuffs and agricultural and mineral raw materials. Up until the end of World War II, the southeastern regions of the Austro-Hungarian Empire remained 'a piece of the Third World in Europe' (Senghaas 1985: 50). In all these countries the growth dynamics were '*exogenously determined* and *dependent*' (Senghaas 1985: 87; emphasis in the original). This 'peripheralization' was characteristic of economies in Europe that were 'not typical colonies under foreign control' and was the result of decisions taken 'within the respective societies themselves' (Senghaas 1985: 155).

But Senghaas argues that other European countries (Britain, Belgium, France, Germany, Austria–Hungary) experienced what he calls an 'autocentric' development, one in which the 'development impetus stems from within' and there is a 'marked bias towards the domestic market' (Senghaas 1985: 29). So, for instance, in Britain, 'the cheapening of foodstuffs owing to the import of inexpensive grain and processed food (cheese, butter, etc.) made possible a rising standard of living for the urban–industrial population and with it a widening of the market for manufactures' (Senghaas 1985: 42). In other countries (Belgium, France, Germany, and Austria–Hungary) it was railroad building that made possible their pursuit of an autocentric development focused principally on the domestic economy.[68]

This seems logical; but, historically, it is not what occurred. Neither in Britain nor anywhere else in Europe was development fuelled for very long by the expansion of the domestic market. In Britain, the import of inexpensive foodstuffs made it possible to keep wages low, increase profits, and invest those profits in export industries and overseas markets. Moreover, treating railroad building and infrastructural development as evidence of autocentric development is problematic. In most cases, railroads were designed to promote exports, and to provide a sop for investment capital, and a means of transporting troops quickly to hinterlands in order to quell trouble or to assert territorial claims. Dismantling internal barriers to trade and other reforms associated with commercialization was not undertaken, as it is often assumed, with a view of developing a large domestic market, but to increase production for export.[69]

Until the twentieth century, the basic structures of society in Europe were more similar than dissimilar to those that existed elsewhere. Industrial expansion, in Europe as elsewhere, dramatically increased overseas sales but left traditional social and political structures largely intact. As everywhere, the expansion of production was undertaken, not by or for a new capitalist bourgeoisie, but by aristocracies and other elites and wealthy groups seeking to expand production while, at the same time, maintaining the class, land, and income structures on which their social power rested.

While no definition of dependent development is likely to meet with universal agreement, the features listed in Table 3.2 are ones that are the most frequently and universally cited as comprising dependent development.

Dependency and world-systems theories maintain that structural relations with the core placed constraints on colonial capitalism, preserving and freezing traditional relations of power and production (see Chapter 1). Paul Baran asserted that partly or wholly self-sufficient economies of some agricultural countries were reoriented toward the production of marketable commodities, but without replacing feudal relations with capitalist relations. These societies live in 'the twilight between capitalism and feudalism' (Baran 1970: 286).

*Table 3.2* Dependent and independent development

| *Dependent development* | *Core* | *Periphery* |
|---|---|---|
| History of colonialism | √ | √ |
| The condition of being a less-developed and not yet well-integrated nation state in an international environment dominated by more developed and homogeneous states[70] | √ | √ |
| Dualism (i.e., the lack of integration of various parts of the domestic economy due to strong linkages between portions of the economy and foreign economies) | √ | √ |
| Dependence on a narrow range of export goods and a few trading partners | √ | √ |
| Dependence on the foreign supply of important factors of production (technology, capital) | √ | √ |
| Specialization in the production of raw materials and primary crops (more generally, limited developmental choices that constrain a country's capacity for setting its own developmental course) | √ | √ |
| Inequality (both of income and of land-tenure structures) and a growing gap between elites and masses | √ | √ |
| Absence of an independent indigenous capitalist bourgeoisie and a dominant role for the state in development | √ | √ |
| Formal but inauthentic, partial, and unstable democracy | √ | √ |

The legacy of this is evident in the problems of contemporary 'third world' development, which are seen as:

> the result of a more protracted transition caused by the fact that the processes of modernization and urban industrialization in the periphery are dependent for a long time on pre-capitalist modes of production in the country-side which have articulated with an externally imposed capitalist mode of production.
>
> (Berger 1994: 262–63)

If European imperial powers limited infrastructural and social investment in other regions to what was compatible with their strategic and commercial aims, this was as true at home as it was abroad – and not only in the backward 'Great Powers' of Europe, such as Austria–Hungary, and Italy; but also in Germany, France, and Britain. In 1914, Britain's industrialization was still sectorally and geographically limited in the way that dualistic colonial and post-colonial economies have been described. Industrialization had taken place in a few small districts of England – in south Lancashire, some sectors of the East Midlands and Yorkshire, Birmingham, and the Black Country (Crouzet 1970: 158, cited in Komlos 2000: 311). Landed and industrial property had become increasingly concentrated. Only in sectors producing for export was there mechanization, skilled labour, and rising productivity and real wages. These sectors did not have a profound impact on the rest of the economy. Revenues from these sectors were not invested in the expansion of production for the home market. There was little attempt to expand or mechanize industries producing goods for domestic household consumption. Instead, production expanded through the development of a circuit of capital that operated among a transnational aggregate of elites and governments. In fact, one could rewrite the history of Europe in the nineteenth and early twentieth centuries as one of successful political policies against industrialization, as an age of industrial counter-revolution (Vieregge 2003: 129–140, cited in Terlouw 2009). Elites everywhere pursued growth only within a specific distribution that preserved elite privileges. Britain's 'patrician hegemony' opposed any 'aggressive development of industrialism' and the social transformation necessary to it (Weiner 1981: 7, 10). Similarly, the main part of Germany's elite, which dominated rural settings and thus the vast majority of both territory and population, opposed industrialization.[71]

Nowhere in Europe during the nineteenth century was a strong, independent industrial capitalist bourgeoisie to be found. In most of Europe, the bourgeoisie was either a foreign class, or politically and economically weak, regionally confined, and dependent on the state or the landholding aristocracy. Development was financed not by the independent indigenous capitalist bourgeoisie of Liberal lore, but by the state, by banks, and by foreign investment.[72] Most European countries in the nineteenth and early twentieth centuries were characterized by a restricted and weakly integrated domestic market. Many, both in the East and in the West, were unable to diversify

*Table 3.3* Britain's nineteenth century industrial expansion: two models compared[73]
(**Boldface** indicates characteristics that predominated throughout the century)

| **The 'European Model'** | **The Dependency Model**[74] |
|---|---|
| **1. The Landowning Class** | |
| **a. Commercialized, Bourgeoisified** | **b. Pre-Bourgeois** |
| • Willingness to sell land for money | • **Concentration of land ownership** |
| • Peasants transformed into a rural proletariat based on wage labour | • **Incomplete proletarianization of peasants; wages in kind; highly repressive labour conditions** |
| • Use of mechanized harvesting | • **Limited mechanization of agriculture** |
| • **Diversification of assets: speculation in non-landed assets (stocks and bonds)** | • Landowner assets remain in landed property |
| • Commercialized distribution of crops | • **High-cost single-crop staple agriculture; lack of flexibility in switching crops**[75] |
| • Commodification of agriculture: large-scale marketing of crops on a regional and global scale | • **Production for local consumption** |
| **2. The Structure of Class and State Power** | |
| • Strong, independent, industrial capitalist bourgeoisie | • **Alliance of capitalist bourgeoisie, state, and landholding aristocracy (and multinational corporations)** |
| • Separation of economic (class) power from political (state) power; creation of bourgeois state and bourgeois law | • **The fusion of economic power and political (state) power for extraction of surplus**[76] |
| **3. The Mode of Production** | |
| **Capitalist** | **Pre-Capitalist**[76] |
| • **Labour is** (1) 'free' of feudal obligations, (2) **dispossessed (separated from the means of production)** | • Labour is (1) **bound by feudal obligations;** (2) in possession of means of production |
| • Surplus is extracted from the dispossessed producer by economic 'coercion'' | • **Surplus is extracted from the dispossessed producer by extra-economic compulsion** |
| • Generalized commodity production | • **Self-sufficient localized** |

| | |
|---|---|
| (production primarily for sale; labour power is itself a commodity)* | **economy supplemented by simple circulation of commodities** |
| • Extended reproduction of capital and rise of organic composition of capital* | • **Simple reproduction where surplus is largely consumed** |
| **4. The Industrial Sphere** | |
| • Liberal, competitive 'bourgeois' ethos | • **Aristocratic values** |
| • Industrial competition | • **Monopolization of industry** |
| • Development of a domestic market for the products of national industry | • **Limited, weakly integrated domestic economy; strong linkages between leading sectors and foreign economies (dualism)** |
| • Diversified industrial structure with numerous linkages, including economically strategic capital goods industries | • **Dependence on a narrow range of export goods and a few trading partners** |
| • Diversification of the export structure, trade partners, and sources of capital and technology | • **Dependence on foreign supply of important factors of production (technology, capital)** |
| • Diffusion and more egalitarian distribution of purchasing power and assets | • **Inequality of income and land structures; growing gap between elites and masses** |
| • **'National' control over the investment of capital and the accumulation process** | • Limited developmental choices |

* Found only in industrial sectors producing for export.

their exports or trading partners until well into the twentieth century. Most adopted from abroad an already developed technology while retaining their 'traditional' social structure, and all were dependent on foreign capital to finance growth. Business and landed interests forged alliances similar in nature and purpose to those forged in the 'third world', and the consequences for class structures and national development were similar as well. Because of the success of these alliances in preserving and reinforcing pre-industrial civil society, on the eve of World War I Europe was still largely 'agrarian, nobilitarian, and monarchic' (Mayer 1981: 129).

## Conclusions

The 'industrial revolution' did not revolutionize technology or transform the means of production. Nor did it bring about any fundamental transformation in the nature of social and political power in Europe (Cain & Hopkins 1993: 24, 37). It was neither produced nor driven by 'Bourgeois Revolutions'. In Britain, its 'net effect' was to systematically 'advantage the older and more conservative sectors' of the wealth structure – 'above all the great landowners and the bankers and merchants of the City of London, rather than the manufacturers and industrialists' (Rubinstein 1983: 17; cited in Cain & Hopkins 1993: 37).[77] Up until the period of the world wars, the traditional aristocracy in Europe retained its wealth and power and played the dominant role in industrial capitalist development. Like its agricultural sector, Britain's financial and industrial sectors were bound by monopoly and restriction. The City of London, in which greater fortunes were made than in the whole of industry, remained 'enmeshed in a pseudo-baronial network of gentlemanly non-competition' (Hobsbawm 1968: 169). In the industrial sphere, traditional corporatist structures – guilds, patronage and clientelist networks – survived in some places and grew stronger. Elsewhere, new corporatist structures were created. As the nineteenth century progressed, industry became increasingly penetrated by feudal forms of organization, and characterized by monopolism, protectionism, cartelization and corporatism; forming small islands within impoverished, backward agrarian economies.

European states did not develop differently from 'the rest' of the world. Thus, to the extent that there was a core, it was the core of a different system than that which is usually posited, a system whose core areas were located in an archipelago of cities, each with its own periphery. Dualistic, externally oriented expansion brought cities, urban commercial centres, and export sectors across the world into closer interdependence, creating dynamic focal points of growth that developed synchronically and interdependently through trans-local interaction and connection. As we shall see in the next chapter, the form of state that became consolidated in the 'core' and 'periphery' was the same, as well.

# 4 City states and nationalism

Previous chapters have argued that capitalism was born global; that it was based on cities, and that it developed through the cross-border expansion of interconnected urban spaces that were essentially global in nature. But if capitalism developed through the expansion, not of national markets and economies, but of cities interconnected across borders, why do we treat the *nation state* as the spatial face of capital accumulation? And if capitalism did not develop national *markets* or *economies*, in what sense is it true to assume that the *states* that emerged concurrently with the development of capitalism were *national* states?

The notion of *national* territoriality, as this chapter will argue, was promulgated as part of an apparatus of economic, political and social control. It emerged in the context of the expansion of production for export and of cross-border commercial networks, the monopolization of land and industry, and the development of new forms of exploitation. It was linked with the struggle of elites to gain greater control of resources within the increasingly differentiated realms – the burgeoning cities and deindustrializing hinterlands – which characterized the territories claimed by states. However, the territorial states that developed in Europe and that, throughout the nineteenth century, were developed and promoted by Europeans there and elsewhere, resembled far more closely the city-state polities of the past 5000 years than the nationally integrated state form of national cultural imaginaries and nation-state ideology.

City states have existed for millennia, and they flourished all along the Silk Road and throughout Asia (as well as in Africa and the Americas). With the westward extension of Asian trade into Europe, city states were established in southern Europe to take advantage of opportunities to extend the Silk Road trade inland to the north and further west. Over time there developed a system of Italian city states with sufficient power to dominate trade throughout the Mediterranean and, eventually, with the emergence of city states to its north and west, this system expanded into a European system. The states that emerged on the Baltic Sea and Atlantic littorals were based on trade and manufacturing (in contrast to the largely rural Swiss city states); and they were principally concerned to secure trade routes and control the growth of rural industry in order to profit from trade linking the Baltic Sea to the Mediterranean along the Atlantic coast.

In the fifteenth century, maritime states along the Atlantic littoral loaded heavy cannon onto the ocean-going ships that had been developed to carry this trade and set out to muscle their way into the Asian commercial world. Having succeeded in this, and in securing vast new opportunities for the pursuit of profit through overseas trade, these states then sought to extend their control over larger territories so as to secure the resources and labour needed for a massive expansion of production for export. But while this produced states with larger territories, these states operated, like city states, to expand and protect external trade; and, as city states typically do, they pursued this through overseas imperial expansion. Cities remained dominant within these larger territorial domains and, with the growth of industrial production, became increasingly powerful both in absolute terms and relative to rural areas. Moreover, the socio-economic, political, and cultural interrelationships that bound cities, in Europe and across the world, to each other remained denser than those that bound together national territories

## I. The nation state and the city state: a comparison

In most discussions, the nation state is generally defined as a 'territorial' state that is in a number of ways fundamentally different from the forms of state that existed in Europe and elsewhere before the eighteenth century (e.g., the feudal state, the multi-national imperial state, the city state, and other smaller states such as princedoms, dukedoms, and emirates).

The nation state is thought to have originated in the modern city states that developed from the medieval towns of Europe. City states are autonomous, self-governing states that are led by a city and, historically, have had centralized political authority and legal systems. They vary in size, from possession of a few square miles of hinterland to huge land and sea empires, such as Rome and Venice. There are four features of the modern nation state that are thought to distinguish it from a city state and, indeed, all other forms of states that preceded its emergence.

The first feature is that the nation state is a territorial state with well-defined borders. But the city state is also a territorial state that operates within well-defined borders. Its opposite is not the territorial state but the *non-territorial* state as, for instance, the nomadic state or the feudal state (a patchwork of, often disconnected, small pieces of land). The idea of a 'territorial state' emerged with the establishment of the Westphalian state, and it was meant to describe a contrast with the feudal state. The term did not then, nor did it ever, signify a contrast with the city state (Hansen 2000: 16; see, also, Finer 1997: Vol. I, 6–7). Like other territorial states, city states 'had a dominant area surrounded by a domain of influence, produced successful economies, employed similar means of domination and surveillance (the fleet and the army, and violence), succeeded as colonial powers ('Venice was just as much a colonial power in the Levant as Holland was in the East Indies'), and established central banks that functioned as lenders of last resort and as 'instruments of power and international domination' (Braudel 1984: 295).

According to conventional accounts of the rise of the modern nation state, the military conquest of cities by rural-based rulers consolidated urban and rural areas into modern centralized states. This is the basis for what is thought to be a second feature that distinguishes the nation state from city states: its subordination of cities and all sectors and subdivisions of its territorial domain to centralized territorial rule. The expansion of trade generated incentives to establish more durable connections between urban centres and their hinterlands, to more securely weld cities to hinterlands and to larger, more militarily powerful territorial domains; to create 'an expanded capacity to monitor, contain, seize, and redistribute resources' within them (Tilly 1994: 26); and to create, as well, financial systems to facilitate this. But, while cities became more closely integrated with their hinterlands, and in some cases were absorbed into neighbouring land empires, they tended to remain dominant. Urban elites and territorial nobles allied to extract rural surplus.[1] By means of capital, urban ruling classes 'extend[ed] their influence through the urban hinterland and across far-flung trading networks' (Tilly 1992: 51), and, as they did so, cities became increasingly powerful both in absolute terms and relative to rural areas.

Land empires were attracted to cities as sources of capital for building armies and for state formation. But the pull of attraction worked the other way as well: cities seeking to better exploit hinterlands were attracted to the administrative and policing capacities of territorial rulers and the security and physical barriers that larger territorial states provide. The attraction, then, was mutual: production and trading require the protection and order that states provide, and states must depend on the wealth generated from production and trading in order to be able to provide protection.

The merging of land power and cities ensured (1) a flow of resources and labour to the cities, and (2) the financing for mass armies needed to protect these larger territorial units. But cities remained or became the dominant element in these units and were their engine of growth. Land empires generally were able to absorb cities only in agrarian regions where they tended to be more susceptible to the predations of neighbours; but major trading cities and city states only fell under the control of external jurisdictions when they lost their positions in international markets.[2]

A third feature thought to be distinctive of modern national states is that they are based on an integrated 'national market'.[3] However, like city states, 'national' territorial states historically have operated mainly to expand and protect external trade. The merging of cities with larger territories was undertaken, not to develop local or 'nationally integrated' markets, but to expand external trade.

The term 'national market' is often used to refer to the integration of standardized production processes and transport and communication systems throughout the territory of a state. The move from short-range, quasi-autonomous regional markets to nationally coordinated ones, and the dismantling of internal barriers to trade and other reforms associated with commercialization were undertaken, not to develop a large domestic market, but to increase production for external markets and to promote and protect foreign and long-distance trade. The unified administration of cities and enlarged territorial domains did not produce an integrated market to serve the needs of the local population; nor was it designed to distribute goods and services for some larger, 'national' public. Transport and communications technologies were not formed for purposes of expanding and integrating the domestic market: their chief function was to provide the technological underpinning of international trade. Railroads and telegraphs linked ports to their hinterlands, and the railway networks were linked by steam ships into an international transport system (Latham 1978: 6).

In Europe, as elsewhere, the building of transport and communication systems facilitated a unified system for the more efficient exploitation of resources for purposes of export. In Britain, better roads and canals and the growth of coastal shipping were used to provision a London population that was steadily increasing with the expansion of foreign trade. London's rapid rise was due to its domination of the export trade (by the mid-sixteenth century, London controlled 90 per cent of the chief export product – cloth). 'By 1700, up to one-half of London's population was employed in jobs relating to shipping and the port' (Lie 1993: 292). In France, Brittany existed as a domestic colony of Paris, with railroads deliberately designed to facilitate the movement of cheap Breton labour into metropolitan France (Loughlin 1985). In Spain, railways were built to facilitate export of mining products. The system radiated from Madrid, with terminal points at the seaports, and had little, if any, impact on the development of other sectors of the economy (Carr 1966; Nadal 1973: 552–553).[4]

Elsewhere, railroads were constructed to open up hinterlands for the export of wheat, tea, rice, cocoa, rubber, diamonds, gold, tin, and copper; or, as in India, to enable easier penetration of the Indian market by English goods (as well as for the large-scale production and export of foodstuffs and raw materials).[5]

While railroads served to promote exports, they also were built with two other purposes in mind. The first was to secure control by central governments over territories, to enable troops to be moved quickly to quell trouble or to assert territorial claims (Latham

1978: 17).[6] The second purpose was as a sop for investment capital. Between 1865 and 1914 almost 70 per cent of British new portfolio investment went into railways, docks, tramways, telegraphs, and telephones, as well as gas and electric works. Most of this went into the enormously capital-absorbing railways (as did the bulk of French and Belgian foreign investment). Railways absorbed 41 per cent of Britain's total international investment.[7] Only the production of modern armaments is more capital absorbing than railroads (the mass production of armaments in the United States, and their export to Europe's great and small powers, began in the 1860s) (Dobb 1963: 296).[8]

If nation states did not develop integrated home markets, they might still differ from city states in their possession of a primary sector. City states are thought to depend on imports of foodstuffs and raw materials, rather than control of their own 'primary' sectors and the accompanying political and social problems that the organization of their production might entail (Braudel 1984: 295). But city states also tended to depend on their own rural hinterlands for food and raw materials. In the Greek *polis* (the term *polis* referred both to the state and its territory) there was a division of labour between the city, the centre of commerce and industry, and the surrounding countryside, which produced agricultural goods and raw materials. Italian cities 'secured supplies of food, water, and raw materials from substantial hinterlands, measuring thousands of square kilometres', over which they exercised 'unchallenged and undivided control' (Parker 2004: 33–34).[9] In sum, in common with 'nation' states, city states also had their own primary sectors.

There is a fourth feature thought to distinguish the modern national state from the city states: a nation state is assumed to be a state in which the political and national unit are congruent (Gellner 1983). In city states, the political identity of the population which (along with its patriotism) is primarily centred on the state, is different from its ethnic identity (language, culture, religion, history, etc.), which it often shares with a number of other states (Hansen 2000: 13). But this is true, too, of nation states. Walker Connor has calculated that in all but 13 of today's states (Austria, Denmark, Germany, Iceland, Ireland, Japan, North and South Korea, Lesotho, Luxembourg, the Netherlands, Norway, and Portugal), ethnic and political identity are *not* congruent; and in six of these 13 exceptions the dominant ethnic group extends beyond the state's borders, as is often the case in city states. If we discard these six states (Austria, Germany, Ireland, North and South Korea, and Lesotho), the total number of people living in a state closely corresponding to the distribution of their ethnic group is less than four per cent – and, if we exclude the Japanese, less than one per cent (Connor 1973: 1).

In fact, the multiculturalism of 'nation states' is the result of their having been formed through a process of expansion that, as Section III will show, is essentially identical to imperialism.

The foregoing discussion is summarized in Table 4.1.

### *City states*

City states have existed in the Americas, throughout Afro-Eurasia, and more-or-less continuously around the Mediterranean for at least 3000 years.[10] Phoenician city states (Byblos, Tyre, Sidon, and Arados) were found throughout the Eastern Mediterranean littoral around 1200 BCE, and over the next 1000 years, they expanded and intensified maritime trade and established a territorial division of labour there. The city-state form was well entrenched in the Mediterranean when it was adopted by the Greeks.

*Table 4.1* A comparison of two forms of territorial state
(**Boldface** indicates the dominant characteristics of nineteenth-century European states)

| The City State | The Nation State |
|---|---|
| 1. **A territorial state with well-defined borders** | 1. A territorial state with well-defined borders |
| 2. **A central city dominates its hinterlands and other cities** | 2. Cities are subordinated to territorial rule |
| 3. **Operates to expand and protect external trade, rather than the development of a home market*** | 3. Based on an integrated 'national market' |
| 4. **Ethnic and political identity are different** | 4. Ethnic and political identity coincide |

* There are exceptions: e.g., the largely rural Swiss city states.

The rise of Rome produced the biggest city state in history. The city absorbed surrounding territories in order to secure itself from external threats, creating 'a large territorial state that gradually eliminated the independence of the other peoples who lived within it' (Parker 2004). The whole process of expansion and consolidation of this vast domain 'was generated by the growth and bound up with the fortunes, of one huge city' (Parker 2004: 63). Its empire, 'even with such giant cities as Alexandria and Antioch, was merely one big hinterland of the capital city, Rome' (Schneider 1963: 133). Rome's oligarchs initially saw land as power, but with the realization 'that trade was a more effective producer of wealth than was agriculture', they set out to conquer the Mediterranean commercial world through the militarization of trade (Parker 2004: 67–68).

Soon after the fall of the Roman Empire in the West (in the fifth century CE), the city state form reappeared in Europe. This first occurred around the shores of the Adriatic, which offered a prime location for trading the products of the Silk Road in the north and west. It was on the swamps, islands, and sandbanks at the head of the Adriatic Sea that Venice was built and, over the course of several centuries, subsequently grew to become 'the largest and most prosperous city in Europe after Byzantium' (Parker 2004: 80). By the fifteenth century, Venice had become part of a wealthy and powerful Italian city-state system whose most important members (Venice, Genoa, Florence, Siena, and Lucca) viewed themselves as the heirs of the city states of ancient Rome and Greece.

During those centuries, older city states flourished and new ones emerged in Asia, Africa, and the Americas. The older city states were those that had developed along the Silk Road in Central Asia (Tashkent, Samarkand, Bukhara, and Ferghana) and in the Tarim Basin (Kucha, Khotan, and Turfan); Chinese city states were established along the northern and southern route of the Silk Road (Shanshan, Yutian, Qiuci, Cheshi, Shule, and Yanqi), and Pyu city states existed in present-day Myanmar from the second century BCE to the mid-eleventh century CE. Newer city states included those established by the Mon people along the Mekong River in the seventh century; Cham city states established by Malay speakers who settled on mainland Asia existed along the seacoast; Sriwijaia, a powerful Malay city state, existed on the islands of Sumatra and Java between the seventh and eleventh centuries; Islamic city states (Melaka, Aceh, and Brunei, among others) were established in Malay/Sumatra between 1450 and 1625,[11] and Thai city states (Ayutthaya, Sukhothai, Lanna, and Thon Buri) flourished at various times after the ninth century.

From approximately 1000 CE, a number of city states stretched along the eastern coast of Africa from Mogadishu in the north to Sofala (in modern Mozambique) in the south (Mombasa, Gedi, Pate, Lamu, Malindi, Zanzibar, and Kilwa). City states in East Africa, in southern Somalia, Kenya, and Tanzania, and in northern Mozambique still existed in the nineteenth century. The Hausa city states, founded in the fifteenth century, lasted until 1804. The city states of the Fante people (Ghana) lasted from the fourteenth to the nineteenth century. Four city states existed in the western delta of the Niger between 1600 and 1800. The Yoruba city states in West Africa (Oyo, Ife, Illorin, and Ibaban) lasted from 1600 until 1900. Twelve to fourteen Kotoko city states that were founded in the fourteenth century also lasted until the twentieth century. In the Americas, the major Mayan cities, Palenque, Tikal, Uxmal, and Chichen Itza, flourished between 250 and 900 CE, and Mayan city states existed in the Yucatan peninsula at the time of the Spanish conquest, as did the three major city states – Tenochtitian, Taxco, and Tiatelolco – that had allied to form the Aztec empire.

In Europe, city states existed to the east and west of Venice: Kievan Rus, founded in 880, was made up of an alliance of small city states in what is today western Russia (Riga, Reval, Dorpat, Pskov, and Novgorod). Muscovy eventually became pre-eminent among these, in part because its princes became allies of and collaborators with the Mongols. The Muscovite state imported Italian artisans, builders, and architects; and German, English, and Dutch engineers and merchants; and, by the end of the sixteenth century, it had conquered western Siberia and captured control of the merchants of the North Asian forests that supplied the fur trade. Norwegian Vikings established city states in Ireland – notably Dublin – in the tenth century CE. City states emerged in Spain, the most important of which were Badajoz, Granada, Zaragoza, Seville, and Toledo, with the breakup of the Ummayad Caliphate in the eleventh century.

During the fifteenth century, the Italian city-state system expanded into a European system of city states that ran through the centre of

Europe 'from northern Italy through the Germany of Danube and Rhine to the crossroads of trade in the Netherlands' (Braudel 1984: 288).

Beginning in the thirteenth century, some 65 cities in what is now called Germany became established as self-governing states. The most important of these were Augsburg, Nuremberg, Magdeburg, Cologne, Frankfurt am Main, Hamburg, Lübeck, Bremen, Gdańsk (Danzig), and Strasbourg. Hamburg was a centre for shipping, publishing, textile production, and banking. Lübeck became the most important harbour of the Baltic Sea, 'the most travelled stretch of water, second only to the Mediterranean' (Schneider 1963: 187).

A cluster of city states also emerged in an area of swamps in the north, in Brugge (Bruges), which, like Venice, was established near the mouth of a great river on a coast of sandbars and marshes. It became closely linked with the Baltic trade and, in 1277, established the first important maritime connection between northern Europe (Brugge) and the Mediterranean (Genoa) (Parker 2004: 163–164).

As Parker describes it, Amsterdam, located in the province of Holland, was, from the outset, 'essentially a city-state, of which the province was the rural part' (Parker 2004: 177); and the Netherlands, as a whole, was in effect a grouping of city states, that 'in the guise of a territorial (nation) state persisted into the 20th century' (Parker 2004: 182).[12] Flanders remained 'a land of city states unified into a sort of federation' (Parker 2004: 169–170).

It is generally assumed that these city states were eradicated at the end of the French Revolutionary wars. In 1797, Venice was conquered by Napoleon Bonaparte, but Lucca remained an independent city state until it voted to join the Kingdom of Italy in 1860; and, until the nineteenth century, Italy consisted of a 'system of small territorial states each dominated by the oligarchy of a single city' (Tilly 1994: 18). Although the Final Act of the Congress of Vienna abolished the German city states in 1815, within the German republic which it created, some cities officially became sovereign city states, including the Free Hanseatic City of Bremen (1806–1811 and again 1813–1871), the Free City of Frankfort Am Main (1815–1866), the Free Hanseatic City of Hamburg (1806–1811 and again 1814–1871), and the Free Hanseatic City of Lübeck (1806–1811 and again 1813–1871). Danzig, which had been absorbed by Prussia in the seventeenth century, became an independent, 'free', city by the League of Nations in 1918.

## II. The aristocratic/urban alliance

According to both Liberal and Marxist historiography, nation states were created in Europe by and for a rising new capitalist bourgeoisie. For Liberals, the nation state represented the coming to prominence of a new, more rational and liberal bourgeoisie. It was an expression of the principles of popular sovereignty, national self-determination, and democracy, and provided the political framework for the establishment of liberal institutions and the gradual extension of liberalism. Marxist accounts of the rise of nation states emphasize the victory of the rising capitalist bourgeoisie in its struggle with the 'feudal' aristocracy, and the establishment of a political framework both for its class rule and for the development of capitalism.[13]

States are the outcome of struggles among different structures and sources of authority. In the consolidation of modern states in Europe, urban merchants and financiers 'typically wielded considerable influence' because they 'entered actively into public finance' and because they controlled markets that supplied state institutions with the resources they needed (Tilly 1994: 6). States 'operate chiefly as containers and deployers of coercive means, especially armed force' (Tilly 1994: 8), and chiefly for purposes of taxation, conscription, and the prevention of rebellion, as well as for protection from external threats.

But cities coordinate and channel capital flows, and states every where depended on the credit facilities of the great commercial families. However, capitalists made cash and credit available only for war or insofar as it 'increased the protection of their own uses of capital' (Tilly 1994: 11). State dependence on commercial revenues enabled merchant classes to use their wealth to gain greater economic freedom and political independence in exchange for financial support. Consequently, merchants not only enjoyed high status but in some countries, such as Holland, 'they *were* the state' (Christian 2004: 394).[14]

City government was immense and complex relative to that of local rural government. In the early commercial cities, merchants had to undertake to provide security for roads, protection from tolls and arbitrary seizures, settle disputes between sellers and buyers, and supervise exchange values. Centralizing monarchs adopted urban forms of fiscal control and laid claim to networks that had been developed by private and municipal organizations. In fact, 'what later became the fields of interstate diplomatic relations – royal coinage prerogatives and monarchical jurisdictions – were primarily shaped by merchants' networks at a time when no prince had the ability or the vision to meet these typically urban needs' (Blockmans 1994: 233).

As Chapter 3 argued, the expansion of industrial production in Europe was everywhere undertaken by aristocracies and other elites and wealthy groups who sought to profit from this expansion while, at the same time, maintaining the class, land, and income structures on which their social power rested. As they took control of the industrial production that had grown up in Europe over several centuries and encroached upon the power of the state, landowners and their merchant allies turned the state back into an apparatus of aristocratic domination.

The expansion of trade led to the concentration of wealth and power in cities, and widened income differentials between interior elites who remained dependent on agricultural taxes, and those who had control of the ports and of direct trade revenues. With the growth of cities, the possession of money became a greater power than the possession of land, further undermining the power of landed elites and transferring power to merchants. However, 'new wealth (manufacturers and industrialists) did not challenge old, but simply bought a landed estate'; and the younger sons of landowners joined the sons of urban tradesmen and master manufacturers among the merchants and professional men, 'thus strengthening the social bonds between landed and other forms of economic and social power' (Morris 1979: 15).

England came to be dominated by an alliance between the great landowners and the bankers and merchants of the City of London. In the eighteenth century, the links between the 'city' and landed society had become more intimate as vast increases in the public debt created a 'stock-and-bondholding aristocracy', and the sons of wealthy landowners and aristocrats were trained for administrative, diplomatic, military, legal, or banking careers. By the 1840s, 'a large fraction of the landed gentry had become directly involved in commercial or financial (but not industrial) activity or in the liberal professions, particularly the law' (Boyce 1987: 19, 20). Merchants who had made their fortunes in the city purchased rural estates and, eventually, made their way into landed society, resulting in 'the urbanization of the surrounding countryside' (Parker 2004: 95–96). In Germany a feudal landed aristocracy and industrial plutocracy merged through frequent intermarriage. Up to 1918, industrial magnates, the landed aristocracy, heads of the army, and the top bureaucracy constituted 'the closely knit ruling system of Germany' (Sohn-Rethel 1978: 52).

In much of Central and Eastern Europe, the bourgeoisie consisted of foreign colonists – usually German, Jewish, or Greek, but also Polish and Italian – who were nationally, as well as socially, different from the surrounding population. Up to the second half of the nineteenth century, and sometimes even into the early twentieth century, many towns in Central and Eastern Europe were German, Jewish, Greek, or Italian enclaves within Slav, Magyar, or Romanian societies. In Poland, Bohemia, and the Slavonic districts of southeastern Austria, the towns were for many centuries exclusively German. Well into the nineteenth century all the larger towns of Hungary were essentially German. Commercial life and industry were controlled by ethnic Germans in Estonia and Latvia. Jews constituted the main urban class in Romania and Poland, as well as in parts of Lithuania. These foreign bourgeoisies represented an international class. Their prosperity was based on their having an international network at their disposal; and 'their primary interest, therefore, was in maintaining the autonomy of the cities and the links among them, rather than in establishing national markets' (Hobsbawm 1962: 166).

## III. State formation in Europe I: imperial expansion at home

Processes of 'nation building' as they unfolded, originally, in Europe bore all the political, economic, cultural, and military features of imperialism and colonialism. They involved territorial expansion from political centres or 'cores', and the absorption of areas with distinctly different traditions and political institutions. Western European states were formed by groups who conquered and colonized territories and subjugated, massacred, expelled, or forcibly assimilated their native populations. Where territories contained ethnically heterogeneous populations, claims were often based on 'historical rights' going back to medieval or even ancient times. Additional claims often enlarged the original territory on the basis of 'strategic' or economic considerations. These territories frequently contained either the most ethnically heterogeneous or the most homogeneously foreign population of the territories claimed by the state. Once statehood was achieved, the ruling nation in the new multinational entity often finished the work (usually already well under way) of expelling, exterminating or forcibly assimilating ethnic minorities and other portions of the population having either separate territorial claims or the potential power to challenge the rule of the dominant group. Later, elite-led 'national' movements, with funds and military assistance provided by existing states, organized crusades to acquire territories for which they had created and advanced cultural or other claims. Cities were at the centre of these processes and, in each 'national' domain, functioned as a seat of imperial power.

*England*, from the sixteenth century, was created and directed by London, with its provincial economies becoming satellites of the capital (Braudel 1982: 365). It then expanded into Ireland, Scotland, and Wales, where Celtic populations, hostile to English culture, were subjugated by military conquest and forcibly united with England in different ways (the British revenue collector was as alien to the inhabitants of Great Britain as the officials of large military/bureaucratic states such as the Romanov or the Habsburg Empires). The English exercised dominance over the commerce and trade of these lands, and all of them – Ireland, as well as Scotland and Wales – sank into the position of 'peripheral' countries (Hechter 1975: 147–150).[15] Ireland, where the English viewed the native population as savages (Hill 1967: 131) and appropriated three-quarters of the land for their own advantage, was totally subjugated to the English market (Cullen 1968: Chs. 2–4; Hechter 1975: 84–95; Plumb 1950: 179). In the eighteenth century, London controlled all of England's production and distribution and handled at least four-fifths of its trade (Braudel 1984: 365–366). In 1914, London was as large as the next 12 cities combined and 'the centre of an imperium that was a city state, not unlike ancient Rome' (Schneider 1963: 229).

*France* was formed by a political–military 'core' located in the region around Paris (the Ile de France) through the sometimes violent subjugation and incorporation of numerous territories: Normandy (1204) and Occitania (1271), in which there lived essentially a different people, with a different (Mediterranean) culture and a different language (*langue d'oc*); and, by 1500, Burgundy, Brittany (a region of Celtic culture), and Aquitaine. These areas were subordinated to the Ile de France for centuries. In the eighteenth century, Montesquieu observed that, 'In France there is only Paris – and a few outlying provinces Paris hasn't yet found time to gobble up' (quoted in de Tocqueville 1955: 72). 'It is no exaggeration to say that Paris *was* France', de Tocqueville wrote at the end of the century, with the metropolis attracting to itself 'all that was most vital in the nation' (de Tocqueville 1955: 72–73). 'Paris', wrote Turgot, 'swallow[s] up all the riches of the state' (*Oeuvres*, 1913: Vol. I, 437; cited in Braudel 1982: 328). The Marquis de Mirabeau observed that the provinces were in 'a state of dependence on the capital, their inhabitants treated as a sort of inferior species' (in de Tocqueville 1955: 72–73). Unequal exchange between Paris and the provinces ensured that Paris would continue 'to grow more handsome and more populous . . . at the expense of the rest of the country' (Braudel 1982: 328).

*Spain*, like France, grew by absorbing kingdoms markedly dissimilar in cultural and legal traditions and institutions, either through dynastic marriage (Castile, Aragon) or annexation by force (Navarre, Granada). *Portugal* built itself up by similar means. In the eighteenth century, Lisbon was the seat of imperial administration, tenuously linked to its rural hinterland, with the monarchy maintaining 'only symbolic ties with the rest of the country' (Hespanha 1994: 194). The creation of *Germany* was achieved under the direction of Prussia and through the military conquest, enforced cultural assimilation, and economic subordination of peoples living in territories annexed from Poland, Denmark, and France. The creation of *Italy* was brought about by the conquest and annexation by Piedmont, a territory not even considered by most of its inhabitants to be part of

Italy,[16] of other provinces on the Italian peninsula. The south was treated as an area for quasi-colonial exploitation by the north,[17] and southerners were considered by many northerners to be a biologically inferior race of barbarians.[18] In the nineteenth century, the Italian peninsula still consisted of a 'system of small territorial states each dominated by the oligarchy of a single city' (Tilly 1994: 18).

## *Imperial, colonial and national states*

Although the term 'imperialism' came to be used exclusively to mean the direct or indirect domination of overseas colonial territories by modern industrial states,[19] the process of building states in Europe and empires (both at home and abroad) was essentially similar. Underlining this similarity, a number of scholars have referred to state-building processes in Europe as 'internal colonialism'.[20] Like colonialism, state building in Europe involved reshaping the social and economic institutions of conquered areas to the needs of a militarily powerful 'core'. This core imposed physical control over culturally distinct groups which were discriminated against on the basis of their language, religion, or other cultural attributes. Often, they were treated as objects of exploitation, 'as a natural resource to be plundered', and with the brutality that states treat conquered foreign countries (Gouldner 1977–1978: 41). The economy of the peripheral area was forced into complementary development to the core, and generally rested on a single primary export. Juridical and political measures similar to those applied in overseas colonies were imposed in order to maintain the economic dependence of these areas. Members of the core monopolized commerce, trade, and credit, while in peripheral areas there was a relative lack of services and a lower standard of living.

Movements to form 'nation states' in Europe during the nineteenth century were thoroughly bound up with imperialism.[21] In fact, in many cases their *stated* aim was not to form 'nation states' but to resurrect or create empires.

At the end of the eighteenth century, Napoleon fused French nationalism with the Roman imperial idea and, as the alleged heir of Charlemagne, united France, Western Germany, Italy, and the Low Countries in a new empire. At the peak of its power (1810), France directly governed all of Germany west of the Rhine, and north Germany eastwards to Lübeck; Belgium, the Netherlands, Savoy, Piedmont, Liguria and Italy west of the Apennines down to the borders of Naples, and the Illyrian provinces from Carinthia down to and including Dalmatia. German nationalists put forth claims to territory regardless of whether the population directly concerned really desired to change its sovereignty.[22]

This served as a template for subsequent 'nationalist' movements in Europe. Many in the pan-German movement demanded 'union' of the Swiss, the Dutch and even the Scandinavians with Germany in a great racial Nordic brotherhood.[23] Italian nationalism became bound up with a mission to 'complete the *Risorgimento*' (unification movement) through expansion into contiguous and overseas territories. This was a theme of Giuseppe Mazzini, a leader of the *Risorgimento*, no less than it was of Mussolini. Mussolini shared Mazzini's hope for a 'Third Rome', which would exercise world leadership as the Rome of the Caesars and the Rome of the Popes had done (Kohn 1955: 81). The champion of Russian pan-Slavism, Nikolai Danilevsky, argued that Russia must create and lead a Slav federation (in order to destroy 'the rotting west' to the benefit of all mankind) consisting of Russia (with Galicia, the Ukrainian parts of Bukovina and Hungary, and the Carpatho-Ukraine added), Trieste, Gorizia, Istria, the major part of Carinthia, Czechoslovakia, Romania, Hungary, Bulgaria, Greece, and Constantinople.[24]

Polish nationalists sought and won from the Peace Conference following World War I a resurrection of the supra-national seventeenth-century Polish commonwealth. Hungarian nationalism, as embodied in Lajos Kossuth's program of 3 March 1848, envisaged not a Magyar nation state, but incorporation of Croatia–Slavonia, Transylvania and the so-called Military Frontier in the Kingdom of Hungary. None of the Balkan nationalist movements that came to the fore in the early nineteenth century, or their Great Power sponsors, was interested in dividing the Ottoman Empire according to the principles of nationality. The ideological cornerstone of Greek national politics until recent times was the *Megali* idea, based on the notion of the resurrection of the glory and power of the Byzantine Empire (Petropulos 1968: 455–457). The *Megali* idea culminated on 4 August 1936, when General Johannes Metaxas established a fascist regime, inaugurating the 'Third Hellenic Civilization', with the Spartan salute as its symbol (Daphnas 1955).

Nationalists and nationalist writers (Fichte, Treitschke, Mazzini, Garibaldi, D'Annunzio, Kossuth, Obradovich, Danilevsky, and others) did not call for political independence of national communities within national frontiers. They demanded the resurrection of the historical empires of Byzantium and Rome, of Charlemagne, Caesar, Dushan, and Simeon. Where there was no imperial past to recall, nationalist writers and leaders called for the widest possible extension of national boundaries, regardless of ethnic considerations and in fundamental opposition to the national idea: the Great Germany Crusade; the Italian fascist crusade to recreate a Roman empire; the Russian pan-Slav movement and, within the pan-Slav movement, movements for a Greater Croatia, Greater Macedonia, Greater Serbia, and Greater Bulgaria. A pan-Celtic movement to unite the Gaels, Welsh, and Bretons was formed in the late nineteenth century; as was the Polish nationalist crusade to resurrect the supra-national Polish Commonwealth; and the Lithuanian ambition to resurrect the Kingdom of Lithuania.

## IV. Imperial expansion abroad

European expansion abroad was characterized by the same activities undertaken by previous city states in armed pursuit of maritime commerce and colonies. It relied primarily on what William Thompson (1999) calls 'the Venetian model': the development of sea power to gain trading privileges rather than territorial possessions.[25]

Venice built a commercial empire through establishing nodes, forts, and trading posts to control other cities, many of which became city states. Among the most important of these were Zara, Spalato, Durazzo, and Ragusa (today's Dubrovnik). Ragusa became, with Venice, one of the two principal city states in the Adriatic (Parker 2004: 87). This was the model of overseas commercial and imperial expansion that was adopted first by Lisbon and then by Amsterdam and London, all of which reproduced small-scale versions of what they themselves constituted in western Eurasia: 'small enclaves oriented to long-distant trade and adjacent to large and more powerful land powers' (Thompson 1999: 156).

As Chapter 3 recounted, these activities began when fleets of Portuguese, Spanish, Dutch, and British warrior merchants, using ocean-going ships that had been developed to carry goods from the Baltic Sea to the Mediterranean along Europe's Atlantic coast, sought to gain control of Asia's trade. To control the Indian Ocean trade, the Portuguese established a chain of forts and commercial outposts along the main sea route which ran between Southeast Asia and the Middle East along the Malabar coast. These included Cochin (1503), Cannalore (1505), Goa (1510), and Malacca (1511). During the mid-sixteenth century, the Portuguese created dozens of fortified trading enclaves from Sofala (in Mozambique) to Macao in Southern China (Darwin 2007: 53). Like Lisbon itself, these were port cities oriented to trade and the exploitation of their own subject territories stretching into the interior: transit points in the export of agricultural products from their hinterlands. From these bases, Portuguese warrior merchants established a loose network of imperial authority over the sea lanes, taxing ships in transit in return for protection. In Indian Ocean ports, rulers were forced to pay tribute and to allow Portuguese military seamen to establish settlements, engage in trade, and acquire local lands. In East Africa, the Portuguese operated within the framework of the independent city states that existed along the coast (Mombasa, Gedi, Pate, Lamu, Malindi, Zanzibar, and Kilwa).

The Spanish, Dutch, and English warrior merchants who swarmed out of Europe were also primarily interested in creating and maintaining enclaves, forts, and trading posts. Spain, in establishing the administrative divisions of 'New Spain', recreated the old city states of pre-Colombian America (Darwin 2007: 64). These were large cities offering sophisticated road and irrigation networks, and systems of slave labour and tribute (Colley 2008: 44). Mayan city states existed in the Yucatan peninsula at the time of the Spanish conquest, as did the three major city states – Tenochtitlan, Taxco, and Tiatelolco – that formed the Aztec empire. Tenochtitlan at that time was larger than any city in Europe. The Spanish created Mexico City in Tenochtitlan in the first half of the sixteenth century, and established a network of urban centres, including Lima, Puebla, Mérida, Oaxaca, Santiago de los Cablleros de Guatemala, Cuzco, Quito, Trujillo, Cali, Bogotá, and the first foundation of Buenos Aires (Portes 1977a: 61). Cities were founded as mining and agricultural settlements, and as harbours. Potosi, the

South American boomtown, was one of the largest cities in the world in 1600. In 1580, there were 225 towns in the Spanish Indies: by 1759, perhaps 13 per cent of the population of Spanish America lived in cities with more than 20,000 inhabitants (Elliot 2006). Spanish settlers had only very limited contact with the Amerindian populations of the interior (Colley 2008: 44). Networks of labour and domination developed 'that were connected to the cities only to the extent that they participated in providing foodstuffs for the Spaniards' and *castas* (mixed-race people), 'generated surplus that could be used for tribute, or were part of the extractive structure' (de Alva 1995: 269).

The Dutch and British East India Companies were 'fashioned in the spirit of the Venetian state-galley system'(Cox 1959: 230). In Venice, large 'merchantman galleys' (*galere da mercato*) had been constructed in the shipyards of the Arsenal, which was run by the Venetian state. Braudel describes these large trading galleys as 'a combination of state enterprise and private association, the latter being a kind of consortium of export merchants' (1984: 126).

The Dutch envisioned securing commercial domination of trade in Asian waters by avoiding territorial control and establishing a network of bases. But violent local succession struggles and rivalries, which constantly embroiled the Dutch in military conflict, shifted their strategy to one of establishing direct rule (Thompson 1999: 165). The British East India Company established trading posts in Madras (1639), Galle (1640), Bombay (1661), and Calcutta (1690). India at that time had two of the largest cities in the world: Delhi and Ahmedabad. Bombay grew as it gained control of India's westbound trade. During the late seventeenth and early eighteenth century, rapid conversion of marsh and forest into rice lands in Bengal, and the huge workforce of cotton weavers and spinners (perhaps one million or more) 'created an exceptionally dynamic economy' (Darwin 2007: 149). It was not until the mid-eighteenth century, that London became 'as extensive, populous and rich' as Murshidabad (the old capital of Bengal), or as Agra, Fatechpore, Lahore, and other cities of the subcontinent.[26] There also emerged two clusters of city states within the ambit of the British Empire: Singapore and Hong Kong, in the Far East; Kuwait, Bahrain, Qatar, and the United Arab Emirates, in the Middle East.

As European military power intensified and extended trading networks, it was cities, not states, that were incorporated into the system: those that linked together the Atlantic trade in the sixteenth century (Lisbon, Seville, Bahia, Havana, Mexico City, Amsterdam, Le Havre, London, and New York); those that tied together circuits of silver in the seventeenth century (Seville, Amsterdam, Acapulco, Manila, Edo [later re-named Tokyo], Guangdong, and Beijing); and the Pacific cities that emerged by the end of the nineteenth century (San Francisco, Sydney, Shanghai, Los Angeles, Hong Kong, Vancouver, and Tokyo). Edo, by 1868, had become one of the largest cities in the world. Treaty ports were the sites of a 'disproportionately large part of the wealth and enterprise of China' (Hubbard 1935: 195). After 1842, the port of Shanghai became the commercial outlet of China's Yangtze basin. Singapore (founded in 1819) grew up as a hub of Southeast Asian trade. The commercial hub of the pampas, Buenos Aires, grew from 300,000 in 1880 to 1.3 million in 1920 (Darwin 2007: 332). Cape Town rapidly expanded to serve as a commercial centre for the diamond and gold mined inland. Melbourne and Sydney emerged on the Australian coast.

The British and Ottoman Empires were intertwined through Bombay, Karachi, Bushire, Basra, Port Said, and Jidda. Ottoman port cities on the Eastern Mediterranean and the Black Sea – Corfu, Salonica, Smyrna (Izmir), Odessa, Alexandria, Beirut, Trabzon, and Trieste – were linked to port cities in Europe: Amsterdam, London, Venice, Genoa, Nantes, Bordeaux, Lisbon, Cadiz, Seville, Rotterdam, and Le Havre. These, and also the great commercial cities of Constantinople and Cairo, experienced continuous population and commercial growth during the nineteenth century. Salonica was an industrial city that manufactured cloth, carpets, soap, and faience. It had silk-weaving and glass-blowing industries and, along with Smyrna, was an important source of cotton for Europe. Trabzon was a centre for exports that came through the Iranian transit trade and the coastal trade along the Black Sea, supplemented by the products of the East Anatolian hinterland (Kasaba, Çağlar, & Tabak 1986: 130–131). Alexandria in the nineteenth century was one of the world's greatest entrepots.

At the beginning of the nineteenth century the world was perhaps about three per cent urban. At its end some 15 per cent of the world's population was urban (Hay 1977: 74).

Imperial and port cities in Europe, and port cities and colonial cities elsewhere, formed a dynamic field of transnational production and exchange. With the expansion of trade around the world, port cities expanded and large new port cities emerged. These developed to serve global trade. They were 'entry or exit points for the movement of goods, labour and capital' and served 'as nodal centres for the reception and transmission of culture, knowledge and information' (Tan 2007: 853). They 'followed similar trajectories – rapid economic growth, physical transformation, and the emergence of an outward-looking, plural population linked to a dense network of maritime connections engendered by international trade' (Tan 2007: 852).[27] British industrial exports were designed to promote this urban 'development'; and throughout the nineteenth century, Britain built, in foreign lands, banks, telegraphs, and other public services, port and city infrastructures, urban dwellings, harbour improvements, docks, rail yards and railroads, customs houses, hotels, clubs, and residences for the prosperous merchant class.

## V. State formation in Europe II: nationalism

The construction of modern 'national' states involved two processes. The first was the creation of more durable connections between urban centres and their hinterlands and 'an expanded capacity to monitor, contain, seize, and redistribute resources' within territorial domains (Tilly 1994: 26). The second, and later, process was the development of an ideology that sought to naturalize those connections and tie the mass of the local population to a bounded political and cultural realm.

The emergence of the notion of *national* territoriality was linked with the struggle of elites to gain greater control of resources within the territories claimed by the state. The territorial entities inscribed with national identities were often divided by linguistic and cultural incomprehension, and by barriers between town and country, classes, and regions. These barriers were not different in kind from those that faced migrants moving between states and continents. By forging societal integration and social solidarities across increasingly differentiated realms, nationalism emerged as a resolution both to internal 'north/south' divides (as, for instance, the Southern Question in Italy) or the 'internal colonial' situation, and to the 'social question'.

The national idea was an elite-constructed *imaginaire* that envisioned cities and their hinterlands as organically related and culturally bound together, and the population throughout the combined terrain as having become, through common heritage, members of a single family.

It emerged in the context of the simultaneous globalizing and localizing dynamic generated by dualistic industrial expansion. Dualistic industrial expansion linked together the cities around the world in a trans-local system of trade and intercultural exchange, but simultaneously reinforced a separate set of rules, processes, and conditions of life for the wider local population. It was in the context of both the mobilization of mass labour forces, and the increasingly different systems for trans-local and local interests and actors, that the national idea emerged. Nationalism pushes the class situation into the background by defining the propertied and propertyless as equal members of a nation. It represents national issues as more important than social, economic, or political ones, maintains that the basis of exploitation is race, not class and 'naturalizes' an image of the world as consisting of whole racially homogenous societies locked into relations of antagonism with other whole racially homogenous societies.

In the eighteenth century, dominant groups in Europe began increasingly to define themselves as 'nations', and, as the European sphere of influence expanded, groups in different countries facing problems similar to those that had given rise to the national idea in Europe adopted the model and adapted it to local conditions. The emergence of national states was a global, nineteenth-century process, developing in Egypt, Thailand, and Japan as much as in the monarchies and empires of Europe (Goldstone 2002: 338). Elites around the world, challenged by the same local pressures, redefined themselves and what they were doing in broadly similar ways. As Chris Bayly has noted, 'what we call "nationalisms" within Europe and "communalisms" or "ethnicities" outside Europe were in fact comparable, and were fashioned to confront similar pressures over a broadly similar period' (Bayly 1989: 174).

Cities are at the intersection of local and trans-local socio-cultural realms and are embedded in webs of connection that ensure that they are never entirely local. They develop at the end of a transport route, or at the junction of two transport routes: thus, 'no city is an island; each is part of a larger network' (Bosworth 2000: 273).

By the mid-eighteenth century, the most advanced cities of Europe had become as fully developed toward capitalist production, class relations, and commerce as were many cities of Asia and Africa.

Europe's integration into Asian trade and commercial networks had generated new sources of wealth and opportunities for the pursuit of profit (see Chapter 2). In the maritime states of northwest Europe, elites sought to monopolize these opportunities by privatizing vast blocs of collectively owned lands of village and town communities, common fields, common pastures, and woodlands; and by deindustrializing the countryside and concentrating industry in cities where large populations could be mobilized and placed under surveillance (see Chapter 3). These changes were undertaken, not to create national markets and broad-based prosperity, but to generate profits for rural landowning and urban elites through an expansion of production for export. With the expansion of urban-based industrial production for export, cities in Europe and throughout the world became increasingly linked together in an interdependent system of trade and inter-cultural exchange. Throughout the world, rural areas were deindustrialized and industry was concentrated in foreign-oriented urban centres leaving local economies, everywhere, limited and weakly integrated.

From the start, national historiography, ideology, and cultural institutions masked the existence of the trans-local/trans-continental character of the elite.[28] Until recently there was a sharp disparity between local cultures that were 'strongly particularized' and a transnational culture of which Latin and French were successively the linguistic vehicles (Bayart 2005: 63). Many scholars have described the pan-regional European elite as more closely tied by culture and concrete interests to an international class than to the classes below them. Even where they had the same nationality and religion, their mode of life had, in all respects, more in common with elites elsewhere than with the lower classes within their own countries.[29] Russian elites spoke French or German, and not Russian, which was a peasant dialect. The Ottoman elite 'identified with an Osmanli culture that was open to Byzantine, Arabic, Persian, Jewish, and Armenian influences, rather than the popular Turkish-speaking culture' (Bayart 2005: 62).

To 'nationalize' themselves, ruling classes in Europe embedded themselves in the culture of the local rural sector. Politically active and nationally self-conscious ruling groups, educated urban classes, and conservative elements extolled the peasant and traditional forms of life of the rural population as the main sources of national culture, and revived peasant costumes, dance, and celebrations as part of its effort to hold down the rural population (Luxembourg 1976: 260, 262). Elsewhere, the theme of extolling traditional ways of life, 'was seen by turns as rural–aspirational (the dominions of settlement), caste-based and princely (the Indian Empire), chiefly and traditional (the crown colonies of rule), and Bedouin and tribal (the Middle East)' (Cannadine 2001: 122).

Everywhere, the idea of 'nation' emphasized features characteristic of lower social strata so as to make the population of a territorial domain 'more distinct from people in adjacent countries' (Lieberman 1999b: 38). The hinterland represented a conservative bulwark against potential radicalism and the growth of new classes in the cities. The conservatism of the peasant mass was a counterweight to the multi-national radicalism of cities; and socially conservative peasants provided a source of soldiers and mercenaries.[30]

While national institutions created bounded political and cultural realms, these realms nevertheless remained open and fluid 'at the top'. There, trans-local networks of elite exchange, and interdependent sites of production transected them and produced a convergence of styles and conditions of life. Nationalism sought to render invisible the trans-local networks that linked together (and sometimes created) the top strata of 'national' societies, and the existence and interdependence of a trans-local social field that, from the start, and continuing to this day, has shaped relations and developmental outcomes across, between and within them.[31]

## Conclusions

The enclosure of urban hinterlands within armed governates enabled elites to monopolize access to local resources, expand trans-local networks of elite exchange, and create, with elites elsewhere, interdependent sites of production. This monopolistic, anti-market accumulation expanded the wealth and power, not of nations, but of cities. Cities were welded to increasingly larger, more militarily powerful territorial domains. However, the deindustrialization of rural areas, concentration of production in cities, and alliances between urban notabilities and rural landowners, ensured that the power of cities increased and remained greater relative to that of their surrounding areas. Thus, throughout processes of territorial expansion and consolidation, cities remained centres of wealth accumulation, culture, and power within the larger territorial units that formed around them. Despite their integration with rural areas or, in some cases, absorption into neighbouring land empires, cities remained dominant. The consolidation of larger territorial domains consequently produced a form of state that more closely resembled the city-state systems of the past than an essentially new and different nationally-integrated state form. What we call the 'nation state' is a unified administration of cities and their hinterlands – not to develop 'national' markets, but to facilitate capital accumulation through exports. The ideology of nationalism and nation states deflected attention from the fact that their chief aim was to promote the expansion of external trade rather than to develop the home market.

As Charles Tilly observes, 'state-led processes created visible, prestigious, transferable models for exploitation and opportunity hoarding'. As a result, 'Throughout the world, administrative structures, constitutions, and declared commitments of regimes to development, stability, and democracy came to resemble each other far more than did the diversity of their material conditions and actual accomplishments' (Tilly 1990: 180). As the next chapter endeavours to show, a global social order emerged with the expansion of industrial production, constituted of horizontal solidarities between groups of elites in different parts of the world. During the nineteenth century, cross-national networks of production were expanded and maintained through the development of an imperial project which became increasingly a collaborative *transnational class* project.

# 5 The imperial 'historic bloc' of the nineteenth century

The last three chapters focused on Europe because of its central role, not in global development, but in historical narratives and theories that this book is concerned to challenge.

Previous chapters have argued that capitalism was monopolistic, anti-market, and global from the start (see Chapter 2), and that what we call the 'Industrial Revolution' principally involved a reorganization of production in Europe to accelerate the globalization of capital and facilitate the further integration of Europeans into the Asian *ecumene* (see Chapter 3). State building processes integrated and enclosed cities and urban hinterlands within armed governates, enabling elites to mobilize the resources and organizational capacities needed to expand their participation in trans-local networks of elite exchange. These state-building processes, in Europe as elsewhere, contributed to building, not national markets and economies, but interdependent sites of production across borders. They produced, not nationally integrated states, but polities that resembled city states; and, as the power of Europeans grew within existing networks of trade, it was largely the city-state form that they helped to maintain, reproduce, or create abroad (see Chapter 4). This chapter argues that these developments were driven by changes occurring in Asia and Africa, and were a reflection of Europe's increasing integration into those areas of the world.

During the sixteenth century, Chinese demand for silver drove a global expansion that increasingly embedded long-distance trade in Asian production processes. Beginning in the seventeenth century, an economic contraction set in, generating crises and conflicts that eventually culminated, in the eighteenth century, with a global war and a quarter century of conflict and revolutionary ferment (1789–1815). At its end, a counter-revolutionary, imperial post-war global order was consolidated, which further expanded and integrated cross-border networks, and which brought governments and elites around the world into closer relations of interdependence. Cross-border expansion left domestic markets weak and poorly integrated, enabling elites to enjoy monopoly profits from overseas sales and to preserve, to a very large extent, the traditional bases of their social and political power. We might conceive of this system of capital accumulation as forming and operating through what Antonio Gramsci called an *historical bloc*: a variety of social forces interconnected across 'national' and international borders, and the complex of values, attitudes, and beliefs that support established social structures and the position of dominant groups at the top of them.[1]

Discussion of this imperial 'historical bloc' begins, in the next section, with its roots in the sixteenth-century Eurasian expansion and global integration, and in the seventeenth century Eurasian crises and eighteenth century world wars that followed.

## I. Eurasian expansion, crisis and war

Between the tenth and fifteenth centuries, a 'vast world market' formed based on a network of mercantile–maritime cities that, across Afro-Eurasia, had become tied together in a 'great interregional commercial network' (Hodgson 1993: 47). This Afro-Eurasian *ecumene*, which extended from the Straits of Gibraltar (north and east of the Sahara desert) to the shores of Hokkaido, consisted of 'a string of societies' that had been 'loosely knit together for millennia' (Lewis & Wigen 1997: 143). But Europe did not play a part in, nor was it greatly affected by, developments in Asia and Africa. These developments only began to impact Europe after the fourteenth century, when the extension of networks of trade from China all the way to England began to transform Europe through devastating diseases and through the collapse of its social structures and of feudal society.

### *Sixteenth century eurasian expansion and global integration*

By the sixteenth century, patterns of trans-national elite connection and exchange linked together political societies, from around the Mediterranean through the Middle East and India to China, in a prosperous and far-flung trading system and an active and important network of intercultural exchange. Within this system, the dynamics of expansion and contraction of power, and of shifting balances of population and resources followed similar rhythms and patterns, shaping the direction of social change across large areas in broadly similar ways. Broadly synchronous developments had enabled its network of mercantile–maritime port cities to attain a more or less similar level of achievement. Across Eurasia, total output had expanded, and agricultural and craft production had become more specialized and commodified. Money had infiltrated rural life, and commercial institutions had matured as 'the growing frequency of transactions encouraged the codification of procedures concerned with money and credit and with the ownership and transfer of goods' (Lieberman 1999b: 57).[2]

Business techniques and technical and material means of production were advanced to a similar degree. India had a sophisticated financial and commercial life, an interconnected credit system and, in Bengal and elsewhere, a long-established system of land taxation. Its marketing of fine cotton and silk fabrics had established 'enduring and structurally important linkages' to Island Southeast Asia and to the world of Islam, from Persia to the Arab lands to the Swahili ports of East Africa'. From Mozambique to Island Southeast Asia, 'well-established and sophisticated Muslim merchant communities' were employing a unified set of commercial and legal practices (Wills 1993: 86). In Africa, there was a range of manufacturing industries 'based on clothing, metal working, ceramics, construction, and food processing'. Kano was a major textile centre – 'a kind of Manchester of West Africa' (Reynolds 1985: 20). Along trade routes, covering distances as great as from the Lake Chad area to Daka or from Kano to the Mediterranean coast, were centres 'for the assembly, breakup, or re-export of shipments' and 'an elaborate system of local agents and commission men; banking and credit facilities, and a code of commercial morality' (Reynolds 1985: 20). In East Africa was a mercantile empire that had rapidly expanded with the rising demand for slaves in the Middle East and for ivory in Europe.

European incursions into the Indian Ocean and in the Americas in the sixteenth century were part of an interconnected Eurasian expansionism that occurred during that century: the consolidation of Ming absolutism, the Ottoman Empire's naval expansion into the Red Sea and the Persian Gulf, and efforts to assert their power in the Indian Ocean; the Safavid unification of 'Greater Iran'; the expansion of Islam into Southeast Asia, Southeast Europe, and sub-Saharan Africa; the creation of a vast new Islamic Empire in North India; Burmese, Thai and Vietnamese imperial expansion; and Japan's fifteenth century commercial expansion and sixteenth-century boom.

There was a phenomenal expansion of the silver trade during that century driven by China,[3] a country 'which contained perhaps one-fourth of the earth's population' and had urban centres of 'up to 1 million inhabitants (five to seven times greater than the largest cities in western Europe)' (Flynn & Giráldez 1995: 208). China remonetized its economy with silver in the sixteenth century after a failed experiment with paper money. Spain mined huge quantities of silver in Potosi (in modern Bolivia) and in Mexico to meet this Chinese demand, and this made Spain a world power in the sixteenth century for a few decades 'and sustained the growth of the whole network of world trade – in northern Europe, in the Mediterranean, on the Mecca pilgrimage routes, into India, and both ways around the world into China' (Wills 2001: 23). Spain shipped it across the Atlantic to Europe. It was then carried by the Portuguese and, later, the Dutch to 'a multitude of routes into Asia' (Flynn & Giráldez 1995: 203). It was also shipped across the Pacific to Manila (founded by Spain in 1571 for this purpose), which established 'continuous trade between America and Asia for the first time in history' (Flynn & Giráldez 1995: 201). Japanese exports of silver to China may have exceeded those coming from the Americas (Flynn & Giráldez 1995: 202). Its expanding silver production made it a key trading partner for the Portuguese and Spanish, and encouraged it to develop new commodities exports – including copper, sulphur, and swords, which then made their way to the Americas, Europe, and West Africa (Darwin 2007: 89). By the end of the sixteenth century, a multi-centric global trade in silver had emerged based on Potosi, Manila, Edo, Beijing, and Seville.

This global expansion produced roughly comparable changes in elite consumption across a number of societies. In Europe, China, Japan, and India, there was 'a striking increase in the quantity and quality of home furnishings, elaborate clothes, eating utensils, and what would today be called "collectibles" among the wealthiest people' (Pomerantz 2000: 127). Upper-class homes in Europe and China became 'increasingly crammed with paintings, sculptures, and fine furniture' (Pomerantz 2000: 131). The opening of new overseas markets for porcelain and silk fuelled the expansion of urban centres in China; and Chinese demand for a wide range of exotic luxury items from Southeast Asia rose sharply (Pomerantz 2000: 159). The passage of most white settlers, as well as of African slaves, to the Americas was financed in order to create luxury exports to Europe and Asia, including Brazilian gold, North American furs, and tobacco and sugar. After the mid-seventeenth century, standards of living among the wealthy became more luxurious (Kellenbenz 1976: 273). Benares and Lucknow in the eighteenth century represented 'huge concentrations of luxury demand' (Pomerantz 2000: 133; citing Bayly 1983: 199); as did European demand for Asian luxuries, and particularly for Indian muslins and calicoes, which were luxury items in Europe.

### *Seventeenth and eighteenth century crises and wars in Europe and Asia*

By the beginning of the seventeenth century, the glut of silver on the Chinese market and the ensuing inflation had produced a global 'price revolution'. The dramatic rise in prices (inflation) caused by the large influx of gold and silver from the New World, and debt problems and fiscal pressures, fuelled a 'general crisis' that generated political instability and war throughout Eurasia and beyond. The silver glut had a devastating effect on Spain. And in India, the Ottoman Empire, Morocco, and Brazil, there were major political crises,[4] the beginning of *Sakoku* (a system strictly regulating commerce and foreign relations) and the Shimabara Uprising (1638) in Japan (where silver exports had fallen off dramatically), and the collapse of the Ming Dynasty in China (1644–1662).

Production processes had become increasingly geared to the development of foreign markets and to building the infrastructure for long-distance trade, disrupting established patterns of social organization and exerting pressures on the relationship between commerce, landed wealth, and patrimonial political authority. Asian commercial growth had begun to intensify conflicts over labour and revenue. In the Ottoman Empire, the growing power of provincial notabilities had triggered a groundswell of tax revolts and rebellions. In the eighteenth century, an unprecedented wave of social conflict swept through Asia and the Middle East. Riots and disturbances were widely recorded 'from the Balkans to the Indonesian archipelago' (Bayly 1989: 189), paralleling the revolts of weavers in Europe, whose position was eroded or who were thrown out of work (Bayly 1989: 189).

In Europe, the end of the great expansion of the sixteenth century triggered a social upheaval that made this 'the darkest era . . . since the catastrophe [i.e., the Plague] of the fourteenth century' (Fischer 1996: 91). The industrial heartland of Europe, Northern Italy, lost its foreign markets, and the woollens, silk, and metallurgical industries of all its cities declined. Venice's economy contracted 'to a regional distribution function' after it lost its spice trade to the Dutch and English, and Northern competitors introduced new, cheaper cloths which quickly dominated Levantine markets (De Vries 1976: 26–7). The reaction to the economic contraction elsewhere in Europe was 'refeudalization – 'an agricultural revolution in reverse' (Braudel 1972: 427). There were civil conflicts in England, France, Spain, Portugal, and Italy; major political crises in the Palatinate, Bohemia, Germania, Catalonia, Ireland, Scotland, Holland, Sweden, the Ukraine, and Muscovy; wars with the Ottoman Empire fought by Venice over Crete (1654–1669) and by the Habsburgs (1593–1606, and 1683–1699); revolutions in England (1649–1660, 1688), a coup d'état in the United Provinces of the Netherlands (1650); revolts in Catalonia (1640), Portugal, Andalusia (1641), and Naples (1647); and, in France, the Fronde (1648–1653), and French wars in the Spanish Netherlands (1667–1668), and against the Dutch Republic (1672–1679). The Thirty Years' War (1618–1648) was one of the most destructive conflicts in European history. The Nine Years' War (1689–1697) became a worldwide event.

There were also conflicts between Asian and North African elites and also 'increasingly bitter struggles of the more powerful kingdoms and states to seize their own share of trade, labour and revenues' (Bayly 1989: 56). There were conflicts between the Dutch and English in their competition to monopolize trade in Indonesia and later in India; and between armed traders from Britain and France competing to find Indian clients. In the eighteenth century, these conflicts produced two global wars: the 'Seven Years' War' (1756–1763), which was simultaneously fought in North America, Europe, India, and the Caribbean; and the 'Napoleonic Wars' (1793–1815). These wars were battles to redistribute the world's resources, and all of them involved the active participation of Asian and North African states (Bayly 1989: 56). Napoleon's empire in Europe (the 'Continental System') was 'an attempt to secure an accessible and regular supply of grain for the French Republic' (Bayly 1989: 58), and a large protected market for France's historic luxury industries and her fledgling textile industry.[5] But it was also designed to shut Britain out of Europe; and with the closure of European markets by Napoleon, Britain struck at France's Caribbean empire and the Dutch East Indian empire, annexed the Cape of Good Hope, appropriated the French and Spanish Indies and the Dutch colony of Java, and sponsored independence for the Latin American republics, thereby bringing the Spanish empire to an end. Following the conclusion of the world war of 1793–1815, an international regime was established to manage the acquisition, through European imperialist expansion, of resources and markets.

## II. The imperial 'historic bloc'

Throughout the sixteenth, seventeenth, and eighteenth centuries, there had been developing, within traditional power structures both in Europe and elsewhere, a new means of producing wealth (industrialism) through exports. By the end of the eighteenth century this had produced a Eurasian world of 'surprising resemblances' (Pomerantz 2000: 29), in which China's Yangtze delta, and parts of Japan, northern India and Europe had achieved comparable levels of commercialization and overall productivity (Bin Wong 1997; Christian 2004: 357; Frank 1998). Asia, with 66 per cent of the world's population, accounted for almost 80 per cent of wealth produced throughout the world (Pomerantz 2000: 49). Europeans were prominent players only in the Atlantic System: in most of the world's major sites of economic and political activity, they were principally intermediaries in the trade of commercial goods produced in Asia (Chinese silk and porcelain, Sumatra spices, Malabar cinnamon and pepper), and silver and slaves. China's economic growth during that century had 'contributed far more to the increase in world GDP than did growth in Britain'.[6]

In the nineteenth century, Europeans began to play a more prominent role in global trade. Europe's 'Industrial Revolution', as discussed in Chapter 3, was a reorganization of economic life that enabled elites to launch a brutal expansion of production for export. It emerged as a result of struggles to deregulate capital and privatize sources and means of producing wealth. It was shaped by the experience of a quarter century of war and revolutionary turmoil in Europe and Asia that began at the end of the eighteenth century and was consolidated, in the nineteenth century, beneath the shadow of those events. For elites and ruling groups everywhere, the Napoleonic Wars had revealed the dangers of a trained and compact mass army. After 1815, Europeans drew many analogies between the mass army of soldiers created in the Great War and the mass industrial army of workers needed to expand industrial production. The French Revolution had given birth to socialism, and its focus, in particular on eradicating private property, seemed, in combination with the revolutionary ferment unleashed by the wars that followed, to threaten an anti-capitalist revolt of the masses.[7] It was in this context that 'disembedded', dualistic economic expansion emerged as a model for industrial expansion. This involved producing huge quantities of goods for export as a means of accumulating wealth. To provide workers with the purchasing power to consume what they produced would have resulted in social levelling and destroyed the class, land, and income structures on which existing structures of social power rested.[8] By producing for export, elites could profit from industrial production without having to democratize consumption at home.

Europeans now played a more prominent role in world trade; but they did not fundamentally change the system of inter-regional trade that had developed over previous centuries. Networks structured by European activities were 'introduced into contexts that already had developed 'spatially extensive trading, tribute, diplomatic, intellectual, migration and travelling networks'; and, in most cases, the networks formed by Europeans were layered on top of them to add 'new levels of complexity' (Lester 2006: 134).

European elites shared with elites everywhere a vision of hierarchy, tradition, and social order. This bound them together with the 'coffee barons' of Brazil and 'sugar barons' of Peru, the Brahmins in India, the Taluqdars of the United Provinces, the Pirs of Sind, the rajas and maharajas and nawabs and nizams that ruled over India's princely states; the Dahomean kings, the king of the Asante in Africa's Gold Coast; the great ruling clans of Kenya, the Bugandan chiefs of Uganda, the emirs of Nigeria; the Sudanese sultans and sheikhs, the kings and chiefs of southern Africa, the Zulu chiefs in Natal, and the pashas of Egypt; the Malay rulers, King Cakobau of Fiji, the Goyigma caste of Ceylon; and the sheikhs, chiefs, and emirs of the Arab lands. Elites were embedded in broadly similar local relations – grounded in the dynamics of setting masses of labour to produce profit for a small number of elites; and through interaction and independence they developed broadly similar interests, capabilities, and policies. As a result of their common relations with the lower classes, and through collaboration, emulation, learning, and the adoption of best practice, they developed a common system of social institutions, relationships, and norms.

What Antonio Gramsci called an 'historical bloc' aptly describes this interconnected system. An historical bloc is a 'social and political space relatively unified through the instituting of nodal points [privileged positions] and the constitution of tendentially relational identities' (Laclau & Mouffe 1985: 136). By the nineteenth century, imperialism had developed the sort of interconnected system that the term 'historical bloc' describes. Imperialism represented a collaborative regime of elite accumulation that operated to expand trans-national networks of production and exchange, bound together a 'series of loosely linked aristocratic fiefdoms' (Bayly 1989: 195), and worked within existing hierarchies, amplifying them and their exploitative potential.[9] The British Empire *at home* was characterized by 'a compact of British elites which crossed the Anglo-Celtic border and overrode the provincial interests and regional patriotisms of England, Scotland, and Ireland' (Bayly 1989: 76). This is how the English had come to govern Wales, Scotland, and parts of Ireland; and this was how the British came to govern their overseas empire

(Cannadine 2001: 69). Just as British local government 'had always depended on the resident aristocracy and gentry, so their chosen partners in South Asia were the "natural leaders": large landowners, men of "property and rank," and of "power and importance," who "exercised great influence" in rural society' (Cannadine 2001: 43–44). The Empire in India included territories directly administered by the British and ruled from Calcutta, and 500 to 600 princely states (roughly one-third of the subcontinent) ruled by local elites who shared with the British a common vision of hierarchy, tradition, and social order (Cannadine 2001: 51). A Bengali intelligentsia enthusiastically supported the British regime, for it provided them with an acceptable livelihood and opportunities for some upward mobility, and was seen by them 'as the channel through which western knowledge and enlightenment had come to India' (Raychaudhuri 1988: 16). English education did not become widespread in India because 'it was forcefully imposed from above by the British colonial state: the education budget was minute', and Lord Curzon, who was perhaps the British Empire's most celebrated Indian Viceroy, 'was strongly committed to curtailing it'. It expanded largely because certain Indian elite groups, overwhelmingly high-caste Hindu, pursued it and invested in it themselves – 'and for their own purposes'. In India, those 'who came to "command" the English language . . . used it (in association with British power) to displace older ruling elites, whose hegemony had been expressed far more in the languages of Indo-Persian culture inflected by Islam' (Washbrook 1998: 302). In this way, a 'metropolitan culture of outreach and replication converged and connected with a colonial culture of aspiration and assimilation' (Cannadine 2001: 98). Elites in Egypt helped to establish Western higher education. In Beirut they dressed in European clothing, knew French or English, built Italianate villas with red-tile roofs and Western furnishings and, in the Ashrafiyya quarter, 'lived like aristocrats in European palaces' (Fawaz 1983: 101–102).

Some perspectives on 'underdevelopment' and ideologies of nationalism, maintain that, in the nineteenth century, the exploitation of societies that today form part of what is called the 'third world' had its basis in *race*, and specifically racialized *external* relations (see Chapter 1, for a discussion). But Europeans viewed the situation of being 'more or less civilized' as an attribute of class, as well as of race: 'depending on context and circumstance, *both* white *and* dark-skinned peoples of empire were seen as superior; or, alternatively, as inferior'. The British were concerned with 'the replication of sameness and similarities originating from home' and the 'construction of affinities' among elites. Their presumption was that society in other parts of the world 'was the same as, or even on occasions superior to', British society (Cannadine 2001: xix). In short, 'these people were no aggregated, collective mass, all regarded as inferior and potentially hostile; they were seen differentially and often individually'. In India, the British strengthened and supported native princes and regarded them as social equals (Cannadine 2001: 18), while collaborating with the Brahmins 'to harden caste status into an administrative system' (Darwin 2007: 15).

As Cannadine points out, 'the whole purpose of the British Empire was', as Lord Lugard observed, 'to maintain traditional rulerships as a fortress of societal security in a changing world'. And in that enterprise, the colour of a person's skin was less significant than their position in the local social hierarchy: 'the really important category was status', and as such it was 'fundamental to all other categories' (Cannadine 2001: 124). This was true, too, of other European imperial powers. The Spanish regarded Amerindian leaders as royal or aristocratic; and, in 1514, the Spanish Crown formally permitted inter-ethnic marriages. By the second half of the sixteenth century, 'wide-spread intermarriage and cross-cultural mating in Latin America were generating new ethnic communities' (de Alva & Jorge 1995: 269). In the Netherlands Indies, the boundary separating 'European' and 'non-European' tended to be poorly defined and to shift. One could acquire European legal equivalence (*gelijkgestelde*) by (1) being Christian, (2) speaking and writing Dutch, (3) having a European upbringing and education, and (4) demonstrating a suitability for European society, or (5) marrying or adopting a European (van Marle 1952: 98, 109; Stoler 1989: 153). The legal category of 'European' during the early twentieth century included within it Japanese, Jews, Arabs, Armenians, Filipinos, naturalized Javanese, the Sudanese wives of Dutch-born bureaucrats, the recognized children of mixed marriages, and Christian Africans, among others (van Marle 1952: 108).

The expansion of networks of production and exchange grew up within, and reinforced and extended, already existing patterns of transnational elite connection and exchange. The transnational elite was transnational in that the interests of its members were linked to sources of power and stability provided by other elites, rather than to resources and markets that were local and national in origin. Not all its members faced the same opportunities or constraints – these were determined by local struggles and social relations; and they entered by different pathways into the system. But their structural location was similar in that they were all extracting surplus. Not all groups of elites carried the same weight in terms of the number and strength of their connections. Not all were autonomous or able to overthrow the domination and hegemony of 'Western' powers. But did they want to? Elites were all parts of the same imperium; and while they often had conflicting interests, these coexisted with their common interest in exploiting the producing class (Lachmann 1990: 411). Although international military power was not exercised by all, the basic antagonism between capital and labour compelled the more militarily powerful elements within the elite to produce policies that reinforced the subordination of labour to capital, and this redounded to the benefit of all (elites in the 'periphery' also benefited by not having to expend resources on, and mobilize industrial capital for, military expansion).

Elites were bound predominantly by relations of cooperation in producing surplus, rather than of inequality and active exploitation, as characterized their relations with subordinate classes. Their concern was not with *vertical* inequality (exploitation) but with inclusion in or exclusion from the overall system (an ability to exploit was an essential criterion for inclusion). Groups of 'national' elites were individuated and differentiated, not hierarchically, but based on different forms of power, and with 'complex gradations' such as are found among the officer corps within the 'military class'.[10] This was a *beside-each-other* differentiation – not the antagonism of a class-based division of labour, as in the system of production. Local systems of power and authority were linked to each other and interdependent: all gained, though not to an equal degree. However, these unequal gains represented 'within-class' inequalities. While elites were united by a fundamental and long-term unity of purpose, this did not mean that there were not shorter term conflicts of interest. The primary interest of elites is to maintain class power. But they also must maintain autonomy against rival elites (Lachman 1990: 412). This is where intra-elite conflict emerges. Inter-state wars have been largely the result of intra-class conflict among dominant classes; usually waged as a last resort, most disputes between the elites of different 'national' formation have been settled by negotiations; and increasingly interstate wars have been regulated by various institutions and laws.

### *Military power*

British power around the world depended for its success on non-Europeans, on the collaboration and mediation, and the military and administrative muscle, of indigenous elites (Robinson 1972: 131). The emphasis usually placed on the superiority of European military power overstates that power and vastly understates the role of alliances.

The idea of European military superiority was advanced by Geoffrey Parker (1996) to explain how small numbers of Europeans were able to defeat large numbers of non-Europeans.[11] Hernan Cortés and a small army of 500 men arrived in Mexico in 1519, and by 1521 had conquered the Aztec Empire, a resource-rich territory of 11 or 12 million people. However, this was not the result of military power but of the demographic devastation caused by Old World diseases (Chanda 2007: 231),[12] and of the ability of Cortés to find allies among subject peoples in many of the smaller city states in Mexico who resented being forced to pay tribute to the Aztec empire (Darwin 2007: 59). When Francisco Pizarro invaded the Inca Empire in 1532 with fewer than 200 men, it was at a time in which the Empire was torn by an intensive civil war (and with no unified army), making it easy for Pizarro to acquire allies.

It took the Dutch three centuries (from Ambon in 1632 to Bali in 1906) to conquer the entire archipelago of Indonesia. The French did not consolidate their rule over most of Vietnam, the Lao states, and Cambodia until the 1880s and 1890s. British invasions of Afghanistan in 1838–1842 and 1879–1880 were unsuccessful; and they did not succeed in gaining control of the interior of Burma until 1885.

The British 'conquest' of India provides, perhaps, the clearest challenge to the 'military superiority' thesis: it took a century, from the Battle of Plassey (1757) to the annexation of Awadh (1856), for huge British armies to conquer India; and they were outnumbered by Indian troops only at Plassey and at Buxar (1764), where they fought against a quarrelsome and divided coalition of forces.

Empire was affordable and sustainable only where it was an essentially collaborative project (Robinson 1972: 131). Spain's empire depended on the 'silverization' of China; and when the value of silver declined, so did Spain's empire (Flynn & Giráldez 1995: 211). The British Empire had to be 'run on the cheap' – i.e., through 'voluntary collaborators' (Cannadine 2001: 124). 'Indirect rule' over India, which was the model for indirect rule elsewhere, depended on the cooperation and support of local elites and rulers as well as tens of thousands of loyal Indian notables, soldiers, policemen, and bureaucrats. British India was run by Indians (Bose & Jalal 1998: 57–66; Cohn 1962; Marshall 2000). An intricate network of local bankers throughout the subcontinent made possible the local recruitment and feeding of a huge mercenary army; and it was the network of Indian merchants throughout the Indian Ocean that enabled the British to station garrisons there.

India was 'the prime fiscal and military base for the spread of British power in Asia' in the late eighteenth and early nineteenth centuries (Wills 1993: 86). By 1815, the Bengal Army raised by the East India Company was 'one of the biggest European-style standing armies in the world' (Bayly 1989: 128). By 1835, the East India Company's Indian armies were much larger than the whole of the British army, at home and abroad (Darwin 2007: 264). Europeans controlled their African spheres with a handful of officials 'heavily reliant on local "collaborators"' (Darwin 2007: 316). 'In what became French West Africa, the *officiers soudanis* carved out their warrior state with an army of African soldiers who were paid in slaves. In British East Africa it was Maasai fighters who helped to coerce Kikuyu and Embu in return for a share of the captured cattle' (Darwin 2007: 315).

Europeans had sufficient military power to create footholds along the coasts of Asia and Africa, but they could not reshape societies and reorganize production throughout large territories by military means. This depended absolutely on political alliances and the collaboration of local ruling groups and elites. Military power was used to win fiscal and commercial concessions. But, where a military presence was established, it was usually to build, consolidate, or preserve political alliances, often either in response to the request, or with the aid and approval, of local elites.

### *Collaboration*

An emphasis on conflict and coercion in European Imperialism airbrushes out of the picture the crucial role of collaboration and consensus and the power and immense wealth of local elites. The claim that elites around the world – usually characterized as intermediaries, representatives, or 'compradores' who were only tangentially related to their own societies – reoriented state policy to benefit foreign or core interests is a key distortion: elites reoriented state policy to benefit the interests of a trans-local class to which they, themselves, belonged. Local economies were reoriented, not to 'meet the requirements of the international economy', but to create the conditions for capital accumulation and its monopolization by elites.

The point is not to downplay the coerciveness of European imperialism or to deny its unique barbarity – the savage wars of repression against the Ceylonese and Burmese, and against the Indian 'mutineers' in 1857, for example – but rather to bring into focus the extent to which imperialism was/is a relation between a cross-national elite and local masses. There are, of course, always people who will collaborate with power-holders in the exploitation of their 'own' communities or communal groups. Jews worked to round up other Jews for transport to Nazi death camps. But the collaboration involved in empire is different. What we call 'collaboration' refers, in this context, to a relationship of interdependence and mutual interest, in which agents were 'working jointly with another' (Robinson 1972) as opposed to working *for* another (Onley 2004). 'Imperialism' was a system of exchange and control that was forged on the basis of common interests and developed within a transnational social field and class structure. Each of its local fields had its dominant and its dominated, its struggles for usurpation and exclusion. Collaborators were crucial to the formation and operation of empire. They were often already in positions of power when they became collaborators, and they remained power-holders and exploiters after their European partners left.[13]

Elites, because they are few, have always sought the military or political aid of external agents in order to prevail in struggles with rivals.

In Asia, tensions between inland kingdoms and coastal 'middleman powers' were 'endemic (Bayly 1989:70), involving competition between coastal commercial communities and inland exporting kings to secure a stable labour force to produce exports. Asian empires and their military nobilities proved unable to control the tensions unleashed by the rapid commercialization of large parts of the Indo-Islamic world in the seventeenth century (Bayly 1989: 188). Local elites collaborated with foreigners in order to prevail in local struggles, and sought to gain autonomy from locally powerful groups by securing alternative sources of revenue. Losers in local wars in the Coromandel (eastern India) coast allied with Europeans in the mid-seventeenth century in an attempt to recoup their positions (Pomerantz 2000: 182). The explosive growth of commercial agriculture on the north coast of Java unleashed a series of conflicts which indigenous rulers and the Dutch struggled together to control, and which ultimately led to Dutch colonial intervention. With a series of civil wars spreading to the interior and threatening the Sultanate of Mataram, the aristocracy of the northern coast 'begged the Dutch company for help and sought to become its vassals' (Bayly 1989: 68). In exchange for aid in their conflict with the princes of the powerful commercial community of the Bugis, the rulers of Kedah in Malaya ceded the island of Penang to the British in 1786 (this became the base of British operations throughout the Eastern seas). In Egypt, Mohammad Ali and his successors sought to use Europeans in their struggles with the Ottoman Sultan (Landes 1958: 93).

Elites also forged alliances in order to acquire or increase their wealth. In Latin America, old fortunes were revitalized and new ones created by coffee, sugar, and beef exports (Portes 1977a: 68). Asian rulers, mistrustful of their own commercial communities, sought to increase their wealth by attracting Portuguese ships to their harbours (Darwin 2007: 56). The Ming authorities in China preferred to allow the establishment of a Portuguese settlement on Macao (from about 1570 to 1638) and use it as a base from which to trade with Japan, rather than to engage themselves directly with the Japanese (Souza 1986). Japan permitted Portuguese merchants to settle in Nagasaki in 1571. Local rulers cooperated with Dutch traders who introduced coffee in west Java in 1707, and local aristocrats helped to make Indonesia one of the world's leading coffee producers (Chanda 2007: 90; Knapp 1986).

'From the beginning', local South Asian rulers 'did not just tolerate' Europeans; 'they employed them, rewarded them with revenue rights, and sought their protection in trade', while at the same time 'teaching them how to exploit the immense talents of the Indian peoples for production, commerce, and warfare' (Wills 1993: 86). In exchange for paying revenue to the British and assisting in maintaining order in the countryside, the Taluqdars of Awadh, mostly local rajas and heads of clans, officials and tax farmers, gained 'many of the rights of the land-owning gentry of Britain' (Pandey 1988: 234). Parsis, who were originally from Iran and who dominated Bombay, were 'natural partners' of the British (Darwin 2007: 264). The British also found it easy to find allies among the great Hindu and Jain banking families (Bayly 1989: 224), and among the Brahmins and Rajputs of the central Ganges valley who had once served the declining Mughal Empire (Bayly 1989: 128).

The Capitulations System enabled Ottoman Sultans to force through changes that strengthened their grip on power (Darwin 2007: 213).[14] Dozens of rulers and governors in eastern Arabia and southern Persia used European merchants as sources for revenues and loans (Onley 2004: 131). The African slave trade was a collaboration between Africans and Europeans: Africa had a long history of slavery and slave trade within Africa, and its slave trade expanded because African kings used slaves as a means of obtaining European and Asian goods for their personal use.[15]

Chinese merchants employed as managers of European and Japanese firms (called 'compradors', *mai-pan*) were among the richest in China. In many cases, compradors made much more than the firms that employed them. A comprador was usually paid a fixed salary, but he accumulated substantial wealth from commissions, being paid both from Chinese and foreign merchants on each business deal (Hao 1970: 90); and he also had use of company funds to finance his own businesses. After the conclusion of the Treaty of Nanking in 1842, the role of the comprador shifted to that of a business assistant (Hao 1970: 48). Overseas, Chinese merchants frequently became 'commercial and political allies of local rulers, whether Asian or European'. Key nodes of commerce and power in maritime Southeast Asia, such as Manila and Batavia, 'were fundamentally dependent on Chinese productive, commercial, and organizational skills' (Wills 1993: 87).

Indian merchants and employees of the Dutch and English East India Companies were connected through an immense web of private trade links (Das Gupta 1979). Chinese merchants active in Southeast Asia were key allies of the Dutch. They facilitated Java's trade with China, contracted with the Dutch to collect various local taxes, and built up Java's sugar industry (Blussé 1986). In the Coromandel, local merchant capitalists provided Europeans with access to the local economy for purchasing textiles and other export commodities, and acted as middlemen between European traders and local weavers, and between Europeans and local governments. In exchange, they paid only half of the customs duty on their imports of broadcloth, silver, coral and rubies, and enjoyed certain status-related privileges that 'could at times outweigh the potential monetary gains involved in their work' (Mukund 1999: 60).

Affluent Arab, Persian, and Indian merchants in the Gulf allied themselves with European governments or companies and worked as 'native agents' or 'native assistants' (*munshis*) to increase their wealth and their political influence and gain protection for their businesses and families (Onley 2004: 130, 131). They gave the Gulf Resident access to the local political systems 'to an extent that would have been otherwise impossible' and obtained, as employees of the British Government or of British companies, the 'protection' and 'good offices' (diplomatic representation and mediation) of British civil and military officers. Their private businesses, as well as their 'ships, goods, families, and staffs were all protected, giving them the same advantages British merchants enjoyed in the Gulf' (Onley 2004: 131).

Christians profited from Aleppo's trade in the seventeenth and eighteenth centuries; Greek Orthodox merchants prospered from shipping and commerce in the eastern Mediterranean; and the Maronite Christians of Lebanon expanded their wealth through the silk trade (Kasaba, Çağlar, Tabak 1986: 133), as did a whole range of brokers operating mostly through or in Beirut. The Mediterranean basin, and the Levant in particular, 'regained some of the importance in world trade that it had lost after the mid seventeenth century' (Kasaba *et al.* 1986: 121).

With European demand, reeled silk became a machine-made good and, from the 1830s, mechanized cotton-spinning mills were established in many Ottoman locations (Quataert 1994: 33–34). Initially the capital was supplied by western Europeans, but they were soon replaced by Ottomans. Most of the investment came from the import–export houses of Marseilles and Lyons, who advanced capital to the silk manufacturers either directly or through local merchants in Beirut who served as brokers. A number of these brokers maintained their own business on the side, and borrowed capital to buy the silk crop, 'sometimes gambling on futures at usurious rates'.[16] They were also able to become very rich by cheaply acquiring Western manufactured goods that were much in demand in the hinterland.

The sea-based network of Sindwork traders and merchants of Hyderabad eventually forged its worldwide web 'by initially taking advantage of the British colonial link between Sindh and Bombay and then across the Western Indian Ocean between Bombay and Egypt' (Bose 2005: 73–74). Gujarati, Marwani and high-caste Bengali traders of the north, Chettis and Tamil Muslims in the south, 'took a leading part in the development of new export trades in cotton, indigo, and opium in alliance with the British houses of agency' (Bayly 1989: 224). 'The rise of Gujarati capitalists in Africa, which occurred in partnership with the Arabs from the turn of the nineteenth century', preceded the European penetration of Africa (Bose 2005: 75). When European factories 'began to desert the Levant' in the late eighteenth century, Levantine merchants took over their position, 'with the names and trading positions of the European houses', and installed their own agents, Greek, Syrian, Armenian, in England and elsewhere (Kasaba *et al.* 1986: 126–127).

### Transnational classes

Similar urban worlds were found across the globe. In Africa, Asia, Europe, and the Americas, cities became focal points of growth, and these, and in particular port cities, increasingly created a global urban landscape in which were found similar processes of class formation, commercialization, industrialization, and cultural practices.[17] A single trading system linked together ports and forts, plantations and mines, for the production and exchange of Argentinian beef, Australian wool, Ceylon tea, Malayan rubber, Brazilian coffee, British textiles, American cotton, Canadian furs, French silk, Finnish timber, Bengali jute, Rhodesian copper, or South African diamonds. Each country had a specialized island of production in a sea of cheap labour. Ports grew into large coastal cities – Buenos Aires, Lagos, Calcutta, Shanghai – with modern buildings, installations, and services. There was an urban-based class of landowners engaged in commercial agriculture for export, an expanding transnational middle class of merchants, businessmen, and financiers; and an urban workforce including dockers, porters, packers, railwaymen, warehousemen, clerks, servers, cooks, and builders.

In Asia, Africa, and Europe alike, wealthy and powerful classes transformed themselves into big capitalist landowners producing for the world market. Hungarian magnates and Polish noblemen used their power to organize production to respond to demands in Amsterdam and elsewhere in order to meet their own demand for luxury goods (Braudel 1982: 271). In the Ottoman Empire, the power of a traditional landlord class was strengthened as additional land was brought under cultivation for export crops. In Egypt, the total cultivated area expanded by 70 per cent during the nineteenth century (see Warriner 1948: 49–50), and most of it was acquired by a few thousand Egyptian landlords who transformed Egypt into a cotton farm in order to profit from overseas sales (Amin 1974: 362). In Mesopotamia, increased demand for exports of grain at the end of the nineteenth century gave tribal chiefs a motive for acquiring land as their personal property (see Warriner 1948: 20–25).

South Asia saw the rise of a powerful class of territorial magnates (thakurs, zamindars), who disposed of the rural surplus and became the socially dominant class in India. In Latin America, independence from Spain and Portugal at the beginning of the nineteenth century transferred power to the large landlords and the local mercantile bourgeoisie interested in exporting. The pre-independence structures remained in place and were reinforced by exchange with the new metropolitan centre, Great Britain, which set up import–export firms and banks all over the continent and financed the public debt of the new states (Amin 1974: 362). In Africa throughout a vast area from Senegal through northern Nigeria to the Sudan, the Muslim Mourid brotherhoods destroyed the dense and integrated network of domestic trade that had been dominated by African traders and reoriented the economy toward the production and export of groundnuts and cotton (Amin 1977: 148–149). Egypt's colonization in the Sudan provided the conditions for a latifundia system of large estates and made available modern techniques, notably large-scale irrigation in the Gezira' (Amin 1977: 148).

The expansion of trade involved a multiplication of class positions that are 'bourgeois', and those who filled these positions established and maintained connections among elites: navigators, merchants, pirates, and merchant-princes; traders, soldiers, diplomats, and clergymen; speculative financiers, bankers, money lenders, and foreign investors. Business practice and culture were diffused through commercial associations, Merchant Societies, and Chambers of Commerce; the international payments 'circuit' which any country could plug into and draw the foreign exchange it needed to pay for its imports; networks of missionaries, merchants, or colonial administrators (informal legal, ecclesiastical, commercial employees, and administrative professional networks also existed) (Laidlaw 2005: 16); global flows of wealth and information; networks of interaction among different services (accountancy, advertising, banking/finance, insurance, management consultancy, law, etc.), and networks of trade and mercantile credit, and of producer centres and markets. All of these were increasingly bound together in the commercial life of different regions. Despite cultural differences, those involved in these mercantile networks had a great deal in common: they were economic liberals who sought freedom to move across jurisdictions and frontiers, resisted the interference of bureaucrats and officials, yet wanted governments to support their enterprises; and were concerned with the sanctity of contracts and property rights, the stability of currencies and the reliability of banks (Darwin 2007: 333).

Eurasian port cities of the nineteenth century were 'cultural hybrids, in which Eastern and Western cultures intermingled. Merchant bankers 'were members of a world community transcending national and religious boundaries', which 'for all its geographical dispersion' was 'a small world, in which everybody who was anybody knew or knew about everybody else of importance' (Landes 1958: 39). The Indian Ocean arena was connected by flows of intermediary capital and migrant labour, streams of Indian professional people and service groups seeking opportunities in colonies other than their own (Bose 2005: 77–78). 'Indian merchants and Muscat Arabs multiplied trade in the Persian Gulf and Red Sea' (Bayly 1989: 226). There was a transnational Chinese business class, and overseas Chinese and Indian capitalists financed the opening of new rice frontiers in the Irrawaddy Delta in lower Burma, the chow Chao Phraya Delta in Thailand, and the Mekong Delta in southern Vietnam (Bose 2005: 78).

Ethno-religious groups were part of a transnational middle class, dispersed in various geographic settings and connected by ties of kinship and common origin and ethnicity: Chinese workers who filled the jobs of traders, clerks, and skilled workers throughout Southeast Asia, Parsis in Bombay; and Parsis, Jews, and Armenians further east; Armenians in charge of the trade networks leading to Persia, Central Asia, and India; a mercantile network consisting of Greek businessmen in the Near East and Black Sea; Lebanese traders in West Africa who occupied posts previously occupied by Africans (who then had to occupy subordinate positions) (Amin 1977: 146). While many studies emphasize the role of minorities in Asia and Africa (as, for instance, that of Jews and Christians in the Ottoman cities), minorities also played a key role in Europe's expansion. Local and foreign intermediaries and agents were as much a part of the social landscape in Europe as they were in other regions of the world.

## III. Core and periphery

A vast accumulation of wealth and power in what today is called the 'third world' pre-dated and continued to grow during the era of European imperialism. The notion of wealth being extracted from the periphery and transferred to the core ignores the fact that the surplus extracted was shared among local and foreign elites.

Moreover, the diffusion of 'modernity' went from East to West. Far from dragging backward peoples towards European-style modernity, Europeans learned about the production of cotton textiles, steel, and other goods from Asia; and they borrowed, adapted, and improved upon its technological and commercial innovations in textile production, metallurgy, astronomy, medicine, and navigation. England followed the classic pattern of import substitution in the development of its cotton industry: it imitated muslins and other materials pioneered by Indian and Chinese manufacturers and imported by the East India Company, and gradually replaced imports with domestic substitutes – assisted, of course, by protection (O'Brien 1982: 11). It was the 'efficiency of Chinese and Indian industry' that pushed European nations towards specialization in commercial services': the reason Europeans specialized in shipping, banking, and insurance services to other continents was in order to pay for their adverse balance of commodity trade with India and China (O'Brien 1982: 10). In 1838, Britain was attempting to redress her trade imbalance with China by selling some 1400 tons of opium to China per year, in exchange for Chinese tea and silk. The opium suppliers were Indians, who grew, harvested, and shipped the opium and became the largest drug dealers in the world. Indian farmers, traders, sailors, and investors were central to the opium trade (Ghosh 2008). It was the Chinese government's attempts to restrict the import of opium into China and the ensuing Opium Wars that led to the Treaty of Nanking in 1842. As Lewis and Wigen point out, India and China simply cannot be said ever to have constituted a cultural periphery; and, except in areas that were depopulated and densely 'settled' by Europeans, the colonized portions of the world never surrendered their cultural autonomy (Lewis & Wigen 1997: 140).

### *Turning points*

Previous chapters have argued that the division defined by conventional historiography between a modern and a backward world misrepresents the history of Europe. But it misrepresents the history of non-European regions as well.

Walt Rostow's *The Stages of Economic Growth* (1960) did much to enshrine the notion of a divide between Europe and the rest of the world (see discussion in Chapter 1). Following Rostow, much development theory tends to assume that 'Western' countries reached a point of 'take-off' to industrial development by the middle of the nineteenth century, while those countries of the developing world that have reached this stage did so only after World War II. But as Lloyd Reynolds argues, 'The chronology, in which Europe and North America develop very early and other countries follow only after a century-long delay, is seriously distorted' (1985: 31). All of the countries of the contemporary third world experienced a slow and more-or-less similar rate of increase in both population and national output during the eighteenth and nineteenth centuries. By the middle of the nineteenth century, many of them were experiencing a sustained rise in per capita output.

What Rostow calls a country's 'take-off' to industrial development is the point in which that country has a substantial development of factory industry. Reynolds uses a different formulation. What Reynolds calls the 'turning point' in growth is the transition from a stationary to a rising trend of per capita outcome. This he dates from the acceleration of agricultural, and sometimes mineral, output and a rising income from exports (Reynolds 1985: 10). There are sound reasons for preferring Reynolds' formulation: one being that it characterized the 'turning point' for many of today's most advanced countries.

With this formulation, Reynolds shows that 'the procession of turning points in Europe *overlaps* heavily with the corresponding procession in the third world'. Between 1850 and 1914, third-world countries were keeping up with the general pace of world trade. In Latin America, North Africa and the Middle East, Sub-Saharan Africa, and Asia, after about 1850 'we observe, in one country after another, a marked rise in the export/GDP ratio'. Between 1883 and 1913, 'exports from the tropical countries grew at almost exactly the same rate as industrial production in various countries' (Reynolds 1985: 26). Participating in the nineteenth century export boom were Argentina, Brazil, Chile, Colombia, Cuba, Mexico, and Peru. The turning points of Ceylon, Burma, Thailand, and Malaya were generally in the 1850s.[18] Egypt in the mid-nineteenth century had a booming cotton export economy. Toward the end of the century, Algeria, Nigeria, Ghana, the Ivory Coast, Kenya, Uganda, Tanganyika, and Southern Rhodesia entered into the intensive-growth process.

Table 5.1 compares Rostow's mostly twentieth-century 'take-off' dates for contemporary developing countries with Reynolds' revised set of nineteenth-century 'turning points. A longer list of Reynolds 'turning points' (1985: 10) is given in Table 5.2.

*Table 5.1* The Nineteenth-century 'turning points' of contemporary third-world countries: Rostow (1960) and Reynolds (1985) compared

| *Country* | *Rostow's 'Take-off'* | *Reynolds' 'Turning Point'* |
|---|---|---|
| Thailand | 1960–1970 | 1850 |
| Argentina | 1933–1950 | 1860 |
| Mexico | 1940–1960 | 1876 |
| Brazil | 1933–1950 | 1880 |
| Taiwan | 1953–1960 | 1895 |

*Table 5.2* A longer list of Reynolds' 'turning points' (Reynolds 1985: 10)

| *Country* | *Turning Point* | *Country* | *Turning Point* |
|---|---|---|---|
| Chile | 1840 | Sri Lanka | 1880 |
| Malaysia | 1850 | Peru | 1880 |
| Thailand | 1850 | Taiwan | 1895 |
| Argentina | 1860 | Columbia | 1885 |
| Burma | 1870 | Nigeria | 1890 |
| Mexico | 1876 | Ghana | 1895 |
| Algeria | 1880 | Ivory Coast | 1895 |
| Brazil | 1880 | Kenya | 1895 |
| Japan | 1880 | South Korea | 1910 |

By the nineteenth century, elites were embedded in broadly similar local relations, and enjoyed similar conditions and styles of life. Elites outside of Europe enjoyed the benefit of lower prices (the 'consumers' rent of the richer men in a poorer society), and had the additional advantage that security costs were met in large part by European taxpayers. As John Mellor points out, 'A dominant, privileged landlord class is likely to be wealthy, with command of all the benefits, through imports and travel, of high-income nations plus the vast privileges of wealth available in a low-income society with its attendant low cost of servants and personal services' (Mellor 1966: 15). Reynolds adjustment to a purchasing-power basis suggests that the 'official' per capita figures for the lowest-income countries should be calculated at three times their current levels to make them comparable with figures for the richest countries (Reynolds 1985: 40).

A key assumption of much development theory is that capital-intensive goods flowed to the periphery, while labour-intensive raw materials flowed from the periphery to the core (Chase-Dunn 1985: 271). But Britain exported a comparatively narrow range of manufactured goods. Its industrial system was based on the exploitation of a limited number of basic raw materials for the production of textiles, heavy industries, coal, iron, and steel, engineering, and shipbuilding. New World metals and transhipped Asian goods that had often been obtained with silver and exotica from the New World (such as sugar and tobacco) 'paid for more of western Europe's imports from the rest of the Old World than did manufactures created wholly within Europe' (Pomerantz 2000: 273).

The 'core' did not import raw materials and minerals necessary for its industrial capitalist expansion, but luxury goods and foodstuffs that made it possible to depress wages. Europe did not need raw materials from other regions. Continental Europe was rich in ores – gold, silver, copper, iron ore, zinc ore, mercury, and quartz (used for glass making); wood (for fuel, for the construction industry, mining and various processing industries), and coal, lead, and tin deposits. Paul Bairoch has argued that the 'core' countries had an abundance of the minerals of the Industrial Revolution (iron ore and coal); they were almost totally self-sufficient in raw materials and, in fact, exported energy to the Third World (Bairoch 1993: 172). The main commodities extracted from the Americas were high-cost items that repaid the costs of long-distance trade: silver (much of which was used to pay for Asian textiles, porcelain, silk, tea, and spices), gold, sugar, tobacco, and chocolate. Britain was an entrepôt – not a final destination – for much of the food products and raw materials it imported. A large part of imports into England were re-exported, including American sugar, tobacco, coffee and rice, and Asian dyestuffs, cotton goods, and tea. By 1815, Britain was re-exporting nearly half of its sugar imports, two-thirds of its coffee imports, and almost all of the calicoes it imported (see the figures in Davis 1979: 31). In addition, it sold American tobacco and rice, and large quantities of Asian cotton goods, silk and tea to Europe, and German linens to America and Africa (Davis 1979: 31).

The notion that the periphery was characterized by a system geared to produce a surplus of raw materials for export *to serve the needs of 'core' countries* obscures the fact that local elites monopolized the production and export of raw materials and used the proceeds for luxury goods, and goods needed for developing and transporting exports, and for protection. Such phrases as 'peripheral country or region X exported raw material goods *to serve the needs of the core*' are a misrepresentation: elites chose to use their land, political power, and means of coercion in order to profit from the sale of goods to other elites. For Europeans and non-Europeans alike, imperialism offered wealth and power and prestige. Entering into alliances with foreigners enabled all parties concerned to monopolize foreign trade and to grow rich or increase their wealth.

Africans re-partitioned Africa in the nineteenth century causing a great upheaval (Blake 1950: 65; quoted in Barraclough 1991: 112). In Upper Senegal and Ashanti gold mined under the orders of the king provided the ruling classes with a means to obtain luxury goods (clothes, drugs, perfumes, dates, and salt), and 'the opportunity to establish and strengthen their social and political power by the acquisition of horses, copper, iron bars, and weapons' (Amin 1977: 143).

In Latin America, independence from Spain and Portugal 'brought few changes except those which accentuated structural imbalances between urban and rural areas and between primary and other cities' (Portes 1977a: 70). As Platt argues, 'it takes a creative imagination and perhaps even "inventive research" to establish a client relationship between Argentina, rich at home and abroad, and a Britain which, in the decade before the First World War, was selling far less to Argentina than it bought' (Platt 1980: 126). Argentina 'maintained a large and increasingly favourable balance of trade' with Britain, its main customer, could borrow 'readily at competitive rates' (Platt 1980: 126),[19] and grew rich exporting wool, grain, mutton, and beef. The terms of trade, which altered in favour of producers of food products in 1896, were particularly favourable to Argentina until 1929 (Ferns 1967: 125).

Egypt's cotton industry had nothing to do with Europeans refashioning Egyptian society to serve the needs of the 'core'. Seeking to increase his revenue through cotton, Muhammad Ali turned almost all of Egypt 'into a huge government farm' (Landes 1958: 75; see, for details, Owen 1969: Ch. 1), and used revenues from cotton for building up an army and a navy so he could increase Egypt's autonomy from the Ottoman Empire (Landes 1958: 75), fight in Arabia against the Wahhabis, and build up a fleet to operate on the Red Sea. He remodelled Egypt's defences, and undertook a costly programme of reform designed to produce a new army trained according to the latest European methods (Owen 1969: 20). He pursued a programme of rapid Westernization, encouraging the introduction of Western techniques, and bringing in European specialists to organize and direct a state programme of modernization. He saw foreigners as collaborators in this project, and agreed to remove many of the disabilities that had encumbered Christian traders with Egypt (Owen 1969: 22). Though Abbas (1849–1854) endeavoured to reverse many of Muhammad Ali's projects, he also strengthened his ties with Britain and France in order to preserve Egypt's autonomy viz. the Ottoman Empire; and his successor, Said (1854–1863), returned to the programme of rapid Westernization promoted by Mohammad Ali (Landes 1958: 81–83). In 1833, there were 33 cotton factories in Egypt. 'With the exception of a few machines brought in from Europe as models, no cotton-spinning apparatus was imported. All the factories used jennies and looms made by Egyptian carpenters, smiths, and turners under the direction of French technicians' (Owen 1969: 44).

The notion that concentrating production on agricultural and raw materials for export blocked autonomous economic development and balanced growth is also false. Many of today's advanced countries were integrated into the world economy as exporters of agricultural and raw materials. The binarism that locates production in the colonies and consumption in the centre is false, as well. All export commodities had an exchange value as well as a use value: all could be exchanged for international currencies. In this sense, these commodities were also 'consumed' by the elites that exported them (Coronil 1996: 64).[20]

Key elements of 'dependency', and aspects of societies that are characterized as 'colonial legacies', pre-date European influence and colonialism. European imperialism did not create global inequality: the world market into which European countries became integrated, 'was already characterized by considerable development differentials' (Senghaas 1985: 9). 'Political discrimination on matters of race had local origins' in the societies of Asia, the Caribbean, and southern Africa (Bayly 1989: 149–150). Except in regions of European settlement where whole indigenous populations were incarcerated and all but physically eliminated, colonial rule was embedded as much in pre-colonial structures as in ones imposed by Europeans.

Capitalist expansion, everywhere, involved the same changes: the breaking down of communal organization; tariff policies that favoured foreign imports and destroyed indigenous handicrafts; immigration policies favouring the export sector; and the promotion of staple-export expansion with a dualistic rather than a wider distribution of benefits. Historically, it has made no difference if these changes were directed by indigenous elites, or by indigenous elites allied with foreigners.

The historiography of contemporary third-world countries emphasizes the role of imperial trade in sweeping away existing industries (artisanal handicrafts) and preventing modern ones from emerging.[21] But as Chapter 3 showed, Europeans were doing the same at home. European governments restricted manufacturing in their imperial holdings; and education, especially secondary and higher education, was undersupported. Chapter 3 also showed that the dualism that is thought to be a legacy of European empire was a core feature of European economies before World War II. Dualism was also a characteristic feature of development in Japan, a country that was never colonized. After the Meiji restoration in 1868, Japanese elites introduced a 'particularly rapacious form of capitalism' that was 'based on a hierarchical social structure and relations of production directly inherited from feudalism' (Sachs 1976: 62–63). Japanese elites imported European technology and, in particular, rapidly Europeanized their weapons technology, while simultaneously reinforcing the system of local political and cultural values. Foreign experts were employed to assist, and Japanese students were sent abroad for technical training; but its agriculture was characterized by 'gross poverty, overcrowding of the land, and debt' (Hubbard 1935: 164). Economic power was concentrated in the hands of landlords; and Japan's industrial expansion and, in particular the expansion of its heavy industries, by the 1930s was fuelled by railroad building in Manchuria and the expansion of military production. In 1880, raw silk and tea made up two-thirds of Japanese exports. The collapse of American demand for silk during the Great Depression had a big impact on Japan. Japan's exports to her most important market, China (Japan supplied roughly 70 per cent of China's imports of cotton piece-goods; Hubbard 1935: 11), also declined precipitously during the Depression. Japan attempted to turn Taiwan into a source of rice for Japanese domestic consumption. Japan formally took over Korea in 1910 and, as in the earlier case of Taiwan, set about to develop the country as an auxiliary to the Japanese economy. An article written in the 1940s observed that there were 'two Japans' living side by side and 'drifting more and more apart', and that this 'dualism' arose from 'the co-existence of large-scale modern industry with primitive handicraft and trade conducted along traditional lines'.[22]

## Conclusions

Cores and peripheries were not properties of individual states or regions. Historically, capitalist development proceeded through the cross-national integration of export sectors rather than through the expansion and integration of national markets. Every state had core and peripheral areas. The core within each state was linked cross-nationally to cores within other states. These cores tended to be more similar than dissimilar, and they drew surplus from their own peripheries using broadly similar means.

On the eve of World War I, most of Europe was still rural and 'pre-eminently pre-industrial', as Arno Mayer has argued (1981: 187, 301); and most of rural Europe had not changed substantially since the Middle Ages. Agriculture was still the single largest and weightiest sector in all the Continental countries.[23] Even after World War I, France drew her wealth principally from agriculture, and approximately half of her population was engaged in agricultural pursuits (Ogg 1930: 185). In 1914 almost half of western Europe's working population was still employed in agriculture (including fishing and forestry), and rural dwellers still made up the largest part of the population in all the countries of continental Europe, except Germany. In many western European industrial countries, the absolute numbers of those employed in agriculture did not decline dramatically until after 1945, when mechanization of production increased significantly.

# 6 The system unravels

## Contraction, conflict and social revolution

During the nineteenth century, a monopolistic system of capital accumulation fuelled a global economic expansion based largely on the production of goods and services for export to an expanding network of elites, ruling groups, and governments around the world. Expanding production for export made it possible for elites to accumulate wealth and, at the same time, limit the scope of industrialization and the growth of organized labour so as to maintain the traditional bases of their social power.

Locally, elites cooperated with 'foreign' class allies in producing surplus; and while European imperial agents competed for clients and markets they did so through practices that during the course of the century assumed the character of an international regime. Thus, while 'there were conflicts, frictions, and collisions at points where empires geographically came together and occasional armed skirmishes outside of Europe,' there were also 'periodic conferences called to settle colonial issues, and countless bilateral treaties and agreements between colonial powers that defined borders on distant continents, transferred territories or populations, and codified the privileges and obligations of each colonial power with respect to the domains of others' (Puchala & Hopkins 1983. 68).

However, during the Great Depression that began in the 1870s, the cooperation that underpinned this system began to dissolve. Depression and agricultural decline triggered the explosive rise of a global 'red tide' and a sharp escalation of imperialist expansion; and, by the early years of the twentieth century, these two sources of tension had begun to undermine the two central features of nineteenth-century global industrial expansion: internal repression and external expansion.

## I. Social conflict, 1815–1914

During the nineteenth century, the organization of production and direction of class formation and political change throughout the world was broadly similar and gave rise to similar forms of conflict.

Some scholars insist that forms of collective struggle in 'the periphery' of the global imperial order of the nineteenth and early twentieth centuries differed from those found in the core (see Chapter 1). They argue that workers in 'the periphery' do not express their identity or articulate their grievances in the way that classical Marxism defines as 'proletarian', but through nationalist, religious, and other discourses. However, as Zachary Lockman points out, 'precisely the same is true in the most developed capitalist countries that are usually held up as the norm' (Lockman 1994: xxix). In Europe, working-class activism was focused both on the marketplace and – because governments appeared to be allied with employers against workers – the political arena. Most strikes and labour disputes were concerned with improving wages, hours, and working conditions. But workers also used the strike as a means of demonstrating for the extension of the franchise; and authorities in various European countries routinely characterized those strikes as 'political'. Working-class activism was also often associated with or interpreted as nationalism (see e.g., Gellner 1983; Hobsbawm 1990; Wallerstein 1997). Historically, class struggles have been embedded in, or have intersected with, ethnic, national, and other communities and identities. Thus, the 'banners' raised in struggles are often those of communal identification rather than those specifically of class identification.

'A wage labour class emerged, to one degree or another, in every part of Africa', and 'this soon led to an organized labour movement' (Orr 1966: 65). Workers employed in small workshops in Damascus engaged in the same forms of labour struggle associated with wage workers employed in the advanced industrial sector; and they represented their interests before the state in ways that were similar to those used by workers in unions after 1908 (Quataert 1994: 36). Sherry Vatter argues that 'Although Damascus's journeymen weavers engaged in disciplined strikes, they do not meet all the Marxist criteria for class-conscious workers', because they retained a sense of communal artisanal identity and legitimized their actions 'in terms of a "moral economy" framework rather than class struggle' (Vatter 1994: 8). However, the same can be said of striking weavers in Europe. Throughout the nineteenth century and around the world, there were ethnic and nationalist, religious and ideological conflicts; riots, insurrections, rebellions, revolutions, uprisings, violent strikes and demonstrations; and brutal repression; and all of these expressed the basic antagonism between monopolists (large plantations, trading companies, and transnational corporations) and working populations seeking to reclaim more of the surplus value they created.

While labour in 'the periphery' was a numerically smaller category in relation to European labour forces, it was, as Frederick Cooper points out, 'an extremely influential one, because the very narrowness of colonial commercial, mining, and industrial channels meant that a small group – in a position to use face-to-face relations to organize – could disrupt the entire import–export economy' (Cooper 1994: 1534).

It is often assumed that labour was more effectively organized in Europe than elsewhere the nineteenth century. But before 1945, Europe's industrial expansion was largely carried out by atomized, low-wage and low-skilled labour forces; they were neither permanent nor full-time, nor represented by national industrial unions. The First International (officially called the International Working Men's Association), founded in 1864, established regular contacts between labour leaders of different countries and, in many countries, inspired trade union organization and helped to formulate some of the ideas that later became the basis of the demands of organized labour. But it was feared by European elites to a degree far beyond its actual strength. It was hardly 'the powerful, well administered, smoothly functioning organization' of legend (Collins & Abramsky 1965: v–vi). The attempt to create working-class internationalism ultimately proved ineffective. The Second International (1889–1914) was much larger than its predecessor, but labour internationalism ultimately proved 'unable to move beyond the exchange of information and a reinforcement of national union identities' (MacShane 1992: 47). It failed to organize the unskilled majority of the working class; and the fact that capitalists were free to take their capital elsewhere made the conditions for forging labour solidarity internationally unfavourable.

Some theorists argue that the forms of labour control used in 'core' and 'peripheral' countries were different. For instance, Immanuel Wallerstein argues that 'free labour, the form of labour control used for skilled work, characterized core countries; whereas coerced labour, used for less skilled work, characterized peripheral areas' (Wallerstein 1974: Vol. I, 127). But other scholars have argued that, both in 'the core' and in 'the periphery', labour regimes and forms of labour (wage, coerced, and semi-coerced) were heterogeneous (Cameron 1976; Rapp 1976; Sella 1977; Stern 1988). Megan Vaughan argues that labour control differed in core and colonial societies because in core countries surveillance and control was directed at individuals, while in colonial societies it was directed at collectivities (Vaughan 1991: 8–12). But by the late 1830s, England had stationed over 30,000 troops on permanent garrison duty in its industrial towns, and beginning in the 1840s, local barracks and a state-controlled system of paramilitary and police forces were established as part of an organization headed by the Home Office, the local military command, and the local Home Office intelligence network (see Foster 1974: Chs. 3 and 4). This system of surveillance and control was directed, not at individuals, but at the lower classes and, particularly, workers and ethnic minorities.

Similar forms of labour struggle, including Luddite, radical, trade unionist, utopian socialist, and democratic were found around the world. Machine breaking (Luddism), a well-known practice in early nineteenth-century Europe, later occurred in the Ottoman Empire, Brazil and China.[1] In Asian centres of trade, population and production, a wage-labour class emerged and, with it, trade unions and modern forms of labour struggle. Organized protests, strikes and the formation of labour movements were 'part of the political and economic life of a number of Middle Eastern countries' (Lockman 1994: xxviii). Strikes and trade-union activity occurred in textiles, mining, transport, and the artisanal sector (tailors, cobblers, bakers, and porters).

The experiences of miners, railwaymen, weavers, and artisans in Anatolia, Damascus, in Egypt and in Europe were fundamentally similar. In England, mechanized weaving and spinning caused a massive collapse of home-based crafts organized under the mercantile 'putting-out system'. Some regions of the country were able to make the transition quickly and, after 1815, textile exports produced in these areas brought about the collapse of European regions active in craft production. But, by the 1830s, 'Alsatian and Swiss producers were almost on a par with Lancashire, and machines built by Escher Wyss of Switzerland were found to be superior in many ways to English ones' (Komlos 2000: 309). Weavers, however, were not the beneficiaries. There was a revolt of silk weavers in Lyon in 1834 in which 300 people were killed in six days of fighting (Goldstein 1983: 147). There was an uprising in Prussian Silesia in June 1844 of about 5000 starving linen handloom weavers, which resulted in 35 deaths (Reichard 1969: 31).

After 1850, weavers and other artisans everywhere 'suffered severely from a flood of cheap, machine-made goods coming from European factories' (Davis 1979: 38). However, before very long factories in Japan, China, and India began to produce cheaper and better goods than Europeans (and Americans) did (McNeill 2008: 5). In the nineteenth century, dyestuffs from India and the Caribbean were replacing those of the Mediterranean; and Chinese silk replaced Italian silk (Davis 1979: 38). Thousands of weavers in Damascus had lost their jobs when relatively inexpensive Western European textiles flooded Ottoman markets in the 1830s and 1840s. But by the end of the 1870s, Damascus' commercial textile sector had regained its earlier strength as a result of expanding rural demand for textiles, the cotton boom of the 1860s, appreciation for better quality, although slightly higher priced, local fabrics, and Ottoman fiscal policies encouraging local industries (Vatter 1994: 5–6).

## The Great Depression, 1873–1886

Beginning in the 1870s, there was a marked deterioration of agricultural conditions and a slowdown in world production and trade. This accelerated economic imbalances in Asia, Africa, Europe, and the Americas, and produced a groundswell of social conflict around the world. There was an explosive rise of violence in rural areas, which proved increasingly difficult to keep in check by repression and emigration. At the same time, in the urban core of the global system, hungry and disenfranchised populations were fuelling a rising 'red tide' of radicals and socialists of various sorts, dissenters, trade unionists, and suppressed national minorities.

In Europe, conditions in rural areas produced an unprecedented upsurge in agrarian agitation and protest in the 1870s. At that time, some 7000 persons owned about 80 per cent of the land in Britain. In 1897, 175,000 people owned ten-elevenths of the land of England, and 40 million people the remaining one-eleventh (Romein 1978: 195). Before World War I (1911–1913) the top five per cent of the British population owned 87 per cent of personal wealth, while the bottom 90 per cent owned 8 per cent (Hobsbawm 1968: 274). Less than four per cent of the population owned 25 per cent of the land of Denmark and France. Ten per cent of landowners held 85 per cent of Italy; less than one per cent of the landowners controlled over 40 per cent of the land of southern and central Spain (Goldstein 1983: 240). In 1907, 0.2 per cent of all farms in Prussia controlled 20 per cent of the arable land (Puhle 1986: 84). In 1900, less than one per cent of the population owned more than 40 per cent of the land in Austria, Hungary, Romania, Germany, and Poland,

The growing land hunger in Europe was reflected, not only by agrarian agitation and protest, but by the massive emigration that began in the final decades of the century. Between 1870 and 1914, 35 million Europeans left the region. Most of the 25 million who left after 1890 departed from southern, central, and eastern Europe, and were displaced peasants and agricultural labourers from Prussia's eastern agricultural regions, from southern Italy, the Austro-Hungarian Empire, and the Balkans (Goldstein 1983: 246).

There was a series of subsistence crises across Asia, Africa, and Latin America (Davis 2001). The Great Famine of 1876–1879 caused a large migration of agricultural labourers and artisans from southern India to British tropical colonies, where they worked as indentured labourers on plantations.[2] In 1896–1897 there was a wave of crop failures across India, Australia, southern Russia, northern Africa, and Spain. 1889–1890 saw a second wave of drought. In 1902, a third wave of drought and famine, 'comparable in magnitude to the 1876–1879 catastrophe, swept over India, northern

China, Korea, Java, the Philippines, northeast Brazil, and southern and eastern Africa' (Davis 2001: 138). In the Ottoman Empire, slow growth rates of agricultural production and foreign trade and declining wheat prices triggered a wave of agrarian unrest from Syria to Algeria in the late 1870s and early 1880s. In Egypt, there was a wave of mortgage foreclosures, and a 'growing number of increasingly desperate landless peasants and service tenants' attacked moneylenders and landowners (Burke 1991: 33). The economic situation in Chile deteriorated in the late 1870s as its wheat exports came up against competition from Argentina, Canada, and Russia, and its income from silver mining and copper dropped.

The modern cartel movement began to develop during the depression years. In addition to traditional corporatist structures – guilds, and patronage and clientelist networks – which had survived in some places and grown stronger during the nineteenth century, new corporatist structures were created. During the Great Depression, industry became increasingly penetrated by monopoly and protection. By 1900, there were no German enterprises of any consequence, except shipbuilding, which were not affected profoundly by the cartel movement (Ogg 1930: 222). After Germany, Austria had the most cartels, many of which were associated with the corresponding German cartels (Curtis 1931: 411). In Belgium, cartels were also developed largely on German models. In France, the cartel generally took the form of a joint selling bureau or *comptoir*, involving price fixing, but not restriction of output, as a rule. In what David Landes aptly calls 'a commercial version of the enclosure movement (1969: 247), Britain answered the cartel movement with the 'combine' which, like cartels, was designed to control the market by eliminating competition and fixing prices. By 1914, cartelization pervaded industry everywhere in Europe (see Halperin 1997: Ch. 7). Between 1921 and 1932 the number of major cartels in Japan increased from 15 to 84. By the 1930s, 70 per cent of all Japanese trade and industry was 'in the hands of fifteen great houses' (Hubbard 1935: 77).

## *Strikes*

The 1850s saw the emergence of the strike as an offensive weapon for the improvement of wages and working conditions; and by the 1870s, the strike had become the 'workers' preferred form of action' (Gillis 1977: 269).[3]

There was a sharp increase in strike activity in Europe in the 1880s as a result of the depression. The rise in the number of strikes in Britain each year of that decade, as shown in Table 6.1 below, was indicative of the general trend.

Between 1870 and 1914 there were strikes by journeymen weavers in Damascus's artisanal sector. In 1879, a strike by weavers to protest a cut in piecework wages led to a work stoppage for four weeks and a reinstatement of their original wages (Vatter 1994: 3). Textile workers went on strike in Pisa in 1873, and in the United States in 1903, 1912, and 1934. There was a strike of 5000 textile workers in London's East End in 1906; and cotton strikes in the Dutch region of Twente in 1923 and 1931–1932.

The decade of the 1870s began, in France, with the rising of the Paris commune in which Parisians led a movement to secede from France; 20,000 were killed or banished during the repression and reprisals. In the United States, a financial panic that had begun in Vienna in 1873, left 25 per cent of New York workers unemployed; by 1878 more than three million people had joined the ranks of the unemployed nationwide. Worker demonstrations (e.g., the 1874 Tompkins Square protest) became common, some so violent that many major cities built armories (Schlager 2003: 91). Another financial panic in May 1893 led to a depression that lasted four years. In the first year of the crisis, several Wall Street brokerage houses collapsed, over 600 banks and 16,000 businesses failed; thousands of farmers lost their land, and national unemployment reached an estimated 20 per cent (Schlager 2003: 92).

There were strikes of miners throughout the 1880s and 1890s. In Belgium, troops were called in to put down rioting miners in Liége and Charleroi and throughout the Borinage in 1886, and there was

*Table 6.1* Strikes in Britain in the 1870s (Bevan 1880: 37)

| *Year* | *Number of Strikes* | *Year* | *Number of Strikes* |
|---|---|---|---|
| 1870 | 30 | 1875 | 245 |
| 1871 | 98 | 1876 | 229 |
| 1872 | 343 | 1877 | 180 |
| 1873 | 365 | 1878 | 268 |
| 1874 | 286 | 1879 | 308 |

an armed uprising of the mining population in 1893. In 1889 there were violent miners' strikes in Ruhr and Silesia. There were miners' strikes in the United States in 1897, 1919, and 1922. In 1893, 300,000 mineworkers went on strike in Britain; coal workers went on strike in 1910–1911 and conducted a national strike in 1912. There were miners' strikes in Germany in 1899, in Mexico in 1906, in Chile in 1907, in South Africa in 1922, in the United States in 1933–1934, and in Zambia among copper miners in 1935.

Strikes of transport workers began in force in the 1880s. There were railroad strikes in the United States in 1877 and in 1888 (the Burlington Railroad Strike). In 1894, the Pullman Strike by the American Railway Union involved 125,000 workers on 29 railroads. Some 12,000 federal troops and 5000 federal marshals clashed with strikers over the course of a week, leaving 34 strikers dead and more than 50 wounded (Schlager 2003: 94). There were dockers' strikes in Great Britain in 1898 and in 1899; and, in 1911, a general strike involving 65,000 port workers at Southampton, Liverpool, Hull, Newport, the Northeast coast, Humber, Leith, Manchester, Cardiff, and London. In the Ottoman Empire, the Great Anatolian Railway strike took place in September 1908. Alexandria tramworkers went on strike in 1900. The 2000 drivers, conductors, and maintenance workshop workers employed by the Belgian-owned Cairo tramway company went on strike in October 1908. In October 1910, railway workers throughout Egypt went on strike, and police and army units were sent in to clear the strikers and to reopen the rail lines to Upper Egypt, which the workers had cut. In July and August 1911, there was another strike of Cairo tramworkers, together with an almost simultaneous tram strike in Alexandria. That year, about 80,000 railway workers, coal porters, lightermen, and carters went on strike in Britain. There was a strike of longshoremen in Changsha (Hunan Province, China) in 1917, a strike lasting five weeks at the Ishikawajima shipyard in Tokyo in October–November 1921, and a strike of railway workers in Sekondi-Takoradi (Gold Coast/Ghana) in 1931.

In March 1900, riots and revolutionary turmoil in Cairo and upper Egypt was violently repressed. That year began a high level of labour violence in the plantation belt of the Dutch Indies. A three-month strike of cigarette rollers in Cairo began in December 1899, another one occurred in 1903. After the 1908 coup, there were 104 strikes between July and the end of the year in the Ottoman Empire (Quataert 1994: 27). In Argentina, the period between 1902 and 1910 was punctuated by a series of massive general strikes leading to the involvement of the state in campaigns of repression. The national government imposed a state of siege to combat strikes on five occasions, and violent confrontations between workers and the police (Rock 1975: 81).

After the turn of the century, industrial disputes in Europe reached unprecedented proportions. Over 1000 strikes per year were recorded after 1906. In *France*, there were violent strikes in 1905–1906 which, on numerous occasions, involved struggles with troops. In 1908, French troops killed 20 strikers and wounded 667 at Nantes (Tilly, Tilly, & Tilly 1975). In *Germany*, the number of industrial disputes escalated from 1468 strikes in 1900 to 2834 in 1912 (Geary 1981: 105). In *Italy*, the number of strikes, strikers, and workdays lost between 1900 and 1914 was about eight times higher than in the 1880s (Bordogna, Cella, & Provasi 1889: 223–224): there were violent strikes in 1901, 1902, 1903, a general strike in 1904, waves of industrial unrest in 1906–1907 and 1910–1913, and violent agricultural strikes in 1901–1906, and in 1908 (Tipton & Aldrich 1987a: 115). The average number of strikes in *Britain* increased from 872 per year in 1911, to 1459 in 1913 (Meacham 1972: 1344, 1347). In *Belgium*, there were massive strikes in 1902 (Goldstein 1983: 264), and a general strike in 1913. In *Russia*, the incidence of strikes, mass protests, police arrests, and killings increased throughout the first decade of the century: in 1901, there were 155 interventions by troops in labour violence; in 1902, troops were used on 365 occasions to crush the peasantry; in 1903, there were 322 interventions by troops involving 'a force far greater than the army of 1812' (Stone 1983: 212–213); in 1912 there were 2032 strikes; and in 1913 there were 3534 strikes, and 100,000 arrests for 'attacks on State power' (Stone 1983: 244).

The 1880s also marked the rise of socialist parties whose essential object was the reconstruction of society in the interest of the wage-earning classes. In the years leading up to World War I, their membership, the number of their candidates elected to representative bodies, and their share of the popular vote, increased by leaps and bounds in Europe. Socialist parties and groups were also formed in the late nineteenth century and the early twentieth century in Argentina, Bolivia, Brazil, Chile, Cuba, Guadeloupe, Martinique, Mexico, Peru, and Uruguay. The first communist parties in Latin America were founded in the wake of the Russian Revolution of 1917. The Mexican Communist Party was the first communist party outside Russia. A communist party was formed in Brazil in 1922. The Partido Socialista del Perú (PSP) was founded in 1928.

Trade-union activity increased with the upsurge of strikes. 1889 saw the development of the New Unionism in Britain, a movement that drew in masses of unskilled workers and women. In 1889–1900 the trade-union movement 'leaped to something like one and a half million members', grew more slowly to about two million, then doubled again to about four million in the great 'labour unrest' of 1911–1913 (Hobsbawm 1968: 165). Between 1910 and 1914 membership in the so-called 'new unions' – dockers, seamen, and general labourers – increased by over 300 per cent (Meacham 1972: 1344).

Trade unions were formed in Japan between 1890 and 1900. The first union organization for workers was formed in Egypt in 1890 following a strike organized by the tobacco workers (cigarette rollers) in Cairo. This branched into several organizations, including the Tailors Workers Union Society in 1901 and the Railway Workers Society in 1908.

Transport unions were formed in South Africa (African dock workers, 1909), Gambia (seamen, late 1920s), Nigeria (railway and port workers, 1931), Gold Coast (motor drivers, 1931); and, during the 1940s, in Kenya and Uganda (Asian railway staff), Tanganyika and Nyasaland (railway workers), Kenya (port, railway, and motor transport workers), and Zanzibar (cart coolies and seamen) (Orr 1966: 78–79). Unions of European workers in South Africa date from the 1880s. By 1900 European workers were organized in South Africa, Rhodesia, Mozambique, Algeria, and Egypt, and by 1910 also in Tunisia (Orr 1966: 65–66). European railway workers were the first to bring trade unions and collective bargaining to Rhodesia, early in the century, and were pioneers in Dahomey, the Ivory Coast, the Sudan, and Ethiopia.

Trade unionism around the world was advanced by European workers. European company executives and their employees did not form 'a seamless community' of colonial interests (Stoler 1989: 135).[4] There was a sharp social and political division among them, and European employees, found in all the large cities of the world, cooperated with indigenous workers in trade unions. In 1909, the lower ranks of the estate hierarchy in the Dutch Indies, having formed a union of European plantation employees (*Vakvereeniging voor Assistenten*), supported indigenous protests, railway strikes, and nationalist organizations (Stoler 1989: 145). In the 1920s multiracial trade unions in Java were found that included lower level Europeans and Indonesian workers (Ingelson 1981: 55; cited in Stoler 1989: 138). Europeans formed and led the first African or mixed trade unions in most of the African territories where there was a European working class (Orr 1966: 89). In South Africa revolutionary socialists (Europeans) organized unions for African workers (Orr 1966: 69). A racially mixed tramworkers' union was organized in Cairo in 1908. Government workers were among the first to organize unions in Egypt, South Africa, the French African territories, and the Belgian Congo. While these unions were sometimes confined to Africans, and sometimes to Europeans; frequently they had a mixed membership (Orr 1966: 78).

Colonial states and foreign companies actively opposed cooperation among European and indigenous workers, as well as inter-racial mixing among workers. There were large populations of European paupers in the colonies. This situation raised two threats: it called into question the status and authority of 'Europe's civilizing mission'; and it raised the prospect of European and non-European labour closing ranks against owners. More than three-quarters of the European population in Barbados were poor whites in the mid-nineteenth century (Stoler 1989: 151). French colonial communities in Northern Africa contained a vast population of lower class Europeans which included many poor whites of non-French European origin (Stoler 1989: 151). Poor whites made up nearly half the European population in India. In 1900 there were some 6000 of them in workhouses (Arnold 1979: 104, 122). In the Netherlands Indies a relief fund for 'needy Europeans' was established in 1891 to support planters and their staff who went bankrupt during the crisis that ensured from a fall of tobacco prices on the world market (*Kroniek* 1917: 51; in Stoler 1989: 151). By the early 1900s, the Netherlands Indies contained tens of thousands of dangerously impoverished Eurasians ('Indos') and 'full-blooded' Europeans, according to government reports.[5]

In Johannesburg, where 'working-class whites and blacks socialized at home and at work', urban planning was designed 'to eradicate 'inter-racial "slum-yards"' and increase the 'social distance between white and black miners' (van Onselen 1982: 39; in Stoler 1989: 138). 'British India and the Netherlands Indies were able to maintain less formalized apartheids' because there 'unfit whites' could simply be sent home (Stoler 1989: 151).

Colonial authorities promoted 'racist ideology, fear of the Other, preoccupation with white prestige, and obsession with protecting European women from sexual assault by Asian and black males' as 'part of the apparatus that kept potentially subversive white colonials in line'. These were not about white supremacy, but were aimed at European underlings in the colonies (Stoler 1989: 138).

### *Imperialist rivalries*

By the 1880s, the increase in European imperialist activity abroad had produced 'a stupendous movement, without parallel in history' (Barraclough 1964: 63–64): *France* in Tunisia (1881), Madagascar (1883–1885, 1894–1901), Indochina (1882–1885), China (1882–1885; 1899–1900), and Morocco (1912); *Britain* in Afghanistan (1878–1880), the Boer Republic of the Transvaal, the Orange Free State (1879, 1899–1902, 1906), the Sudan (1881, 1885–1895, 1896–1900), Burma (1885–1886), India's northwest frontier (1897–1898), Uganda (1897–1901), and Sierra Leone (1898); *Germany* in southwest Africa (1903–1908); *Russia* in Transcaspia (1878–1881) and, with the Japanese, in Korea and Manchuria (1904–1905); *Italy* in the Ottoman Empire (1885), Abyssinia (1894–1896), and Libya (1911–1917); the *Netherlands* in the Achinese sultanate (1873–1908), the Malay Archipelago (1891–1894), the Congo (1892–1894), and Abyssinia (1894–1896); and all of them in China (1894–1901).

By the early twentieth century, the best markets had already been formally annexed or informally established as spheres of influence. As the potentialities of overseas outlets diminished, imperialist ambitions focused increasingly on Europe. In 1914, European states were still each other's best customers (Landes 1969: 241); and it was Europe, itself, that consequently became the target of the fiercest imperialist rivalries.

The Central and Eastern European nations, which had no colonial possessions and little hope for overseas expansion, decided that they, too, 'had the same right to expand as other great peoples and that if [they were] not granted this possibility overseas, [they would] be forced to do it in Europe' (Arendt 1958: 222–223).[6] German manufacturing output, which was quickly overtaking that of earlier industrial producers, sought markets abroad. But expansion in Latin America was checked by the United States, while expansion in China was no longer possible after the Russo-Japanese War in 1905, and plans to develop the Baghdad Railway and to secure the Portuguese colonies were checked by the British. In his famous 'hammer and anvil' speech of 1899, the German Reich Chancellor Bernhard von Bülow angrily declared, 'We cannot allow any foreign power, any foreign Jupiter to tell us: "What can be done?" The world is already partitioned'. This was only the first of what would be a series of increasingly pressing demands for the re-division of the globe (Kennedy 1980: 311).

## II. The system unravels, 1914–1945

There are a number of parallels between the world war of 1793–1815 and the world war that began in 1914.

Both wars came after a long period of expansion (the 'long sixteenth century', the 'long twentieth century'), followed by periods of contraction and conflict that culminated in an imperialist world war. In the earlier war, France had declared its intention to acquire its 'natural frontiers' and had sought to acquire German and Italian lands; while landlocked countries, e.g., Austria, sought outlets to the sea. In World War I, all the belligerents sought vast extensions of their territories: Austria–Hungary to divide Russian Poland with Germany, and Serbia with Bulgaria, annex Montenegro and control Albania and Venetia (Meyer 1955: 135); Germany to acquire substantial territories in Eastern Europe, retain some form of effective control of Belgium, and annex the French coal region of Briey-Longwy;[7] and Bulgaria to get Macedonia. Secret treaties concluded among the Allies provided for British acquisition of Southern Mesopotamia; Baghdad, Haifa, and Akka in Syria; a 'neutral' zone in Persia, and part of the German colonies; French acquisition of Syria, the Adana Vilayet, territory in Asia Minor, Alsace-Lorraine, the Saar

Valley, territories on the left bank of the Rhine, and a part of the German colonies; Romanian acquisition of Transylvania, the Banat and Bukovina; and Russian acquisition of Constantinople, Bosphorus and Dardanelles, the Sea of Marmora, Imbros and Tenedos in the Aegean, full liberty in Northern Persia, Ispahan and Yezd, Trebizond, Erzerum, Van and Bitlis, further territory in Asia Minor, and those parts of Poland which were under the rule of Prussia and Austria in 1914.[8]

In the French Revolutionary and Napoleonic Wars, the experience of blockade (of its European markets) had turned the focus of British expansionist ambitions to overseas territories. Conversely, the experience of a naval blockade in the 1914 war shifted German imperial ambitions from overseas to Europe. After the war, many Germans held that 'the enemy had been able to win only by resorting to the "unfair" method of the "hunger blockade"' (Hardach 1977: 30). The result was, therefore, to steer Germany after the war to a policy of expansion in Europe. In both wars, the belligerents endeavoured to undermine each other by fomenting or aiding revolts within each other's colonies or spheres of interest: the attack by the British on Spain's American Empire and their support for independence movements in the northern regions of Spanish South America; the support within Africa and the Ottoman Empire for a revolt by non-European elites that was carried out in separatist struggles and that, ultimately led to decolonization.

During the earlier war, the 'spectre of the international threat to property' from the French Revolutionary campaigns, together with slave and peasant revolts from within, combined to produce a 'Great Fear' across Eurasia and the Americas.[9] During the 1914 war, the Bolshevik Revolution, and the crescendo of strikes and groundswell of demonstrations and uprisings in support of it, instilled a fear in wealthy classes around the world which decisively shaped the postwar decades. Following the end of war in 1815, there was, everywhere in Europe, a period of restoration and reaction: a 'white terror' in France conducted by royalist gangs, often led by nobles, and which murdered thousands of former Jacobins, Bonapartists, Protestants, and Jews, and a long period of Ultra reaction; martial law provisions (in the Six Acts) introduced in 1819 in Britain; the abrogation of Liberal constitutions and the imposition of strict press and publication censorship (the Carlsbad Decrees) in Prussia, a revolt of the Guard at St. Petersburg in 1820, and a conservative and clerical reaction in Piedmont (Droz 1967: 87).

'Just as the "ideas of 1789" became potent when they were identified with the power of France, so the association of communism with the Soviet Union transformed it from the doctrine of a small subversive minority into a world movement, backed, as time passed, by an increasingly formidable economic and military power' (Barraclough 1964: 206). And just as the supreme object of the great powers after 1815 had been to prevent another French Revolution or a general European revolution on the French model, the supreme object of the powers after 1917 became to contain the spread of Bolshevism in Europe.

After the French Revolution, it was an accepted fact that revolution in a single country could become a European phenomenon. Thus, at the conclusion of the Napoleonic Wars, the kings and aristocracies of Europe formed an *internationale*, a 'Concert of Europe' (concluded in 1815 among Great Britain, Russia, Austria, and Prussia, and, later, France) for the purpose of suppressing revolutionary uprisings throughout the region.[10] After World War I, it was generally believed that conflicts involving labour were a threat to world peace.[11] Concerned to defend their common way of life, the owning classes of all countries joined together, fighting side by side with 'foreign' class allies to suppress dissident and revolutionary elements from among their own countrymen. France, Britain, Czechoslovakia, Germany, the United States, Poland, and Japan fought with Russian conservatives to overturn the Bolshevik Revolution in Russia.

## *The Cold War begins, 1917–1945*

For all governments and ruling elites, war in 1914 came at a time of particularly intense domestic difficulties. The first half of the year had seen a marked rise in the intensity of both political and economic strikes in Russia (Haimson 1964: 628). A massive confrontation between employers' organizations and labour unions was looming on the horizon in Germany; the socialist leader, Jean Jaurès, was assassinated in France; and Britain seemed on the verge of actual civil war over the question of Irish home rule. Even as they declared war, European governments were unsure whether workers would voluntarily join the war effort, or whether oppressive measures would be needed to induce them to participate. On the day war was declared, there were anti-war demonstrations in Moscow, St. Petersburg, and a number of other industrial centres in Russia. Reservists in the provinces demonstrated with red flags, revolutionary songs, and cries of 'Down with the War!' (Hardach 1977: 219). During August, two million Russians got married in order to avoid being drafted into the army (P. Kennedy 1987: 237). In Britain, the National Transport Workers Federation passed a resolution demanding the general strike 'in the event of national war being imminent'.[12] In Italy, a general strike was called in opposition to tax increases intended to pay for the looming war (Tipton & Aldrich 1987a: 115).

However, governments everywhere in Europe succeeded in inducting their workers into national armies. Many accounts of this period assume, as many contemporary observers did, that working-class participation in the war effort represented a victory of nationalism over socialist solidarity.[13] But this was decidedly not the case. Throughout the war, labour struggles continued unabated and, in many places, increased both in number and intensity.

In Britain, workers in the Clyde, and 10,000 miners in South Wales went on strike in 1915; and a rebellion began in Ireland in April 1916. An average of 1000 workers were on strike each month in Germany in 1915; in 1916, the average was 10,000 (Hardach 1977: 183). In 1916, there were 240 strikes, affecting 124,000 workers; in 1917, there were more than twice as many strikes (562) involving more than four times as many strikers (651,000) (Carsten 1982: 124–25).

In January 1917, a strike movement in St. Petersburg, escalated and spread to other cities. In February, when army units stationed in the cities refused to fire on the strikers, a coalition of the Constitutional Democrat Party (the 'Cadets' or Liberal bourgeois) and the moderate Socialists secured the abdication of the Tsar and formed a provisional government. In October, the provisional government was removed and replaced with a Bolshevik government. Throughout Europe, events in Russia triggered massive strikes and demonstrations, involving millions of workers, in solidarity with revolutionaries and workers in

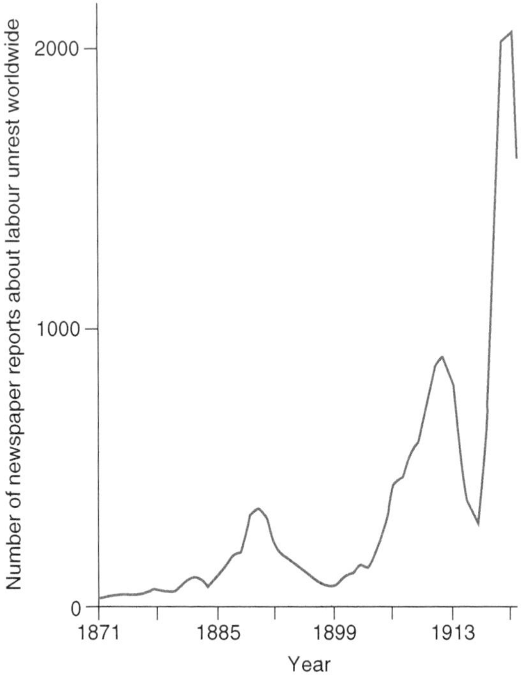


*Figure 6.1* World Labour Unrest, 1870–1914 (taken from Silver 2003, p. 126).[14]

Russia. A great wave of strikes shook the munitions industry and the armed forces in France. Strikes and rioting in industrial centres were suppressed by the military in Spain. In Britain, a strike movement that spread to some 48 towns and involved some 200,000 workers threatened to paralyze the war industries. A general strike and insurrection in Turin, Italy, involved some 50,000 workers in five days of street fighting, and led to hundreds of casualties (Tilly *et al.* 1975). In Germany, a million munitions workers went on strike in February to demand peace with Russia, and six companies of infantry were required to restore order in Hamburg after two days of rioting. In April 1917, between 200,000 and 300,000 workers went on strike, closing down more than 300 armament works in Berlin (Carsten 1982: 124–25).

Violent uprisings continued into 1918. In October, there was open mutiny in Germany. Near Metz, a whole division of the territorial army refused to go back to the front, and thousands of soldiers did not return from their leave. A mutiny of sailors at Wilhelmshaven and other ports spread to Kiel, where most of the ships in the harbour hoisted the red flag, and dockyard workers struck in sympathy with the mutineers. The revolution spread to the ports along the coast of the Baltic and the North Sea, to Lübeck, Hamburg, and Bremen. On 7 November, Kurt Eisner, the leader of the Independent Social Democratic Party (USPD), proclaimed a revolution in Munich, and the king and his family fled the city. Two days later, Phillip Scheidemann, a Social Democratic Party (SPD) member of the government, proclaimed the German Republic from the balcony of the parliament building in Berlin (Carsten 1982: 215–226).[15]

### *Retrenchment and counter-revolution*

Following World War I, Western states confronted newly organized and more powerful labour movements at home, as well as a Bolshevik revolution abroad.

The war accomplished what the much-feared *Internationale* had failed to do. The war was a watershed in the development of socialism and of organized labour as a force. By 1918, labour's wartime mobilization and participation had increased its relative power within European societies. It was to deter labour from setting up a rival workers' peace conference that European leaders set up an International Labour Office;[16] and it was labour's new power and the threat of social revolution that impelled European leaders to accede to the establishment of the League of Nations.

Left-wing parties and movements emerged throughout Europe, and trade-union membership skyrocketed as unskilled and agricultural labour and women joined its ranks for the first time. Following the war, skilled and unskilled labour, workers of different occupations, anarchists and socialists, social democrats and communists, revolutionaries and reformists, closed ranks. A more or less continuous round of demonstrations, riots, violent strikes, and street fighting, as well as coups, rebellions, and revolutions swept through France, Britain, Germany, Italy, Switzerland, and eastern and southeastern Europe.

Trade-union membership doubled in Britain (from four to eight million; Geary 1981: 151–55); in Italy, having doubled during the war, it nearly doubled again by 1920. By the autumn of 1919, the membership of the National Federation of Agrarian Workers had more than doubled to reach 475,000 militant members. and a year later increased to almost 900,000 (Maier 1975: 47). By 1920, Europe had 34 million trade unionists (Ogg 1930: 759–797). Mass communist parties emerged in France, Germany, and Italy; and Hungary briefly became a communist country. In 1919, a new revolutionary movement – the Third International – was formed under the auspices of Lenin and the Russian Bolsheviks. In Britain, 'The fear of serious social unrest, even revolution' was 'widespread among the propertied classes' early that year, and was 'accentuated by considerable unrest in the army, navy and police' (Wrigley 1990: 24). When the red flag was raised on the town hall in Glasgow, the British War Cabinet feared that a Bolshevik revolution was being attempted (Mayer 1967: Ch. 5). In 1923 a year of communist riots in Germany culminated in an attempted communist revolution at Hamburg. The first Labour government took office in Britain in 1923, and the Left triumphed in France in 1924. Socialist parties came to power in Sweden in 1920, in Denmark in 1924, and in Norway in 1927.

Beginning with the 1919 peace settlement in Eastern Europe, which was designed to create a *cordon sanitaire* of new states between Germany and Russia, the European territorial order was revised in order to defeat socialism. The attention of the negotiators at the conferences was riveted on the Allied war against the Bolsheviks in Russia and on communist revolutions in Germany and Hungary. Decisions taken at the conference regarding Germany, Polish border disputes, political arrangements in the Baltic, and settlement of the 'Eastern Question' were shaped by concerns about the spread of Bolshevism from the Soviet Union (Baker 1922: 64).

Workers had reason to believe that, through their patriotism and sacrifices, they might win the rights for which they had struggled for over a century. Their struggle continued, both during and after the war; and socialist solidarity continued to be an important means of advancing it. It was widely acknowledged that the war could not be won if workers did not support it. It seems reasonable to assume that, when the working classes joined up with national armies, they did so to advance their own struggle for economic and political rights.[17]

However, governments set about restoring pre-war monopoly capitalism and shoring up its social structures. Pre-war trends towards industrial concentration were carried forward in the corporatist structures that emerged throughout Europe after the war. As a number of scholars have noted, these represented an attempt to apply the organization of feudal society to the industrial sphere (Berghahn 1988; Bowen 1947; Elbow 1953; Gulick 1940). The aim of fascist corporatism was to ensure that economic expansion would be contained within traditional hierarchical social forms (Crouch 1986: 193; Linz, 1984: 105–106). It attempted to recreate traditional, paternalistic, and rural ways of life and relations of authority in the industrial sphere, and recalled key features of feudal society: the fundamental antagonism between landlord and peasant, the exercise of power over the peasantry through economic exploitation and politico-legal coercion, and the ideological vision of an organic society of orders.[18] Corporative institutions were established in Belgium, Holland, Italy, Norway, and Sweden; and full-fledged corporatist regimes came to power in Germany, France, Austria, Portugal, Spain, and Poland. Corporatist structures everywhere were concerned with labour control, and with containing the popular sector through electoral restrictions, limitations on the right to strike, and the corporatization of unions.

European governments suspended parliaments and outlawed opposition parties, censored the press and limited assemblies. In Italy (1922), Portugal (1926), the Baltic states (1926), Hungary (1919), Poland (1926), the Balkan countries (1923, 1926, 1929), Belgium (1926, 1935), Germany (1934), Austria (1934), the Netherlands (1935), Switzerland (1935), and Spain (1936), parliamentary democracy was destroyed.

During the intervening years, and 'from Nigeria to India to Ireland', there was 'a rash of revolts, tribal unrest, nationalism, and Bolshevik intrigue' (Fisher 2009: 261)[19]. Throughout their colonial sphere from Jamaica to Malaya, and especially in India, the British crushed labour unions and jailed trade unionists (Thompson 2004: xiv). In Japan, rice riots and a wave of strikes and other labour disputes broke out at the end of World War I. In 1914 there had been only 49 labour unions in Japan, but by 1919 there were 187, with a total membership of 100,000.

There was an explosive growth of socialist and communist movements in the Middle East. Industrial expansion in the region during the war had led to a sharp rise in the labour force and in labour militancy. The Cairo tramwaymen were the first to go on strike, and were soon joined by the workers of the Egyptian State Railways, the government press, the Arsenal and government workshops, the Cairo light company, the Alexandria tramways, postal, port, lighthouse and customs workers, taxi and carriage drivers, the Hawamdiyya sugar refinery workers, and others. Between 1919 and 1921, 81 strike actions took place in Egypt (Deeb 1976: 74). By 1922, there were 38 workers' associations in Cairo, 33 in Alexandria, and 28 in the Canal Zone. The Palestine Communist Party (PCP) was formed in 1921; a Lebanese Communist Party and a Syrian Communist Party emerged in the 1920s, and the Iraq Communist Party (ICP) was founded in 1934.

In 1919 in Sierra Leone, government railway workers, employees of the Public Works Department, and some 2400 African policemen went out on strike (Orr 1966: 78). There was an upsurge of trade-union organization in France's African territories following the French Peoples' Front agitation of 1936 (Orr 1966: 68). In 1919, an economic crisis of great severity generated violent and numerous strikes and clashes in Argentina, and these culminated in the *Semana Trájica,* a series of riots, led by anarchists and communists, resulting in massacres that took place during the week of 7 January 1919. By the 1930s, the socialists had established an important and relatively stable position within the Buenos Aires electorate (Rock, 1975: 70). In Columbia, the army massacred more than a thousand striking banana workers in 1928.

In the second half of 1918 food riots and looting swept through the Madras Presidency. In the 1920s 'the emerging trade union movement joined forces with the larger anti-colonial political struggle' opening up 'a whole new arena of urban radical action' (Chattopadhyay 2006: 166).[20] In the first months of 1924, a strike in the Bombay textile industry forced the great majority of its 82 textile mills to close (Kooiman 1980: 1223). In December 1925, leading trade unionists in Bombay formed the Bombay Textile Labour Union (BTLU), which began with a membership of about 5000 but within a year had about 10,000 members (Sen 2000: 2565). Labour intensification and the threat of redundancy and unemployment precipitated a mammoth general strike in 1928 (26 April to 6 October) in the Bombay mill industry, during which the communist-dominated Girni Kamgar Union (GKU) was formed and established its leadership over the mill workers. Between 1929 and 1937, mills cut money wages by more than 20 per cent and threw almost 52,000 workers out of employment (Goswami 1997: 571). During these years, the communists as well as the Congress socialists made considerable inroads into the mill areas, where their task was made easier by the savage wage cuts and retrenchment undertaken in textile industries during the Depression (Goswami 1997: 568). A three-month long strike involving 272,000 workers started in July 1929 (Goswami 1997: 560). A three-month strike that started in Bombay in February 1937 involved almost 220,000 workers (76 per cent of the labour force) (Goswami 1997: 560).

After a rapid and simultaneous price rise in most of the world during the 1920s, the 'Great Depression' of 1929 hit all parts of the world at the same time. Unemployment and its repercussions increasingly posed a fundamental challenge to the existing order. It eventually engulfed all of Europe except the Soviet Union. The depression spread through the tropical Far East, paralyzing commerce and production. Mines and plantations were closed and abandoned, and many Europeans returned home. Commercial enterprises that continued to operate reduced costs by replacing European employees with natives or foreign orientals. The threat posed by large numbers of European paupers overseas continued, despite the profusion of relief agencies and community efforts; and by the 1930s, white pauperism had reached crisis proportions (Stoler 1989: 152).

### *'Appeasement'*

Throughout the interwar years the spectre of revolution haunted Europe's governments and ruling classes. As elites closed ranks to stem the rising 'red tide', European society became increasingly polarized between a newly powerful left and a resurgent, ultra-conservative and militant right.[21] British and French 'appeasement' policies reflected this polarization, and led the way to another world war.

'Appeasement' may be defined as 'a foreign policy that seeks to propitiate an aggrieved rival by making concessions over matters otherwise likely to lead to war' (Palmer 1983: 25). The term has been applied to attempts by the British government to satisfy Hitler's demands between 1936 and 1939. But Britain *did not* 'appease' Germany during the interwar years: it actively aided and encouraged the revival and expansion of German power in Europe. As Frederick Schuman points out, every effort was made to assist or condone the aggrandizement of the fascist states and to subvert all attempts on the part of their victims or rivals to offer collective resistance (Schuman 1942: 332). In fact, the British 'were often closer adherents to German expansionist policy than the Germans themselves' (Gilbert & Gott 1963: 35).

Troops from Czechoslovakia, Greece, Britain, the United States, France, Poland, Canada, Serbia, Romanian, Italy, China, Finland, India, and Australia had attempted to squash the Bolshevik menace through military means (1918–1920). Fear of social revolution at home had impelled them to abandon this effort. However, the rise of fascism offered a line of attack against Bolshevism. Britain and France made every effort 'to assist or condone' fascist Italy's attempts to strengthen itself in Africa and the Mediterranean, and Germany's quest to secure mastery of Central Europe (Schuman 1942: 332). And they supported Japan's drive to 'save China from Bolshevism' in 1927.

Germany under Hitler based its foreign policy on opposition to Bolshevism, and sought to make common cause with the Western powers against the Soviet Union. After Hitler came to power, Britain rescheduled debts, rolled over loans, and enabled Germany to openly and rapidly build a powerful military machine (see, e.g., Bonnell 1940: 64–66; Einzig 1941: 74–78, 116–119; Schmidt 1986: 88–89). In 1933, Hitler withdrew Germany from the League of Nations after it refused to accede to his demand for an increase in German rearmament. The five permanent members of the Council of the League – Britain, France, and the three fascist powers (Germany, Italy, and Japan) – then joined together in two new overlapping associations, the Four Power Pact (1933)[22] and the anti-Comintern Pact (1936). With Britain and France now engaged in an alternative grouping with the fascist powers, and with the strength and prestige of the League fatally diminished, the League ceased to play any effective role in European affairs. The anti-Comintern Pact, formed by Germany and Japan in 1936 (Italy joined in 1937), declared the hostility of its signatories to international communism, and formalized opposition to communism as the basis of German foreign policy.

Germany, formally allied with France and Great Britain, and, with their acquiescence, now began to openly and rapidly re-arm. In 1935, the year Germany declared itself a bulwark against Bolshevism, the German government reintroduced conscription. This was the first formal repudiation of a clause of the peace treaty. The British and French governments did nothing more than issue protests. From then on, German rearmament was a fully open matter and was carried out with vigour and speed. Hitler ended the restrictions placed on Germany by the treaty by the end of 1937.

The resurgence of German power in Europe proceeded through Hitler's step-by-step dismantling of the restrictions placed on it by Versailles. At each step of the way, it could have been halted by an alliance between the western powers and the Soviet Union. At each step this option was rejected. 'Blinkered by anti-Communism – the same anti-Communism which led Lord Halifax to welcome Germany as 'a bastion against Bolshevism' – neither the British nor the French 'made a serious attempt to reach agreement with Stalin' (Mazower 1998: 75). Instead, Britain and France allowed Germany to reoccupy the Rhineland and to openly rearm after 1934. Between 1936 and 1939 they allowed the fascist powers a free hand in the Spanish civil war. In 1938, they acquiesced to the union of fascist Germany and fascist Austria, though they had refused in 1919 and during the 1920s to allow a union of Austria with the German Weimar Republic when it was proposed by a socialist-dominated Austrian government. In 1938 the powers refused to make common cause with the Soviet Union against Hitler's demands regarding the Sudetenland. They took no action when Nazi Germany then proceeded to absorb the whole of Czechoslovakia. The following year, they extended full diplomatic recognition to Spain's fascist regime, even before the civil war had drawn to a close. When Hitler invaded Poland the following year, they declared war on Germany but took no action. Instead, the allies prepared for war with the Soviet Union in Finland, while allowing Germany to proceed virtually unimpeded with its conquest of Poland, Norway, Denmark, Belgium, and the Netherlands. France, herself, capitulated with hardly a struggle. Only then, when Britain was left alone to face Nazi Germany, did she finally enter into an alliance with the Soviet Union.

## Conclusion

In the years leading up to the 1914–1918 war in Europe, the two central features of industrial production – internal repression and external expansion – were rapidly coming into conflict. Economic depression, a rising 'red tide', and increasing intra-elite rivalry and conflict combined to produce a multi-lateral war in Europe. After 1815, there had been few multilateral great power conflicts in Europe because Europe's monarchs and aristocracies feared that such conflicts would call into use the mass armies that, during and immediately after the Napoleonic Wars, had triggered revolutionary upheavals and threatened to destroy the social order. But, in 1914, European states, confronted with an existential threat, were forced, once again, to deploy the weapon of mass destruction introduced in the previous world war (the Napoleonic Wars): the *lévee en masse*. The war forced European governments to mobilize the masses for war and for the expansion of industrial production needed to support it – precisely what a century of external expansion had enabled them to avoid. The mobilization of the masses for war in 1914 set in motion a social revolution that began in 1917 and, thereafter, swept through all of Europe.

The Bolshevik Revolution unleashed a wave of more intense social conflict and revolutionary activism, and it catalyzed what became a European and, after 1945, a global response to the 'rising red tide' that had threatened the pre-war system of capital accumulation: fascist corporatism. In Europe, this response not only failed to staunch the revolutionary currents unleashed by the mass mobilization of 1914: it came perilously close to permitting a takeover of Europe by fascist Germany. This led to a second world war and to the emergence of the 'three worlds' that were to become the focus of 'development' theory: a world that briefly compromised with labour and adopted national capitalism; a communist world; and, nearly everywhere else, a world characterized by variations on the themes of the pre-war order.

# 7 The post-World War II interregnum

During the nineteenth and early twentieth centuries, broadly similar social and economic structures emerged throughout the world. This changed after 1945. Between 1914 and 1945, the mobilization of mass armies to fight two hugely destructive wars in Europe, and the enormous industrial expansion that governments undertook to support them, triggered a social revolution that transformed social structures and put economies on a fundamentally different footing. As a consequence of these events, in some areas of the world – in Europe, in a few Asian countries where similar changes were imposed, and in 'areas of new settlement' (the United States, Canada, Australia, and New Zealand) – conditions of life began rapidly to diverge from those found everywhere else in the world.

It soon became a commonplace to characterize the world as divided into 'developed' and 'developing' countries. In 'the West', this division was attributed, not to recent and revolutionary transformations, but to a further evolution of processes that had purportedly defined the separation of 'the West' from 'the rest' beginning in the sixteenth century. However, it was only after 1945 that the set of conditions that defined the 'developed' countries emerged and produced, in those countries, phenomenal growth and a relatively broad-based prosperity. 'Developed' countries were those that had (1) experienced a breakdown of their traditional social structures through land and other reforms and as a result of war or external agents (all of Europe, Japan, Taiwan, and South Korea), (2) earlier experienced a significant decline in the power of landowners as a result of one of the bloodiest wars in human history (the United

States in the 1860s), or (3) never had an entrenched landed elite (Australia, Canada, and New Zealand).

By the early 1950s, the binary of 'developed' and 'developing' countries had given way to a tripartite division of the world which assigned capitalist countries to a 'developed' *first world*, and the Soviet Union and communist countries of Eastern Europe to a separate *second world*. The rest of the world – comprising some three-quarters of the world's population in areas covering two-thirds of the surface of the Earth (Mason 1997) – was the 'developing' *third world*. Here, as a result of a massively funded, sustained, and coordinated global effort, pre-war social structures were preserved for more than half a century, and remain today largely intact.[1] But the existence of 'three worlds' was brief: by the 1970s and 1980s, the countries of the 'first' and 'second' worlds themselves began rapidly returning to pre-war patterns and structures. The immediate post-World War II period might be seen, then, as an interregnum: two or three decades during which social revolutionary changes in a few areas of the world suspended the operation of historically 'normal' patterns of capitalist social reproduction.

## I. The 'advanced' world: social revolution and the nationalization of capital

In Russia, the revolution of October 1917 brought about a sharp and decisive break with the past. The revolution produced a system that rapidly industrialized a very backward and undeveloped country. In 1913 the Tsarist Empire was producing four per cent of the world's industrial output. Between 1917 and 1935, the industrial output of large-scale industry increased 5.7 times, eight-fold in Turkmenia, and 8.5 times in Kirgizstan (Lane 1971: 93–94). By the eve of World War II, the USSR was producing 19 per cent of world industrial output (Rostow 1978: 52–53). In the 1930s, when the Great Depression had engulfed all of Europe except the Soviet Union, the country enjoyed full employment. The USSR introduced social assistance for the first time in November 1917, and a complete social insurance system in 1922 (in the Labour Code of November of that year). By the eve of World War II, Russia had more doctors per thousand of the population than Germany, France, and Britain (Marwick 1974: 102). A system of paid holidays was introduced in the 1930s. The Soviet system achieved universal literacy, one of the best technological education systems in the world, free education and healthcare, and security in old age (Getty 2000: 115). It also put the first man in space.

After World War I, and despite the profound dislocations that had resulted from the war, leaders and ruling classes in all Western European countries succeeded in re-establishing and maintaining the pre-war *status quo*.[2] However, following the Great Depression, mass mobilization for war and industrial expansion for a second massively destructive European war, led to the collapse of social and economic structures throughout Europe. In Western Europe, governments were forced into a political accommodation with working-class demands that made a restoration of the pre-war system impossible. There, economies were restructured on the basis of a social democratic compromise that required social democrats to accept private ownership of the means of production and capitalists to use the profits they realized from this to increase productive capacity and to allow labour to share in productivity gains (Przeworski 1979: 56). States adopted social democratic and Keynesian goals and policy instruments that, before the war, would never have been accepted by the wealthy classes; and they resumed the welfare and regulatory functions they had relinquished at the beginning of the nineteenth century. Wages rose with profits, making higher mass consumption possible for new mass consumer goods industries.

*Table 7.1* Share of major industrial countries in world industrial production (per cent)

| | *Great Britain* | *France* | *Germany* | *USSR* | *United States* | *Japan* |
|---|---|---|---|---|---|---|
| 1870 | 32 | 10 | 13 | 4 | 23 | — |
| 1881–1885 | 27 | 9 | 14 | 3 | 29 | — |
| 1896–1900 | 20 | 7 | 17 | 5 | 30 | 1 |
| 1906–1910 | 15 | 6 | 16 | 6 | 35 | 1 |
| 1913 | 9 | 7 | 12 | 4 | 42 | 3 |
| 1936–1938 | 9 | 5 | 11 | 19 | 32 | 4 |
| 1963 | 5 | 4 | 6 | 19 | 32 | 4 |

Source: Rostow (1978: 52–53).

Workers also achieved the political rights for which they had fought for over a century. It is generally assumed that, before the wars, most Western European societies 'were either political democracies, or well on the way toward becoming so' (Chirot 1977: 222). But European 'democracy' before 1945 was a severely limited form of representative government. Political institutions were generally designed to increase the power of traditional forces against the lower classes; and they were generally successful in achieving that end. Hereditary transmission of socio-political status was widespread; and parliamentary institutions functioned more like royal courts.[3] Political institutions were continually compromised by efforts to preserve privilege and forestall the acquisition of power by subordinate groups and classes, and by extra-legal patronage systems, corruption, and violence.

Everywhere in Europe electoral systems were based on a highly restricted, means-tested suffrage that excluded the great majority of adults. Only men over the age of 25 or 35 were able to vote. Since life expectancy in Europe before World War I was between 41 and 55 years of age,[4] that meant that only men in the last third of their life (in today's terms, men over 54 years of age) could vote (Goldstein 1983: 241). Universal adult suffrage would have enfranchised 40–50 per cent of each country's population; but, in 1910, only some 14–22 per cent of the population was enfranchised in Britain, Sweden, Switzerland, Belgium, Denmark, the Netherlands, and Germany. The number of people who were actually permitted to vote, however, was lower because restrictions on, and biases against, working-class organizations and parties, three-class and other weighted and plural voting systems, and open balloting made it futile for poor people to vote. The figures listed in Table 7.2 are consequently *higher* than the percentage of the population that was actually permitted to vote.

By 1914, Norway was the only country in Europe with full universal and equal suffrage; and France had universal and equal *male* suffrage. After the war, Denmark, Finland, the Netherlands, and Sweden established full suffrage; Germany and Austria did too, but only briefly. By the eve of World War II, Britain can be added to the list, though instances of plural voting remained. It was only after 1945 that, for the first time, equal, direct and secret suffrage became

*Table 7.2* Percentage of European population enfranchised, 1910

| | | | |
|---|---|---|---|
| Finland | 45 | Austria | 21 |
| Norway | 33 | Sweden | 19 |
| France | 29 | UK | 18 |
| Spain | 24 | Denmark | 17 |
| Bulgaria | 23 | Portugal | 12 |
| Greece | 23 | Romania | 16 |
| Serbia | 23 | Russia | 15 |
| Germany | 22 | Netherlands | 14 |
| Belgium | 22 | Italy | 8 |
| Switzerland | 22 | Hungary | 6 |

Source: Lieven (1992: 222).

the norm throughout Western Europe. Parties representing labour became legitimate participants in the political process for the first time, as well. Labour and socialist parties formed governments and joined ruling coalitions in Britain and France, and socialists regularly participated in coalition governments in Austria, Switzerland, Belgium, the Netherlands, Sweden, Norway, and Denmark. Socialists ruled in coalition governments in Italy and West Germany in the 1960s; and formed the first left-wing government in the history of West Germany in 1969.

After 1945, Western European economies were characterized by sustained growth and by a more equitable distribution of income.[5] In contrast to pre-war economic policies, post-war policies focused on expanding domestic markets through increased production, increasing and regulating domestic investment, and raising the level of working-class earnings and welfare. While there was a strong growth in the volume of exports, the expansion of domestic markets for domestic goods and services ensured that, until the 1960s, the proportion of resources devoted to exports declined. During the 1950s and 1960s, these policies produced unprecedented growth. Production grew much faster and with less interruption than in any previous period (Schonfield 1965: 61). In most of Western Europe, industrial production had surpassed pre-war levels by 1947 (Aldcroft 1978: 148). Between 1850 and 1913, output per head in the most advanced countries of Western Europe had grown by not more than 1.5–2 per cent a year: between 1950 and 1973, it grew in those same countries by 3–4 per cent per year (Lewis 1978b: 33). Between 1950 and 1970, total output increased at 3.5 per cent each year in Belgium, 4.2 per cent in Switzerland and 5 per cent in Austria and the Netherlands (Ricossa 1973: 291).

Eastern Europe in 1945 was composed of countries that, in most cases, were economically backward relative to Western Europe. But by the early 1950s, these countries were experiencing unprecedented and rapid economic growth and increasing affluence. Beginning in 1945, they had undergone a social revolution that completely changed the system of property relationships. In many countries, large estates were 'confiscated from the former owners without compensation and redistributed free among the peasants' (Aldcroft 1978: 170). Within one generation, rapid economic, and especially industrial, growth shifted a majority of labour and capital into non-agricultural activities (Lampe & Jackson 1982: 576). Workers enjoyed healthcare, education, and other social services, and lower housing rents and greater security of employment compared with the situation that had existed before the war. In the German Democratic Republic (GDR) real wages more than tripled in this period; in Bulgaria, Yugoslavia, and Romania they rose by over 150 per cent (Aldcroft 1978: 212–15).

After World War II, Eastern Europe countries experienced the same structural changes as Western European countries and, like them, enjoyed an unprecedented period of rapid industrial development and increasing affluence in the 1950s and 1960s. However, they did not achieve democracy: their autocratic structures of power remained during the decades of the Cold War. But because of the social structural changes that had occurred after World War II, the countries of Eastern Europe – unlike those of the 'third world' – were eventually able to achieve by means of a 'velvet revolution' the political changes that had occurred in the 'first world'.

'Development' theory has focused on the causes and conditions of growth and prosperity in the capitalist 'first-world' countries. Consequently, a great deal of attention has been directed towards explaining Western Europe's post-war boom. The factors most frequently cited are Marshall Aid, the creation of regional institutions and trade liberalization, the influx of foreign labour, and war-induced institutional and technological changes and 'learning'. The violent upheavals of war, and the social revolutions that occurred during and immediately following the wars, are generally not cited as factors in Europe's phenomenal post-war growth.

Marshall funds played a prominent role in Western Europe's post-war recovery. But investment capital had not been lacking before the war: Britain, France, Germany, and Austria had made enormous amounts of capital available to each other and to other European countries; and Eastern Europe, whose post-war boom had much in common with Western Europe's, did not receive any Marshall funds. Western Europe's rapid post-war growth was well underway by the time regional and international organizations had abolished trade restrictions among their members. It has been argued that the availability of large supplies of labour fuelled Europe's phenomenal growth (e.g., Kindleberger 1964). This ignores the fact the Western Europe before the war suffered, not from insufficient labour, but from persistent unemployment, even during the 1920s (Landes 1969: 390–1); and large numbers of (lower cost) foreign workers had been available, and had been used in significant numbers (Strikwerda 1993: 1122).

Some scholars argue that the adoption by governments in Western Europe of policies that oriented investment and production towards domestic markets after the war was a result, not of social revolutionary pressures, but of 'learning'. They argue that, as a result of their wartime role in managing economies and encouraging industrial expansion, governments had 'learned' how to create the mass demand necessary to base industrialization on the expansion of the internal market (e.g., Kuznets 1964). But government-induced demand creation had been a key feature in Europe's nineteenth-century industrial expansion, and, everywhere in Europe, it had substituted for a home market for industrial goods (Morris & Adelman 1988: 123–124).

Post-war changes that broadened the distribution of income and expanded domestic markets were the result not of 'learning' but of a social revolution. The politically conservative economist Joseph Schumpeter expressed this succinctly: a decisive shift in the balance of class power throughout Europe had compelled 'a massive capitulation' to social democracy; and it was this that explained, not only the transformation that had taken place in Western Europe, but its apparent permanence:

> The business class has accepted 'gadgets of regulation' and 'new fiscal burdens', a mere fraction of which it would have felt to be unbearable fifty years ago. . . . And *it does not matter whether the business class accepts this new situation or not. The power of labour is almost strong enough in itself* – and amply so in alliance with the other groups that have in fact, if not in words, renounced allegiance to the scheme of values of the private-profit economy – *to prevent any reversal* which goes beyond an occasional scaling off of rough edges.
>
> (Schumpeter 1976: 419–420; my emphasis)[6]

In Europe, previous regional conflagrations had been followed by restorations (the Napoleonic Wars, the revolutions of 1830 and 1848, and World War I). But after World War II, a shift in the balance of social power, and consequent changes throughout the class structure, made restoration impossible.

Not only were the radical changes in the structure of European economies the outcome of a social revolution but, as Carr pointed out, they owed much to 'the Soviet example' (Carr 1947: 44). Key elements of the social democratic agenda formed the basis of the changes instituted throughout Europe after 1945, and Soviet policies were a model for them. Virtually every European country introduced some form of economic planning.[7] Britain also implemented, at least in part, other key elements of the social democratic agenda: substantial nationalization (of the coal industry, electricity and gas, railways and road transportation, iron and steel, and the Bank of England), socialized medicine, the extension of welfare, the dismantling of empire, and the narrowing of income differentials. French government officials and business executives accepted the view, long promoted by labour leaders and widespread in the resistance, that some form of state planning was necessary to avert the economic crises of the preceding decades, as well as nationalization, big public investments, 'economic and social democracy', and state control over cartels, prices, and capital movements. Post-war governments also promoted measures of income redistribution and social welfare on a scale unknown before (Hoffmann 1961: 49–50).

It was the threat of a radicalized international labour movement protected and supported by the USSR that brought about the adoption of labour reforms, not only in Europe but elsewhere in 'the West'. The 'new deal', which introduced these reforms in the United States, was in part meant 'to steal the thunder of radicals who looked to Moscow and therefore could not be ignored'. The right to work and to a living wage is not liberalism, but socialism. Women's rights and racial integration were planks of the Communist Party platform long before mainstream American parties took them seriously. 'It was communists who first went to the American South and began organizing African-Americans and poor whites around issues of social justice' (Getty 2000: 116)

If we assume that policy-makers in Western Europe 'learned' how to create the mass demand needed to expand the internal market after World War II, then why, for over 65 years, has this better or different understanding of demand management not been used by ruling groups, or by multitudes of international 'development' agencies and initiatives, to promote the expansion of domestic markets in Asia, the Middle East, Africa, and Latin America?

## II. The 'Third World': the reproduction of dualism

The 'third world' consists of most of the world. It encompasses the three-quarters of the world's population that did not directly participate in the world wars and that did not experience the massive slaughter and destruction that Europe suffered as a result of them. In areas that were not directly involved in the fighting, governments did not mobilize mass armies, and undertook, at best, only a limited expansion of industry to exploit whatever profit opportunities the wars offered. In those areas the crises that arose during the Great Depression and the era of the world wars led, not to a social revolution, but only to a retrenchment of traditional structures.

The occurrence or non-occurrence of social revolutionary change during or after the world wars was the crucial factor in explaining the diverging fortunes of 'developed' and developing' countries. A comparison of Latin America and 'first-world' countries before and after the world wars will help to bring this into sharper focus.

### *Latin America*

On the eve of World War I, the regions of Latin America and Europe had, as a whole, achieved comparable levels of development and economic wellbeing. Latin America's richest countries were as rich as Europe's richest, and its poorest countries were *not as poor*. In Argentina and Uruguay the standard of living was well in excess of that of Britain, France, Belgium, and Germany. In the decades before World War I, the annual rate of growth of exports in Argentina and Uruguay, and in Brazil, Ecuador, Peru, Colombia, and Mexico, was greater than that of Britain, Belgium, and France (see Halperin 1997: Statistical Appendix). Between 1913 and 1950, annual average GDP growth was 1.9 per cent for the countries which today are the advanced capitalist countries; in Latin America it was 3.5 per cent (Maddison 1991: 17), and its manufacturing production almost doubled between 1937 and 1950 (Maizels 1970: 24).

It was only after 1945 that a gap opened up between these two regions, even though, in both, the rate of growth increased. In Latin America, total output rose at an annual rate of 4.9 per cent and output per capita by 2.4 per cent between 1945 and 1955.[8] There was also an unprecedented inflow of foreign investment into Latin America after 1945. Its rate of savings was not much below that of the advanced Western countries, and it had no shortage of entrepreneurs and skilled labour. Its production of goods and services increased by 60 per cent between 1945 and 1958; and manufacturing industry expanded its production by 90 per cent. While, at times, monetary instability afflicted some countries, inflation-ridden countries such as Brazil developed at a more rapid rate than fairly stable ones, such as Cuba (Ahumada 1963: 115).

However, the structure of power in most countries in the region changed little after World War II and, as a result, Latin America's growth was no match for the phenomenal and unprecedented surge of post-war growth experienced by European and other 'first' and 'second' world countries. Power remained concentrated in the hands of landed classes who saw no reason to develop an internal market, widen the geographic and sectoral spread of economic growth, and support the emergence of new classes (Lewis, 1978b: 11).

To sharpen the comparison and eliminate factors such as post-war Marshall Aid and regional organizations, we can consider the cases of Argentina and Australia. A comparison of these two countries is particularly instructive because their production and export structures were similar and the timing of their development was the same. They both began to grow rapidly in the 1850s by selling the same commodities – cereals, wool, and meat; and by 1913, GNP per capita in both countries was among the world's top ten.

In 1914, Argentina was one of the richest countries in the world. It had a temperate climate, an integrated national territory, vast stretches of fertile soil, large deposits of petroleum, easy access to the sea, a literate and fairly homogeneous population, adequate access to foreign technical knowledge, numerous and talented entrepreneurs; an adaptable, skilled workforce; average wages comparable with many parts of Western Europe, and relatively better opportunities for social mobility (Rock 1975: 67). Between 1880 and 1910, the value of Argentina's exports had increased six-fold; total production had grown at an annual average of 5 per cent per year, population by 3.4 per cent, the crop area by 8.3 per cent, and the railway system by 15.4 per cent (Rock 1975: 1). Its debt burden was less than that of Australia, Canada, and New Zealand, and the British had less influence in Argentina than they did in Australia and Canada. By 1916, Argentina also had a democratic political system, with universal, secret, and compulsory suffrage for males at 18 years of age, and no qualifications in terms of income, property, or literacy. Between 1916 and 1930 voter turnout leaped from approximately 20 per cent to more than 65 per cent, and thereafter oscillated between 50 and 80 per cent. Elections for the House of Representatives were direct. In 1916, presidential power passed smoothly from long-entrenched Conservatives to the leader of the largely middle-class Radical Party. The Radical Party won presidential elections in 1922 and 1928. By 1930, Argentina equalled Canada in leading the world's exports in grain and attracting massive European investment and hard-working European immigrants. By 1944, the net value of manufacturing output surpassed the net value of agricultural and livestock production, and more people were employed in industry than in agriculture.

Argentina's economic growth, its wealth, and its abundant human and material resource advantages had made it as 'developed' as

Australia before the world wars. After 1945, it continued to maintain an adequate rate of domestic capital formation and attracted significant foreign investment in its manufacturing sector.[9] However, after World War II, the fortunes of Australia and Argentina diverged: Australia ascended into the ranks of the 'first world', while Argentina became part of the vast, global 'third world'. What factors both differentiate these cases and can explain this divergence?

One factor is that while in Argentina's politics were dominated by a commercial–agrarian oligarchy, Australia had no landed aristocracy. There, urban communities dominated politics and used their power to protect industrial profits and wages (Lewis, 1978b: 25). As the depression hit Argentina in 1930, a military revolt by the armed forces put an end to nearly seven decades of civilian politics and the gradual liberalization of the oligarchic order, and placed control of the government firmly in the hands of the old landowning elite that had appropriated 'millions of hectares of the best pampaen land' (Lewis 1978b: 144). As in the rest of Latin America, in Argentina little change took place in land institutions after the world wars. Land reforms introduced in Latin America in the 1950s and 1960s were brought to a halt by a continent-wide anti-land-reform movement (Feder 1970; Hough *et al.* 1982; Ruhl 1984; Wise 1983). In the 1960s about 94 per cent of the total arable land in Latin America was owned by seven per cent of the landholders. In the 1980s, with the exception of Cuba, land tenure systems in Latin America were still characterized by large estates (Theisenhusen 1980); and there were more poor and illiterate people than in 1950.

The disruption of international markets during the world wars and the Great Depression of the 1930s affected both Australia and Argentina. Both economies were closely integrated with international markets during this period. The disruption of international markets created incentives in both countries to industrialize 'while maintaining the rural sector as the most important producer of hard currency through exports' (Gallo 2006: 15). Both countries 'engaged in strong industrial policies during the postwar period and subsequent decade' (Gallo 2006: 18). But, after the end of World War II, 'things changed abruptly' (Gallo 2006: 18). Argentina was afflicted with political turmoil and instability.

In a number of Latin American countries, import substitution policies (ISI) were pursued between 1945 and 1971. The decline of

Latin America's exports during the Great Depression had decreased its ability to finance imports of manufactured goods and encouraged it to produce, or increase the domestic production of, previously imported manufactured goods. ISI emphasized production for the domestic market, and higher wages and levels of domestic consumption. But in the absence of a broader distribution of income and effective land reform, the growth of the domestic market was limited. Import substitution policies never dispossessed the old commercial–agrarian oligarchies and, in the 1970s, there was a return to export promotion. In the absence of land and labour reforms, a shift into production of manufactures did not substantially diminish the basic dualism of the economy (more on this in Chapter 8). The shift back to export-led industrialization led, in the 1980s, to a dramatic fall in economic growth, and to debt crisis and terrible social costs.

### *The Middle East*

The end of empires and decolonization during and after the world wars changed political structures and government institutions. But it did not involve any social revolutionary transformation. Nor did it displace or destroy the global elite networks that had developed over previous centuries. A brief discussion of the Middle East provides an illustration of what occurred in imperial and colonial territories.

In the Middle East, the end of empire and the establishment of independent states changed the political structure of the region, but left social structures essentially the same.

The social and economic structures that characterize most of the Arab part of the region today are similar to the ones that existed in those areas prior to the world wars. Arab economies – those of both oil-producing and non-oil-producing countries, such as Jordan, Syria, Egypt – are dualistic: centred on dynamic but restricted foreign-oriented enclaves which have little, if any, impact on their larger, and largely 'traditional', non-industrial economies. There is little, if any, investment outside the export sector: profits are either reinvested within it or exported; and improvements in technology do not diffuse outwards beyond it to agriculture or to small industry. Cultural, educational, legal, and political spheres are also dualistic, creating societies that are structurally divided by different rules, processes, and institutions. Elites are as wealthy as elites in 'first-world' countries (or actually more so), and their standards and patterns of consumption are similar to those of elites elsewhere. At the same time, and despite all its abundant wealth, the region's average annual growth in GDP per capita is converging at lower than the average for 'developing' countries. Between 1960 and 1990 it was the only region in the world to exhibit a net drop in productivity. It has a steadily declining share of the global economy, and GNP growth 'lags badly' relative to other developing regions (Cordesman 2001). Adding to its relatively low, and relatively more volatile, rate of per capita GDP, rapid population growth and the ten-fold increase in the population living in urban areas since 1950 (from 27 per cent of the total population in 1950 to 61 per cent today) as a result of the absence of effective land reform, has produced high unemployment. Among Arab youth, unemployment is twice the world average (UNESCO 2011).

But what of the 'nationalist' revolutions in Egypt, Iraq, Syria, and Yemen; and the independence movements in Tunisia and Libya that, in the 1950s and 1960s, supposedly brought about a 'historic change' in those countries? A broadly similar story might be told with respect to all of them. Like their old regimes, their new ones continued to build up export industries within restricted foreign-oriented enclaves, to enjoy 'Western' standards and styles of living, and to purchase massive amounts of weapons to police their populations and prevent changes to their largely subsistence economies and impoverished societies. For more than half a century, the basic structures of these societies have remained largely intact.

The Egyptian 'revolution' of 1952 overthrew the monarchy and brought a group of military officers led by Gamal abd-ul Nasser to power. Nasser established a regime that offered the Egyptian propertied classes and their foreign allies a better guarantee of social stability. The British made no attempt to use their troops in the Canal Zone to intervene on behalf of the king and, along with the French and United States governments, helped the new regime consolidate its power. The United States was keen to replace elites it saw as too weak to withstand the communist challenge by military officers who were thought to be tougher anti-communists and less susceptible than civilian and educated elements to the appeals of 'radical nationalism' (Springborg 1993: 25). The CIA had brought Syria's Husni al-Zaim to power in 1949 in a coup d'état; and they supported the coup by Nasser's Free Officers which brought down the Egyptian monarchy in 1952. They later strengthened the rule of Saddam Hussein, a leader of the Ba'th Party faction that seized power in Iraq in a coup in July 1968.[10]

Nasser and the Ba'thist parties of Iraq and Syria called their governments 'Arab Socialist'. But, 'Arab Socialism' was a corporatist ideology which was, like 'National Socialism' and others that had emerged in Europe earlier in the century concerned, above all, with containing and co-opting independent bourgeoisies and labour movements.[11] Nasser moved immediately to repress all political and trade-union organizations and suppress communist and other leftist elements. In addition to 'progressive' military officers in Arab countries, the United States found allies among the former military officers who established 'modernizing' dictatorships in Iran (Reza Shah), Pakistan (Ayub Khan), and Turkey (Mustapha Kemal). Kemal, whose policies served as a model for those of the Shah of Iran, introduced a corporatist nationalism, amended the penal code in 1935 and 1936 to punish strikes and all propaganda on behalf of communism, introduced a law in 1938 banning all associations organized on the basis of class and, in 1946, closed down all unions and socialist parties (Ahmad 1994: 142).

As in Egypt, the bureaucratic and military elites that came to power in nationalist 'revolutions' and coups elsewhere proved either unwilling or unable to transform the bases of traditional social and political power. They suppressed movements and groups calling for leftist, liberal, or progressive politics, and they consolidated and reproduced the enclave-like, dualistic economic expansion that had developed in the nineteenth century. They institutionalized a corporatist, ethnic- and religious-based, and selectively anti-imperialist, nationalist politics that brought labour organization under state control, targeted minorities and foreign elements that had been instrumental in developing communist parties and labour movements in the region, and ensured that the wealth generated from exploiting national resources in alliance with Western business interests would be limited in its distribution, locally, to only a narrow elite.

Decolonization movements were co-optive and conservative, not revolutionary or transformative. Nationalism was used by elites, as it had been used by elites in Europe, to gain state power. Nationalism and independence movements had united workers and peasants against colonial rule and for radical social change. But those who hoped these would advance their struggle for economic and political rights were sidelined after their activism was no longer needed. As colonial empires were dismantled, the imperial system was modernized and made more efficient. Local structures and the transnational social and economic relationships that had tied elites together remained substantially the same. However, new means of control were introduced: local regimes replaced garrisoned imperial troops, and occasional interventions took the place of ongoing colonial administration. As had been the case in Europe during the nineteenth century, in the newly 'independent' states established after World War II, nationalist elites that succeeded in gaining state power pursued a programme of capitalist expansion that consolidated dualism. They continued to build up export industries within restricted foreign-oriented enclaves, and to accumulate wealth and enjoy Western standards and styles of living without transforming their largely traditional and non-industrial economies and societies.

## III. The Cold War: containment and the 'development' project

Elites and ruling groups in the 'third world' had considerable help in blocking socio-economic change after World War II. Working closely with each other and with the United States and other 'first-world' countries, they closed ranks to contain the spread of national capitalism, socialism, and communism, and to implement 'development' programmes that maintained their pre-World War II structures.

### *The containment of 'national capitalism'*

Most accounts of the Cold War emphasize geopolitics and ideology, and the bipolar superpower competition that began at the end of

World War II. But the Cold War began after World War I with military invasions of the Soviet Union by Japan, Canada, the United States, Britain, and other countries; and when the Cold War resumed after World War II, it was fought as much against national capitalism in Western Europe and elsewhere, as against socialism and communism.

It is generally recognized that one of the motives for the Marshall Plan 'was to forestall the advent of a "socialist" Europe' (Heilbroner & Milberg 1996: 49).[12] But American elites also feared the domino effect of national capitalism, and Marshall funds were deployed against this enemy of 'free' capital as well as against socialism and communism.[13] Thus, just as after World War II, the countries of Eastern Europe were closely supervised by the Soviet Union, those of Western Europe were closely supervised by the United States. The United States severely limited the direction of policies in Western European countries by the conditions of American aid, and by the imposition of severe restrictions and outright embargoes on exports to the socialist countries. More generally, these countries were under the rule of an international monetary system that remained imperial. The gold standard effectively limited their ability to control their own money supply and to practice the sort of demand-management strategies Keynes advocated; and eventually they were brought under the direct financial surveillance of international financial institutions that gave them little room to manoeuvre.

After 1945, the United States promoted decolonization in order to foreclose a restoration of trading blocs by European states (although it did not give independence to the colonies that it held itself at the end of World War II). However, all of the colonial powers attempted to hold on to their colonies after World War II.[14] The British elite converted their empire into a self-governing Commonwealth consisting of the former British 'dominions' and India; and sought to restore the role of the City of London as the banker and financier of the 'developing' countries. 'Despite the shortage of manpower in the civilian economy', Britain kept over 800,000 men in the armed services in 1948; and, along with their large navy and air force, and their network of bases, this enabled them to retain their status as a military power (Darwin 2009: 546). In the Middle East Britain reasserted its position in Iraq, Jordan, Iran, and in Egypt and the Suez Canal Zone, hoping to manage the region's affairs and to play the role of regional 'guardian'. But the Suez War (1956) was generally seen as the end of this hope. This proved to be a landmark event in the transfer of responsibility for much of the British Empire to the United States and the beginning of the formation of an American 'informal empire'. In the 1950s and 1960s, the United States took over the 'jumble of British treaties, alliances, protectorates, colonies, bases, gunboats and garrisons' that made up Britain's 'undeclared empire' in the Middle East (Darwin 2009: 602); as well as the monarchies that the British had created or protected in Brunei, Buganda, Tonga, Lesotha, and Swaziland (Cannadine 2001: 175).

### *The containment of socialism and communism*

After World War II, the United States government and its allies pursued a policy of containment and encirclement of the USSR and China, and took military action against China (1945–1946), Cuba (1959–1961), Vietnam (1961–1973), and Korea (1950–1953). The United States also poured grants and credits into 14 countries encircling the USSR and China: Japan, South Korea, Taiwan, India, Iran, Pakistan, Vietnam, the Philippines, Greece, Yugoslavia, Austria, Turkey, West Germany, and Italy. These countries together received nearly $51 billion between 1946 and 1978 – 50 per cent of the $101 billion given to 77 countries during those years. South Korea and Taiwan *each* received more in United States aid between 1946 and 1978 (nearly $6 billion) than the whole of Africa ($5.6 billion) over the same period (Mason 1997: 435).

As part of its policy of geo-strategic encirclement and containment, the United States also financed revolutions in several 'vulnerable' East Asian countries facing either the Soviet Union or China. The Supreme Command for Allied Powers (SCAP), which remained in Japan for six years following the war, initiated and implemented a land reform that reduced the power of landlords and doubled the proportion of those who farmed their own land (Darwin 2007: 448). It also encouraged protection and subsidies, and heavy government regulation of foreign investment by transnational corporations (Chang 2008: 61). Following the victory of the People's Republic of China in 1949, the United States implemented similar agrarian reform laws in the autonomous province of Taiwan, and it did the same in South Korea following the Korean War (1953–1956). As a result of the successful United States-imposed land and democratic reforms, these countries 'went through the fastest economic and social transformation in human history' (Chang 2003b: 121). All three experienced vigorous industrial growth stimulated by the development of a vibrant domestic market; and all grew *less* unequal (in contrast to patterns elsewhere). However, the policies and reforms that had produced these outcomes in 'frontline' states, were elsewhere characterized as 'communism' and strenuously opposed.

The 'Communist threat' was defined in the 1950s, by a study group led by Harvard political scientist W. Y Elliott, as any independent economic policies of socialist or nationalist countries proceeding 'in ways that reduce their willingness and ability to complement the industrial economies of the West' (quoted in Chomsky 1985: 58).[15] This definition of 'Communist threat' seems to have been widely employed by governments and ruling groups around the world. In the Americas, Europe, Asia, and Africa, elites closed ranks to eradicate, not only communists and socialists, but *any* element calling for democracy and land reform, including liberal, left-of-centre, and other reformist groups and movements. The United States and its allies supported coups and took military action against governments that tried to steer development along socialist and nationally independent paths: in Guatemala (1953), Iran (1953), Tanzania (1965–1985), Indonesia (1958), Cuba (1959–1961), Congo (1964), Laos (1964–1973), Peru (1965), Cambodia (1969–1970), Jamaica (1972–1980), Chile (1973), Grenada (1982), Nicaragua (1980s), Libya (1986), and El Salvador (1980s). Britain and the United States also intervened in civil wars in Jordan (1957), Lebanon (1958, 1982), and Yemen (1962–1969); and in the Dhufar Rebellion in Oman in the 1960s and 1970s, the overthrow of the Qasim regime in Iraq (1963), border conflicts between North and South Yemen, and Kurdish rebellions in Iraq in the 1970s.

Nationally embedded capital, land reform, and the expansion of domestic markets had brought about dynamic growth in Japan and the 'Asian Tigers'. However, this was attributed by the United States, its allies, and international organizations and development agencies as the result, not of social revolutionary changes, but of market-driven forces or policies applicable only to those countries.[16] Nowhere else were these policies either promoted or allowed to take place.

Instead, 'development' prescriptions promoted policies that restricted domestic markets, repressed labour, and prevented the emergence of the nationally integrated economies and Fordist mass consumption that had come to characterize the United States and other 'first-world' countries after World War II. Elites in these countries recognized that land and labour reforms worked to increase the all-round productive capacity of economies, and that this created new 'first-world' states that, like Japan, competed with the older ones. Moreover, in most countries, as in the United States and in Europe, local elites had no interest in pursuing such policies, for reasons elaborated previously (see Chapter 3, and further discussion below and in Chapter 8).

## *The development project*

In Europe, a thorough-going reconstruction took place on the basis of redistributive policies that, before the world wars, had been effectively blocked; and this led to dynamic and sustained growth. However, leaders of Western European and other capitalist countries did not promote these policies in other parts of the world. In fact, they became actively involved in preventing their adoption and in promoting policies that consolidated and maintained the structures that had characterized their own societies before 1945. These policies became the core of what came to be defined and promoted as 'development' after 1945.

'Development' is a relatively new notion. While 'development' is often treated as the outcome of processes or patterns of change that 'happen in history', the term was introduced into public discourse after World War II in association with, and for the promotion of, a specific post war project and set of policies. The British had used the term for a brief period before the war to mean the engineering of a slow and controlled process of change in their colonies and dependencies; and, after the war, the ruling elites and governments of newly independent countries articulated 'development' as a key policy goal. These elites, retreating colonial bureaucrats, and a wide set of 'first-world' elites shared a broadly similar vision of what 'development' would entail (in fact, development experts have often been colonial administrators who returned to the former colonies in new clothing (Frey 2011).

We can say, then, that 'development' is a post-World War II project of governments, ruling groups, and elites throughout the world. A 'project' consists of policies and strategies that seek to give shape to and control processes of social change. Post World War II 'development' created and operated through a transnational 'development community' consisting of the staff of donor and recipient country development ministries, multilateral 'aid' agencies, financial institutions non-governmental organizations, and academic and non-academic consultants.[17] Whatever its stated goals, after a half-century its outcome has been to prevent the sort of social revolution that transformed the conditions of life in the 'developed' world. Instead, it has succeeded in developing demand among elites and governments, principally for weapons; and in reconstituting and reproducing dualistic economies that, beginning in the nineteenth century, had linked the export sectors of economies around the world.[18]

Immediately after World War II, the United States government sought the involvement of American scholars in 'non-Western' studies. Stimulated by Truman's Point Four Program, the American academy conceptualized almost all areas outside the Atlantic Alliance as 'backward', a term that suggests the goal of 'catching up' and that had the directly political function of providing a rationale for active Western involvement, guidance, and tutelage. Centres dealing with Africa, the Middle East, and North Africa, and to a lesser extent Asia and Latin America, proliferated with the help of non-governmental organizations (such as the Social Science Research Council), which funded workshops and conferences, fellowships and grants, summer training institutes, scholarly exchanges, and publications, and forged links between government and universities, and among researchers, practitioners and policy-makers (Gendzier 1985: 18).[19] A discipline or field of 'development studies' was also built up with encouragement and funding from governmental, international, and private agencies.

### *The transnational elite: Intra-elite conflict and compromise in the Interregnum*

Between 1914 and 1945, the more-or-less continuous crisis in Europe enabled elites outside of Europe to better their position in relation to European ruling groups by seizing control of the apparatus of colonialism and wresting a larger share of political power for themselves. Consequently, between the late 1940s and the 1960s a number of previously colonized states became independent.

But nationalist, anti-colonial, and independence struggles were essentially civil wars fought among different factions of trans-national elite. They resulted, in Africa and most of Asia with the conclusion of an intra-elite compromise: 'western' ruling groups of decolonization and political independence, accepted in exchange for a commitment by 'third world' elites committed themselves to open markets, and to the slow, piecemeal, autocratically governed development of export sectors both to pay for weapons imports from the United States and the UK, and to accumulate personal wealth, and finance conspicuous 'industrialization' projects as a means of maintaining their legitimacy. As had been the case with intra-elite struggles in Europe, elites outside of Europe used nationalism to articulate their demands, win the support of the lower classes, gain state power, and embark on a programme of capitalist expansion that consolidated dualism. Once in control of state power, these 'nationalist' elites continued to build up export industries within restricted foreign-oriented enclaves. They used revenues from exports (and/or foreign aid) to purchase masses of weapons from Britain and the United States, and this enabled them to protect these enclaves and to accumulate wealth safe from the mass misery that grew up and has remained all around them.

Thus, while 'development' had been a mobilizing part of nationalism, it subsequently became an instrument of elite legitimacy and plunder; and while 'nationalist' elites took over the positions held by foreigners and minorities and the functions they performed, the overall aims for which they used them remained the same: a 'program of capitalist modernity' that 'sharpened inequalities' (Prakash 1994: 1476). Despite the appearance of change following decolonization in Latin America, the Middle East, Africa and Asia, it was only elites that were 'incorporated into the global political–economic order on favourable terms': the vast majority of the world's poor were not (Berger 1994: 268). Local 'national' systems remained open and fluid at the top, closed and static at the bottom. Elites remained economically, socially, and culturally oriented towards North America and Western Europe, where they maintained bank accounts, business links, and homes, and sent their children to school (Berger 1994: 268). Thus, throughout the world conditions at the top continued to change in tandem and to converge while, at the bottom, they tended to diverge.

Frantz Fanon saw nationalism as the ideology of those who

wanted to take over the colonial structure rather than dismantle it (Fanon 1966: 30). In some places, nationalism had already begun to achieve this before 1945. The 'All-India' national congress, an annual meeting of provincial associations, represented an Anglo-literate 'national' elite that had arisen predominantly from the upper and middle castes 'and from inside the pursuits and professions that were closest to the institutions of the (colonial) state: administration, law, commerce, English-language journalism, teaching staffs of universities and colleges' (Aijaz 1992: 76). The use of English by these elements and its limited availability to working classes played a role in maintaining social privilege and reproducing class structures. 'The Congress represented this elite and its distinctive (and elitist) demands. It had no mass support – and no desire for it' (Darwin 2009: 199). The independence struggle no more than partially engaged the mass of the Indian peasantry (Arnold 1984: 173–174). Congress leaders 'came around to the view that if the peasants' struggle was allowed to continue', it might hinder the development of the national movement against the British. 'The interests of that "larger" struggle, the need for "national unity", necessitated the shelving of such sectional struggles for the time being' (Pandey 1988: 276). Instead, Indian nationalists demanded more railways and bourgeois law – 'English rule without the Englishman', as Ghandi characterized these demands in 1909 (Ghandi 1963: 15; cited in Chakrabarty 1992: 8). In contrast with post-1949 *China*, post-1947 *India* failed to undertake 'direct and massive public action to improve living conditions.' By 1980 there was a 15-year difference in the average life expectancy in the two countries (Bose 1997: 55–56). Prime Minister Jawaharlal Nehru (1947–1964) promoted the idea that a paternalistic technocratic elite could guide a nationalist and socialist development; but the main beneficiaries of this period were private industrial and commercial groups and bureaucratic and professional elites directly or indirectly connected to the political elite (see Kohli 1987).

Elsewhere, decolonization proceeded in conjunction with the formation and transformation of an elite to which political power could safely be transferred (Unger 2011: 241).[20] United States President Harry Truman and his advisors envisioned a gradual but steady process of national independence spreading across the 'third world', with power passing peacefully from retreating European colonial officials into the hands of pro-Western, anti-communist 'indigenous elites' (Barstelmann 2001: 68–69). Thus, from the 1950s, efforts to educate elites in the decolonized world featured prominently in private and public American 'development' policies. In the 1940s, the Carnegie Corporation and the British Colonial Office planned and administered educational policies in African territories under British rule. Secondary education, reserved for only a minority, was designed to support the 'preservation and adaptation of the Great Tradition of Western society to the conditions of a new world' (Unger 2011: 246; quoting Harvie Branscomb).[21]

But if elites throughout Asia and Africa have allied with 'Western' elites to contain socio-economic change, how do we explain their tendency to espouse anti-imperialist and anti-Western ideologies?

In the Middle East and elsewhere, nationalist, anti-imperialist and anti-Western rhetoric has been used to legitimize the extirpation of 'Western' working-class and left-intellectual influences, and to foreclose the adoption of 'Western' reforms and the spread of 'Western' standards and styles of life to other classes. Having established their legitimacy by opposing colonial and imperial powers, ruling groups and elites continually reproduce this foe by emphasizing racism and imperialism, rather than social justice. Thus, intellectuals and radical scholars who blame colonialism and imperialism, and 'dependency' and 'dependent' development, for continuing poverty and 'underdevelopment', are 'paradoxically much more useful for the state than for the people' (Jewsiewicki 1989: 5).[22]

And what about the 'non-aligned movement' and Bandung? The 'Bandung Era' (1950s–1970s) began with the Asian–African Conference held in Bandung, on the island of Java in Indonesia in 1955. At the conference, a number of countries calling themselves 'the non-aligned nations' attempted to form a united front to negotiate with industrialized nations for better conditions of international trade, and for the creation of international mechanisms for maintaining fair prices for raw materials, cash crops and foodstuff. By 1970, this initiative appeared to have exhausted itself. Then, in 1974, came a call for a New International Economic Order (NIEO). The NIEO Declaration of 12 December 1974 called for the establishment of a world order based on equity, sovereign equality, independence, and cooperation. The initiative came from the presidents of oil-producing nations (Algeria, Iran, Mexico, and Venezuela) who demanded a unilateral reduction in Northern trade barriers and international commodity agreements (ICAs) for coffee, sugar, and rubber. Given the enclave character of oil- and mineral-exporting economies, it is not unreasonable to assume, as Rajeev Patel and Philip McMichael argue, that it was, at least in part, 'an intensification of the development project inasmuch as it called for Northern concessions geared to increasing external revenues available to Third World elites' and to 'strengthening the sovereignty of the rentier state' (Patel & McMichael 2004: 244). In 1981, United States President Ronald Regan unilaterally declared the death of the NIEO at the Cancun Summit on International Development.

## Conclusion

In Europe, 'development' was achieved, not gradually, but within a short period of time and as a result of much violence and destruction – by means of revolution (in Russia) and wide-scale, massively destructive war (in all of Europe). In Australia, Canada, and New Zealand the landowning classes were circumscribed from the start, and so revenues were not used solely to enrich traditional landowning classes and their allies as they were in Europe and elsewhere.[23] In the United States, where a strong landowning class developed in the south, a struggle between landowners and industrialists culminated in one of history's bloodiest civil wars and the victory of the industrial capitalist bourgeoisie. As a result, smallholder patterns of land ownership evolved there. In Japan, a massive and spectacularly successful land reform, imposed by the Allied powers after World War II, led to the transformation of its economy and society.[24] The Japanese reform transformed its backward, feudal rural economy, brought about a transfer of political power, and increased the all-round productive capacity of the economy by the creation of substantial effective demand in agriculture and by the increased supply of domestic food and raw materials (Ladejinsky 1959). The same reforms were paid for by the United States and implemented in Taiwan and South Korea.

These were the 'first-world' and 'second-world' countries which were able to participate fully in the historically unprecedented boom of the 1950s and 1960s. However, the changes that had effectively 'nationalized' capital and led to the expansion and integration of domestic markets in the 'first' and 'second' world countries were prevented from occurring elsewhere. Instead, elites and ruling groups in 'first' world and newly independent and 'developing' states closed ranks to eradicate socialism, contain democracy, and consolidate dualistic structures in what became, as a result, a vast, global 'third world'. The 'development' project maintained and reproduced dualistic economies and reconstituted networks of elite exchange around an Anglo-American military–industrial complex. 'Development' was concerned not with promoting capitalist development, but with maintaining the pattern of monopoly capitalism that had predominated everywhere before the world wars. Thus, the term 'third world' applied, not to societies characterized by their common levels, paths, or timing of development, but to those in which social democratic/Keynesian or communist/socialist policies were to be proscribed.

The existence of these different 'worlds', however, was brief. In the late 1970s, 'first-world' countries began to roll back the restrictions on capital mobility and to eliminate regulatory agencies and social welfare programmes that, after World War II, had produced the conditions of life associated with 'first-world' development. At the end of the 1980s, the 'second world' adopted similar measures. These changes are the basis of what we call 'globalization'. But its dominant trend is *not* towards integration of the second and third worlds into the first world, but just the opposite: the *re*integration, of the first and second worlds into a system of local and trans-local relations similar to the one that, in those areas of the world, pre-dated the crisis of the world wars and the great depression. Consequently, as time goes on, the 1950s and 1960s may appear to have been a brief interlude in the history of the worldwide expansion of capitalism.

# 8 Globalization redux

The immediate post-World War II decades saw the establishment, for the first time, of nationally embedded economies, though only in a relatively few countries ('first' and 'second' world countries). However, transnational linkages and relations that had been consolidated during the nineteenth century continued to operate through a variety of institutions and alliances; and, in what came to be known as the 'third' world, these enabled ruling groups to maintain the disembedded capitalist economies that had characterized all countries before the world wars.

In recent decades, industrialization in the third world, and the conviction that globalization is bringing about a levelling of economic circumstances (a 'flat' world), has led scholars to proclaim the imminent emergence of one world. The presumption is that, in this world, the conditions of life that exist in the advanced countries of the 'first' world will exist everywhere: they will not only continue to characterize today's first-world countries, but will also be enjoyed by the countries that were previously part of the 'second' and 'third' worlds.

This chapter considers this claim. The current acceleration of capitalist globalization parallels, to an almost uncanny extent, that which began at the end of the eighteenth century (see Chapter 3), reminding us that change is not unidirectional: while it may bring progress, it also may bring retrogress (a return to or repetition of a former and less socially progressive condition) or regress (a change from better to worse). Consequently, this chapter reflects on the nature of current trends of change and on their likely outcome in light of the account of modern history elaborated in previous chapters.

## I. Industrialization without 'development'

One of the most pervasive and durable beliefs of the post-war era is that economic growth in the countries of the third world will bring about the conditions of life that exist in the advanced countries of 'the West'. In the 1970s and 1980s, the third world had made little progress towards this goal.[1] However, by the end of the 1980s it appeared that levels of industrialization in the first and third worlds were converging. A number of scholars and practitioners at that time assumed that we would soon be seeing the end of the 'third world' as a political, economic, and ideological entity;[2] and in the 1990s, an increasing number of scholars appeared to agree.[3] The basis of their optimism was data on two indices of industrialization – manufacturing as a proportion of per capita GDP, and the ratio of non-rural to total population. These data showed that, according to the first indicator, the 'third world' had 'not just caught up but *overtaken* the "first world" in degree of industrialization'; and that, with respect to the other, 'it had further reduced the gap by one quarter' (Arrighi, Silver, & Brewer 2003: 15). These data are shown in Table 8.1.

However, despite converging levels of industrialization, it soon appeared that the divide in income and wealth between the 'first' and 'third' worlds was, in fact, widening.[4] It might be said, then, that what countries of the third world have achieved since World War II is industrialization without 'development' – i.e., without the conditions of life that exist in the first world.

Scholars have responded to this unexpected outcome of half a century and more of 'development' in a number of ways. One response has been to emphasize the necessity of greater market freedom: to argue that third-world countries will achieve the conditions of life

*Table 8.1* Convergence of 'first' and 'third' world levels of industrialization: two indices

| | *% GDP in Manufacturing* | | *% Non-Rural to Total Population* | |
|---|---|---|---|---|
| | *1980* | *1995* | *1980* | *1995* |
| **First World** | 24.3 | 20.4 | 75.4 | 78.2 |
| **Third World** | 25.6 | 25.6 | 30.6 | 42.5 |

Source: World Bank (1999).

found in the first world by eliminating state interference that prevents markets from working efficiently. However, 'first-world' conditions of life were achieved, not as a result of greater market freedom, but though the establishment, after World War II, of a relatively more nationally 'embedded' capitalism involving greater restrictions on capital, and an increase in state regulatory and welfare functions (see Chapter 7).

A second response has been to reiterate arguments concerning the legacy and continuing relevance of imperialism. Imperialism *is* relevant to understanding development outcomes. However, arguments about the impact of imperialism on contemporary development tend to advance a partial and misleading conception of what imperialism is and how it operates. The usual assumption is that imperialism is an external relation between national societies. But imperialism is a regime of elite accumulation that, historically, has been essentially transnational and collaborative and which, before the world wars, operated to produce broadly similar structures everywhere (see Chapter 5). The supposedly idiosyncratic and distorted 'dependent' capitalism that is assumed to be a legacy of imperialism in contemporary 'third-world' countries is simply capitalism as it existed everywhere before the world wars: in countries that were colonies, dependencies, and 'spheres of influence' (both in Europe and elsewhere), and those that were not. The differences that distinctions between 'independent' (non-colonial) and 'dependent' (colonial/post-colonial) development are meant to capture emerged only after World War II.

There have been two other responses to the dilemma of 'industrialization without development' which, rather than attempting to explain this outcome, attempt, instead, to redescribe or reconceptualize what we mean by 'development'. One of these responses is the United Nations Development Programme's Human Development Index (HDI). The HDI combines measures of real GDP per capita with measures for social development or human welfare, which highlights just what standard national measures obscure: the distribution of wealth and material wellbeing. But it neither explains nor prescribes a remedy for the disparities that the index reveals. The other response has been to reduce expectations of 'development': departing from normal usage, it uses the term development instead, to describe 'a modest increase in "industrialization" . . . an improved capacity to produce textiles, sports shoes, furniture, or even a solid GDP based on the export of resources, agricultural products, or low-tech industries' (Mason 1997: 409). Neither of these responses provide an explanation of or prescription for, overcoming 'underdevelopment'. However, they are more useful than the first two. While the first two depend for their support on a profoundly erroneous interpretation of modern history, the second two are descriptively accurate, advance realistic expectations, and have a firm basis in the history of actually existing capitalism.

The arguments of previous chapters provide a different explanation and, as this chapter will discuss, imply a different strategy for overcoming underdevelopment. Third-world countries were never forced, willing, or allowed to adopt the policies that produced broad-based, nationally embedded economic growth in the 'first world', and, consequently, remained dualistic after 1945. Since industrialization produces different outcomes in nationally integrated and dualistic economies, comparing levels of industrialization is misleading. In dual economies, leading sectors remain largely alien to other sectors and so restrict the growth of the domestic economy. Consider, in this light, the comparative data on the rural sectors of today's first and third world countries shown in Table 8.2. Taken together, the sectoral and comparative data presented in Tables 8.1 and 8.2 illustrate why industrialization in the countries of the third world has not brought about the conditions of life found in the first world.

In dualistic economies, the industrial sector does not act as an engine of growth for the rest of the economy, so neither wealth nor material wellbeing are generated or distributed 'nationally'. State policies ensure this outcome by maintaining a system that is organized, not to expand and integrate national societies and economies, but to expand export sectors and link them to external markets (see Chapter 3). Third-world countries that have levels of industrialization comparable to those of first world countries have achieved this by concentrating productive resources in cities and mobilizing them for foreign trade rather than (as in the first world) for the expansion of the domestic market. Consequently, a large proportion of the workforce remains concentrated in low-productivity agriculture. For those who are rural and poor, which in many third-world countries is the majority of the population,[5] conditions of life are not significantly different than when the industrial age began more than 200 years ago.

*Table 8.2* Rural/agrarian sectors

| | *1997** | | | *1997* | | *Eve of World War I†* | |
|---|---|---|---|---|---|---|---|
| | *% of total labour force in agriculture* | *% of GDP from agriculture* | | *% of total labour force in agriculture* | *% of GDP from agriculture* | *% of total labour force in agriculture* | *% of GDP from agriculture* |
| Ethiopia | 86 | 50 | Japan | 7 | 2 | 63 | 38 |
| Nepal | 83 | 40 | France | 5 | 2 | 43 | 35 |
| Kenya | 80 | 26 | Germany | 4 | 1 | 38 | 18 |
| China | 72 | 18 | United States | 3 | 2 | 31 | 17 |
| India | 64 | 29 | UK | 2 | 2 | 12 | 8 |
| Indonesia | 55 | 20 | | | | | |
| Pakistan | 52 | 26 | | | | | |
| Philippines | 46 | 17 | | | | | |
| Nigeria | 43 | 32 | | | | | |
| Peru | 36 | 7 | | | | | |
| Mexico | 28 | 5 | | | | | |
| Brazil | 23 | 8 | | | | | |

* Data both first and th rd world: United Nations Statistics, 2000; *World Development Indicators 1998* (World Bank 1998).

† Date are for the following years (1912), France (1910), Germany (1910), UK (1911) source is Kuznets (1957: 73). For the United States, the data for the percentage of GDP from agriculture are for 1904–1913 (Kuznets 1957: 73), and that for the percentage of the total labour force in agriculture is for 1900 (Dimitri, Effland, & Conklin 2006).

The next section will argue that, while a convergence between the first and third worlds *is* taking place, this is a result *not* of the industrialization (and end) of the third world, but of the denationalization of capital in (and disappearance of) the first and second worlds.

## II. Denationalizing capital: the end of the 'first' and 'second' worlds

The existence of 'three worlds' of development following World War II was brief. In the 1970s, 'first-world' countries began to roll back restrictions on capital mobility and to eliminate regulatory agencies and social welfare programmes that, after World War II, had produced the conditions of life associated with 'first-world' development. At the end of the 1980s, the 'second world' (the Communist world) adopted similar measures. These changes are the basis of what we call 'globalization'

In 1968, a series of uprisings and demonstrations throughout the world marked the beginning of the end of the post-World War II order. In the United States, the activities of anti-Cold War/Viet Nam and civil rights movements upset the balance of power on which the post-war Keynesian compromise had depended. This began a policy shift that deregulated capital and began a broader process of disembedding the United States economy. In the 1970s, governments in other first-world countries introduced similar measures to eliminate restrictions on capital mobility and dismantle regulatory agencies and social welfare programmes. These measures were characterized as a necessity demanded by the emergence of 'globalization'; but government policies were designed, not to *adjust* to new, global circumstances, but to *promote* them. By the end of the 1980s, a drastic 'shock-therapy' version of these policies was introduced in second-world countries and quickly reinstated the dualistic and monopoly capitalist structures that had characterized their economies before the world wars. The dismantling of nationally embedded economies in 'first' and 'second' world countries brought the brief post-World War II interregnum to an end. By the 1990s, the introduction of greater market freedom had produced rising income inequality throughout both the first and second worlds (Alderson & Nielsen 2001; Gustafsson & Johansson 1999; OECD 2008).

The return to pre-war policies brought about the re-emergence of pre-war transnational spatialities. Productive resources became concentrated, once again, in cities and substate regions; and global trade and technology flows and capital movements were restored to their former prominence. This is what we call 'globalization'. Though the features that comprise it are characterized as 'new', they are not new but only newly salient; they have not recently emerged, but only re-emerged with the adoption by governments of a variety of restructuring initiatives designed to reinstate, deepen, or extend pre-war structures.

### *The 'crisis' of capitalism and the end of the 'first' world*

The Keynesian–Fordist compromise that developed in the United States starting with the New Deal required far less of a concession by capital than did the Keynesian social democratic compromises forged in Europe. The United States had enjoyed both a higher level of domestic investment and faster growth than Western European economies (Schonfield 1965: 5–6); and Keynesian policies also functioned as a welfare programme for the mass production of armaments which, in the United States, had begun in the 1860s and, thereafter, had become an increasingly important part of its economy. Most importantly, American industry had few competitors, so the higher wages conceded as part of its fordist compromise could be paid for by higher prices. By the 1960s, however, competition from Europe and Japan had begun to erode the advantage that American industry had enjoyed and to narrow its profit margins.[6] At the same time that international competition began to act as a constraint on pricing, labour militancy and political radicalism in the United States as a result of mass conscription for the Viet Nam war made reducing wages politically untenable.

The introduction of mass conscription for the Viet Nam war increased American domestic opposition to the Cold War and expanded and radicalized its Civil Rights movement. After the world wars and their social revolutionary consequences, governments in Europe had replaced mass conscription armies with professional armed forces; and, having observed the consequences of Europe's wartime mobilizations, elites all around the world appeared committed to avoiding mass mobilizations either for war or industry. But the United States government, desperate to prevail in its war in Viet Nam (1955–1975), raised a mass conscription army in the 1960s. In light of Europe's experience in the world wars (see Chapter 7), the consequences for the United States seem predictable: the war politicized and radicalized masses of people and unleashed powerful pressures to extend and expand civil rights. These pressures undermined the New Deal coalition on which the Keynesian–Fordist compromise with labour rested; a coalition that had been forged, in part, on the basis of a North–South agreement to maintain the racial *status quo*. With the expansion of the Civil Rights movement, wealthy southerners fled the Democratic Party for the Republican Party and, by sowing fear and racism, succeeded in bringing a majority of white Southerners with them. Not only did the delicate balance of power on which the New Deal coalition rested dissolve, the unity of labour also fractured as rank-and-file members of unions in Northern cities resisted demands to integrate housing, schooling, and unions.

In 1968, civil rights riots exploded in New York, Washington DC, Cincinnati, Chicago, Kansas City, Louisville, and Baltimore. These, and an escalation of anti-Viet Nam/Cold War protests in the United States, appeared to be part of a world revolution that cut across the tripartite division of the world system at the time – across the West, the Communist bloc, and the 'third world' (Wallerstein 2006: 84).[7] The impact of these events around the world, the spectacle of social revolutionary activism and of an aggressive counter-revolution in the United States, made 1968 a turning point in the post-World War II order.

Within a few years, a decisive shift in policy had denationalized capital throughout the first world and laid the foundations for a rapid return to transnational capitalism – capitalist accumulation organized beyond the territorial boundaries of the nation state. Needing to borrow abroad to pay both for Viet Nam and for social programmes to assuage growing domestic political volatility (the 'Great Society'), the United States, which by 1973 had become the world's largest debtor nation, abandoned the gold-standard system and removed its capital controls. Germany also ended capital controls that year, and at the end of the 1970s Japan and the UK ended theirs. The OECD countries and the European Community removed theirs beginning in the early to mid-1980s.

The crisis of capitalism in the 1970s recalls the discussion in Chapter 2 of the 'crisis of feudalism' which began in Europe in the thirteenth century. The term 'crisis' describes a general calamitous situation that occurs at a particular time and place. But, as Chapter 2 argued, what historians call the 'crisis of feudalism' was not a *general* crisis, but a crisis only for aristocratic landowners.

The Black Death had undermined feudal mechanisms of economic exploitation and created a crisis for landowners; but by levelling the social field, it had also inaugurated a period of great opportunity and prosperity for the mass of the European population. Like this earlier crisis, the crisis of the 1970s occurred at a time in which most people in the United States were enjoying a better standard of living. Caught in a profit squeeze by competition abroad and labour militancy at home, United States capitalists pressed for a shift of policies that would enable them to escape the implications of the Keynesian–Fordist compromise in a 'sealed-off domestic context' (van der Pijl 1998: 119).

The lifting of capital controls in the 1970s launched a colossal wave of capital exports. Before this, American capital exports had been relatively small (British capital exports in the nineteenth century had amounted to 10 per cent of GDP; at their peak, those of the United States had been around two per cent of GDP); and they had supported an overall system of welfare, income equality, and higher wages at home. The capital exports that began in the late 1970s, however, were part of an overall shift that involved downsizing workforces and resetting corporate activity 'at ever lower levels of output and employment' (Williams, Williams, & Haslam 1989: 292). The bargaining power of labour was weakened by making the relationship between firms and workers more 'flexible', and by subcontracting and outsourcing, plant closings and layoffs, concessionary bargaining and union-busting, and the internationalization of production through direct foreign investment. By the early 1990s, the deregulation of industry and markets, abandonment of exchange controls, privatization of state assets, and curtailment of welfare functions had resolved the 'crisis of capitalism' by producing growing inequality, rising poverty, and widespread homelessness.[8]

Previous chapters have argued that, except for the 1950s and 1960s, capitalism has always and everywhere been externally oriented – not because it contains an inevitable crisis involving

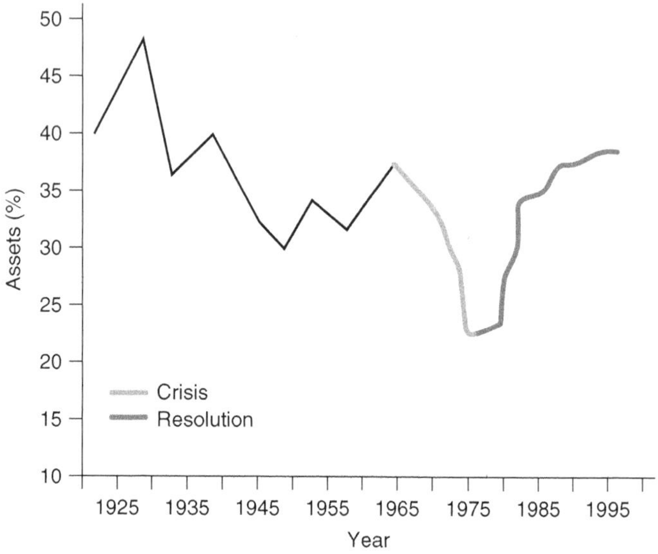


*Figure 8.1* 'Crisis' and resolution. portion of assets (real-estate assets, securities and monetary holdings, and durable consumption goods) held by the richest one per cent of households (per cent) in the United States: 1922–1998.

Source for data: Duménil and Levy (2004: 139).

overproduction, underconsumption, and a falling rate of profit – but because of an ongoing conflict between capitalists and workers and a recurring social logic of elite reproduction (see Chapters 2 and 3).

Chapter 3 argued that elites who sought to profit from industrial production were reluctant to provide workers, through higher wages and inward investment and development, with a standard of consumption high enough to absorb the output of what they produced. They feared that this would lead to social levelling and dissolve the basic relation of capital (the subordination of labour to capital). Consequently, before the world wars industrial production everywhere was organized to produce commodities for consumption abroad. Everywhere, dominant classes pursued an externally oriented industrial expansion that limited the geographic and sectoral spread of development and the growth of organized labour. Britain used capital exports to develop purchasing power and demand among foreign governments and elites for British-made ships, guns and ammunition, and for railway and canal and other transport, as well as for communication and business infrastructure and services.

Just as the output of Britain's industrial production had been designed largely for ruling groups and governments in the nineteenth century so, too, is the massive output of today's increasingly integrated Anglo-American military–industrial complex.[9]

Much analysis of the American empire after the Cold War has focused on the enlargement of America's military arsenal as a means of furthering American economic and political interests around the world. But what is of pre-eminent concern to American elites is the *export* of armaments, rather than their deployment for purposes of control or coercion. The mass production of armaments became an important part of the American economy in the nineteenth century. After World War II, American weapons exports were maintained by military-related spending by the United States government, and by allied rearmament, the deployment of American troops and weapons abroad, foreign military aid, and United States government assistance to allies which was recycled in the United States in the form of military purchases. During the 1970s, the rise in oil prices provided additional purchasing power among Arab elites for American weapons.[10] After the Cold War ended, any pretence that the defence establishment was actually defensive in posture was gradually abandoned (Bacevich 2002: 98).[11]

Today, the American and British economies have become increasingly dependent on exporting weapons and defence-related infrastructure and services. The United States and the UK are the largest arms exporters in the world, a factor of central importance to their 'special relationship' and to their foreign policies. Governments in both countries use similar means of creating demand for the products and services of their military sectors and defence-related firms: American taxpayer dollars fund American foreign aid and development assistance to expand the role of the military in third-world countries and to create purchasing power abroad for American weapons; and the UK government loans out British taxpayers' money through its Export Credit Guarantee Department to fund foreign purchases of British-made arms. American and UK foreign policy is also shaped by their financial and business services sector.

The U.K.'s financial and business services companies are the biggest exporters of capital and 'the most aggressive proponents of forcing open banking and public services at home and abroad' (Foster 2005).

### *The end of the 'second world'*

Many of the social revolutionary changes that occurred in the 'first world' after 1945 also occurred in the countries of the 'second world'. However, while they experienced rapid, broad-based growth and other benefits of first-world countries, their political and economic structures developed within an environment dominated by Cold War military threats and containment policies. The collapse of Communist party rule in the second world in the 1980s brought the Cold War to an end. The economies of Russia and the countries of eastern Europe were rapidly restructured through policies that Milton Friedman characterized as 'shock treatment' or 'shock therapy'. This involved the institution of a sweeping, quick, all-at-once free-market programme designed to rapidly dismantle socialist structures and replace them with the dualistic, capitalist monopoly ones that had prevailed in those countries before the world wars.

In Russia, 'shock-therapy' policies succeeded in producing an extremely polarized distribution of income with, at one pole, extreme wealth for a small number of citizens, the majority of them former members of the Communist Party; and, at the other pole, a very low level of wages. The deindustrialization, degeneration, and decay that resulted from these policies has been so extreme as to amount to a virtual 'demodernization' of the country (Cohen 2000: 41). The economy is tightly controlled by crony capitalists and criminal syndicates, the export lobby, and domestic security services. While the Soviet Union had produced industrial goods and manufacturing tools for the developing world, shock-therapy policies have swiftly converted Russia into an exporter of natural resources. Seventy per cent of total exports in capitalist Russia consists of raw commodities, and the country now imports the higher value-added goods it had previously produced for itself (Cooper 2009: 9). Finally, market freedom has produced, not democracy, but an authoritarian super-presidency that recalls the Russian tsarist regime that existed on the eve of the

1917 revolution, along with elements of tsarist imperialism and the Greater Russia nationalism of the nineteenth century. These features of capitalist Russia are often held to be a legacy of communism; but all of them are characteristic of capitalist systems that are found throughout history.[12]

Reforms aimed at instituting greater market freedom were introduced in nearly all Eastern European countries beginning in the 1960s; and, within a decade, these reforms had widened income differentials and produced a class stratification system that became in many ways similar to that of Western capitalism (Parkin 1969: 255–274).

Yugoslavia, which instituted market reforms earlier and far more radically than the other socialist countries (Landy 1961), also became the most politically volatile among the Eastern European countries and the scene of the greatest communal violence. By the end of the 1970s, the economies of Eastern European countries had begun to slow dramatically. To increase the efficiency of their economies, governments imported advanced technology from Western countries and borrowed from Western banks, governments, and international agencies in order to pay for it. But the slow growth of the world economy in the late 1970s and 1980s made it difficult to repay these loans, and the burden of debt contributed to severe economic crises in Poland, Romania, and Yugoslavia, and to increasingly difficult conditions throughout Eastern Europe (Tipton & Aldritch 1987: 248–252).

In 1989, a wave of demonstrations swept through Eastern Europe. These were the prelude to relatively peaceful 'velvet revolutions' which that year brought about a change of government in Poland, Czechoslovakia, the German Democratic Republic (GDR), Romania, and Bulgaria. These revolutions were initiated by elements within Eastern Europe's increasingly deproletarianized communist parties – those elements that were best positioned to take advantage of marketization and capitalist forms of ownership, and who therefore sought to accelerate the conversion of Eastern European economies to market systems.[13] The revolutions produced a further decline in living standards, and societies became much more visibly stratified. Alongside new entrepreneurial classes, armies of the unemployed emerged for the first time in the post-World War II Eastern European order. The transition rapidly led to massive increases in inequality within individual countries. In 1988, Eastern Europe was

*Table 8.3* Regional gini coefficients in 1988 and 1993*

| | *1988* | *1993* |
|---|---|---|
| Africa | 42.7 | 47.2 |
| Asia | 55.9 | 61.8 |
| Latin America and Caribbean | 57.1 | 55.6 |
| Eastern Europe/Former Soviet Union | 25.6 | 46.4 |
| Western Europe, North America, Oceania | 37.1 | 36.6 |

Source: Milanovic (1999: 21). For the list of countries included in each region, see Milanovic (1999: 11).

* Common-sample countries; distribution of persons by US dollars of purchase power parity income/expenditures per capita.

the most equal region of the world. By 1993, inequality within Eastern European countries had far surpassed that of Western European and North American countries.

Many of the changes that scholars have been describing since the 1970s actually represent a return to pre-world-war structures. To a large extent, this has been driven by neo-liberal policies designed to restructure markets and integrate them into global commodity chains. Neo-liberal restructuring measures have been promoted under different banners. They were introduced in first-world countries at the end of the 1970s under the banner of 'globalization'; and later, when applied in more brutal fashion in Eastern Europe and Russia, they were called 'shock therapy' or 'fast-track' transitions from socialist to capitalist market systems. They have been promoted more-or-less continually and under a variety of other banners as a means of deepening and extending dualistic economies in the rest of the world (through 'structural adjustment, 'democratization', and 'civil society' initiatives or regime change), and of eliminating constraints on capital wherever else they might be found around the globe (through post-war and post-disaster 'reconstruction').

## III. Post-Keynesian accumulation strategies: Reintegrating the three worlds

As in the first and second worlds, neo-liberal restructuring has been pursued in the third world through 'structural adjustment programmes, as well as though post-war and post-disaster reconstructions. When Milton Friedman coined the term 'shock treatment' or 'shock therapy' it was to describe, not only the free-market measures promoted in Russia and Eastern Europe, but also the exploitation of a crisis for the same purpose.[14] Like war and ethnic cleansing, crises such as Sri Lanka's 2004 tsunami and Hurricane Katrina in the United States provide a clear field for neo-liberal restructuring by blocking residents displaced by these disasters from returning and rebuilding.

Neo-liberal restructuring has also been pursued through 'democratization' and 'civil-society' initiatives. The achievement of democracy in Western Europe and other countries is associated with an increase in the power of working classes relative to that of other classes, a relatively more nationally embedded capitalism, the development of purchasing power among a mass domestic citizen workforce, the expansion and integration of domestic markets and policies designed to increase domestic investment, a more equitable distribution of income, and the resumption by states of the welfare and regulatory functions that they had relinquished at the end of the eighteenth century. But this is not what is being promoted by the democratization initiatives of Western governments, NGOs, and international organizations. Nor do these changes feature prominently in the vast literature exploring 'requisites' or 'prerequisites' of democracy'.

Democratization initiatives have been promoted by business interests with the aim of restoring or creating institutional mechanisms that allow them access to policy-making (Conaghan, Malloy, & Abugattas 1990). The parliamentary institutions and electoral systems that are counted as successes of these initiatives do not, and are not designed to, facilitate citizen deliberation, participation, and engagement. Nor do civil-society initiatives provide the mass of the population with an independent, autonomous voice. Instead, they have promoted institutionalized forms of participation that have worked to strengthen a narrow range of foreign-oriented interests and to contribute to the marginalization or weakening of trade unions, farmers and fishermen's associations, and ethnic, religious, or caste associations.[15]

Neo-liberal policies represent a return to pre-Keynesian/Fordist policies. Instead of the strategic state action prescribed by

Keynesianism and used successfully in Western Europe, the United States, and the East Asian 'tigers', neo-liberalism prescribes:

1. freeing the market from state control and regulation to allow total freedom of movement for capital, goods and services; and greater openness to international trade and investment, and the lifting of price controls
2. reducing government expenditures and its role, overall, by cutting public funding for social services such as education and healthcare, and reducing government investment in such things as the maintenance of roads, bridges, the water supply, etc.
3. privatization: selling state-owned enterprises, goods and services to private investors, including banks, key industries, railroads, toll highways, electricity, schools, and hospitals.

Neo-liberalism sees itself as the heir to liberalism – the dominant economic doctrine of the late nineteenth and the early twentieth century; and its agenda is clearly of 'nineteenth-century vintage' (Chang 2003a: 3). It calls for the dismantling of state planning and of government regulation of economic activities. It portrays these policies as 'new', and as necessary to meet the challenges of a 'new' global world. This discourse echoes the theme of disjuncture and difference that has been, throughout the ages, propagated by conquerors to invalidate pre-conquest legal and other claims to possessions and privileges and to provide a basis for a new definition of property rights in conquered areas (see Chapter 1). It masks the fact that, under whatever banner they are introduced, neo-liberal policies are designed to reconstruct key aspects of the pre-world war international political and economic order and, in particular, its guarantee of international, as opposed to national, property rights (Lal 2003).

The discourse of 'globalization' (like that of 'nationalism' and 'development') has been developed and consciously used as a political tool. The development of this discourse launched scholars into 'globalization' as a field of inquiry well in advance of their having imagined or discovered the subject themselves (Cumings 1999: 182). One of the manifestations of globalization that scholars have discovered is the emergence of a transnational capitalist class (TCC). William Robinson (2004) has argued that this class emerged with changes in economic organization that undermined the foundations of post-World War II industrial policies and inspired elites to view their interests within a global, rather than national, frame of reference (see also Robinson & Harris 2000). Leslie Sklair has described this TCC as the driving force behind the growing transnational corporate and international institutional emphasis on free trade and, in most developing countries, the shift from import substitution to export promotion strategies since the 1980s. He argues that the TCC is transnational (or global) in that the economic interests of its members are increasingly globally linked rather than exclusively local and national in origin. They have outward-oriented global rather than inward-oriented local perspectives on most economic, political and cultural–ideological issues, and this has been facilitated by patterns of higher education (increasingly in business schools), similar life styles, and consumption of luxury goods and services: exclusive clubs and restaurants, ultra-expensive resorts, private forms of travel and entertainment, and increasing residential segregation in wealthy gated communities secured by armed guards and electronic surveillance (Sklair & Robbins 2002: 84).

Previous chapters have challenged the notion that a transnational capitalist class has only recently emerged (see Chapters 1 and 5). They argued that the expansion of capitalism proceeded, from the start, through an essentially transnational class; and, even though capital was nationalized in a few areas of the world in the twentieth century as a result of the world wars, transnational linkages and relations were maintained by a variety of institutions and alliances that regulated trade and technology flows and capital movements, and expanded transnational circuits of capital and commodities, institutions and forms of accumulation. Anti-revolutionary 'development' coalitions, the OECD, the Group of Seven, Bretton Woods institutions, and the International Monetary Fund and International Bank for Reconstruction and Development (World Bank), as well as NATO and other transatlantic and trans-Pacific security systems, played a key role both in maintaining transnational linkages and relations within the, now, United States-led 'historic' bloc, and in promoting fundamentalist market policies throughout it (Hoffman 2004: 118).

The resurfacing of transnational structures, linkages, and relations has generated a flood of studies. But rather than seeing these phenomena as having emerged from a return to previous policies, most scholars see them as having emerged from fundamentally new conditions. What scholars describe as a fundamental change in the nature of space – new transnational connections and social spaces, the weakening of the significance of national territorial space and the yielding of national spaces to cross-national flows, and the increasing significance of 'deterritorialization', 'supraterritoriality', and 'spaces of flows' (Arrighi 1994; Castells 1996; Hannerz 1996; Hoogvelt 1997; Pries 2001; Taylor 2003) – while descriptively accurate, misrepresents these phenomena as something new and historically unprecedented.[16] These changes are policy driven – the outcome of deliberate choice and collective effort on the part of elites concerned, not with responding to fundamentally new conditions and challenges, but with maintaining a specific distribution of resources that subordinates labour and preserves elite privileges.

### *Post-Keynesian spatial policies: the re-emergence of global city regions and city states*

Previous chapters have argued that capitalism was born global (Chapter 2), that it developed through the cross-border expansion of interconnected urban spaces which were essentially global in nature (Chapter 3), and that its most characteristic political form was the city state (Chapter 4). Dualistic, externally oriented expansion in the nineteenth century had brought cities, urban commercial centres, and export sectors across the world into closer interdependence, creating dynamic focal points of growth that had developed synchronically and interdependently through trans-local interaction and connection. As trading networks expanded, it was cities, not states, that were incorporated in the system. The nation state became the spatial face of capital accumulation only after World War II and in a few countries (in the first and second worlds) where Fordist–Keynesian and social democratic policies generated and distributed wealth and material wellbeing *nationally* rather than within urban-based export sectors.

The changes that occurred in a few areas of the world after the world wars represented a departure from historical patterns of capitalist expansion. These changes were not a natural outcome of industrialization or rising GDP, but the result of state regulatory policies that made investment and production serve the expansion and integration of national markets. However, this was to be only a brief interregnum and, with its end, pre-war structures and patterns have quickly resurfaced. As a result of policies that are restructuring national economic spaces, productive resources are, once again, being concentrated in and by world cities and mobilized for foreign trade. This has restored globalization to its former prominence, along with the transnational flows, networks, and organizations that have always characterized it.

Post-Keynesian spatial policies are really *pre*-Keynesian: they are policies that resurrect pre-Keynesian structures and, specifically, the interconnected urban spaces through which capitalism operated before the world wars.

## *Global City Regions*

At the end of World War II, every European state was marked by sharp regional inequalities: Italy's Mezzogiorno, Spain's Andalusia, France's western and southern regions, West Germany's agricultural peripheries and border zones, Belgium's Limburg coal-mining district, the Dutch northeastern peripheries, Denmark's northwestern regions and islands, the Scandinavian North, western Ireland, and much of Northern Ireland. Table 8.4 shows these regional inequalities in a few Western European countries.

After World War II, governments introduced policies to alleviate these regional inequalities by spreading growth 'as evenly as possible across the entire surface of each national territory' (Brenner 2004: 51). Regional industrial and infrastructural policies introduced between

*Table 8.4* Regional inequality in Europe before 1945 (per capita income of region relative to national average)

| | | | | |
|---|---|---|---|---|
| **Sweden** (1930) | Stockholmstad | **264.2** | Gotlands | **58.1** |
| **France** (1864) | Paris Region | **175.1** | Britanny | **62.1** |
| **Netherlands** (1938) | North Holland | **141.2** | Drenthe | **50.0** |
| **Germany** (1926) | Hamburg | **154.8** | East Prussia | **69.5** |
| **Italy** (1928) | Piedmont | **155.6** | Sicily | **69.7** |

Source: Williamson (1965).

the 1950s and 1970s were designed to 'rechannel employment and growth capacities into underdeveloped regions and rural peripheries throughout the national territory' (Brenner 2004: 135, 137). Government policies in Britain promoted the economic regeneration of its coal-mining regions of south Wales, northern England, west Cumberland, and central Scotland (the Distribution of Industry Acts of 1945); in 1966, an Industrial Development Act broadened this initiative to areas 'encompassing 40 per cent of British territory and 20 per cent of the total population' (Brenner 2004: 141). Projects introduced in the Netherlands in the 1960s sought to disperse industry, population, and employment from the western Randstad regions (Amsterdam, Utrecht, Rotterdam, and the Hague) to the depressed peripheral regions of the north, east, and south. French post-war regional policies were designed 'to decentralize industrial capacities and employment out of the dominant Paris region and into major provincial cities, towns, rural areas, and border zones' (Brenner 2004: 141). Italy's Southern Italy Development Agency was established in 1950 to promote agricultural modernization and industrial growth throughout the south. West Germany's Spatial Planning Law of 1965 promoted 'equal life conditions' across the entire national territory – targeting, in particular, rural peripheries and eastern border areas.[17]

The introduction of post-Keynesian spatial policies by Western European states in the early 1980s reversed these post-World War II trends and have actively *intensified* 'uneven geographical development' through the strengthening of 'globally linked city-regions' (Brenner 2004: 16).[18] According to Parag Khanna, today just 40 'city-regions' account for two-thirds of the world economy and 90 per cent of its innovation (Khanna 2009).

## *Global cities*

Like other structures that have become newly salient with the dismantling of national economies, the re-emergence of what scholars today are calling 'global cities' are being described as fundamentally different from cities that existed in past centuries.[19] Saskia Sassen describes today's global cities as deploying capabilities once associated with nation-states for new purposes. She describes them as 'command points in the organization of the world economy' (Sassen

1994: 4), and as different from the cities through which global trade was organized in the past because, she argues, they were 'produced in a context where most territory is encased in a thick and highly formalized national framework marked by the exclusive authority of the national state' (Sassen 2003: 5). Sassen associates the 'national' with Keynesian policies aimed at strengthening the 'national' economy, 'national' consumption capacity, and the educational level of 'national' workforces (Sassen 2003: 8–9). If these policies and outcomes are of such recent vintage it is difficult to see why they should be assumed to exercise so powerful and durable a force.

Studies of world cities conceptualize them as representing a 'reterritorialization' of state power or 'rescaling' of the state so as to produce a type of state in which the national and urban converge (Brenner 2004). While this is generally seen as transforming the nation state into a fundamentally new form of state, it actually represents a return to a previous state form: the city state. City states already have this national–urban scaling, which explains why they are seen as more agile geopolitical units in today's 'new' global economy. The fact that they are not 'constrained by the tensions inherent in the national-versus-urban politics of non-city states' means they are better able to mobilize strategic resources. Moreover, since they were, from the start and have remained, intertwined in global networks, they have enjoyed 'a head start on other "global cities"' (Olds & Yeung 2004: 508). A number of scholars have highlighted the success of previous world cities which became city states after World War II. For example, Singapore, which became a highly industrialized city state after the war, played a significant role in the evolution of modern Southeast Asia (Parker 2004:12), and today is producing 18 per cent more manufacturing output per capita than the United States (Chang 2008: 215). Elaborating on this theme, Manuel Castells surmises that the revival of the city state 'could be the necessary complement to the expansion of a global economy'. As he points out, there is a 'tradition of European cities as city states leading the pace to the modern age' (Castells 1994: 30).

Arguments developed in earlier chapters suggest that 'European cities as city states led the pace', in the nineteenth century, to an era of monopolistic, anti-market accumulation (see Chapter 4). Today, as in the past, globalization has been characterized by increasing concentration and monopoly, by a global merger wave set in motion by capital in its search for ways to avoid the free market and strengthen monopoly positions (Nitzan 2001: 245). Recalling themes from previous chapters, Peter Taylor has argued that today's global cities facilitate monopolistic, anti-market accumulation; and that spatial networks and hierarchies capped by 'world cities' are the geographic counterpart of the increasing concentration of power and wealth in the hands of global monopolies (Taylor 2000).

That world cities linked to post-Keynesian spatial policies in first-world countries are not newly emerging, but re-emerging, can be seen by their resemblance to structures found in third-world countries. These countries never adopted the policies which produced broad-based, nationally embedded growth in the first world. In these countries, economies remained dualistic after World War II. With economic growth contained within urban-based export sectors, the centrality and overriding prominence of their cities never receded: they enjoyed a high degree of autonomy[20] and, in some cases, played a major role in the world economy. Today, most of the world's largest cities are in third-world countries: of the world's 16 largest cities, each with more than 10 million inhabitants, 12 are in the third world (Mexico City, Mumbai, and Sao Paulo are among the world's five largest) (Gugler 2004: 3).

Today's new global cities and regions are similar to third-world cities in a number of ways. Manuel Castells describes Europe's global cities – he calls them 'information cities' – as 'dualistic'. He argues that they have 'a structural tendency to generate a polarized occupational structure (Castells 1994: 29–30). At one pole is a cosmopolitan elite, 'living on a daily connection to the whole world (functionally, socially, culturally)'; at the other pole is 'the tribalism of local communities, entrenched in spaces that they try to control' as their last stand against the macro-forces that shape their lives (Castells 1994: 30). Structural unemployment or a downgrading of the social conditions of manual labour occurs particularly where labour unions are weak and the institutions of the welfare state have been undermined by political assaults (Castells 1994: 29–30). This dualism is reinforced wherever downgraded jobs are filled by immigrant workers, as in Western European societies where a massive import of foreign workers began to form a new 'sub-proletariat' by the end of the 1960s. For the most part, these workers are found 'in the least attractive and worst paid manual jobs' (Castles 1984: 149). Unrepresented in the government and unorganized, they have been unable to bring effective pressure on either employers or governments for higher wages, shorter hours, and better working conditions. Those from poorer lands, in particular, are often content with or resigned to poorer living conditions, creating, as David Landes observed, 'a situation reminiscent, in small, of the industrial slums of the early nineteenth century' (Landes 1969: 501). China's rapid urban development in recent years has been described in similar terms. Less than 0.5 per cent of Chinese households now own over 60 per cent of the nation's personal wealth, while 'the 150 million-odd migrant workers building China's gleaming cities and the millions more in antiquated rural factories live in Dickensian squalor' (Chanda 2007: 313). Today, cities all around the world – 'Los Angeles and Miami, Moscow and Madrid, Bogota and Kuala Lumpur' (Castells 1994: 19) – are fundamentally dualistic, characterized by 'elite enclaves in which offices, hotels, luxury housing, high-scale infrastructure, and up-scale shops and restaurants have displaced low-income residents' (Gugler 2004: 10).

## Conclusions: re-envisioning 'development'

This book has sought to challenge key features of the highly ideological and profoundly erroneous account of global development that became widely accepted after World War II.

Rather than focusing on *national* phenomena, it has emphasized the extent to which *transnational* class configurations and networks interpenetrate the frames that localize human interactions. While there is increasing awareness today of transnational structures of social power, these have been wrongly associated with a 'new' global era, rather than with structures of social power that have been developing over centuries. This book has highlighted the ways in which an essentially transnational and 'horizontal' structure of social power has shaped modern global development, its role in the origins of capitalism (Chapter 2) and the shift to large-scale industrial production (Chapter 3); in the construction and reconstruction of city states and the emergence of the resource-mobilizing ideology of nationalism and national states (Chapter 4); in the imperial order of the nineteenth century (Chapter 5), during the rise of social revolutionary pressures from 'below' in the nineteenth and early twentieth centuries (Chapter 6) and during the post-World War II interregnum (Chapter 7).

This book also challenges the binary divisions that are at the heart of so many conventional accounts of global development and that tend to obscure the more-or-less similar global development that took place up until the world wars of the twentieth century. Recent research and writing on world history provides abundant evidence of cross-setting similarities in processes and outcomes of growth in world history that, when combined, helps to dissolve distinctions conventionally drawn between 'Western' and 'non-Western' historical development, and between 'developed' and 'developing' worlds. Accounts of global history organized around fictive binary divisions obscure the extent to which the obstacles to broad-based prosperity and sustained growth are generally the same everywhere. Neither the legacy of imperialism, and the nature of post-colonial international relations, nor changes in technology, capital, or markets, has transformed the nature of the set of choices confronting societies. As Colin Duncan points out,

> anybody who can read Dickens and has seen pictures of Malaysian slums is capable of getting the basic diagnosis right. It is still perfectly clear overall that an enormous number of very poor people are making things for a comparatively small number of very comfortable people. Absolutely nothing fundamental has changed
>
> (Duncan 2000: 187–188).

The implication to be drawn from the arguments presented in this book is that the main obstacle to broad-based prosperity is a structure of social power that restricts the growth of national economies. Production predominantly for external rather than internal markets promotes internal structures of inequality. Neither the size nor the nature of the export sector is what is at issue. What is at issue is whether export policies promote the development of the domestic market and support an overall system of welfare, income equality, and higher wages at home; or whether they suppress workers' incomes and domestic demand, and stunt domestic markets.

Conventional accounts of global development tend to treat the distinctions that defined a division between 'advanced' and 'developing' countries after 1945 as a further evolution of processes that began with the 'rise of the West' in the sixteenth century (or earlier). Placing Europe's decisive advance centuries earlier than it actually happened airbrushes out of *history* the social revolution that transformed Europe during the world wars of the twentieth century, and out of *theory* the importance of social revolution for the achievement of broad-based prosperity and democracy.

The conditions of life associated with 'development' did not occur 'naturally' or automatically. The key requirements of economic development are a continuous rise in per capita output in the long run and the balanced distribution of the steadily rising national income among *all sectors* of the population. Redistribution of income in favour of lower income groups requires that the production of goods and services for which there is a demand among the lower income groups, especially foodstuffs, expands more rapidly than production of non-essential goods; this is unlikely to happen, however, in the absence of land reform. But 'a land reform whose purpose is primarily to redistribute income and political power is unlikely to occur without a quick overthrow of the landlord class and immediate changes in tenure systems' (Mellor 1966: 163–164). Redistributive reform requires speed, like the sweeping, quick, all-at-once land reform programme that was implemented in Japan and in the 'Asian Tigers'. Land reform, if it is at all meaningful in scope and intensity is, by its very nature, revolutionary change (Carroll, 1970: 103).[21]

Economic development also requires a change in the structure of employment: workers must be assured of an increasing share in the productivity increments that take place in each sector. But privileged classes resist measures that would ensure this – such as those that enable trade unionism to develop as an effective instrument of working-class representation.

Thus, broad-based development is usually not possible or sustainable without a relatively more egalitarian and fluid structure of social power than exists in the contemporary 'third world' and that existed in today's 'advanced' countries before World War II. This requires a drastic alteration of existing social structures and trends.

But because privileged classes tend to resist measures that require them to relinquish their privileges,[22] radical social transformation rarely takes place in the absence of war or natural disaster. Relatively broad-based prosperity was achieved during the 1950s and 1960s in countries that (1) never had an entrenched landed elite (e.g. Canada, New Zealand, Australia), or had previously seen a significant decline in the power of landowners as a result of civil war (i.e., the United States in the 1860s), and those that (2) experienced a breakdown of traditional social structures and massive land reforms as a result of war (most of Europe in the course of the world wars), or as a result of the imposition of a massive United States-financed land reform (Japan, Taiwan, and South Korea, following the wars).

Globalization is a matter of deliberate organization and collective effort on the part of elites concerned to maintain a specific distribution of resources that subordinates labour and preserves elite privileges. The discourse of globalization emphasizes the necessity of governments to adapt to newness and difference, a necessity that forecloses choice. But government policies are designed, not to adopt to new circumstances, but to promote them.

The claim that changes in the global economy are *inducing* changes in politics and the nature of political authority depoliticizes the policies of governments and hides the processes of class conflict and social struggle that animate them. Keynesian policies created national markets; post-Keynesian policies are dismantling them. Neither set of policies was 'induced' by technology or the logic of capital or markets. Both are related to class and class struggle.

Some have argued that a 'global civil society' is needed in order to resist global capital and secure democratic governance throughout the world, because national initiatives are too small to do so effectively.[23] However, history reveals just the opposite. Redistributive policies were gained through the achievement, locally, of democratic control of the state. It was through national mobilizations that the rights of citizenship, democratic governance, and economic justice were won in the West. It is there that today they are being lost.

Because elites are few in number; they have always had to organize transnationally in order to remain dominant within their own countries. But lower classes have *mass* which, as Marx pointed out, is the one factor of success at their command. This mass becomes strong when it is compact and united. Global forces achieve concrete existence only at specific national and local sites and can usually be effectively opposed only there. While citizen movements have benefited from transnational ties, they have won concessions only when they mobilized domestically against national elites. Thus, the struggle for real democracy of citizens over elites is most likely to succeed at the national level.[24] If efforts to 'globalize' the struggle take precedence over, and divert energies from, national and grass-roots struggles, campaigns to preserve, strengthen, and extend bottom-up democracy may be undermined. In recent decades, fewer and fewer people have been joining political parties, and more have joined environmental, peace and human rights groups such as Greenpeace and Friends of the Earth, Amnesty International, and the anti-nuclear movement (Anheier, Glasius, & Kaldor 2003: 15). Historically, national organization has always been a pre-condition of genuine internationalism from below. National state governments must be held accountable.

Basic social logics tend to recur. Similar patterns in different parts of the world are part of an integrated set of global processes which, themselves, emerge from similar choices made and similar struggles fought in different local settings. The conditions that generate these patterns are similar, as are the dynamics by which they operate, and the possibilities for change.

The notion that globalization today is new, or that its dynamics and outcomes are different from those that characterized globalization in the past, recycles the themes of disjuncture and difference that in the past have been elaborated as a rationale for voiding prior claims, obligations, and rights. Characterizing changes as fundamentally 'new' and 'different' diverts consideration from whatever elements of continuity, retrogress, or regress it might contain. Globalization defines not a disjuncture or difference, but the end of a brief interregnum and a return to transnational, as opposed to nationally embedded, capitalism. History tells us that globalization may lead not to the integration of the second and third worlds into the first world, but perhaps to the opposite: the *re*-integration, of the first and second worlds into a system of local and trans-local relations similar to the one that, in those areas of the world, pre-dated the crisis of the world wars and the great depression.

# Notes

## 1 Global development

1. Wolf described the consequences for his own discipline. Cultural anthropology, he pointed out, began as world anthropology and sought to develop a global culture history. It was concerned 'with the evolution of culture on a global scale', and with global interconnections (Wolf 1982: 13). Today, it divides its subject matter into distinctive cases, each conceived of as an integrated and bounded system with its society and its characteristic culture, set off against other equally bounded and culturally distinctive systems.
2. The term 'historiography' as used here refers to a body of historical work on a specialized topic.
3. As Colin Leys observes, 'It was implicit that the development that was being discussed was not socialist'; but its capitalist character went unacknowledged: capitalist development was simply 'development' (Leys 1996: 11). 'Development' cuts across many levels, but the term has been usually used to refer to patterns of a nation's growth. Scholars and practitioners concerned with the contemporary 'developing' world articulate themes that produce this 'working definition' of the term:

   a. 'Economic transformation, in the direction of sustained and rapid increases in the national product' and a measure of autonomy in decisions affecting future growth'.
   b. 'Social transformation, in the direction of a more egalitarian distribution of income and widespread access of the population to "social goods" such as education, health services, adequate housing, recreational facilities, and participation in decision-making'.
   c. 'Cultural transformation, in the direction of reaffirmation of national identity and traditions. Emergence, in elites and masses alike, of a new self-image which dispels feelings of second-rate nationality and external subordination' (Portes 1977b: 109).

4. Pessimism and doubt about whether the ever-expanding productive capacity of society leads to human happiness was expressed by the classical theoreticians of liberalism. As Björn Hettne points out, 'classical' nineteenth century views of industrial development were ambivalent: Weber's concerns about bureaucratization, Durkheim's concept of anomie, Marx's concern with alienation. However, in post-World War II modernization theory, 'the negative pole of the polarity shifted to "traditional society," whereas *Gesellschaft* came to be seen as desirable' (Hettne 1995: 51; quoting Wolf 1982: 12).
5. As Ha-Joon Chang argues, the 'official history of capitalism' tells a substantially fictitious story about the development of the world economy over the last few centuries (2002: 13–19); and it is this story that informs current debates about economic development.
6. With apologies to McNeill, who actually wrote:

    > 'the stately structure raised at the close of the nineteenth century to accommodate European history still stands. The roof may be leaky and the plumbing deplorable, but in the absence of any alternative housing. . . . the Victorian edifice continues to give shape to what . . . graduate students learn and what their teachers choose to emphasize amidst all the buzzing . . . confusion of the accessible European past' (1974: 3–4).

7. Among the most notable twentieth-century historians are: Arnold Toynbee, who was concerned to eliminate distinctions between East and West, and Asia and Europe; Marshall Hodgson, who sought to develop a broad vision of global connections and cultural processes; William McNeill, who focused on the emergence of western domination within the developing global system; Fernand Braudel (and, based on his work, the American sociologist, Immanuel Wallerstein), who offered a conception of the whole system grounded in studies of capital and commodity exchange emphasizing cross-cultural connections. But all focus primarily on Europe.
8. This phrasing is borrowed from Andrew Sherratt (2000: 116) who notes that 'bounded structures are secondary phenomena arising from the properties of networks'.
9. See Lewis & Wigen (1997, chapter 3) for a discussion.
10. As, for instance, during the Crusades and in accounts of the capture of Jerusalem in Palestine, which came four years after the proclamation of an ideology of crusade by Pope Urban II at the end of the eleventh century (1095).
11. This was facilitated by the decision of China's imperial court to halt the construction of seagoing ships and to make overseas voyaging illegal in the fifteenth century. The reasons for this are still being debated.
12. Reinhard Koselleck notes that the promulgation of simplified binarisms

or dualistic forms – pairs of concepts which 'divide all of humanity into two groups with opposing modalities' – recurs throughout history (Koselleck 1985: 165). Examples used in the past are Hellene–Barbarian and Christian–Heathen, which degraded the whole of humanity beyond Hellas or Christianity.

13. In fact, Europe's discovery of America owed much to the Muslim doctrine of the sphericity of the Earth, a theory to which scholars had long subscribed at the Islamic centre of scientific studies at the University of Toledo, and one accepted by Christopher Columbus (Bozeman, 1994: 415).
14. European scholars began working with Spanish collections as early as the tenth century, but far more after the twelfth century, translating philosophical and scientific literature almost exclusively from Arabic, rather than Greek texts. It was not until the fall of Constantinople in 1453 that Greek scholars brought to Western Europe knowledge of their own (Greek) civilization. Roger Bacon relied on Arabic translations in developing his contributions to optics, astronomy, the natural sciences and chemistry (Sarton 1957: 83). Copernicus relied on the Arabic translation of Ptolemy's *Almagest* (Sarton 1957: 57).
15. The production of more goods and services and the concomitant rise in *national* income, measured in terms of an estimate of the total money value of all the final goods and services produced in a given one-year period by the factors of production located either within a particular country's borders (gross domestic product – GDP), or owned by a particular country's residents (gross national product – GNP).
16. There are different conceptions of 'development', but most equate development with national economic growth. Some see development as an international relation, based in an international division of labour (Amin 1974, 1976b; Frank 1967; Wallerstein 1974), on imperialism or a 'historical bloc' of forces (Cox 1987; Gill 1990; Wolf 1982). Some are state-centrist but recognize the importance of trans-local circuits (e.g., Polanyi 1944). But, as will be argued further on, the non-national ontologies they suggest continually become subsumed by and assimilated to the national frame.
17. Leys 1996: 5. Leys argues that this was in order to avoid seriously engaging the work of Marx which, during the Cold War, 'was not merely considered unscientific, but in the USA could easily cost you your job' (1996: 6).
18. Dependency writings in the 1970s delineated a variety of alternative paths possible to capitalist development in the periphery, including the 'semi-peripheral', 'dependent', 'associated-dependent' and 'unequal' paths. (See, e.g., Amin 1976; Cardoso 1973; Cardoso & Faletto 1979; Evans 1979; Wallerstein 1997.) Cardoso and Falletto (1979) also delineated different forms of dependency. The theorization of these various types of peripheral development continued to undergo

refinement in the 1980s and 1990s (see, e.g., Becker *et al.* 1987; Hettne 1990; Kay 1989; Larrain 1989).

19. Braudel is generally considered to have been the founding father of global history. Wallerstein was instrumental in establishing the Fernand Braudel Center at Binghamton University (SUNY) in 1976. Some of Braudel's arguments, not featured in Wallerstein's perspective, are incorporated in the approach elaborated further on in this chapter.
20. The period of Wallerstein's study is 1450–1640; but Gourevitch selects 1700 as one of the dates because 1640 proves troublesome for a variety of reasons.
21. Its complexity and sophistication were evident in the technology of shipping and navigation, social organization of production and marketing, and the institutional arrangements for conducting business, such as partnerships, mechanisms for pooling capital, and techniques for monetization and exchange.
22. See, for example, Abu-Lughod (1989), Bairoch (1988), Chase-Dunn and Hall (1993), Frank and Gills (1993), and Schneider (1977).
23. Paul Bairoch points out that, for Europeans, 'What defined luxury food as luxuries (what defined their price) was essentially the impossibility of growing them in temperate climates, which led to long-distance trade with different countries and different cultures' (1988: 195).
24. A debate ensued about the theoretical implications of Wallerstein's 500-year history of the capitalist world system versus Frank and Gills' 1000 years of world-system history. The debate, as Frank and Gills point out, 'is really about how to write world system history . . . about continuity versus discontinuity' (Frank & Gills 2000: 4). Their use of the term 'world system' (without the hyphen) refers to a Eurasian social formation that is larger than Wallerstein's 'world-system', and that has a far longer history. It is used more generally by those exploring the contours and dynamics of macro-sociological relationships over time.
25. Edward Said's book, *Orientalism* (1977) is considered by many to be its founding work. Said argued that 'the Orient' was a construct of 'the West' that shaped the real and imagined existences of those subjected to the fantasy; and that, in turn, this 'othering' process used the Orient to create, define, and solidify the 'West'. The result, as Said notes in *Culture and Imperialism* (1993) is that, while former imperial powers may have physically left the lands they had ruled for decades and centuries, they still dominate them ideologically, culturally, and intellectually.
26. The 1988 *Selected Subaltern Studies* reader edited by Ranajit Guha and Gayatri Spivak, with a foreword by Edward Said, defined the theoretical and methodological contributions of the project. The original subaltern studies collective of scholars were South Asian historians working primarily within a Gramscian tradition. The term 'subaltern' is taken from the writings of Antonio Gramsci (1881–1937), whose perspective

on the political and cultural basis of hegemony has had an important impact, in particular, on Marxist thinking. The term 'subaltern' refers to persons or groups of inferior rank and station, and thus can be employed in discussions of race, class, gender, sexuality, ethnicity, and religion, and 'to signify the centrality of dominant/dominated relationships in history' (Prakash 1994: 1477).

27. See, e.g., Chakrabarty 1992, 2000; Gupta 1998; Prakash 1996; and, for an overview, see Young 2001.
28. One might argue that post-colonial historiography, which appropriates every moment and variety of popular protest and resistance to the anti-colonial struggle, also empties subaltern consciousness and experience of its specificity. Ahmed Aijaz points out that post-colonial theory is the creation of Western-educated intellectuals drawn, generally, from the upper classes of their home countries; so it is not clear why they are better able to reflect the consciousness of the masses (Aijaz 1992: 196). There will be more discussion of this point in Chapter 7.
29. On the intimate relationship between nationalism and class see, e.g., Gellner 1983; Hobsbawm 1990; Wallerstein 1997.
30. In a detailed study of developing countries, Morris and Adelman concluded that 'domestic dominance of government policy' does not assure 'widely beneficial economic growth' (1988: 210).
31. As Eric Wolf pointed out, 'the world of humankind constitutes a manifold, a totality of interconnected processes; and inquiries that disassemble this totality into bits and then fail to reassemble it, falsify reality' (1982: 3).
32. See, e.g., Susan Strange's discussion of structures of power – key structures through which power is exercised: the *security structure*, which provides protection to human beings; the *production structure*, the primary means of creating value and wealth in a society; the *finance structure*, which determines who has access to money, how, and on what terms; and the *knowledge structure*, which 'determines what knowledge is discovered, how it is stored, and who communicates it by what means to whom and on what terms' (Strange 1994: 121).
33. Elites in the third world enjoy the same level of income and standard of living as elites in the developed countries (Sunkel 1973: 150).

## Chapter 2 The origins and development of capitalism

1. Following in this tradition, Max Weber defined capitalism as an economic system based on the production and rational exchange of goods within a market framework (1978: Vol. II, 920, 922). Werner Sombart (1902) equates capitalism with market society.
2. Agricultural wage labour was found throughout the Roman Empire. In the Empire's most important province, Egypt, wage labour played a major role on commercial estates. Peter Temin argues that 'despite

Rome's use of slavery, free hired labour was the rule, not the exception, in the rest of the early Roman empire' (2004: 516).

3. For classical political economists, competition in the market is an ideal mechanism for maximizing welfare; while, for Marx, the basic objective of capitalism is to maximize capital accumulation, and this does not necessarily lead to the production of goods and services that people want and need.
4. These accounts, also referred to as 'demographic', or 'neo-Malthusian', or 'neo-Ricardian' explanations, build on Emmanuel Le Roy Ladurie's (1976) definition of the basic mechanisms and consequences of population shifts in early modern Europe.
5. Wallerstein argues that a point of diminishing returns was reached after nearly a millennium of surplus expropriation within the feudal mode of production; unfavourable climatological conditions that lowered the productivity of the soil, and increased epidemics.
6. As Stephen Sanderson observed, *contra* Dobb, 'the game of spiralling status emulation was played by landlord classes throughout the agrarian world without necessarily resulting in increased levels of exploitation and peasant flight' (Sanderson 1994: 27).
7. Brenner seems to acknowledge this in stating that 'changes in relative factor scarcities consequent upon demographic changes exerted an effect on the distribution of income in medieval Europe only as they were, so to speak, refracted through the prism of changing social-property relations and fluctuating balances of class forces' (Brenner 1982: 21).
8. Real wages doubled in most countries and cities during the century following the first occurrence of the plague. As land became more abundant relative to labour, prices of agricultural goods declined relative to manufactured goods, especially in relation to manufactured goods with high labour content. Land rents as well as interest rates went down both in absolute terms and relative to wages. Landowners began to lose, while incomes of labourers, peasants, and women rose (Pamuk 2007: 294).
9. In Britain, the crisis in seigneurial incomes was exemplified by the Wars of the Roses (1455 and 1485).
10. As Claudio Katz describes it, aristocratic attempts to restore feudal controls over the cultivators 'were met by violent peasant resistance organized village by village and built upon the long years of experience of conflict against the lords' (1993: 372).
11. Patricia Croot and David Parker argue that such innovations were necessary for the survival of smaller farms that lacked the capital for large sheep flocks, the typical cash generator of sixteenth century England (Croot & Parker 1985: 80). There are cases in which even open-field villages successfully adopted new crop-rotation and breeding techniques (see Havinden 1962; Jones 1974, and the works cited there; and O'Brien 1977).

12. Tom Williamson maintains that, in any case, crop yields in the period 1700–1870 'were largely independent of farm size'. In fact, 'on average, large farms actually produced *lower* yields than small ones because small farms were generally found in areas of more fertile soil and large ones in less favoured areas' (Williamson 2002: 19–20).
13. There is an ongoing debate about categories of labour and labour conditions which count as wage labour or proletarianization. According to Ann Kussmaul (1981), when farms used outside labourers in the mid-eighteenth century, up to one-half were so-called 'servants in husbandry' who were hired on an annual contract, lived in the farmer's house, and were paid room and board plus a little spending money. Adding family farms to this, no more than 30 per cent of agricultural labour was done on the basis of wages (cited in Albritton 1993: 431).
14. Fully commodified labour power is characterized by the following:

    (1) Workers are fully separated from all means of production and have no means of support outside their wage; this means they must be paid a 'subsistence' wage and paid frequently (usually weekly) in money form.
    (2) The relation between capital and labour is totally impersonal in the sense that capital treats labour simply as a commodity input.
    (3) Labour must, at least in principle, be mobile in order to be able to respond to changes in supply and demand in the labour market.
    (4) No form of extra-economic coercion interferes with the labour market, whether from labour, capital, landlords, the state, or any other interventionist source (Albritten 1993: 424).

15. 'The lengthening of the workday . . . permits an expansion of the scale of production without any change in the amount of capital invested in machinery and buildings' (Marx 1990: 529).
16. See, for a discussion, Marx (1990: 517–118) and, as cited there, annual *Reports of the Inspectors of Factories, Reports of the Children's Employment Commission*, and *Reports on Public Health*, published in London.
17. In irrigation and many other agricultural technologies Europe 'lagged behind China, India, Japan, and parts of Southeast Asia' (Pomerantz 2000:45). According to Pomerantz, Europeans applied lessons learned from India and China to their tropical colonies, but not at home until well into the nineteenth century (Pomerantz 2000: 45).
18. According to Perry Anderson, Absolutism was essentially 'a redeployed apparatus of feudal domination, the new political carapace of a threatened nobility . . . in the epoch of transition to capitalism' (1974: 18, 42).
19. Before 1800, most of what was exported from the New World, other than gold and silver, was luxuries: furs, tobacco, and sugar (Pomerantz

2000: 192); from the East, the main exports to Europe were spices, jewellery, textiles, porcelains, tea, silks, paintings, lacquerware, metalwork, and ivory.

20. Early modern Europe's main source of grain, timber products, and raw materials for textiles (Kellenbenz 1976: 326).
21. The term 'born global' has been applied to firms. It challenges the assumption that firms build a stable domestic position before starting international activities (for an explication see Knight & Cavusgil 1996).
22. For good introductions to Braudel's work see Helleiner (1990), and Germain (1996). Wallerstein's conception of capitalism as a world system was inspired by Braudel's argument that capitalism occupies the uppermost of these levels, above the spheres of local and national life. However, Wallerstein ignores key elements of Braudel's conception of capitalism and how it develops.
23. This borrows from John Lie's definition of 'region' (Lie 1993: 278).
24. As Braudel notes, '[T]he extraordinary thing is that such images should still be with us today in the language spoken by politicians and journalists, in works of popularization and in the teaching of economics, when doubt long ago entered the minds of the specialists' (1984: Vol. III, 628–629).
25. This war was misnamed by German historians as the 'Seven Years' War' – it actually lasted for nine (Fischer 1996: 135).
26. The common people regarded the 'moral economy' as the birthright of 'free born Englishmen': the belief that members of the community had the right, enforceable by law, of basic material security, either through labour at a fair wage or through poor relief, and protection from violence, theft and extreme oppression. Closely associated with this belief was the conviction that members of the community possessed certain rights, enforceable in law, including that of subsistence, if not through labour at a fair rate of pay then through poor relief (Thane 1990: 7). In France, ' Liberty, Equality, and Fraternity' – the 'Rights of Man' – was a call, not to new ideas, but for a return to the moral economy. One of the fundamental articles of the Declaration of the Rights of Man and of the Citizen proclaimed that subsistence for the poor was a fundamental right; it declared that 'Public relief is a sacred debt'.
27. Many historians assume that England did not experience a form of state corresponding to the absolute monarchies of the continent because English monarchs could not take the property of their subjects without their consent in Parliament. But continental absolutism was also based on the rights of property.
28. In the first half of the sixteenth century, many European towns and governments produced new ordinances for the relief and regulation of the poor. Most of the schemes and regulations represented a 'forceful introduction of secular authority into the field of social welfare and placed at least part of the responsibility for organizing poor relief in lay

hands'. In addition, most of them 'centralized control of a miscellany of existing charitable institutions and mechanisms' (Slack 1988: 9).
29. Pat Thane points out that 'There is a real question as to whether the vastly richer Britain of the twentieth century is relatively more or less generous to its poor than the England of the seventeenth and eighteenth centuries' (1998: 55). Paul Slack thinks it likely 'that Englishmen gave more to the poor in 1700 than they had ever done; and that they gave a greater part of it through an organized system of public welfare and not through private charity, of whatever kind' (Slack 1988: 172).
30. By the beginning of the eighteenth century, all cites with a population of more than 5000 had an *hôpital general*. The monarchy financed a system of *ateliers de charité* in the 1770s to provide supplementary income to the able-bodied poor, primarily in the countryside in months when there were no opportunities for work (Lis & Soly 1979: 200–209).
31. The legal measures were never fully implemented, however, because of resistance from aristocratic office-holders whose job it was to apply them (Zöllner 1982: 18).
32. Based on the feudal mode of production, in which heavy extraction of surplus from small producers is applied through extra-economic coercion and economic growth is primarily extensive – through the expansion of the area under cultivation.

## 3 Industrialization and the expansion of capital: core and periphery redefined

1. In the 1980s, a number of prominent economic historians questioned the empirical validity and theoretical utility of the notion. (see, e.g., Cameron 1981, 1985; Crafts 1983; Fores 1981; Harley 1982; North 1981: 162). Cameron (1985) provides a brief survey of the scholarly objections voiced at the time Arnold Toynbee invoked the phrase, in his *Lectures on the Industrial Revolution*, published in 1884. De Tocqueville had used the phrase as early as 1850–1851 in his *Souvenirs* (1978: 113–114), but it may have been used earlier by others.
2. Karl Polanyi's analysis of Europe's nineteenth-century market system (in *The Great Transformation*, 1944) inspired the notion of markets as embedded and disembedded. Polanyi argued that, before the rise of the unregulated market system at the end of the eighteenth century, exchange relations were governed by principles of economic behaviour (reciprocity, reallocation, and householding) that were 'embedded' in society and politics. At the end of the eighteenth century, however, states began to institute changes that formed the basis of the disembedded capitalist development that characterized Europe's nineteenth-century industrial expansion.
3. Moreover, anti-machinery riots between 1776 and 1823 'very considerably delayed the introduction there of the spinning jenny, scribbling engine, and flying shuttle' (Charlesworth *et al.* 1996: 24).

4. The term, 'Absolutism' was used by those who became opposed to centralized administration when monarchs attempted to introduce reforms that encroached on aristocratic power and privilege. However, in historical writing, the term 'absolutism' is used to refer to states that supposedly had a centralized administration applying laws uniformly over all the inhabitants of a territory. More on this in Note 7, below.
5. Attempts by elites to end their subordination to 'absolutist' states occurred in different ways. Aristocrats in France attempted to seize the state in 1789, triggering a move against them by bourgeois elements and an uprising of urban workers and peasants. The restoration that followed consolidated a conservative absolutism more compatible with the interests of aristocrats and elements allied with them. Revolutions broke out in what is now Belgium (1789), Switzerland (1792), the Netherlands (1794), Poland (1794), and Ireland (1798). Ruling oligarchies fell at the hand of French armies in many parts of Italy and Switzerland, including Genoa (1797), Venice (1797), and Berne (1798). Sweden's King Gustavus III was assassinated (1792), as was Russia's Czar Paul I (1801).
6. Adam Smith coined the term 'mercantile system' to describe the system of political economy that sought to enrich the country by restraining imports and encouraging exports. While mercantilist policies were concerned to expand exports and limit imports (in order to accumulate bullion), industrial capitalist policies sought the same end (in order to maintain the existing social system).

   Friedrich List, in his book *The National System of Political Economy* (1841) argued that countries must first develop their domestic markets before opening themselves up to international competition. The book had an enormous impact on German conservatives, who extracted from List's argument the need for protection, but rejected his prescription regarding the development of the domestic market (see Cowan & Shenton 1995).
7. The term 'absolutism', 'a commonly used pejorative political catchword in western European political discourse' during the eighteenth century (Blänkner 2005), was meant to convey 'absolute power' – which, in the middle ages and early modern period, denoted 'a regime where the ruler is not limited by institutions outside the kingship itself' (Bonney 1987: 94). Only France, Spain, and Austria are considered to have actually achieved this ideal. But even these states continued to be conglomerates where different systems operated. Under Louis XIV, France was a patchwork of political–legal structures, in which local and provincial institutions (estates, parliaments, sovereign courts) provided a counterbalance to monarchical power (see Morrill 1978).
8. This 'unfree' market was, according to Braudel, 'fairer' and 'more truly competitive' than what anti-Absolutist groups characterized as the 'free' market (Braudel 1982: 412–413).

9. The rentier capitalism 'which arose from the ownership of land by a numerically small elite' was initially the most important form of capitalist wealth in Britain (Cain & Hopkins 1993: 24).
10. Especially where they were needed to meet demand for luxury articles such as tapestries and porcelain; or where mass production for military needs was needed (Kellenbenz 1976: 247, 248).
11. In the first half of the eighteenth century, home industries increased their output by 7 per cent, export industries by 76 per cent; and then between 1750 and 1770 by another 7 per cent and 80 per cent, respectively (Hobsbawm 1968: 26). See also Deane and Cole (1967: 78) and Mathias (1983: 94).
12. This excludes goods produced both for the home market and for export: e.g., high-quality furniture, tools and utensils, glass, as well as building materials.
13. To paraphrase Perry Anderson's previously quoted description of the Absolutist state.
14. Though, the degree of discipline involved in the transition to industrial capitalism 'would hardly have been conceivable' without, in addition to new forms of exploitation, 'the authoritarian attitudes and laws' of an earlier time (Gillis 1983: 165).
15. As discussed in Chapter 2, both the classical and Marxist traditions assume that, in capitalism, competition drives the capitalist to improve the productivity of labour by technical means. But in monopoly conditions, there is no pressure on capitalists to do this.
16. Coal increased from 49 million tons in 1850 to 147 million tons in 1880. There were 200,000 coal miners in Britain in 1850, half a million in 1880, and 1.2 million in 1914 (Hobsbawm 1968: 116).
17. American shipbuilding expanded at a faster rate than British shipbuilding, and, by 1860, it had almost caught up.
18. For example: the Siemens–Martin open-hearth furnace (1867), which made it possible to increase productivity; the Gilchrist–Thomas process (1877–1878), which allowed the use of phosphoric ores for steel manufacture.
19. 'In order to effect a fall in the value of labour-power, the increase in the productivity of labour must seize upon those branches of industry whose products determine the value of labour-power, and consequently either belong to the class of customary means of subsistence or are capable of supplying the place of those means . . . But an increase in the productiveness of the labour in those branches of industry which supply neither the necessaries of life, nor the means of production for such necessaries, leaves the value of labour-power undisturbed' (Marx 1990: Vol. I, 432).
20. In the contractions of the late 1860s (in textiles especially) and mid-1870s (industry-wide), employers attempted to cut labour costs by increasing performance, and the question of the nature and size of the

workload, and the replacement of skilled by unskilled and semi-skilled hands, supplanted wages as the major issue in labour disputes (Landes 1969: 319).

21. The value of labour was also reduced by forcing workers to consume poorer quality food, as, for instance, making them dependent on the potato crop for sustenance, which allowed them to survive on the lowest possible wage. The encroachment of potatoes on bread 'precipitated 'a regular dietary class-war' (Thompson 1975: 145).
22. In France and Germany the first factories were state prisons, 'whose purpose was both to make money and to discipline the inmate population' (Gillis 1983: 162).
23. The French National Assembly's *Decree upon the Organization of Trades and Professions* of 14 June 1791 prohibited all combinations, strikes, and agreements between workers to refuse to work, or between employers to refuse to give work except on specified conditions. The Act of 29 June 1871 gave legal recognition to trade unions (Trade Union Act 34 and 35 Victoria, c.31). But another Act of the same date (Criminal Law Amendment Acts 34 and 35, Victoria, c.32) re-established the previous situation in a new form (Marx 1990: Vol. I, 903).
24. See Chapter 2 for a discussion.
25. This connection 'appears irrefutable'. The reorganization of public support beginning in the 1770s occurred in places where the expansion of labour-intensive industries was occurring (Lis & Soly 1979: 205).
26. Workshops were connected to workhouses and orphanages in Hamburg, Berlin, and Copenhagen (Kellenbenz 1976: 247).
27. Wage rates and poor relief were used to keep 'a fluid supply of labour near at hand' in the towns, and were 'manipulated in the interests of farmers to maintain an adequate supply of labour to meet the highest seasonal demands' (Mock 1981: 26).
28. Beginning in the last decade of the seventeenth century, the economics literature suggests that most thinkers of the period were in favour 'of increased consumption, both by the middle class and the working classes' as an incentive for 'enterprise and industriousness' (Perrotta 1997: 296).
29. Developments in China, Japan, and Europe were strikingly similar in this respect. Between 1500 and 1750, the consumption of 'non-essentials' by ordinary Chinese rose. Japan's sumptuary edicts complained of peasants eating too well, using expensive specialty woods, and having overly decorative clothing, umbrellas, and gold, ivory, and silver ornaments; of people in farming villages buying 'furniture, medicines, and other specialised luxury goods from far away, while village stores stocked a variety of ready-made perfumes, hair oils, incense, and paper' (Burke 1993; cited in Pomerantz 2000: 131). Pomerantz notes that it 'remains unclear how much "luxury" consumption there was among

plebeians'; but that it 'probably drew disproportionate comment' from the upper classes even when the total amount, as with tea and sugar, 'remained quite small' (2000: 135). 'Even in England, it seems unlikely that working-class consumption of tobacco, tea, and sugar was of much significance before the 1840s' (Pomerantz 2000: 151).

30. The concern became to reduce wages to a minimum of 'subsistence'. Pre-Smithian economists generally advocated higher wages, which they defined as 'subsistence wages': 'the wage for the simplest work that ensured that the worker was well-fed, well-clothed, and well-protected from the elements'; and that not only covered the worker's annual costs, but allowed him 'to be free on holidays' (Perrotta 1997: 303; citing James Steuart [1767] 1966: 273, 275).
31. Increased consumption of tea and sugar was thought to waste the time and destroy the industry of the labouring class. Snuff-taking, tea and dram drinking, and ribbons, ruffles, and silks, were seen as responsible for high labour and servants' wages (Furniss 1965: 153; see also 154–156). Trade of sugar, tea, and coffee was for the upper classes; but the consumption of these items had 'spread slowly down the social scale' (O'Brien 1982: 10).
32. For instance, Rousseau and his adherents contended that luxury and increased consumption had corrupted French culture and had made men physically weak and caused them to forget civic virtue. However, the traditional luxury of the aristocrats, 'which had been a means of legitimating the political power of the nobility and was therefore part of the old social order', was not condemned (Perrotta 1997: 308). For a review of the eighteenth century debates on luxury, see Berg and Eger (2003: 7–27) and Berry (1994: 126–176).
33. Employers called into use the language and protocols of military operations. They saw themselves as 'captains' of industry and their task as one of 'conscripting, training, and commanding' an industrial 'army' which they housed in large-scale, multi-family tenements or rental 'barracks'. In Prussia, miners wore uniforms and saluted their supervisors (Gillis 1983: 154).
34. Private property had become 'enshrined as an absolute right in the struggles against Stuart and French absolutisms' (Ward 1977: 56).
35. Labour organization had played an important role in radical movements in France and England during the 1790s; and demobilization after the war contributed to the renewal of *sans-culotte* and trade union activity in France. Republican, liberal, or reformist army officers in Italy, Germany, Russia, and Spain joined the ranks of secret societies and radical movements (e.g., the Italian Carbonari, German Conditionals, Russian Decembrist conspiracy); officers and foot soldiers alike figured prominently in revolts and putsches in 1819, 1822, 1825, 1834, 1839, and 1844, and in the Europe-wide revolutions in 1820, 1830, and 1848.

36. See Halperin (2004, Appendix A3) for a chronology of insurrections, rebellions, revolutions, uprisings, violent strikes, riots, and demonstrations in Europe following 1789–1945.
37. By this is meant 'masses raised by universal conscription, armed and equipped by large-scale state-intervention in industry' (Howard 1961: 9). See, for an overview of this issue, Howard (1961: 8–39). Russia conscripted large numbers of men for the Crimean War; but contrast a description of the forces raised for that war (Royle 1999: 91–92) with the account of the French mobilization in 1870–1871 (and its connection to the rising of the Paris Commune) in Taithe (2001: esp. 6–13, 22–28, 38–47).
38. It seems unlikely that owners of wealth would not be conscious of the externalities associated with the application of large masses of labour to industrial production. But if they were not, would they have remained unconscious of this danger after Marx spelled it out for them in the widely read and endlessly cited *Communist Manifesto*? Marx, as in much of his writing, was perhaps only reflecting a general perception of his times when he wrote that

    > *The advance of industry . . . replaces the isolation of the labourers . . . by their revolutionary combination, due to association. The development of Modern Industry, therefore, cuts from under its feet the very foundation on which the bourgeoisie produces and appropriates products.* (Marx 1967: 93–94).

39. Jules Ferry, the founder of the modern French colonial empire expressed the general view in a speech delivered in 1883:

    > *The great states of modern Europe, the moment their industrial power is founded, are confronted with an immense and difficult problem, which is the basis of industrial life, the very condition of existence – the question of markets. Have you not seen the great industrial nations one by one arrive at a colonial policy? And can we say that this colonial policy is a luxury for modern nations? Not at all . . . it is, for all of us, a necessity, like the market itself.* (quoted in Langer 1931: 286–287).

40. See, e.g. Cairncross (1953: 225), Cameron (1961: 123, 152), Lévy (1951–1952. 228), Lewis (1972: 27 58), Sée (1942: 360), and Trebilcock (1981).
41. Britain devoted a substantially smaller proportion of her national output and savings to home investment than did any of her major competitors (Floud 1981: 12–17). There was a brief home investment boom near the end of the nineteenth century when an abrupt paralysis of the market for foreign loans occurred (one of the proximate causes of the Great Depression of the 1870s–1890).

42. Committee on Finance and Industry, Macmillan Report (1931), p. 171.
43. Lenin recognized that profitable investment opportunities could be provided at home with an adequate and sustained rise in the consumption of the masses. But, as John Strachey notes, this was, for Lenin, only 'a theoretical possibility to be dismissed as utterly incompatible with the real balance of power in any capitalist society' (Strachey 1959: 117).
44. See, also, Cain (1979), Davis and Huttenback (1988), and Engerman (1994). For Germany, see Wehler (1969); for France, see Langer (1931), and Wesseling (1997).
45. A. K. Cairncross asserts that French industry was 'starved for capital' (1953: 225). The issue was a matter of debate from at least the 1830s. See, Landes (1954: 260, n9). See also Kindleberger (1964), Lévy (1951–1952), and Sée (1942).
46. The minerals prominent in tropical trade today did not come to the fore until the end of the nineteenth century. Minerals amounted to only 13 per cent of tropical exports in 1913, compared with 29 per cent in 1965, and were prominent in the exports only of Peru and Mexico (Lewis 1978a: 201). Moreover, Britain's terms of trade were unfavourable throughout the nineteenth century and, until around 1920 (see figures in Strachey 1959: 149–151), while terms of trade improved for the less developed countries throughout that period. It was only in the 1950s, and again in the 1980s, that terms of trade in primary goods deteriorated (Bairoch 1993: 113–114). The exception – and, as Arthur Lewis points out, it is an important one for Latin America (and for arguments developed in this chapter concerning cheap food imports) – is terms of trade for sugar which, relative to manufactured goods, deteriorated by 25–35 per cent between 1830 and 1910.
47. W. Stanley Jevons' Law of Indifference states that, under ideal market conditions – perfectly homogeneous goods, a legal framework that provides for the enforcement of contracts and property rights, and traders who are knowledgeable profit maximizers – people are indifferent about what they buy or sell and with whom they trade (Jevons 1931: 90–92).
48. This can be seen today in regard to patent monopolies. The logic of patent monopoly is to have a safe and secure distribution system aimed at selling smaller numbers of expensive medicines to a wealthy class, rather than trying to distribute large numbers of cheap medicines at a few cents a day to the many poor. When large pharmaceutical companies speak about 'growing the market' in developing countries, it is the wealthy segment of the market they have in mind' (Drahos & Braithwaite 2002: 6).
49. British overseas investment – in particular British railway and harbour and ship building for Baltic, and later North American, grain – produced a backflow of cheaply produced raw materials and foodstuffs that did not compete with domestic English agriculture and drove domestic working-class wages down. Britain imported a third of its food after

1870, including nearly half of its bread grains (Barratt Brown 1970: 66; E. H. P. Brown 1968: 166).

50. In the 1850s, 'mass flight from the land – to railways, mines, cities and overseas – produced a welcome rural labour shortage and slightly higher wages' (Hobsbawm 1968: 84).
51. Britain's 'industrial revolution' was limited to the export sector and to the great centres of the export industry in the North and 'Celtic Fringe'.
52. Charles I of England (1600–1649) had launched a major programme of warship building and created a fleet of powerful ships; and shipbuilding became the basis for the expansion of industrial growth in Britain (R. Davis 1979: 64), fuelled by massive state investment in naval and military power.
53. See, e.g., Baran (1957), Chase-Dunn 1975, Evans (1979), and Portes (1985). This is a prominent theme in studies of the 'periphery'. Fernando Henrique Cardoso and Enzo Faletto state that their influential study of Latin American development 'does away with the idea that class relations in dependent countries are like those of the central countries during their early development' (Cardoso & Faletto 1979: 22). They describe Latin American societies as characterized either by a structure of 'oligarchic-bourgeois domination' centred on the alliance of a national bourgeoisie of local producing groups (plantation and mine owners, merchants and bankers) with local traditional oligarchies and bureaucratic–military states usually opposed to 'any effort to convert the dominant paternalism into a more efficient bureaucracy'; or by a weak bourgeois sector and oligarchic groups of large landholders linked to mining and plantation enclaves (Cardoso & Faletto 1979: 66–73).
54. See e.g. Blum (1978: 422–24), Cannadine (1990: 391–444), and Maier (1975).
55. E.g., Wallerstein (1974, 1991). 'Far from the bourgeoisie having overthrown the aristocracy, we have instead the aristocracy becoming the bourgeoisie' (Wallerstein 1991: 58).
56. There are numerous variations of this schema. Coates distinguishes between two different patterns of capitalist development. In 'First-Wave' capitalism, 'indigenous middle classes set the pace of economic change, presiding over an industrialization process'. In 'Second-Wave' capitalism, the move from feudalism to capitalism was fused and, as a result, industrial bourgeoisies were weaker and modernizing aristocracies were stronger (Coates 2000: 227). Lenin (1917) used the same set of characteristics to define two different roads: the 'American' and 'Prussian' roads (note, however, that only one of these roads is found in Europe). See, also, Kees van der Pijl's two-road schema based on a similar set of distinctions (1998: 78–79).
57. The classic study is the one by Lefebvre (1991 [1976]). See also Cobban (1971), Furet (1971), Rudé (1989), and Soboul (1962).

58. The *ancien regime* began the breakup of large estates into a multiplicity of small proprietorships long before 1789; and they introduced standing armies, a permanent bureaucracy, national taxation, a codified law, and the beginnings of a unified market. Johnson maintains that the number of landed proprietorships in France was scarcely smaller before 1789 than it was in the 1970s (Johnson 1979: 155). Nor were the ideas and values promulgated in the Revolution the product of a new and revolutionary class. De Tocqueville observed that 'many of the sentiments and opinions' which he had always regarded as products of the Revolution, and 'many of the customs commonly thought to stem from it exclusively had already entered into our mores' (1955: ix).
59. Chirot 1977: 223. A number of Marxist scholars once accorded to the bourgeoisie the central role in England's seventeenth-century revolutions. Hill (1940) and Stone (1972) are the standard accounts, but both have revised their views. Stone later argued for a more complex model of causes, but maintained that the result of the events of the 1640s was a bourgeois revolution (Stone 1981); Hill (1981) later conceded that the Revolution was not brought about or intended by the bourgeoisie. Both agree that the Revolution nonetheless resulted in establishing the political supremacy of the bourgeoisie after 1688. See also Clark (1985, 1986) and Hexter (1961).
60. As Max Weber (1927) recognized, it was the centralized bureaucracy, not the rational businessman, that exemplified the industrial age. Rationalized systems of social organization do not revolutionize social structures; they only function as a means to the furtherance of existing structures.

    Throughout the nineteenth century, the nobility in Europe was an expanding, not a declining, class. From 1871–1918, the German emperor created over a thousand new nobles. The English peerage increased by the creation of 200 new peers between 1888 and 1914 (Tipton & Aldritch 1987a: 77). Spain had 118 grandes and 535 other titled nobles in 1787. By 1896 the number had nearly doubled to 207 and 1206 (Herr 1977: 99).
61. The practice of gerrymandering and disproportionate allocation of seats retained, for most of Europe, a clear overrepresentation of conservative rural voters, throughout the century and the subsequent one.
62. It is often assumed that the repeal of the Corn Laws (1846) marked the end of the power of the landlords in Britain. But the Corn Laws had not been shoring up a declining sector; they were retaining the high profits generated during the Napoleonic War years. Wheat prices did not fall until the onset of the Great Depression in the 1870s (see Hobsbawm 1968: 197).
63. After World War I, the Labour Party was still unable to gain significant strength in rural areas. Labour propagandists were refused halls or

muted by the presence of the local squire in their audience. In 1929 the Labour Party did not carry a single predominantly rural district (Gosnell 1930: 19).

64. Ogg (1930: 174), citing the report of a Land Enquiry Committee, appointed in 1912 to investigate wages, hours, housing, and conditions of land tenure.
65. In France, the small peasant plots were inadequate to the needs of their owners, and their size made it impossible to introduce the kinds of improvements needed to make them more productive. Production continued to be for local rather than national consumption.
66. According to a semi-official Land Enquiry Committee report in 1912; cited in Ogg (1930: 174).
67. See, for a discussion of these elements in European development, Halperin (1997: especially Chs. 1,2, 3, 4, and 7).
68. Belgium used its own capital and resources to finance and build railroads at home which, thereafter, made it possible to pursue a 'dynamic export offensive'. In Germany, railroad building 'gave the development process a lasting impetus' (Senghaas 1985: 29).
69. See Hobsbawm (1968: 111–15). This will be discussed further in Chapter 4.
70. This follows the distinction drawn by Caporaso (1978) between 'dependence' and 'dependency,' which distinguishes between the external reliance of well-integrated nation states on one another ('dependence'), and the integration of less-developed and less-homogeneous societies into the global division of labour ('dependency'). Interactions among the former, he argues, have consequences different from interactions among the latter.
71. German landowners feared that the expansion of employment in factories would increase both the danger of socialism and the power of the Polish population. Through their opposition, they were able to hamper industrial development plans in the 1890s and to prevent their revival after 1902. (See, e.g. Tipton 1976: 115–116. See also Richter 1938: 48–52). Much of the politics of the time was dominated by fear of industrialization; but most explanations treat this as an aberration to the general trend towards modernization and industrialization.
72. The state played an active role in the industrial development of Britain, France, Belgium, Scandinavia, Germany, Italy, Eastern Europe, and Russia. See Berend and Ránki (1976: Ch. 4), Gerschenkron (1962: 119–152), Henderson (1958), Jörberg (1973), Mathias (1983: Chs. 3–5), Mori (1979), Pounds (1959), Price (1981: 159–168), and Supple (1973).
73. This table is based on Halperin (2004, Ch. 3).
74. For a complete list of elements comprising 'dependent development' and a discussion of each, see Halperin (1997, Ch. 5).
75. This was true of wheat production, for example, which comprised half of Britain's grain output in 1870 (Mathias 1983: 316).

76. Locally, state-controlled systems of paramilitary and police forces, and concentrations of regular troops on permanent garrison duty in working-class areas of industrial towns; elsewhere, the opening up and control of territories for exploitation by armed aggression.
77. Rubinstein 1983: 17; in Cain and Hopkins 1993: 37. The European 'Age of Reform' was an age of 'pragmatic conservatism rather than liberalism'. Chris Bayley argues that Britain's great Reform Act of 1832 'did little to challenge aristocratic domination of politics, indeed it may have been designed to perpetuate it' (1989: 236).

**4 City states and nationalism**

1. Commercial and landed classes merged in the Italian city states; in the Netherlands, where a commercial and industrial bourgeoisie ran the cities and the Dutch nobility maintained power in the rural provinces; England was characterized by a synthesis between the merchants of London and landowners (Tilly 1994: 12).
2. Jane Jacobs argued that cities are the means by which economies expand and diversify. They grow by trading, not with a rural hinterland, but with other cities (Jacobs 1969: 35), and by myriad borrowings (with necessary improvisations) of what has been successful in other cities (1969).
3. The term 'national market' denotes 'the economic coherence achieved within a given political unit'. The unit, here, corresponds to the 'territorial state', which might also be called the 'nation state' (Braudel 1984: 277). Tilly has argued that, after 1700, the 'national' state became the dominant form of rule in Europe: a state that controlled a well-defined continuous territory, was relatively centralized and differentiated from other organizations, and sought to monopolize the means of coercion (Tilly 1994: 4–5). Braudel distinguishes the *Stadtwirtschaft*, the city-based economy such as existed in medieval Italian and German city states and in Amsterdam, from the *Territorialwirtschaft*, based on an integrated 'national market', as developed in England. He maintains that in the eighteenth century England became a compact and densely woven national market within the British Isles as a whole (Braudel 1982: Vol. III, 368).
4. The Bombay to Thana line was constructed in 1853 to link the cotton fields of the Deccan to the port of Bombay. Other lines were built to link the coalfields of the northeast to Calcutta. The construction of the East Indian railway brought the coalfields of Bengal and Bihar to life, and led to the establishment of engineering works at railway junctions and of modern ironworks at Barakar (Bengal) (Hubbard 1935: 242).
5. In the Malayan peninsula, railroads were built in the 1880s and 1890s to connect the major tin-mining towns on the west coast to ports; and later to transport latex from rubber plantations to the ports. In Java, lines

linked the port of Samarang to the main area of sugar plantations; in Batavia to tea and coffee and sugar plantations; in Sumatra, to facilitate the export of tobacco and coal; in South Africa to bring diamonds from Kimberley and gold from Johannesburg to the ports.

6. Military considerations after 1857 motivated the network that linked Madras, Bombay, Calcutta, Delhi, and Lahore. In French Indo-China a line was built, for political considerations, from Saigon through the most densely populated part of the country in the south. The conquest of Tonkin required building, for military purposes, another line in the North.
7. Port facilities and roads took up another 5 per cent; 23 per cent went to other kinds of public utilities and public works; 12 per cent went to mining and extractive industries. About 15 per cent went into 'miscellaneous outlets, of which plantations must have been important'. The remaining 4 per cent 'was channelled into manufacturing (Latham 1978: 54–55).
8. Hobsbawm argues that, in fact, 'many of the railways constructed were and remained quite irrational by any transport criterion, and consequently never paid more than the most modest profits, if they paid any at all. This was perfectly evident at the time . . .'. What was also evident is that investors were looking 'for any investment likely to yield more than the 3.4 per cent of public stocks.' Railway returns eventually settled down at an average of about 4 per cent (Hobsbawm 1968: 111, see also pp. 113–115).
9. Each Italian city subjugated its own *contado*, a dependent territory or peripheral hinterland that then became an integral part of the city state (Tilly 1994: 18). These *contados* were subject territories and under the authority of the city that provided taxes, recruits for the army, and food supplies, as well as a buffer for the defence of the city.
10. The first city states were in Sumer (fourth millennium BCE).
11. These were called *negeri*, a Sanskrit word meaning 'city' but which in modern Malay has come to mean 'state' (Reid 2000).
12. Antwerp became the main port for the trans-shipment of gold and silver from the New World. It became a great money market and financial centre, and played a central role in the economy of the Spanish Empire. However, it did not become a city state. At the end of the sixteenth century, its fortunes declined with those of Spain and, by the early years of the seventeenth century, Amsterdam had emerged to take its place.
13. The 'Marxist' view of nationalism was systematized not by Marx and Engels, but by their successors. The classic Marxist work on the subject is Bauer (1907). Lenin provided the basic formulation:

    *Throughout the world, the period of the final victory of capitalism over feudalism was linked up with national movements. The economic basis of these movements is that in order to achieve*

> *complete victory for commodity production the bourgeoisie must capture the home market, must have politically united territories with a population speaking the same language* (Lenin, n.d.: Vol. IV, 250).

14. In the Netherlands, a commercial and industrial bourgeoisie ran the cities, while the Dutch nobility maintained power in the rural provinces. While 'the source of political power was officially located in the province, the economic and demographic power that underlay it was that of the city' (Parker 2004: 179). The rich merchants of Amsterdam dominated the province of Holland, which supplied up to 60 per cent of the revenues of the federal treasury. So, in effect, the merchants of Amsterdam controlled the state itself (Parker 2004: 177).
15. In 1968, these areas still ranked generally lowest among British regions in employment, housing, education, health, environment, and personal income (Hammond 1968).
16. In fact, the Piedmontese traveller who went to Florence, Rome, or Venice, used to say that he was going to Italy (Graf 1911: 5–6). Though some Italian provinces had allied with Piedmont as a means of gaining autonomy from other overlords (e.g., Sicily from Naples), they were annexed by Piedmont against their will (D. M. Smith 1971: 33).
17. The north, Gramsci wrote, was an 'octopus' which enriched itself at the expense of the South, 'its economic increment in direct proportion to the impoverishment of the economy and the agriculture of the South' (1971: 71).
18. This was a widespread current of thought. Alfredo Niceforo writes:

> *Within the single womb of a political Italy two societies exist, wholly different in their level of civilization, in their social life, in their moral colour: northern Italy on the one hand, and southern Italy on the other; in a word,* two Italies, *quite distinct. While one of these two Italies, that of the north, can be seen to possess the physiognomy of a more diffuse, fresher, more modern civilization, the other Italy, that of the south, possesses a moral and social structure which recalls primitive, perhaps even barbarian times, with a social structure typical of inferior civilizations . . .'.* (Niceforo 1890: 296–299).

19. The original meaning of 'imperialism' referred to the personal sovereignty of a powerful ruler over numerous territories, either in Europe or overseas. See Koebner and Schmidt (1965).
20. Numerous scholars have underlined the similarity between processes of nation-building and the colonial situation, including Fernand Braudel (1984: 42, 328–352), Maurice Dobb (1963: 194, 206–207, 209), Antonio Gramsci (1957: 430), Alvin Gouldner (1977–1978), Michael

Hechter (1975: 30–33), Oscar Jásci (1929: 185–212), and Eugen Weber (1975: 490–493).

21. As Eric Hobsbawm (1990) has recounted, Liberal discourse regarding nation states in Europe during the nineteenth century focused on optimum size and economic viability, rather than any cultural criterion.
22. The annexation by Germany of French Alsace-Lorraine in 1871 against the will of the population, was justified by Heinrich Treitschke, as follows:

    *We Germans . . . know better than these unfortunates themselves what is good for the people of Alsace, who have remained under the misleading influence of the French connection outside the sympathies of new Germany. We shall restore them to their true selves against their will* (quoted in Macartney 1934: 100).

23. The classical work on the Pan-German League is Wertheimer (1924).
24. From *Russia and Europe* (1871) a collection of Danilevsky's articles (cited in Kohn 1946: 200). Similar plans were proposed by Rostislav Fedeeyev in his *Opinion on the Eastern Question* (1871).
25. Although, as he notes, Venetians did not invent it.
26. Goody (1996: 113), quoting Robert Clive, who established the East India Company's military and political supremacy in Bengal.
27. Tan Tai-Yong is here describing Singapore and Calcutta, but the description applies to port cities everywhere.
28. Cities that were not economically important were often designated or created as capital cities to reinforce the national project, as distinct from the trans-local economy. Examples include the Hague (rather than Amsterdam), Washington DC (rather than New York) and, after World War II, Bonn (rather than Berlin).
29. The French nobility, for instance, considered itself to be a separate nation, one tied to an international aristocracy rather than to the French classes below them. The Comte de Boulainvilliers, a French nobleman, argued at the beginning of the eighteenth century that France was divided into 'two races that have at bottom nothing in common. They speak a common language, but they have neither common rights nor a common origin' (*Histoire de l'Ancien Gouvernement de la France*, 1727, Tome I, p. 33; quoted in Arendt (1958: 162).
30. As Gramsci emphasized, in Italy, rural magnates and petty bourgeoisie maintained a hold over the peasantry, and were able 'to mobilise peasants in the service of reactionary and conservative causes' (Arnold 1984: 159). Consequently revolutionary movements originating in the cities were in danger of being crushed by peasant soldiers, as they were in Turin in 1917 by peasant soldiers from Sardinia (Arnold 1984: 157).

31. Nationalism, as Eric Hobsbawm has shown, is a dual phenomenon. From above, it can be seen as part of a defence of protection and privilege, a quest to control 'free' labour, and (as shall be discussed in Chapter 6) to improve the terms on which 'national' capitals are integrated into the world circuit of capital. A significant aspect of nationalist historiography and doctrines has to do with the expansion of citizenship rights to larger parts of the population – however, these rights remained elusive in 'the west' until after World War II, and continue to remain so in nation states around the world. From below, nationalism can be seen as part of a 'revolt to escape proletarianization', a quest for social justice and rights of citizenship. Disadvantaged groups joined nationalist movements in order to acquire democratic rights, as Hobsbawm (1990) has argued.

## 5 The imperial 'historic bloc' of the nineteenth century

1. See Gramsci (1971: 366, 377); and, for a discussion, Sassoon (1987: 119–126). The understanding of imperialism as a monopolistic system of capital accumulation builds on conceptions developed by Lenin (1939) and Max Weber. For Weber, imperialism was a monopolistic system of control pursued by groups who 'sought monopoly profits instead of being content to manufacture and exchange goods in a formally free market'. This, for Weber, was a 'predatory' form of capitalism 'that was as old as capitalism itself' (in Mommsen 1980: 20).
2. See, also, Bayly (1989), Bin Wong (1997), Chaudhuri (1990), Frank (1998), Goldstone (1991), Lieberman (1993a, 1999), Pomerantz (2000), and Wink (1990).
3. For an explanation of why China came to a prefer silver as a means of valuation and exchange, see Geiss (1979).
4. For China, see Cartier (1981) and Wilkinson (1980); for Japan, see Innes (1980); for Turkey, see Sahillioglu (1983); and for Russia, see Blum (1956). See also Adshead (1973), Atwell (1986, 1990), Goldstone (1988), Lieberman (1993b), Reid (1990), Richards (1990: 625), Steensgard (1990), and De Vries (1976).
5. Napoleon envisioned transforming the Kingdom of Italy (Northern Italy) entirely into an economic dependency and a supplier of cotton for France's textile industry (Heckscher 1964: 297). Naples, in the words of the French envoy there, was to be 'France's richest colony' (in Heckscher 1964: 277).
6. 'This increase in total output was not '"merely" extensive growth, driven by increases in population and territory'. There was substantial productivity-raising innovation and restructuring of the economy' (Goldstone 2002: 349–350).
7. During the sixteenth and seventeenth centuries, more and more of the land and resources in settled countries had become private property. The pace of enclosures in northwest Europe had accelerated, and 'certain

types of private property had grown in importance' in Asia and Africa (Bayly 1989: 190).

8. Sumptuary laws, official documents, records of elite complaints, and public pronouncements about excessive popular consumption attest to the ubiquity of this concern throughout the world.
9. In the United States there were no pre-existing hierarchies, but they increasingly emerged in the south, and later on in the north during the so-called 'gilded age'.
10. This is borrowed from Gramsci, who observes that, within this military class there is a shared culture of aspiration and assimilation, in which the lower strata 'typically display the most enthusiastic *esprit de corps*, and manifest the greatest conceit' (Gramsci 1971: 13).
11. William Thompson summarizes the 'thesis' as follows. In the sixteenth century, western Europeans revolutionized the way they conducted their warfare. This included gunpowder-based weapons, large standing armies, and sailing ships 'with the increasing ability to fire on opponents at some distance' and which 'enabled them to control strategic sea lanes' (W. Thompson 1999: 146). This enabled them to resist Ottoman expansion in the sixteenth and seventeenth centuries, and to extend their control over the Americas, Siberia, most of Indonesia, much of India, and parts of coastal Africa (W. Thompson 1999: 146–147).
12. Chanda 2007: 231. 'In 1563, Portuguese colonizers brought smallpox to Brazil, where it wiped out entire indigenous peoples'. In the territory of the modern United States, an indigenous population of some two million was reduced to 750,000 by 1700. By 1820, they numbered about 325,000 (Chanda 2007: 232).
13. For a discussion of the word 'collaboration', see Atmore (1984), Bose & Jalal (1998), Marshal (1979), Osterhammel (1997), R. Robinson (1972, 1978, 1984, 1986), and Warbury (1981).
14. After the Ottomans captured the Syrian coast in 1517, they allowed French merchants to continue to operate in that area under a system known in Europe as 'capitulations'. These later provided commercial and judicial privileges to all Europeans in the Empire. They regularized customs duties on European manufactured goods and allowed European merchants to purchase goods anywhere in the Empire. They had detrimental effects on centres of local production, but they benefited local merchants in port cities like Beirut (Fawaz 1983: 73–74).
15. The Kongolese paid for European goods with slaves: those taken in wars beyond their borders, those condemned to slavery after committing crimes, and those procured by 'extorting gifts of slaves from the rich and noble' (Wills 2001: 33). The capture and trade of slaves provided a principal source of economic surplus for numerous state structures that evolved in western and eastern Africa as, for instance, in Dahomey where, during the eighteenth and nineteenth centuries, the state 'seemed to be entirely dependent upon slave trade, war, and enslavement' (Jewsiewicki 1989: 23).

16. For example, brokers would borrow capital from European merchants at a rate of 6 per cent and then loan it out to peasants at rates varying between 20 per cent and 100 per cent, with the crop as collateral. Or 'they bought the cocoons in advance for, say, 12 piastres and resold the silk at harvest for 18 piastres' (Fawaz 1983: 66–67).
17. The characteristic processes and structural outcomes that resulted from this exchange included accumulation, infrastructure investment, market integration, demographic change and population movements, urbanization, institutional change, agricultural and manufacturing productivity growth, and inequality trends. See, for example, Bengtsson, Campbell, & Lee (2004), Brenner and Isett 2002, Huang (1990, 2002), Li (1998), Pomeranz (2002, 2000), and Wong 2003.
18. Though Ceylon's coffee exports can be dated from the 1830s. A rising flow of rice exports came from Burma and Thailand. Malaya exported tin and rubber.
19. Platt asks: 'Could Britain have really moulded the economies of Latin America to suit her own needs? Was there some machinery in existence at the time by which such a major undertaking could be planned and put into effect?' (1980: 120). As Ferns points out, 'Argentina became a highly specialized producer because it was profitable to do so, and those who profited most had no motive to seek alternative policies' (1967: 125).
20. See, too, Mintz (1985) on sugar production and consumption.
21. 'The colonial authorities did little to shelter domestic handicrafts from competition from imported factory goods. They were also typically hostile to domestic industrialization, preferring continued import of manufactures from the metropolis' (Reynolds 1985: 42).
22. Hubbard (1935: 126), quoting an article entitled 'Japan and the World', in *The Spectator*, October 26, 1943.
23. For most of the nineteenth century, British agriculture remained the biggest branch of the economy by far in terms of employment. In 1891 it still employed more than any other industrial group. Only in 1901, with the growth of the transport industry and metal industries complex, did it cease to be the largest branch of the economy in employment terms (Hobsbawm 1968: 195).

## 6 The system unravels: contraction, conflict and social revolution

1. See, for example, Eng (1990), Meade (1989), and Quataert (1986).
2. Total famine mortality estimates vary from 6.1 to 10.3 million (Davis 2001: 7). These deaths resulted, at least in part, because the commitment of colonial administrators to free trade led them to abandon, or fail to replenish, traditional food reserves; in the face of the extraordinary weather conditions of the 1870s and 1880s, these reserves would have

been inadequate; however, they might have saved many lives (Davis 2001).

3. The gradual replacement of riots by strikes was noted by observers in the early 1870s (see, e.g., Potter 1870: 34–35; 1871: 535).
4. See, also, Breman (1987), Callaway (1987), Comaroff (1985), Comaroff and Comaroff (1986), Gordon and Meggitt (1985), and D. Kennedy (1987).
5. *Encylopaedie van Nederlandsch-Indie* (1919: 366–368); in Stoler (1989: 150–151).
6. Hannah Arendt (1958: 222–223), quoting Ernst Hasse of the Pan-German League.
7. Letter to Count Czernin, 17 August 1917, cited in Mowat (1927: 98).
8. These treaties were published in the official journal of the Soviets, and in the *Manchester Guardian*. A good summary can be found in Baker (1922: Vol. I, Ch. 2).
9. The French Revolution unleashed slave revolts throughout the Caribbean empires of Britain, France, and Spain between 1791 and 1808. In 1791, a slave revolt on Saint Domingue (Haiti), France's richest colony, ignited a 12-year revolution.
10. English translation is in Hertslet (1891: i, 375, Article VI).
11. The constitution of the International Labour Organisation states that '[C]onditions of labour exist involving such injustice, hardship, and privation to large numbers of people as to produce unrest so great that the peace and harmony of the world are imperilled' (in Zilliacus 1946: 234–235).
12. National Transport Workers Federation, *Report of the Third Annual General Council Meeting*, June 1913, London, p. 31.
13. See, for example, Braunthal (1967: 355), Carr (1945: 20–21), and Schumpeter (1950: 353); and for other works see Doyle (1997: 317–319, esp. p. 318, fn9).
14. A discussion of the procedures used to create this database is given in Silver (2003, Appendix A).
15. Soon after, Karl Liebknecht, a leader of the Spartacus Group, proclaimed the 'German Socialist Republic' from the balcony of the royal palace.
16. The League imposed upon all its members the obligations of becoming members of the ILO, and of performing the duties involved by such membership. However, the ILO was a 'stabilizing action' intended to induce the workers to content themselves with 'positive promises for the future' instead of 'achievement at the moment' (Zilliacus 1946: 234–235).
17. Eric Hobsbawm has argued this view persuasively (1990: esp. 120–130). See, also Benson (1989: 162).
18. The aim of the Vichy Regime's network of corporate committees and councils was made explicit by Marshal Petain: 'Step by step we will

progress toward the establishment of a corporatism which, taking into account the evolution in the social and economic domain, will recall in many respects the close solidarity which formerly existed among the remarkably conscientious workers of our old families' (quoted in Elbow 1953: 183).

19. See Darwin (1981), Fisher (2000), Fromkin (1989), and Jeffrey (1984).
20. For accounts of the post-war industrial unrest, see Basu (2004), Ray (1979), and Sarkar (1989).
21. As Arno Mayer has noted, 'Whenever politics operates under the influence of the specter of revolution', as it did after March 1917, 'societies become much more polarized' (Mayer 1969: 4).
22. The Four-Power Pact, concluded in Rome in 1933, provided that Britain, France, Italy, and Germany, as the four great powers of Europe and on the basis of equality among themselves, should be responsible for the organization of Europe and the preservation of peace.

## 7 The post-World War II interregnum

1. The expression 'third world' was first used in 1952 by the French demographer Alfred Sauvy. Sauvy's allusion was to the *tiers état* (third estate) of French society before the Revolution of 1789, which was at that time made up of people deprived of privileges. See, for a discussion, Melkote and Steeves (2001: 21–22).
2. See Chapter 6. For a detailed discussion of these changes and of the post-World War I restoration, see Halperin (1997: Chs. 5–7).
3. Britain's House of Lords, a hereditary body monopolized by the great landowning families, had absolute veto power over legislation proposed by the House of Commons until 1911 (Lieven 1992: 205).
4. The low of 41 was found in Austria and Spain; the upper limit of 55 in Sweden, Denmark, and Norway (Goldstein 1983: 241).
5. There is near unanimity that, in Britain, income was distributed more equally. Before World War I (1911–1913) the top 5 per cent of the population owned 87 per cent of personal wealth, and the bottom 90 per cent owned 8 per cent; in 1960 the top 5 per cent of the population owned 75 per cent of personal wealth, and the bottom 17 per cent owned 8 per cent (Hobsbawm 1968: 274).
6. In Western Europe, conservative parties were as committed to the welfare state and to government action to ameliorate social problems as were their leftist opponents. British Conservative leader Harold Macmillan argued for 'the Socialist remedy' wherever 'private enterprise had exhausted its social usefulness, or where the general welfare of the economy requires that certain basic industries and services need now to be conducted in the light of broader social considerations than the profit motive will supply' (Marwick 1974: 198).

7. See, for the influence of the Soviet example on 'planning', Hobsbawm (1996: 96–97). Of course, the type and extent of planning varied considerably, and not all changes in all countries evolved from a study of the Soviet example.
8. United Nations, Department of Economic and Social Affairs (1956: 3); see also Bairoch (1975: 184) and Kuznets (1971: 30–31).
9. During the 1960s, American investment in Argentina nearly tripled (from $427 million in 1960 to nearly $1.2 billion in 1968), with more than 90 per cent of it going to the most rapidly expanding sectors of the manufacturing industry – chemicals and petrochemicals, transportation, metallurgy, machinery, electrical equipment, and petroleum (Smith 1989: 34).
10. For the CIA's dealings with al-Zaim and Nasser, see Copeland (1969), Eveland (1980), and Little (1990). According to a member of the Free Officers, several days before the movement seized power, a United States Colonel at the American Embassy in Cairo assured an intermediary that the United States would not intervene against the movement as long as it was not communist. (Interview with Khalid Muyihi al-Din by Rifa'at Al-Sa'id, Cairo, 23 March 1980; cited in Ismail & Al-Sa'id 1990: 72). On United States support for Saddam, see Davis (1993).
11. The doctrines of the Ba'th Party are given in Michel Aflaq and Salahaddin al-Bitar, *al-Qawminyah al-'Arabiyah wa mawqifuha min al-shuyu'iyah* [Arab Nationalism and its Stance Toward Communism] (Damascus, n.d.); and Michel Aflaq, *Fi Sabil al-Ba'th* [For the Sake of the Ba'th] (Beirut: Dar al-Tali'ah, 1963).
12. Block (1977) provides much detail and a good analysis of United States policies towards and relations with Western European countries immediately after World War II.
13. American concern focused both on Western Europe and on Greece and the eastern Mediterranean. Assistance programmes linked to these concerns included the European Recovery programme, Greek Turkish Aid, Interim Aid to Austria, France, and Italy; the Mutual Defence Assistance Program, Chinese and Korean aid, and the Marshall Plan.
14. Post-World War II colonial wars included Palestine (1945–1949), Indonesia (1945–1949; 1963–196), Indochina (1946–1954), Madagascar (1947), Malaya (1947–1952), Korea (1949–1953), Kenya (1952–1954), Tunisia (1952–1954, 1961), Morocco (1953–1956), Algeria (1954–1962), Suez (1956), Cyprus (1955–1959; 1963–1964, 1974), Western Sahara (1957–1958), Congo (1960–1964), Goa (1961), Chad (1962–1992), Angola (1962–1963), Yemen (1963–1967), Mozambique (1965), and Malvinas/Falklands (1982).
15. Russian and Soviet studies programmes at Columbia, Harvard, and MIT were established as a means of gathering information about the Soviet Union, with funding from the CIA, as well as from the United States Air Force and private foundations (Simpson 1999: xvii). The Soviet

Division of the Office of Strategic Services was relocated to Columbia University and became the basis of its Russian Institute founded in September 1946. Harvard's Russian Research Center, established in 1947 with a Carnegie Corporation Grant, maintained a deep involvement with the CIA, the FBI, and other intelligence and military agencies (see Diamond 1992). MIT's Center for International Studies was underwritten by the CIA which, in the early 1950s, had a hand in its choice of projects and in its hiring (Cumings 1999: 171–172).

16. The World Bank, in its *East Asian Miracle* report published in 1993 advised other developing countries *not* to adopt the interventionist policies pursued in Japan and Korea – attributing the success of such policies to factors idiosyncratic to those two countries (Chang 2008: 216).
17. On the 'development project' see, e.g., McMichael (1996a: 13–76, 1996b); and So (1990: Ch. 1). See, also, the essays in Chomsky et al. (1997) and Simpson (1999).
18. Many scholars have contributed to the recognition that 'development' is used as an ideological tool by dominant powers, development agencies and rulers (e.g., Escobar 1995; Ferguson 1996). There were theorists and practitioners of all sorts around the world concerned with contributing to the improvement of the lives of the majority of the world's peoples. Many of the thinkers who contributed to development thinking dissented from orthodoxy in the course of their own intellectual development (see Simon 2009). However, given the vast institutional, ideational, and financial resources devoted to shaping 'development' in line with the interests that motivated the 'development project', the concerns and interests of all actors involved were necessarily shaped by the concerns which created those institutions and ideas, and so brought about the same result. For the influence of funding from military, intelligence, and propaganda agencies on key individuals and groups, scholarly societies, foundation grants committees, tenure decisions, and the contents of academic journals, see Chomsky *et al.* (1997), Crawford and Biderman (1968, 1969), Diamond (1992), Feldman (1989), Simpson (1994, 1999); Trumpboar (1989), and Uliassi (1971).
19. For the origins of area and international studies in the early years of the Cold War see, e.g., Diamond (1992), Nader (1997), and Simpson (1999). For collaboration between universities, non-governmental organizations, and intelligence agencies, see Cumings (1999).
20. The Carnegie Corporation, Rockefeller Foundation, and Ford Foundation, all of which received their funds from private companies, were among the most influential organizations to engage in efforts to educate elites in the third world.
21. Harvie Branscomb (Carnegie Corporation), 'Memorandum on the Corporation Program in the Dominions and Colonies', 18 October 1943 CUL, RBML, CCNY, Series I.D, Box 4, Folder 6.

22. Ahmad Aijaz observes that 'the select Western-educated academic elite' who came as graduate students and then joined humanities and social sciences faculties, tended to come from upper classes in their home countries that had been beneficiaries of colonialism, and so 'sought narratives of oppression not connected to class' (Aijaz 1992: 196).
23. In these countries, there was no pre-existing landed elite, and the colonists displaced, overwhelmed or destroyed prior inhabitants.
24. Before the reform 54 per cent of the cultivated land was owner-operated; after the reform 92 per cent was owned by farmers. Between 1947 and 1949 the government bought and resold 5.8 million acres of land. Three years after the beginning of the reform approximately three million peasants had acquired land. On the Japanese land reform, see *Economic Survey of Asia and the Far East* (United Nations Economic Commission for Asia and the Far East 1950: 188–189) and *Agricultural Geography of Europe and the Near East* (Department of Agriculture 1951: 187–189).

## 8 Globalization redux

1. This, and the absence of consensus about the reasons for it, precipitated a 'crisis' in the field of development studies. See, e.g. Arndt (1987), Caporaso (1980), Hirschman (1981), Lal (1983), Leeson (1988), Mouzelis (1988), Ranis and Schultz (1988), Seers (1979), Sen (1981), Streeten (1983) and Toye (1987).
2. This trend of thought probably began with Nigel Harris's 1986 book, *The End of the Third World: Newly Industrializing Countries and the Decline of an Ideology.*
3. See, for example, Arnold (1993), Burbach and Robinson (1999); Held, McGrew, Goldblatt, & Perraton (1999: 8, 177, 186–187), Hettne (1995), Hoogvelt (1997), and Robinson and Harris (2000). The general argument was that a levelling of the conditions of life in the first and third worlds meant that the geographic breakdown of the world into north–south, core–periphery or First and Third worlds, 'while still significant', was 'diminishing in importance' (Burbach & Robinson 1999: 27–28).
4. In September 1997 the United Nations Conference on Environment and Development reported that:

   > *the total number of people in the world living in poverty has increased. Income inequality has increased among countries and also within them, unemployment has worsened in many countries, and the gap between the least developed countries and other countries has grown rapidly in recent years* (United Nations General Assembly, A/RES/S-19/2, 19 September 1997. Available at: www.un.org/documents/ga/res/spec/aress19-2.htm (accessed 12 December 2012).

5. Rural poor as percentage of total population in today's 'third-world' countries, 1997: Nepal (88), Ethiopia (82), India (72), China (68), Kenya (67), Pakistan (63), Indonesia (59), Nigeria (56), Philippines (41), Peru (27), Mexico (26), and Brazil (19) (United Nations Statistics, 2000; World Bank 1998).
6. A decline in the United States' share of world manufactured exports, and an intensification of import competition in the American home market began in the 1960s. See, for a discussion, Coates (2000: 28–32).
7. That year there were protests in Mexico City, London, Rome, Paris, Dakar, West Berlin, New York, Warsaw, Madrid, Belgrade, Tokyo, Prague, Rio de Janeiro, and Sao Paulo. Street battles between students and riot police in Paris in May of that year were followed by a general strike that involved 10 million workers and closed down most businesses in the country. In Italy, demonstrations that month at the Universities of Milan and Trento spread and eventually paralyzed the Italian university system. Soviet troops sent to Prague to crush reforms engaged in street battles with students. See, also Arrighi, Wallerstein, & Hopkins (1989), Harman (1988), Katsiaficas (1987), and Watts (2001).
8. One in every 10 Americans was receiving federal food stamps. The infant mortality rate for African Americans in the 1990s was 17.7 deaths per 1000 live births – as compared with Jamaica (17.2), Trinidad (16.3), and Cuba (16) (Bello 1994: 95–97).
9. British Aerospace (BAE) now derives more of its income from the US Defense Department than from the British Ministry of Defence. According to the 2005 UN World Investment Report, BAE Systems is one of the world's top arms producers, generating £12 billion in annual sales of warplanes, avionics, submarines, surface ships, radar, electronics, and guided-weapons systems to 130 countries (Lilley 2003). The British and American oil and banking sectors are also very closely linked: British Petroleum (BP) has merged with the American Oil Company (Amoco), and the bulk of the banks (and bank capital) of the City of London (the main world centre for trading in equities, derivatives, and foreign exchange) are American (Lilley 2003).
10. It also widened the American lead over its closest competitors, and devastated the Soviet economy.
11. In a speech at Johns Hopkins University in 1993, entitled 'From Containment to Enlargement', Clinton's national security advisor Anthony Lake, announced that the 'defensive phase of US strategy', which 'never intended to be more than temporary', had ended (quoted in Bacevich 2002: 98).
12. In order to capture the diverse forms of democracy that have emerged along with neo-liberal restructuring in recent decades, researchers have defined new subtypes: 'authoritarian democracy', 'neopatrimonial democracy', 'military-dominated democracy'; and 'limited', 'oligarchical', 'controlled', 'restrictive', 'illiberal', 'guarded', 'protected', and 'tutelary' democracy.

13. See, for example, von Lazar (1966), Lipski (1989–1990: 19–21), Taborsky (1961: 32–37), and Tismeneanu (1989: 31).
14. The specific crisis was that faced by Chileans: a violent coup by Pinochet and hyperinflation. Friedman advised Pinochet to strike quickly and hard: tax cuts, free trade, privatized services, cuts in social spending, deregulation.
15. '"Civil society" is a highly elitist, liberal concept and inclusion within it (especially within its British meaning) has depended – and still depends – on factors of class as much as of "nationality"' (Washbrook 1998: 307). The notion of 'civil society' was originally articulated in the context of a movement by an essentially transnational elite of wealth and property owners. During the nineteenth century, 'some (powerful, property-holding) non-Europeans were long established as part of a common "civil society" with bourgeois Europeans – in the case of British India, even sitting as members of imperial councils in Calcutta and Delhi and the imperial parliament in London' (Washbrook 1998: 307).
16. A number of scholars have pointed out that transnational linkages were perhaps at their height during the nineteenth century. See, for example, Bayley (2007: 343) and Hirst and Thompson (1996).
17. See, for example, Albrechts and Swyngedouw (1989), Clout (1981), Hirschman (1958), Holland 1976, Martin (1989), Martin and Sunley (1997), Myrdal (1957), Sabel (1994), and Swyngedouw (1997).
18. On growing regional inequalities in western Europe, see, Donaldson (2006), Keating (1998, 2001), Kloosterman (2001), MacLeod (2001), MacLeod and Jones (2001), and Paasi (2003).
19. Academic debate on world cities was launched by Friedmann (1986). See, especially, Sassen (1994, 1997, 2007) and Yeoh (1999) for overviews.
20. These would include, for instance, Buenos Aires, Brazilia, Addis Ababa – a chartered city having the status of both a city and a state; the Emirate of Abu-Dhabi, Emirate of Dubai, Emirate of Ajman, Emirate of Sharjah, Emirate of Ras al-Khaimah, Emirate of Fujairah, Emirate of Umm al-Qaiwain. There are also numerous federally administered cities. In India: Delhi and Puducherry, which have been given partial statehood, and Chandigarh, a Union Territory. In Pakistan: Islamabad (Islamabad Capital Territory). In Malaysia: Kuala Lumpur, Putrajaya, and Labuan, an offshore international financial centre. Also, Mexico City (the Mexican Federal District, Mexico), Abuja (Federal Capital Territory, Nigeria).
21. *Evolutionary* policies that aim at reforming landlord–tenant systems can only benefit tenant farmers if tenants have equality of bargaining power with landlords. This depends on the availability of non-farm job opportunities that provide tenants with alternative means of livelihood; and on their having opportunities to acquire a relatively high level of education (Mellor 1966: 260–261).

22. There is, as Rueschemeyer, Stephens, and Stephens (1992: 60) point out, a 'near-universal tendency of the powerful to preserve their position'.
23. David Held has argued that the economic order now 'stretches beyond the control of a single state (even of dominant states)' and of democratic institutions located at the national level, and so 'democracy must become a transnational affair' (Held 1991: 32–34).
24. Concrete analysis of actual agents engaged in struggles to re-embed economies under democratic societal control show that successful anti-globalism actions and mobilizaions such as defeating the Multilateral Agreement on Investment and the Zapatista struggle, represented victories for *national* and *local* political mobilizations which were loosely coordinated by a small number of activists in transnational advocacy networks (Laxer & Halperin 2003).

# References


Abu-Lughod, J. L. (1989). *Before European Hegemony. The World System A.D. 1250–1350*. New York: Oxford University Press.

Adshead, S. A. M. (1973). The seventeenth century general crisis in China. *Asian Profile*, 1:2.

Ahmad, A. (1992). *In Theory*. London: Verso.

Ahmad, F. (1994). The development of working-class consciousness in Turkey. In: Z. Lochman (Ed.), *Workers and Working Classes in the Middle East: Struggles, Histories, Historiographies*. Albany, NY: State University of New York Press; pp. 133–164.

Ahumada, J. (1963). Economic Development and Problems of Social Change in Latin America. In: E. De Vries & J. Medina Echavarria (Eds.), *Social Aspects of Economic Development in Latin America*, Vol. I. Paris: UNESCO.

Aijaz, A. (1992). *In Theory: Classes, Nations, Literatures*. London: Verso.

Albrechts, L., & Swyngedouw, E. (1989). Challenges for regional policy under a *flexible* regime of accumulation. In: L. Albrechts, F. Moulaert, P. Roberts, & E. Swyingedouw (Eds.), *Regional Policy at the Crossroads: European Perspectives*. London: Jessica Kingsley.

Albritton, R (1993). Did agrarian capitalism exist? *The Journal of Peasant Studies* 20(3): 419–441.

Aldcroft, D. H. (1978). *The European Economy, 1914–1970*. London: Croom Helm.

Alderson, A., & Nielson, F. (2001) Globalization and the Great U-Turn: Income Inequality Trends in 16 OECD Countries. Conference paper, American Sociological Association.

Allen, R. C. (1992). *Enclosure and the Yeoman. The Agricultural Development of the South Midlands, 1450–1850*. Oxford: Oxford University Press.

de Alva, K., & Jorge, J. (1995). The postcolonialization of the (Latin) American experience: A reconsideration of 'colonialism,' 'postcolonialism,' and 'mestizaje'. In G. Prakash (Ed.), *After Colonialism: Imperial Histories and Postcolonial Displacements*. Princeton, NJ: Princeton University Press; pp. 241–275.

Amin, S. (1974). *Accumulation on a World Scale. A Critique of the Theory of Underdevelopment*. New York: Monthly Review Press.

Amin, S. (1976a). *Accumulation on a World Scale: A Critique of the Theory of Underdevelopment*, Vol. 2. London: Monthly Review Press.

Amin, S. (1976b). *Unequal Exchange*. New York: Monthly Review.

Amin, S. (1977). Underdevelopment and dependence in Black Africa – Origins and contemporary forms. In: J. Abu-Lughod & R. Hay Jr. (Eds.), *Third World Urbanization*. London: Methuen; pp. 140–150.

Anderson, P. (1974). *Passages from Antiquity to Feudalism*. London: Verso.

Anderson, P. (1979). *Lineages of the Absolutist State*. London: Verso.

Anheier, H., Glasius, M., & Kaldor, M. (Eds.). (2003). *Global Civil Society 2001*. Oxford: Oxford University Press.

Arendt, H. (1958). *The Origins of Totalitarianism*. New York: Meridian.

Arndt, H. W. (1987). *Economic Development: The History of an Idea*. Chicago, IL: University of Chicago Press.

Arnold, D. (1979). European orphans and vagrants in India in the nineteenth century. *The Journal of Imperial and Commonwealth History* 7(2): 104–127.

Arnold, D. (1984). Gramsci and peasant subalternity in India. *Journal of Peasant Studies* 11: 155–177.

Arnold, G. (1993). *The End of the Third World*. New York: St. Martin's Press.

Arrighi, G. (1994). *The Long Twentieth Century: Money, Power, and the Origins of Our Time*. London: Verso.

Arrighi, G., Silver, B., & Brewer, B. (2003). Industrial convergence, globalization, and the persistence of the north–south divide. *Studies in Comparative International Development* 38(1): 3–31.

Arrighi, G., Wallerstein, I., & Hopkins, T. (1989). *Anti-Systemic Movements*. London: Verso.

Aston, T. H., & Philpin, C. H. E. (Eds.). (1985). *The Brenner Debate: Agrarian Class Structure and Economic Development in Pre-industrial Europe*. New York: Cambridge University Press.

Atmore, A. E. (1984). The extra-European foundations of British imperialism: Towards a reassessment. In: C. C. Eldridge (Ed.), *British Imperialism in the Nineteenth Century*. London: Macmillan; pp. 106–125.

Atwell, W. (1986). Some observations on the seventeenth century crisis in China and Japan. *Journal of Asian Studies* 45: 223–244.

Atwell, W.S. (1990). A seventeenth-century 'general crisis' in East Asia? *Modern Asian Studies* 24(4): 661–682.

Bacevich, A. (2002). *American Empire: The Realities and Consequences of US Diplomacy* Cambridge, MA: Harvard University Press.

Bairoch, P. (1975). *The Economic Development of the Third World Since 1900*. London: Methuen.

Bairoch, P. (1988). *Cities and Economic Development: From the Dawn of History to the Present*. Chicago, IL: University of Chicago Press.

Bairoch, P. (1993). *Economics and World History: Myths and Paradoxes*. London: Harvester.

Baker, R. S. (1922). *Woodrow Wilson and World Settlement*. New York: Doubleday.

Baldy, E. (1922). *Les banques d'affaires en France depuis 1900*. Paris: Librairie Générale de Droit et de Jurisprudence.

Baran, P. A. (1957). *The Political Economy of Growth*. New York: Monthly Review.

Baran, P. A. (1970). On the political economy of backwardness. In: R. I. Rhodes (Ed.), *Imperialism and underdevelopment*. New York: Monthly Review Press; pp. 285–301.

Barraclough, G. (1964). *An Introduction to Contemporary History*. Harmondsworth: Penguin Books.

Barraclough, G. (1991). *Main Trends in History* (expanded and updated by M. Burns). New York: Holmes and Meier.

Barratt Brown, M. (1970). *After Imperialism*, revised edn. London: Merlin Press.

Barstelmann, T. (2001). *The Cold War and the Color Line*. Cambridge, MA: Harvard University Press.

Bartlett, R. (1993). *The Making of Europe: Conquest, Colonization and Cultural Change*. Princeton, NJ: Princeton University Press; pp. 950–1350.

Basu, S. (2004). *Does Class Matter? Colonial Capital and Workers' Resistance in Bengal, 1890–1937*. New Delhi: Oxford University Press.

Bauer, O. (1907). In: M. Adler & R. Hilferding (Eds.), *Die nationalitätenfrage und die sozialdemokratie*. Vienna: Volksbuch Handlung Ignaz Brand.

Bayart, J. F. (2005). *The Illusion of Cultural Identity*. London: Hurst.

Bayly, C. (1983). *Rulers, Townsmen and Bazaars. North Indian Society in the Age of British Expansion, 1780–1870*. Cambridge: Cambridge University Press.

Bayly, C. A. (1989). *Imperial Meridian: the British Empire and the World, 1780–1830*. London: Longmans.

Bayly, C. (2007). Distorted development: The Ottoman Empire and British India, circa 1780–1916. *Comparative Studies of South Asia, Africa and the Middle East* 27(2): 332–344.

Becker, D. G., Frieden, J., Schartz, S. P., & Sklar, R. L. (1987). *Postimperialism: International capitalism and development in the late twentieth century*. Boulder, CO.: Lynne Rienner.

Becker, G. (1969). *Human Capital*. New York: Columbia University Press.

Bello, W. (1994). *Dark Victory: The United States, Structural Adjustment and Global Poverty*. London: Pluto.

Bengtsson, T., Campbell, C., & Lee, J. Z. (2004). *Life Under Pressure: Mortality and Living Standards in Europe and Asia, 1700–1900*. Cambridge, MA: MIT Press.

Benson, L. (1989). *The Working Class in Britain, 1850–1939*. London: Longman.

Benton, L. (1996). From the world-systems perspective to institutional world history: Culture and economy in global theory. *Journal of World History* 7(2): 261–295.

Berend, I. T., & Ránki, G. (1976). *Economic Development in East-Central Europe in the 19th and 20th Centuries*. New York: Columbia University Press.

Berg, M., & Eger, E. (2003). The rise and fall of the luxury debates. In: M. Berg & E. Eger, (Eds.), *Luxury in the Eighteenth Century: Debates, Desires and Delectable Goods*. Palgrave Macmillan, Basingstoke; pp. 7–27.

Berger, M. T. (1994). The end of the 'third world'? *Third World Quarterly* 15(2): 257–275.

Berghahn, V.R. (1988). Corporatism in Germany in historical perspective. In: A. Cox & N. O'Sullivan (Eds.), *The Corporate State: Corporatism and State Tradition in Western Europe*. Aldershot: Edward Elgar; pp. 104–122.

Berry, C. J. (1994). T*he Idea of Luxury: A Conceptual and Historical Investigation*. New York: Cambridge University Press.

Bevan, G. P. (1880). On the strikes of the past ten years. *Journal of the Royal Statistical Society* 43: 35–54.

Bigo, R. (1947). *Les banques françaises au cours de XIXe siècle*. Paris: Sirey.

Bin Wong, R. (1997). *China transformed: Historical Change and the Limits of European Experienc*e. Ithaca, NY: Cornell University Press.

Blake, J. W. (1950). The Study of African History. *Transactions of the Royal Historical Society, Series IV* XXXII: 49–69.

Blänkner, R. (2005). Absolutism. In: J. Chastain (Ed.), *Encyclopedia of 1848 Revolutions*, 2nd edn. Available at: http://www.ohiou.edu/~Chastain/ac/absoluti.htm (accessed 12 December 2012).

Block, F. L. (1977). *The Origins of International Economic Disorder*. Berkeley, CA: University of California Press.

Blockmans, W. P. (1994). Voracious states and obstructing cities: An aspect of state formation in preindustrial Europe. In: C. Tilly & W. P. Blockmans (Eds.), *Cities and the Rise of States in Europe A.D. 1000 to 1800*. Boulder, CO: Westview; pp. 218–250.

Blum, J. (1956). Prices in Russia in the sixteenth century. *Journal of Economic History* 27: 182–199.

Blum, J. (1978). *The End of the Old Order in Rural Europe*. Princeton, NJ: Princeton University Press.

Blussé, L. (1986). *Strange Company: Chinese Settlers, Mestizo Women, and the Dutch in VOC Batavia*. Riverton, USA: Foris Publications.

Bois, G. (1985). Against the neo-Malthusian orthodoxy. In: T. H. Aston & C. H. E. Philpin (Eds.), *The Brenner Debate: Agrarian Class Structure and Economic Development in Pre-industrial Europe*. New York: Cambridge University Press; pp. 107–118.

Bonnell, A. T. (1940). *German Control over International Economic Relations, 1930–1940*. Urbana, IL: University of Illinois Press.

Bonney, R. (1987). Absolutism: what's in a name? *French History* 1(1): 93–117.

Bordogna, L., Cella, G. P., & Provasi, G. (1989). Labor conflicts in Italy before the rise of fascism, 1881–1923: a quantitative analysis. In: L. Haimson & C. Tilly (Eds.), *Strikes, Wars, and Revolutions in an International Perspective: Strike Waves in the Late Nineteenth and Early Twentieth Centuries*. Cambridge: Cambridge University Press; pp. 217–246.

Borthwick, B. M. (1980). *Comparative Politics of the Middle East*. Englewood Cliffs, NJ: Prentice-Hall.

Bose, S. (1997). Instruments and idioms of colonial and national development. In: F. Cooper & R. Packard (Eds.), *International Development and the Social Sciences: Essays on the History and Politics of Knowledge*. Berkeley, CA: University of California Press; pp. 45–63.

Bose, S. (2005). *A Hundred Horizons: The Indian Ocean in the Age of Global Empire*. Cambridge, MA: Harvard University Press.

Bose, S., & Jalal, A. (1998). *Modern South Asia: History, Culture, Political Economy*. London: Routledge.

Bosworth, A. (2000). the evolution of the world-city system, 3000 BCE to AD 2000. In: R. A. Denemark, J. Friedman, B. K. Gills, & G. Modelski

(Eds.), *World System History: The Social Science of Long-Term Change*. London: Routledge; pp. 273–274.
Bowen, R. H. (1947). *German Theories of the Corporative State. With Special Reference to the Period 1870–1919*. New York: McGraw-Hill.
Boyce, R. W. D. (1987). *British Capitalism at the Crossroads, 1919–1932*. Cambridge: Cambridge University Press.
*Bozeman,* A. B. (1994). *Politics and Culture in International History: From the Ancient Near East to the Opening of the Modern Age*, 2nd edn. New Brunswick: Transaction Publishers.
Braudel, F. (1972). *The Mediterranean and the Mediterranean World in the Age of Philip II*. New York: Collins.
Braudel, F. (1982). *The Wheels of Commerce, Civilization and Capitalism, 15th–18th Century*, Vol. II, (trans. S. Reynolds). New York: Harper and Row.
Braudel, F. (1984). *The Perspective of the World. Civilization and Capitalism, 15th–18th Century*, Vol. III (trans. S. Reynolds). New York: Harper and Row.
Braunthal, J. (1967). *History of the International:* Vol. I, *1864–1914*. New York: Praeger.
Brayshay, M., Cleary, M., & Selwood, J. (2007). Social networks and the transnational reach of the corporate class in the early-twentieth century, *Journal of Historical Geography* 33: 144–167.
Breman, J. (1987). *Koelies, Planters en Koloniale Politiek*. Dordrecht: Foris.
Brenner, R. (1976). Agrarian class structure and economic development in pre-industrial Europe. *Past and Present* 70: 30–75.
Brenner, R. (1977). The origins of capitalist development: A critique of neo-Smithian Marxism. *New Left Review* 104: 25–92.
Brenner, R. (1982). The agrarian roots of European capitalism. *Past and Present* 97: 16–113.
Brenner, R. (1993). *Merchants and Revolution: Commercial Change, Political Conflict and London's Overseas Traders, 1550–1653*. Cambridge: Cambridge University Press.
Brenner, N. (2004). *New State Spaces: Urban Governance and the Rescaling of Statehood* London: Oxford University Press.
Brenner, R., & Isett, C. (2002). England's divergence from China's Yangzi delta: Property relations, microeconomics, and patterns of development. *Journal of Asian Studies* 61(2): 609–662.
Brown, E. H. P. (1968). *A Century of Pay*. London: Macmillan.
Burbach, R., & Robinson, W. (1999). The *fin de siecle* debate: Globalization as epochal shift. *Science & Society* 63(1): 10–39.

Burke, E. (1991). Changing patterns of peasant protest in the Middle East, 1750–1960. In: F. Kazemi & J. Waterbury (Eds.), *Peasants and Politics in the Modern Middle East*. Miami, FL: Florida International University Press; pp. 24–37.

Cain, P. (1979). Capitalism, war and internationalism in the thought of Richard Cobden. *British Journal of International Studies* 5: 229–247.

Cain, P. J., & Hopkins, A. G. (1993). *British Imperialism, Innovation and Expansion 1688–1914*. London: Longman.

Cairncross, A.K. (1953). *Home and Foreign Investment, 1870–1914*. Cambridge: Cambridge University Press.

Callaway, H. (1987). *Gender, Culture and Empire: European Women in Colonial Nigeria*. Oxford: Macmillan Press.

Cameron, R. (1961). *France and the Economic Development of Europe*. Princeton, NJ: Princeton University Press.

Cameron, R. (1976). Review of 'The Modern World-System: Capitalist Agriculture and the Origins of the European World-economy in the Sixteenth Century', by Immanuel Wallerstein. *Journal of Interdisciplinary History* 7: 140–144.

Cameron, R. (1981). The Industrial Revolution: A misnomer. In: J. Schneider (Ed.), *Wirtschaftskrafte und Wirtschaftwege: festschrift für Hermann Kellenbenz*, Vol. V. Stuttgart: Komission bei Klett-Cotta; pp. 367–376.

Cameron, R. (1985). A new view of European industrialization. *The Economic History Review* 38(1): 1–23.

Cannadine, D. (1990). *Decline and Fall of the British Aristocracy*. London: Penguin Books.

Cannadine, D. (2001). *Ornamentalism. How the British saw their empire*. London: Oxford University Press.

Caporaso, J. (1978). Dependence, dependency, and power in the global system. *International Organization* 32(1): 13–43.

Caporaso, J. (1980). Dependency theory: Continuities and discontinuities in development studies. *International Organization* 34(4).

Cardoso, F. H. (1973). Associated-dependent development: Theoretical and practical implications. In: A. Stepan (Ed.), *Authoritarian Brazil: Origins, Policies, and Future*. New Haven, CT: Yale University Press.

Cardoso, F. H., & Faletto, E. (1973). *Dependencia e desenvolvimento no America Latina: Ensaio de interpretacao sociologia*. Rio de Janeiro: Editora Zahar.

Cardoso, F. H., & Faletto, E. (1979). *Dependency and Development in Latin America* Berkeley, CA: University of California.

Carr, E. H. (1945). *Nationalism and After*. London: Macmillan.

Carr, E. H. (1947). *The Soviet Impact on the Western World.* New York: Macmillan.

Carr, R. (1966). *Spain, 1808–1939.* Oxford: Clarendon Press.

Carroll, T. F. (1970). *Land Reform in Peru.* United States Agency for International Development.

Carruthers, B. G. (1996). *City of Capital: Politics and Markets in the English Financial Revolution.* Princeton, NJ: Princeton University Press.

Carsten, F. L. (1982). *War Against War: British and German Radical Movements in the First World War.* Berkeley, CA: University of California Press.

Cartier, M. (1981). Les importations de métaux monétaires en Chine: Essai sur la conjoncture chinoise. *Annales E.S.C.* 36: 454–466.

Castells, M. (1996). *The Rise of the Network Society.* Cambridge, MA: Blackwell.

Castells, M. (1994). European cities, the informational society, and the global economy, *New Left Review* 204: 18–32.

Castles, S. (1984). *Here for Good: Western Europe's New Ethnic Minorities.* London: Pluto Press.

Chakrabarty, D. (1992). Postcoloniality and the artifice of history: Who speaks for 'Indian' pasts? *Representations* 37(Winter): 1–26.

Chakrabarty, D. (2000). *Provincializing Europe: Postcolonial Thought and Historical Difference.* Princeton, NJ: Princeton University Press.

Chanda, N. (2007). *Bound Together. How Traders, Preachers, Adventurers, and Warriors Shaped Globalization.* New Haven, CT: Yale University Press.

Chang, H. J. (2003a). Introduction. In: H. J. Chang (Ed.), *Rethinking Development Economics.* London: Anthem Press; pp. 1–18.

Chang, H. J. (2003b). The East Asian Development Experience. In: H. J. Chang (Ed.), *Rethinking Development Economics.* London: Anthem Press; pp. 107–124.

Chang, H. J. (2008). *Bad Samaritans: The Myth of Free Trade and the Secret History of Capitalism.* New York: Bloomsbury Press.

Charlesworth, A., Gilbert, D., Randall, A., Southall, H., & Wrigley, C. (1996). *An Atlas of Industrial Protest in Britain, 1750–1990.* London: Macmillan.

Chase-Dunn, C. (1975). The effects of international economic dependence on development and inequality. *American Sociological Review* 40: 720–739.

Chase-Dunn, C. (1985). The system of world cities, A.D. 800–1975. In: M. Timberlake (Ed.), *Urbanisation in the World-Economy.* Orlando, FL: Academic Press; pp. 269–292.

Chase-Dunn, C., & Hall, T. D. (1993). Comparing world-systems: concepts and working hypotheses. *Social Forces* 71(4): 851–886.

Chattopadhyay, S. (2006). The Bolshevik menace: Colonial surveillance and the origins of socialist politics in Calcutta. *South Asia Research* 26(2): 165–179.

Chaudhuri, K. N. (1990). *Asia Before Europe: Economy and Civilization of the Indian Ocean from the Rise of Islam to 1750*. Cambridge: Cambridge University Press.

Chirot, D. (1977). *Social Change in the Twentieth Century*. New York: Harcourt, Brace Jovanovich.

*Chomsky*, N. (1985). *Turning the tide: U.S. Intervention in Central America and the Struggle for Peace*. Boston, MA: South End Press.

Chomsky, N., Nader, L., Wallerstein, I., Lewontin, R. C., & Ohmann, R. (1997). *The Cold War and the University: Toward an Intellectual History of the Postwar Years*. New York: New Press.

Christian, D. (2004). *Maps of Time: An Introduction to Big History*. Berkeley, CA: University of California Press.

Clark, C. (1957). *The Conditions of Economic Progress*, 3rd edn. London: Macmillan.

Clark, J. C. D. (1985). *English Society, 1688–1832*. New York: Columbia University Press.

Clark, J. C. D. (1986). *Revolution and Rebellion: State and Society in England in the Seventeenth and Eighteenth Centuries*. New York: Cambridge University Press.

Clarkson, L. A. (1971). *The Pre-Industrial Economy in England, 1500–1700*. London: Batsford.

Clout, H. (1981). *Regional Development in Western Europe*, 2nd edn. Chichester: John Wiley.

Coates, D. (2000). *Models of Capitalism: Growth and Stagnation in the Modern Era*. Cambridge: Polity.

Cobban, A. (1971). *The Social Interpretation of the French Revolution*. Cambridge: Cambridge University Press.

Cohen, S. F. (2000). *Failed Crusade: America and the Tragedy of Post-Communist Russia*. New York: Norton.

Cohn, B. S. (1962). Political systems in eighteenth century India: The Banaras region, *Journal of the American Oriental Society* 82:3, 312–320.

Collas, H. (1908). *La Banque De Paris Et Des Pays-Bas*. Dijon: Barbier-Lèon Marchal.

Colley, L. (2008). A tale of two empires (review of J. H. Elliot, *Empires of the Atlantic World: Britain and Spain, 1492–1830*, Yale University Press, 2006). *New York Review of Books* LV(12): 43–46.

Collins, H., & Abramsky, C. (1965). *Karl Marx and the British Labour Movement*. New York: Macmillan.

Comaroff, J. (1985). *Body of Power, Spirit of Resistance*. Chicago, IL: Chicago University Press.
Comaroff, J., & Comaroff, J. (1986). Christianity and colonialism in South Africa. *American Ethnologist* 13(1): 1–22.
Committee on Finance and Industry (1931). *Report of the Committee on Finance and Industry* [Macmillan Report]. Cmd. 3897. London: HM Stationary Office.
Conaghan, C. M., Malloy, J. M., & Abugattas, L. A. (1990). Business and the 'boys': The politics of neoliberalism in the central Andes. *Latin America Research Review* 25(2).
Connor, W. (1973). The politics of ethnonationalism. *Journal of International Affairs* 27: 111–121.
Cooper, F. (1994). Conflict and connection: Rethinking colonial African history. *American Historical Review* 99: 1516–1545.
Cooper, W. H. (2009). *Russia's Economic Performance and Policies and their Implications for the United States*. Washington, DC: Congressional Research Service.
Copeland, M. (1969). *The Game of Nations: The Amorality of Power Politics*. New York: Simon and Schuster.
Cordesman, A. H. (2001). *Stability and Instability in the Middle East: Economics, Demography, Energy, and Security*. Three reports. Available at http://csis.org/files/media/csis/pubs/economicdemographic.pdf(accessed 12 December 2012).
Coronil, F. (1996). Beyond occidentalism: Toward nonimperial geohistorical categories. *Cultural Anthropology* 11(1): 51–87.
Cowan, M., & Shenton, R. (1995). The invention of development. In: J. Crush (Ed.), *Power of Development*. London: Routledge.
Cox, O. C. (1959). *Foundations of Capitalism*. New York: Philosophical Library.
Cox, R. W. (1987). *Production, Power, and World Order. Social Forces in the Making of History*. New York, Columbia University Press.
Crafts, N. F. R. (1983). British economic growth, 1700–1813: A review of the evidence. *Economic History Review* 36: 177–199.
Crafts, N. F. R. (1985). *British Economic Growth during the Industrial Revolution*. Oxford: Clarendon Press.
Crawford, E., & Biderman, A. (1968). *Political Economics of Social Research: the Case of Sociology*. Springfield, VA: Clearinghouse for Federal Scientific and Technical Information.
Crawford, E., & Biderman, A. (1969). *Social Scientists and International Affairs*. New York: John Wiley and Sons.
Croot, P., & Parker, D. (1985). Agrarian class structure and the development

of capitalism: England and capitalism compared. In: T. H. Aston & C. H. E. Philpin (Eds.), *The Brenner Debate: Agrarian Class Structure and Economic Development in Pre-industrial Europe.* New York: Cambridge University Press; pp. 79–90.

Crouch, C. (1986). Sharing public space. In: J. A. Hall (Ed.), *States in History*. Oxford: Basil Blackwell.

Cullen, L. M. (1968). *Anglo-Irish Trade 1660–1800*. Manchester: University of Manchester Press.

Cumings, B. (1999). *Parallax Visions: Making Sense of American–East Asian Relations at the End of the Century*. Durham, NC: Duke University Press.

Curtis, R. E. (1931). *The Trusts and Economic Control*. New York: McGraw-Hill.

Daphnas, G. (1955). *Greece Between the Wars, 1923–1940*. Athenai: Ikaros.

Darwin, J. (1981). *Britain, Egypt and the Middle East: Imperial Policy in the Aftermath of War, 1918–1922*. New York, St. Martin's Press.

Darwin, J. (2007). *After Tamerlane. The Global History of Empire since 1405*. London: Penguin.

Darwin, J. (2009). *The Empire Project: The Rise and Fall of the British World System, 1830–1970*. Cambridge: Cambridge University Press.

Das Gupta, A. (1979). Indian Merchants and the Decline of Surat: c. 1700–1750. Wiesbaden: Franz Steiner Verlag.

Davis, E. (1993). The Persian Gulf war: myths and realities. In: H. Amirahmdi (Ed.), *The United States and the Middle East: New Directions in Foreign Policy*. Albany, NY: SUNY Press; pp. 251–285.

Davis, L. E., & Huttenback, R. A. (1988). *Mammon and the Pursuit of Empire*. New York: Cambridge University Press.

Davis, M. (2001). *Late Victorian Holocausts: El Niño Famines and the Making of the Third World*. London: Verso.

Davis, R. (1979). *The Industrial Revolution and British Overseas Trade*. Leicester/Atlantic Highlands, NJ: Leicester University Press/Humanities Press.

Deane, P. (1979). The First Industrial Revolution, 2nd edn. New York: Cambridge University Press.

Deane, P., & Cole, W. A. (1967). *British Economic Growth, 1688–1959: Trends and Structure*, 2nd edn. Cambridge: Cambridge University Press.

Deeb, M. (1976). Bank Misr and the emergence of the local bourgeoisie in Egypt. In: E. Kedourie (Ed.), *The Middle Eastern Economy: Studies in Economics and Economic History*. London: Frank Cass; pp. 69–86.

Diamond, S. (1992). *Compromised Campus*. New York: Oxford University Press.

Dimitri, C., Effland, A., & Conklin, N. (2006). *The 20th Century Transformation of U.S. Agriculture and Farm Policy*. USDA Economic Information Bulletin No. EIB-3; p. 2. Available at: http://www.ers.usda.gov/publications/EIB3/eib3.pdf (accessed 12 December 2012).

Dobb, M. (1963). *Studies in the Development of Capitalism*, revised edn. New York: International Publishers.

Dodgson, R. S. (1977). A spatial perspective. *Peasant Studies* 6: 8–19.

Donaldson, A. (2006). Performing regions: territorial development and cultural politics in a Europe of the Regions. *Environment and Planning* 38: 2075–2092.

Dorwart, R. A. (1971). *The Prussian Welfare State before 1740*. Cambridge, MA: Harvard University Press.

Dos Santos, T. (1970). The structure of dependence. *American Economic Review* 60: 235–246.

Doyle, M. W. (1997). *Ways of War and Peace: Realism, Liberalism, and Socialism*. New York: W.W. Norton.

Drahos, P., with Braithwaite, J. (2002). *Information Feudalism: Who Owns the Knowledge Economy?* London: Earthscan.

Droz, J. (1967). *Europe Between Revolutions, 1815–1848*. Ithaca, NY: Cornell University Press.

Duménil, G., & Levy, D. (2004). *Capital Resurgent: Roots of the Neoliberal Revolution*. Cambridge, MA: Harvard University Press.

Duncan, C. A. M. (2000). The centrality of agriculture: History, ecology, and feasible socialism. *Socialist Register*, 187–204.

Einzig, P. (1941). *Appeasement, Before, During and After the War*. London: Macmillan.

Elbow, M. H. (1953). *French Corporative Theory, 1789–1948*. New York: Columbia University Press.

Elliot, J. H. (2006). *Empires of the Atlantic World: Britain and Spain, 1492–1830*. New Haven, CT: Yale University Press.

Eng, R. Y. (1990). Luddism and labor protest among silk artisans and workers in Jiangnan and Guangdong, 1860–1930. *Late Imperial China* 11(2): 63–101.

Engerman, S. (1994). Reflections on 'The Standard of Living Debate': New arguments and new evidence. In: J. James & Mark Thomas (Eds.), *Capitalism in Context*. Chicago, IL: University of Chicago Press; pp. 50–79.

Escobar, A. (1995). *Encountering Development: The Making and Unmaking of the Third World*. Princeton, NJ: Princeton University Press.

Evans, P. (1979). *Dependent Development.* Princeton, NJ: Princeton University Press.

Eveland, W. C. (1980). *Ropes of Sand: America's Failure in the Middle East.* New York: W. W. Norton.

Fanon, F. (1966). *Wretched of the Earth* (trans. C. Farrington). New York: Grove.

Fawaz, L. T. (1983). *Merchants and Migrants in Nineteenth Century Beirut.* Cambridge, MA: Harvard University Press.

Fedeeyev, R. (1871). *Opinion on the Eastern Question.* London: E. Stanford.

Feder, E. (1970). Counterreform. In: R. Stavenhagen (Ed.), *Agrarian Problems and Peasant Movements in Latin America.* Garden City, NY: Doubleday; pp. 173–223.

Feldman, J. (1989). *Universities in the Business of Repression.* Boston, MA: South End Press.

Ferguson, J. (1996). *The Anti-Politics Machine: Development, Depoliticisation and Bureaucratic Power in the Third World.* Cambridge: Cambridge University.

Ferns, H. S. (1967). *Argentina.* London: Ernest Benn.

*Finer, S.* E. (1997). *The History of Government from the Earliest Times: The Intermediate Ages.* Oxford: Oxford University Press.

Fischer, D. H. (1996). *The Great Wave: Price Revolutions and the Rhythm of History.* Oxford: Oxford University Press.

Fisher, J. (2000). The interdepartmental committee on Eastern unrest and British responses to Bolshevik and other intrigues against the Empire during the 1920s. *Journal of Asian History* 34(1): 1–34.

Fisher, J. (2009). A call to action: The Committee on British Communities Abroad, 1919–20. *Canadian Journal of History* 44(2): 261–286.

Floud, R. (1981). Britain 1860–1914: A survey. In: R. C. Floud & D. N. McCloskey (Eds.), *The Economic History of Britain Since 1700.* Vol. 2: *1860 to the 1970s.* Cambridge: Cambridge University Press; pp. 1–26.

Flynn, D., & Giráldez, A. (1995). Born with a 'silver spoon': The origin of world trade in 1571. *Journal of World History* 6(2): 201–222.

Fores, M. (1981). The Myth of a British Industrial Revolution. *History* 66(217): 181–198.

Foster, J. (1974). *Class Struggle and the Industrial Revolution.* London: Weidenfeld.

Foster, J. (2005). State Monopoly Capitalism Alive, Vulnerable and Dangerous. Available at: http://www.politicalaffairs.net/state-monopoly-capitalism-alive-vulnerable-and-dangerous (accessed 12 December 2012).

Frank, A. (1967). *Capitalism and Underdevelopment in Latin America*. New York: Monthly Review Press.

Frank, A. (1972). The development of underdevelopment. In: J. Cockcroft, A. Frank, & D. Johnson (Eds.) *Dependence and Underdevelopment: Latin America's Political Economy*. New York: Doubleday Anchor Books.

Frank, A. G. (1990a). A theoretical introduction to 5,000 years of world system history. *Review* 13: 155–248.

Frank, A. G. (1990b). The thirteenth-century world system: A review essay. *Journal of World History* 1: 249–256.

Frank, A. G. (1998). *Reorient: Global Economy in the Asian Age*. Berkeley, CA: University of California Press.

Frank, A. G. (2001). Review of 'The Great Divergence: Europe, China, and The Making of the Modern World Economy' by Kenneth Pomeranz, Princeton: Princeton University Press 2000. *Journal of Asian Studies* 60(1): 180–182.

Frank, A. G., & Gills, B. K. (Eds.). (1993). *The World System: Five Hundred Years or Five Thousand?* London: Routledge.

Frank, A. G., & Gills, B. K. (2000). The Five Thousand Year World System in Theory and Praxis. In: R. A. Denemark (Ed.), *World-System History: the Social Science of Long-Term Change*. New York: Routledge; pp. 3–23.

Frey, M. (2011). Dutch elites and the end of empire. In: M. Frey & J. Dülffer (Eds.), *Elites and Decolonization in the Twentieth Century*. Basingstoke: Palgrave Macmillan; pp. 56–73.

Friedman, T. L. (2005). *The World is Flat: A Brief History of the Twenty-First Century*. New York: Farrar, Straus and Giroux.

Friedmann, J. (1986). The world city hypothesis. *Development and Change* 17(1): 69–83.

Fromkin, D. (1989). *A Peace to End All Peace: The Fall of the Ottoman Empire and the Creation of the Modern Middle East, 1918–1922*. London: Owl Books.

Furet, F. (1971). Le catéchisme de la révolution française. *Annales* 26: 255–289.

Furniss, E. (1965 [1920]). *The Position of the Laborer in a System of Nationalism*. New York: Kelley.

Gallo, A. (2006). Argentina–Australia: Growth and Divergence in the Twentieth Century. Paper delivered at the XIVth International Economic History Congress Helsinki, Finland, 21–25 August 2006.

Geary, D. (1981). *European Labour Protest, 1848–1939*. London: Croom Helm.

Geiss, J. P. (1979). Peking under the Ming, 1368–1644. PhD dissertation, Princeton University, Princeton, NJ.

Gellner, E. (1983). *Nations and Nationalism*. Ithaca, NY: Cornell University Press.
Gendzier, I. (1985). *Managing Social Change*. Boulder, CO: Westview.
Germain, R. D. (1996). The worlds of finance: A Braudelian perspective on IPE. *European Journal of International Relations* 2(2): 201–230.
Gerschenkron, A. (1962). *Economic Backwardness in Historical Perspective*. Cambridge, MA: Harvard University Press.
Getty, J. A. (2000). The future did not work. *Atlantic Monthly* March: 113–116.
Ghosh, A. (2008). *Sea of Poppies*. New York: Farrar, Straus and Giroux.
Gilbert, M., & Gott, R. (1963). *The Appeasers*. Boston, MA: Houghton Mifflin.
Gill, S. (1990). Two concepts of international political economy. *Review of International Studies* 16(4): 369–381.
Gillis, J. R. (1983). *The Development of European Society, 1770–1870*. Boston: Houghton Mifflin.
Goldstein, R. (1983). *Political Repression in Nineteenth Century Europe*. London: Croom Helm.
Goldstone, J. A. (1988). East and West in the seventeenth century: Political crises in Stuart England, Ottoman Turkey and Ming China. *Comparative Studies in Society and History* 30(1): 103–142.
Goldstone, J. (1991). *Revolution and Rebellion in the Early Modern World*. Berkeley, CA: University of California Press.
Goldstone, J. (1998). The problem of the 'Early Modern' world. *Journal of the Economic and Social History of the Orient* 41(3): 249–284.
Goldstone, J. (2002). Efflorescences and economic growth in world history: Rethinking the "Rise of the West" and the Industrial Revolution. *Journal of World History* 13(2): 323–389.
Goody, J. (1996). *The East in the West*. Cambridge: Cambridge University Press.
Gordon, R., & Meggitt, M. (1985). The decline of the Kipas. In: R. Gordon & M. Meggitt (Eds.), *Law and Order in the New Guinea Highlands: Encounters with Enga*. Hanover, NH: University Press of New England; pp. 39–70
Gosnell, H. F. (1930). *Why Europe Votes*. Chicago, IL: University of Chicago Press.
Goswami, O. (1997). Jute mill strikes of 1929 and 1937 seen through other's eyes. *Modern Asian Studies* 21(3): 547–583.
Gouldner, A. W. (1977–1978). Stalinism: A study of internal colonialism. *Telos* 34: 5–48.
Gourevitch, P. (1978). Review: The International System and Regime

Formation: A Critical Review of Anderson and Wallerstein. *Comparative Politics* 10(3): 419–438.

Graf, A. (1911). *L'Anglomania e l'influsso inglese in Italia nel secolo XVIII*. Turin: E. Loescher.

Gramsci, A. (1957). *The Modern Prince and Other Writings*. London: Lawrence and Wishart.

Gramsci, A. (1971). The intellectuals. In: Q. Hoare & G. N. Smith (trans. and Eds.), *Selections from the Prison Notebooks*. New York: International Publishers; pp. 3–23.

Guha, R., & Spivak, G. (Eds.). (1988). *Selected Subaltern Studies*. New York: Oxford University Press.

Gugler, J. (2004). Introduction. In: J. Gugler (Ed.), *World Cities beyond the West: Globalization, Development, and Inequality*. Cambridge: Cambridge University Press; pp. 1–26.

Gulick, C. A. (1940). *Austria from Hapsburg to Hitler*, Vol. II. Berkeley, CA: University of California Press.

Gupta, A. (1998). *Postcolonial Developments: Agriculture in the Making of Modern India* Durham, NC: Duke University Press.

Gustafsson, B., & Johansson, M. (1999). In search of smoking guns: What makes income inequality vary over time in different countries? *American Sociological Review* 64: 585–605.

Haimson, L. (1964). The problem of social stability in urban Russia, 1905–1917. *Slavic Review* 23: 619–642.

Halperin, S. (1997). *In the Mirror of the Third World: Capitalist Development in Modern Europe*. Ithaca, NY: Cornell University Press.

Halperin, S. (2004). *War and Social Change in Modern Europe: The Great Transformation Revisited*. Cambridge: Cambridge University Press.

Hammond, E. (1968). *An Analysis of Regional Economic and Social Statistics*. Durham: University Of Durham, Rowntree Research Unit.

Hannerz, U. (1996). *Transnational Connections*. London: Routledge.

Hansen, M. H. (2000). Introduction. The concepts of city-state and city-state culture. In: M. H. Hansen (Ed.), *A Comparative Study of Six City-State Cultures. An Investigation Conducted by the Copenhagen Polis Centre. Historisk-filosofiske Skrifter 27*. Copenhagen: Royal Danish Academy of Sciences and Letters.

Hao, Y. P. (1970). *The Comprador in Nineteenth Century China: Bridge Between East and West*. Cambridge, MA: Harvard University Press.

Harley, C. K. (1982). British industrialization before 1841: Evidence of slower growth during the Industrial Revolution. *Journal of Economic History* 42(2): 267–290.

Hardach, G. (1977). *The First World War, 1914–1918*. Berkeley, CA: University of California Press.

Harman, C. (1988). *The Fire Next Time: 1968 and After*. London: Bookmarks.

Harris, N. (1986). *The End of the Third World. Newly Industrializing Countries and the Decline of an Ideology*. Harmondsworth: Penguin Books.

Havinden, M. A. (1962). Agricultural progress in open-field Oxfordshire. *Agricultural History Review* 9: 73–83.

Hay, R., Jr. (1977). Patterns of urbanisation and socio-economic development in the third world: An overview. In: J. Abu-Lughod & R. Hay, Jr. (Eds.), *Third World Urbanization*. London: Methuen; pp. 71–101.

Hechter, M. (1975). *Internal Colonialism. The Celtic Fringe in British National Development, 1536–1966*. Berkeley, CA: University of California Press.

Hekscher, Eli (1955). *Mercantilism*, 2nd edn. London: George Allen and Unwin.

Heckscher, E. F. (1964). *The Continental System*. Gloucester, MA: Peter Smith.

Heksher, E. (1955). *Mercantilism*, 2nd edn. London: George Allen and Unwin.

Held, A., McGrew, A., Goldblatt, D., & Perraton, J. (1999). *Global Transformations. Politics, Economics and Culture*. Stanford, CA: Stanford University Press.

Held, D. (1991). *Democracy and the Global Order*. Cambridge: Polity.

Helleiner, E. (1990). Fernand Braudel and international political economy. *International Studies Notes* 15(3): 73–78.

Henderson, W. O. (1958). *The State and the Industrial Revolution in Prussia: 1740–1870*. Liverpool: Liverpool University Press.

Herlihy, D. (1997). *The Black Death and the Transformation of the West*. Cambridge: MA: Harvard University Press.

Herr, R. (1977). Spain. In: D. Spring (Ed.), *European Landed Elites in the Nineteenth Century*. Baltimore, OH: Johns Hopkins University Press.

Hertslet, Sir E. (1891). *The Map of Europe by Treaty*. London: Harrison and Sons.

Hespanha, A. M. (1994). Cities and the state in Portugal. In: C. Tilly & W. P. Blockmans, (Eds.), *Cities and the Rise of States in Europe A.D. 1000 to 1800*. Boulder, CO: Westview; pp. 168–183.

Hettne, B. (1990). *Development Theory and the Three Worlds*. Harlow: Longman.

Hettne, B. (1995). *Development Theory and the Three Worlds*, 2nd edn. Chelmsford: Longman.

Hexter, J. H. (1961). The myth of the middle class in Tudor England. Reprinted in *Reappraisals in History*. Chicago, IL: University of Chicago Press; pp. 71–116.

Hill, C. (1940). *The English Revolution of 1640*. London: Lawrence and Wishart.

Hill, C. (1967). *Reformation to Industrial Revolution, A Social and Economic History of Britain, 1530–1780*. London: Weidenfeld and Nicholson.

Hill, C. (1981). A bourgeois revolution? In: J. G. A. Pocock (Ed.), *Three British Revolutions: 1641, 1688, 1776*. Princeton, NJ: Princeton University Press; pp. 109–139.

Hilton, R. (1969). *The Decline of Serfdom in Medieval England*. New York: St. Martin's Press.

Hirschman, A. (1958). *The Strategy of Economic Development*. New Haven, CT: Yale University Press.

Hirschman, A. (1981). The rise and decline of development economics. In: A. O. Hirschman (Ed.), *Essays in Trespassing*. Cambridge: Cambridge University Press; pp. 1–24.

Hirst, P., & Thompson, G. (1996). *Globalization in Question*. Cambridge: Polity Press.

Hobsbawm, E. (1962). *The Age of Revolution 1789–1848*. New York: Mentor.

Hobsbawm, E. (1968). *Industry and Empire*. London: Penguin.

Hobsbawm, E. J. (1975). *The Age of Capital 1848 1875*. Great Britain: Weidenfeld and Nicolson.

Hobsbawm, E. (1990). *Nations and Nationalism since 1780: Programme, Myth, Reality*. Cambridge: Cambridge University Press.

Hobsbawm, E. (1996). *The Age of Extremes*. New York: Pantheon Books.

Hobson, J. A. (1902). *Imperialism: A Study*. London: Allen and Unwin.

Hodgson, M. G. S. (1993). *Rethinking World History: Essays on Europe, Islam, and World History*. Cambridge: Cambridge University Press.

Hoffman, J. (2004). *Citizenship Beyond the State*. London: Sage.

Hoffmann, S. (1961). The Effects of World War II on French Society and Politics. *French Historical Studies* 2: 28–63.

Hoffman, W. G. (1955). *British Industry, 1700–1950* (trans. W. O. Henderson & W. H. Chaloner). Oxford: Basil Blackwell.

Holland, S. (1976). *Capital versus the Regions*. London: Macmillan.

Hoogvelt, A. (1997). *Globalisation and the Post Colonial World: The New Political Economy of Development*. London: McMillan.

Hough, R., Kelley, J., Miller, S., Derossier, R., Mann, F. L., & Seligson, M. A. (1982). *Land and Labor in Guatemala: An Assessment*. Guatemala City: Ediciones Papiro.

Howard, M. (1961). *The Franco-Prussian War.* London: Rupert Hart-Davis.

Huang, P. C. (1990). *The Peasant Family and Rural Development in the Yangzi Delta, 1350–1988*. Stanford, CA: Stanford University Press.

Huang, P. C. C. (2002). Development or involution in eighteenth-century Britain and China? A review of Kenneth Pomerantz's *The Great Divergence: China, Europe, and the Making of the Modern World Economy. Journal of Asian Studies* 61(2): 501–528.

Hubbard, G. E. (1935). *Eastern Industrialization and Its Effect on the West.* London: Oxford University Press.

Hufton, O. (1974). *The Poor of Eighteenth-Century France: 1750–1789.* Oxford: Clarendon Press.

Innes, R. L. (1980). The Door Ajar: Japan's Foreign Trade in the Seventeenth Century. PhD dissertation. Ann Arbor, MI: University of Michigan.

Jacobs, J. (1969). *The Economy of Cities.* New York: Random House.

Jásci, O. (1929). *Dissolution of the Hapsburg Monarchy.* Chicago, IL: University of Chicago.

Jeffrey, K. (1984). *The British Army and the Crisis of Empire 1918–1922.* Manchester: Manchester University Press.

Jevons, W. S. (1931). *The Theory of Political Economy*, 4th edn. London: Macmillan.

Jewsiewicki, B. (1989). African historical studies academic knowledge as 'usable past' and radical scholarship. *African Studies Review* 32(3): 1–76.

Joad, C. E. M. (1951). What I still believe. *The New Statesman and Nation* 19: 557–558.

Johnson, A. A. (1979). *The Disappearance of the Small Landowner.* Fairfield, NY: A. M. Kelly.

Jones, E. L. (1974). *Agriculture and the Industrial Revolution.* New York: Wiley.

Jörberg, L. (1973). The Industrial Revolution in the Nordic countries. In: C. M. Cipolla (Ed.), *The Fontana Economic History of Europe. The Emergence of Industrial Societies – 2.* Glasgow: William Collins.

Kasaba, R., Çağlar, K., & Tabak, F. (1986). Eastern Mediterranean port cities and their bourgeoisies: Merchants, political projects, and nation-states. *Review* X(1): 121–135.

Katsiaficas, G. (1987). *The Imagination of the New Left: A Global Analysis of 1968.* Boston, MA: South End Press.

Katz, C. J. (1993). Karl Marx on the transition from feudalism to capitalism. *Theory and Society* 22(3): 363–389.

Kay, C. (1989). *Latin American Theories of Development and Underdevelopment.* London: Routledge.

Keating, M. (1998). *The New Regionalism in Western Europe: Territorial Restructuring and Political Change*. Cheltenham: Edward Elgar.

Keating, M. (2001). Rethinking the region: Culture, institutions and economic development in Catalonia and Galicia. *European Urban and Regional Studies* 8: 217–234.

Kellenbenz, H. (1976). *The Rise of the European Economy: An Economic History of Continental Europe from the Fifteenth to the Eighteenth Century*. London: Weidenfeld and Nicolson.

Kennedy, D. (1987). *Islands of White: Settler Society and Culture in Kenya and Southern Rhodesia, 1890–1939*. Durham: Duke University Press.

Kennedy, P. (1980). *The Rise of the Anglo-German Antagonism, 1860–1914*. London: Allen & Unwin.

Kennedy, P. (1987). *The Rise and Fall of the Great Powers: Economic and Military Conflict from 1500–2000*. New York: Vintage Books.

Khanna, P. (2009). The next big thing: Neomedievalism. *Foreign Policy*. Available at: http://www.foreignpolicy.com/articles/2009/04/15/the_next_big_thing_neomedievalism (accessed 12 December 2012).

Kindleberger, C. (1964). *Economic Growth in France and Britain, 1851–1950*. Cambridge, MA: Harvard University Press.

Kloosterman, R. C. (2001). Clustering of economic activities in polycentric urban regions: the case of the Randstad. *Urban Studies* 38: 717–732.

Knapp, G. J. (1986). Coffee for cash: The Dutch East India Company and the expansion of coffee cultivation in Java, Ambon and Ceylon, 1700–1730. In: J. van Goor (Ed.), *Trading Companies in Asia, 1600–1830*. Utrecht: Hes; pp. 33–49.

Knight, G. A., & Cavusgil, S. T. (1996). The born global firm: A challenge to traditional internationalization theory. *Advances in International Marketing* 8: 11–26.

Koebner, R., & Schmidt, H. D. (1965). *Imperialism. The Story and Significance of a Political Word, 1840–1960*. Cambridge: Cambridge University Press.

Kohli, A. (1987). *The State and Poverty in India: The Politics of Reform*. Cambridge: Cambridge University Press.

Kohn, H. (1946). *Prophets and People*. London: Macmillan.

Kohn, H. (1955). *Nationalism: Its Meaning and History*. Princeton, NJ: Princeton University Press.

Komlos, J. (1998). The New World's contribution to food consumption during the Industrial Revolution. *Journal of European Economic* History 27(1): 67–84.

Komlos, J. (2000). The Industrial Revolution as the escape from the Malthusian trap, *Journal of European Economic History* 29(2–3): 307–331.

Kooiman, D. (1980). Bombay communists and the 1924 textile strike. *Economic and Political Weekly* 15(29): 1223–1236.

Koselleck, R. (1985). *Futures Past: On the Semantics of Historical Time* (trans. K. Tribe). Cambridge, MA: MIT Press.

Kriedte, P. (1983). *Peasants, Landlords, and Merchant Capitalists. Europe and the World Economy, 1500–1800*. Cambridge: Cambridge University Press.

*Kroniek* [Chronicle]. (1916–1939). Oostkust van Sumatra-Instituut. Amsterdam: J. H. de Bussy.

Kussmaul, A. S. (1981). *Servants in Husbandry in Early Modern England.* Cambridge: Cambridge University Press.

Kuznets, S. (1957). Quantitative aspects of the economic growth of nations – II. Distribution of national product and labor force. *Economic Development and Cultural Change* 5(4 Suppl.): 1–111.

Kuznets, S. (1964). *Postwar Economic Growth.* Cambridge, MA: Belknap Press.

Kuznets, S. (1971). *Economic Growth of Nations: Total Output and Production Statistics*. Cambridge, MA: Harvard University Press.

Lachmann, R. (1990). Class formation without class struggle: An elite conflict theory of the transition to capitalism. *American Sociological Review* 55: 398–414.

Laclau, E., & Mouffe, C. (1985). *Hegemony and Socialist Strategy*. London: Verso.

Ladejinsky, W. (1959). Agrarian revolution in Japan. *Foreign Affairs* 38: 95–109.

Laidlaw, Z. (2005). *Colonial Connections, 1815–45: Patronage, the Information Revolution, and Colonial Government.* Manchester: Manchester University Press.

Lal, D. (1983). *The Poverty of Development Economics*. London: Institute of Economic Affairs.

Lal, D. (2003). In defense of empires. *Economic Affairs* 23: 14–19.

Lampe, J. R., & Jackson M. R. (1982). *Balkan Economic History, 1550–1950*. Bloomington, IN: Indiana University Press.

Landes, D. S. (1954). Social attitudes, entrepreneurship and economic development: A comment. *Explorations in Entrepreneurial History* 6(4). 245–272.

Landes, D. S. (1958). *Bankers and Pashas: International Finance and Economic Imperialism in Egypt*. Cambridge, MA: Harvard University Press.

Landes, D. (1969). *The Unbound Prometheus.* Cambridge: Cambridge University Press.

Landy, P. (1961). Reforms in Yugoslavia. *Problems of Communism* Nov.–Dec.

Lane, D. (1971). *The End of Inequality? Social Stratification under State Socialism*. Harmondsworth: Penguin.

Langer, W. L. (1931). *European Alliances and Alignments, 1871–1890*. New York: Alfred A. Knopf.

Larrain, J. (1989). *Theories of Development*. Cambridge: Polity Press.

Latham, A. J. H. (1978). *The International Economy and the Underdeveloped World, 1865–1914*. London: Croom Helm.

Latour, B. (1996). On interobjectivity. *Mind, Culture and Activity* 3(4): 228–245.

Laxer, G., & Halperin, S. (2003). *Global Civil Society and Its Limits* (co-edited with G. Laxer). London: Palgrave/Macmillan.

von Lazar, J. (1966). Class Struggle and Socialist Construction: the Hungarian Paradox. *Slavic Review* 25.

Le Roy Ladurie, E. (1976). *The Peasants of Languedoc* (trans. John Day). Urbana, IL: University of Illinois Press.

Leeson, P. F. (1988). Development economics and the study of development. In: P. F. Leeson & M. M. Minogue (Eds.), *Perspectives on Development: Cross-disciplinary Themes in Development Studies*. Manchester: Manchester University Press; pp. 1–55.

Lefebvre, G. (1974). *The Coming of the French Revolution* (trans. R. R. Palmer). Princeton, NJ: Princeton University Press.

Lefebvre, H. (1991 [1976]). *The Production of Space*. Cambridge, MA: Blackwell.

Lefebvre, H. (2003). Space and the state. In: N. Brenner, B. Jessop, M. Jones, & G. MacLeod (Eds.), *State/Space: A Reader*. London: Blackwell; pp. 84–100.

Lenin, V. I. (1917). *The Agrarian Programme of Social-Democracy in the First Russian Revolution, 1905–1907*. Petrograd: *Zhizn i Znaniye*.

Lenin, V. I. (1939). *Imperialism*. New York: International Publishers.

Lenin, V. I. (1973 [1917–1918]). Introduction. In: I. N. Bukharin (Ed.), *Imperialism and World Economy*. New York: Monthly Review Press.

Lester, A. (2006). Imperial circuits and networks: Geographies of the British Empire. *History Compass* 4(1): 124–141.

Lévy, M. (1951–1952). *Historie Èconomique Et Sociale De La France Depuis 1848*. Paris: les Cours de Droit, Institut d'Erudes Politiques.

Lewis, A. (1972). The historical record of international capital movements to 1913. In: J. H. Dunning (Ed.), *International Investment: Selected Readings*. Harmondsworth: Penguin.

Lewis, A. (1978a). *Growth and Fluctuation, 1870–1913*. London: George Allen & Unwin.
Lewis, A. (1978b). *The Evolution of the International Economic Order*. Princeton, NJ: Princeton University Press.
Lewis, M. W., & Wigen, K. E. (1997). *The Myth of Continents: A Critique of Metageography*. Berkeley, CA: University of California Press.
Leys, C. (1996). *The Rise and Fall of Development Theory*. Bloomington, IN: Indiana University Press.
Li, B. (1998). *Agricultural Development in Jiangnan, 1620–1850*. London: Palgrave Macmillan.
Lie, J. (1993). Visualizing the invisible hand. *Politics & Society* 21: 275–306.
Lieberman, V. (1993a). Local integration and Eurasian analogies: Structuring Southeast Asian history, c. 1350–c. 1830. *Modern Asian Studies* 27(3): 475–572.
Lieberman, V. (1993b). Was the seventeenth century a watershed in Burmese history. In: A. Reid (Ed.), *Southeast Asia in the Early Modern Era: Trade, Power, and Belief*. New York: Cornell University Press; pp. 214–249.
Lieberman, V. (1999a). Introduction: Eurasian variants. In: V. Lieberman (Ed.), *Beyond Binary Histories: Re-Imagining Asia to c. 1830*. Ann Arbor, MI: University of Michigan Press; pp. 1–18.
Lieberman, V. (1999b). Transcending east–west dichotomies: State and culture formation in six ostensibly disparate areas. In: V. Lieberman (Ed.), *Beyond Binary Histories: Re-Imagining Asia to c. 1830*. Ann Arbor, MI: University of Michigan Press; pp. 19–102.
Lieven, D. (1992). *The Aristocracy in Europe, 1815–1914*. New York: Macmillan.
Lilley, S. (2003). BAE System's dirty dealings. *Special to CorpWatch* 11 November 2003. Available at: http://www.corpwatch.org/article.php?id=9008 (accessed 12 December 2012).
Linz, J. (1984). Interests and politics in Spain. In: P. J. Williamson (Ed.), *Varieties of Corporatism*. New York: Cambridge University Press.
Lipski, J. J. (1989–1990). In defense of socialism. *Across Frontiers* Fall/Winter.
Lis, C., & Soly, H. S. (1979). *Poverty and Capitalism in Pre-Industrial Europe*. Sussex: Harvester Press.
Little, D. (1990). Cold war and covert action: The United States and Syria, 1945–1958. *The Middle East Journal* 44(1): 51–75.
Lockman, Z. (1994). Introduction. In: Z. Lockman (Ed.), *Workers and Working Classes in the Middle East: Struggles, Histories, Historiographies*. Albany, NY: State University of New York Press; pp. xi–xxxi.

Loughlin, J. (1985). Regionalism and ethnic nationalism in France. In: Y. Mény & V. Wright (Eds.), *Centre–Periphery Relations in Western Europe*. London: Allen & Unwin.

Luxembourg, R. (1976). *The National Question*. New York: Monthly Review Press.

Macartney, C. A. (1934). *National States and National Minorities*. London: Oxford University Press.

MacLeod, G. (2001). New regionalism reconsidered: Globalization and the remaking of political economic space. *International Journal of Urban and Regional Research* 25, 804–829.

MacLeod, G., & Jones, M. (2001). Renewing the geography of regions. *Environment and Planning* 19: 669–695.

MacShane, D. (1992). *International Labour and the Origins of the Cold War*. Oxford: Clarendon Press.

Maddison, A. (1991). Economic and social conditions in Latin America, 1913–1950. In: M. Urrutia (Ed.), *Long-Term Trends in Latin American Economic Development*. Washington DC: Inter-American Development Bank; pp. 1–22.

Maier, C. (1975). *Recasting Bourgeois Europe*. Princeton, NJ: Princeton University Press.

Maizels, A. (1970). *Growth and Trade*. London: NIESR.

Mann, M. (1986). *The Sources of Social Power: Volume 1, A History of Power from the Beginning to AD 1760*. London: Cambridge University Press.

van Marle, A. (1952). De groep der Europeanen in Nederlands-Indie. *Indonesie* 5(2): 77–121; 5(3): 314–341; 5(5): 481–507.

Marshall, P. J. (1979). Masters and Banians in eighteenth-century Calcutta. In: B. B. King & M. N. Pearson (Eds.), *The Age of Partnership: Europeans in Asia before Dominion*. Honolulu: University Press of Hawaii.

Marshall, P. J. (2000). Presidential Address: Britain and the world in the eighteenth century: III, Britain and India. *Transactions of the Royal Historical Society, Series VI* 10: 1–16.

Martin, R., & Sunley, P. (1997). The post-Keynesian state and the space economy. In: R. Lee & J. Wills (Eds.), *Geographies of Economies*. London: Arnold; pp. 278–289.

Martin, R. (1989). The new economics and politics of regional restructuring: the British experience. In: L. Albrechts, *et al.* (Eds.), *Regional Policy at the Crossroads*. London: Jessica Kingsley; pp. 27–51.

Marwick, A. (1974). *War and Social Change in the Twentieth Century: A Comparative Study of France, Germany, Russia and the United States*. New York: St. Martin's Press.

Marx, K. (1967). *Communist Manifesto*. London: Penguin.

Marx, K. (1990). *Capital: Critique of Political Economy*, Vols. I–III. London: Penguin.

Mason, M. (1997). *Development and Disorder: A History of the Third World since 1945*. Hanover, NH: University Press of New England.

Mathias, P. (1983). *The First Industrial Nation*, 2nd edn. New York: Methuen.

Mayer, A. J. (1967). *Politics and Diplomacy of Peacemaking: Containment and Counterrevolution at Versailles, 1918–1919*. New York: Knopf.

Mayer, A. J. (1969). *The Political Origins of the New Diplomacy, 1917–1918*. New York: H. Fertig.

Mayer, A. (1981). *The Persistence of the Ancien Regime*. New York: Pantheon Books.

Mazower, M. (1998). *The Dark Continent: Europe's Twentieth Century*. London: Penguin.

McMichael, P. (1996a). *Development and Social Change: A Global Perspective*. Thousand Oaks, CA: Pine Forge Press.

McMichael, P. (1996b). Globalization: Myths and Realities. *Rural Sociology* 61: 25–55.

McNeill, W. H. (1974). *The Shape of European History*. London: Oxford University Press.

McNeill, W. (1982). *The Pursuit of Power: Technology, Armed Force, and Society Since A.D. 1000*. Chicago, IL: University of Chicago Press.

McNeill, W. H. (2008), Globalization: Long term process or new era in human affairs? *New Global Studies* 2(1): 1–9.

Meacham, S. (1972). The sense of an impending clash: English working-class unrest before the First World War. *American Historical Review* 77(5): 1343–1364.

Meade, T. (1989). Living Worse and Costing More: Resistance and Riot in Rio de Janeiro, 1890–1917. *Journal of Latin American Studies* 21: 241–266.

Melkote, S. R., & Steeves, H. L. (2001). *Communication for Development in the Third World: Theory and Practice for Empowerment*. New Delhi: Sage.

Mellor, J.W. (1966). *The Economics of Agricultural Development*. Ithaca, NY: Cornell University Press.

Menocal, M. (2002). *The Ornament of the World: How Muslims, Jews and Christians Created a Culture of Tolerance in Medieval Spain*. Boston, MA: Little, Brown.

Meyer, H. C. (1955). *Mitteleuropa in German Thought and Action, 1815–1945*. The Hague: Martinus Nijhoff.

Milanovic, B. (1999). *True World Income Distribution, 1988 and 1993: First Calculation Based on Household Surveys Alone*. Policy Research Working Paper 2244. Washington DC: World Bank. Available at: http://go.worldbank.org/LZJR56KYD0 (accessed 12 December 2012).

Mingay, G. E. (1994). *Land and Society in England, 1750–1980*. London: Longman.

Mintz, S. (1985). *Sweetness and Power: The Place of Sugar in Modern History*. New York: Penguin Books.

Mock, W. (1981). *The Emergence of the welfare state in Britain and Germany, 1850–1950*. London: Taylor & Francis.

Mohanty, C. T. (1995). Epilogue. Colonial legacies, multicultural futures: Relativism, objectivity, and the challenge of otherness. Colonialism and the postcolonial condition. *PMLA* January: 108–118.

Mohanty, C. T., Russo, A., & Torres, L. (Eds.). (1991). *Third World Women and the Politics of Feminism*. Bloomington, IN: Indiana University Press.

Mommsen, W. J. (1980). *Theories of imperialism* (trans. P. S. Falla). New York: Random House.

Moore-Gilbert, B. (1997). *Postcolonial Theory: Contexts, Practices and Politics*. London: Verso.

Mori, G. (1979). The process of industrialization in general and the process of industrialization in Italy. *Journal of European Economic History* 8(1): 61–82.

Morrill, J. S. (1978). French absolutism as limited monarchy. *Historical Journal* 21: 961–972.

Morris, C., & Adelman, I. (1988). *Comparative Patterns of Economic Development, 1850–1914*. Baltimore, MD: Johns Hopkins University.

Morris, R. J. (1979). *Class and Class Consciousness in the Industrial Revolution*. London: Macmillan.

Mouzelis, N. (1988). Sociology of development: Reflections on the present crisis. *Sociology* 22(1): 23–44.

Mowat, R. B. (1927). *A History of European Diplomacy, 1914–1925*. New York: Longman, Green.

Mukund, K. (1999). *The Trading World of the Tamil Merchant: Evolution of Merchant Capitalism in the Coromandel*. Channai: Orient Longman.

Myrdal, G. (1957). *Rich Lands and Poor*. New York: Harper & Row.

Nadal, J. (1973). The failure of the industrial revolution in Spain 1830–1914. In: C. M. Cipolla (Ed.), *The Fontana Economic History of Europe: Emergence of Industrial Societies*, Vol. 2. Glasgow: William Collins.

Nader, L. (1997). The phantom factor: Impact of the cold war on anthropology. In: N. Chomsky (Ed.), *The Cold War and the University: Toward an Intellectual History of the Postwar Years*. New York: New Press; pp. 107–146.

Nell, E. (1977). Population, the price revolution and primitive accumulation. *Peasant Studies* 6: 32–40.

Niceforo, A. (1890). *L'Italia barbara contemporanea*. Palermo: Sandron.

Nitzan, J. (2001). Regimes of differential accumulation: Mergers, stagflation and the logic of globalization. *Review of International Political Economy* 8(2): 226–274.

North, D. C. (1981). *Structure and Change in Economic History*. New York: W. W. Norton.

O'Brien, P. K. (1977). Agriculture and the industrial revolution. *Economic History Review* 30: 166–181.

O'Brien, P. (1982). European economic development: The contribution of the periphery. *Economic History Review* 35(1): 1–18.

O'Brien, P. (2000). The reconstruction, the rehabilitation, and reconfiguration of the British industrial revolution as a conjuncture in global history. *Itinerario* 22(3/4): 117–134.

OECD (Organisation of Economic Cooperation and Development). (2008). *Growing Unequal? Income Distribution and Poverty in OECD Countries*. Paris: OECD Publishing.

O'Hanlon, R. (1988). Recovering the subject: Subaltern studies and histories of resistance in colonial South Asia. *Modern Asian Studies* 22:1, 189–224.

Ogg, F. A. (1930). *Economic Development of Modern Europe*. New York: Macmillan.

Olds, K., & Yeung, H. W. C. (2004). Pathways to global city formation: a view from the developmental city-state of Singapore. *Review of International Political Economy* 11(3): 489–521.

Onley, J. (2004). Britain's native agents in Arabia and Persia in the nineteenth century. *Comparative Studies of South Asia, Africa and the Middle East* 24(1): 129–137.

van Onselen, C. (1982). *Studies in the Social and Economic History of the Witwatersrand 1886–1914*, Vol. I. New York: Longman.

Orr, C. A. (1966). Trade unionism in colonial Africa. *The Journal of Modern African Studies* 4(1): 65–81.

Osterhammel, J. (1997). *Colonialism: A Theoretical Overview*. Princeton, NJ: Markus Wiener.

Owen, E. R. J. (1969). *Cotton and the Egyptian Economy, 1820–1914*. Oxford: Clarendon Press.

Paasi, A. (2003). Region and place: regional identity in question. *Progress in Human Geography* 27: 475–485.

Palmer, A. (1983). *The Penguin Dictionary of Twentieth-Century History, 1900–1982*, 2nd edn. London: Penguin.

Pamuk, S. (2007). The Black Death and the origins of the 'Great Divergence' across Europe, 1300–1600. *European Review of Economic History* 11: 289–317.

Pandey, G. (1988). Peasant revolt and Indian nationalism: The peasant movement in Awadh, 1919–22. In: R. Guha & G. Spivak (Eds.), *Selected Subaltern Studies*. New York: Oxford University Press.

Parker, G. (1996). *The Military Revolution: Military Innovation and the Rise of the West, 1500–1800*. Cambridge: Cambridge University Press.

Parker, G. (2004). *Sovereign City: the City-State through History*. London: Reaktion Books.

Parkin, F. (1969). Class stratification in socialist societies. *British Journal of Sociology* 20: 355–374.

Parry, B. (2004). *Postcolonial Studies: A Materialist Critique*. London: Routledge.

Patel, R., & McMichael, P. (2004). Third worldism and the lineages of global fascism: The regrouping of the global South in the neoliberal era. *Third World Quarterly* 25(1): 231–254.

Perrotta, C. (1997). The preclassical theory of development: Increased consumption raises productivity. *History of Political Economy* 29(2): 295–326.

Petropulos, A. (1968). *Politics and Statecraft in the Kingdom of Greece*. Princeton, NJ: Princeton University Press.

van der Pijl, K. (1998). *Transnational Classes and International Relations*. London: Routledge.

Pirenne, H. (1958). *A History of Europe*. Garden City, New York: Doubleday.

Pirenne, H. (1969). *Economic and Social History of Medieval Europe*. New York: Harcourt, Brace.

Platt, D. C. M. (1980). Dependency in nineteenth century Latin America: An historian objects. *Latin American Research Review* 15(1): 113–130.

Plumb, J. H. (1950). *England in the Eighteenth Century*. Harmondsworth: Penguin.

Polanyi, K. (1944). *The Great Transformation: The Political and Economic Origins of Our Time*. New York Farrar and Rinehart.

Polanyi, K. (1944). *The Great Transformation*. New York: Rinehart.

Pomerantz, K. (2000). *The Great Divergence: China, Europe, and the Making of the Modern World Economy*. Princeton, NJ: Princeton University Press.

Portes, A. (1977a). Urban Latin America: The political condition from above and below. In: J. Abu-Lughod & R. Hay, Jr. (Eds.), *Third World Urbanization*. London: Methuen; pp. 59–70.

Portes, A. (1977b). On the sociology of national development: Theories and issues. In: J. Abu-Lughod & R. Hay, Jr. (Eds.), *Third World Urbanization*. London: Methuen; pp. 108–127.

Portes, A. (1985). Latin American class structures: Their composition and change during the last decades. *Latin American Research Review* 20(3): 7–40.

Portes, A., Castells, M., & Benton, L. (Eds.). (1989). *The Informal Economy: Studies in Advanced and Less Developed Countries*. Baltimore, OH: Johns Hopkins University Press.

Potter, G. (1870). Strikes and lockouts from the workman's point of view. *Contemporary Review* 15: 525–539.

Pounds, J. G. (1959). Economic growth in Germany. In: H. Aitken (Ed.), *The State and Economic Growth*. New York: Social Science Research Council.

Prakash, G. (1994). Subaltern studies as postcolonial criticism. *American Historical Review* December: 1475–1490.

Prakash, G. (1996). *After Colonialism: Imperial Histories and Postcolonial Displacements* Princeton, NJ: Princeton University Press.

Price, R. (1981). *An Economic History of Modern France, 1730–1914*. London: Macmillan.

Pries, L. (Ed.). (2001). *New Transnational Social Spaces*. London: Routledge.

Przeworski, A. (1979). The material bases of consent. *Political Power and Social Theory* 1: 21–63.

Puchala, D. J., & Hopkins, R. F. (1983). International regimes: Lessons from inductive research. In: S. Krasner (Ed.), *International Regimes*. Ithaca, NY: Cornell University Press.

Puhle, H. J. (1986). Lords and peasants in the Kaiserreich. In: R. G. Moeller (Ed.), *Peasants and Lords in Modern Germany*. Boston, MA: Allen & Unwin; pp. 81–109.

Quataert, D. (1986). Machine breaking and the changing carpet industry of western Anatolia, 1860–1908. *Journal of Social History* 13: 473–489.

Quataert, D. (1994). Ottoman workers and the state, 1826–1914. In: Z. Lockman (Ed.), *Workers and Working Classes in the Middle East. Struggles, Histories, Historiographies*. Albany, NY: State University of New York Press; pp. 21–40.

Quataert, D. (1996). The social history of labor in the Ottoman Empire. In: E. Goldberg (Ed.), *The Social History of Labor in the Middle East*. Boulder, CO: Westview Press; pp. 19–36.

Randall, A., & Charlesworth, A. (2000). The moral economy: Riots, markets, and social conflict. In: A. Randall & A. Charlesworth (Eds.), *Markets, Market Culture and Popular Protest in Eighteenth-Century Britain and Ireland.* Liverpool: Liverpool University Press; pp. 1–32.

Ranis, G., & Schultz, T. P. (Eds.). (1988). *The State of Development Economics: Progress and Perspectives.* Oxford: Basil Blackwell.

Rapp, R. (1976). Review of *The Modern World-System: Capitalist Agriculture and the Origins of the European World-Economy in the Sixteenth Century*, by Immanuel Wallerstein. *Journal of Economic History* 36: 801–803.

Ray, R. (1979). *Urban Roots of Indian Nationalism: Pressure Groups and Conflict of Interests in Calcutta City Politics 1875–1939.* New Delhi: Vikas.

Raychaudhuri, T. (1988). *Europe Reconsidered: Perceptions of the West in Nineteenth-Century Bengal.* Delhi: Oxford University Press.

Read, D. (1964). *The English Provinces, 1760–1960.* New York: St. Martin's Press.

Reddy, W. M. (1987). *Money and Liberty in Modern Europe: A Critique of Historical Understanding.* Cambridge: Cambridge University Press.

Reichard, R. W. (1969). *Crippled from Birth: German Social Democracy, 1844–1870.* Ames, IA: State University Press.

Reid, A. (1990). The seventeenth-century crisis in Southeast Asia. *Modern Asian Studies* 24(4): 639–659.

Reid, A. (2000). 'Negeri'. The culture of Malay-speaking city-states of the fifteenth and sixteenth centuries. In: M. H. Hansen (Ed.), *A Comparative Study of Six City-State Cultures. An Investigation Conducted by the Copenhagen Polis Centre. Historisk-filosofiske Skrifter 27.* Copenhagen: Royal Danish Academy of Sciences and Letters; pp. 417–429.

Reynolds, L. G. (1985). *Economic Growth in the Third World, 1850–1980.* New Haven, CT: Yale University Press.

Richards, J. F. (1990). The seventeenth-century crisis in South Asia. *Modern Asian Studies* 24(4): 625–638.

Richter, F. (1938). *Preussiche Wirtschaftspolitik in den Ostprovinzen.* Köningsberg: Ost Europa.

Ricossa, S. (1973). Italy 1920–1970. In: C. M. Cipolla (Ed.), *The Fontana Economic History of Europe: Contemporary Economies* – 1. Glasgow: William Collins.

Robinson, R. (1972). Non-European foundations of European imperialism: Sketch for a theory of collaboration. In: R. Owen & B. Sutcliffe (Eds.), *Studies in the Theory of Imperialism.* London: Longman; pp. 117–142. [Reprinted in Wm. R. Louis (Ed.). (1976). *The Robinson and Gallagher Controversy.* London: New Viewpoints; pp. 128–151.

Robinson, R. (1978). European imperialism and indigenous reactions in British West Africa, 1880–1914. In: H. L. Wesseling (Ed.), *Expansion and Reaction*. Leiden: Leiden University Press; pp. 141–163.

Robinson, R. (1984). Imperial theory and the question of imperialism after empire. *Journal of Imperial and Commonwealth History* 12: 42–54.

Robinson, R. (1986). The excentric idea of imperialism, with or without Empire. In: W. J. Mommsen & J. Osterhammel (Eds.), *Imperialism and After: Continuities and Discontinuities*. London: Allen & Unwin; pp. 267–289.

Robinson, W. I., & Harris, J. (2000). Towards a global ruling class? Globalization and the transnational capitalist class. *Science & Society* 64(1): 11–41.

Robinson, W. I. (2004). *A Theory of Global Capitalism. Production, Class, and State in a Transnational World*. Baltimore, OH: Johns Hopkins University Press.

Rock, D. (1975). *Politics in Argentina, 1890–1930: The Rise and Fall of Radicalism*. London: Cambridge University Press.

Romein, J. (1978). *The Watershed of Two Eras*. Middletown, CT: Wesleyan University Press.

Rostow, W. W. (1960). *The Stages of Economic Growth: A Non-Communist Manifesto*. Cambridge: Cambridge University Press.

Rostow, W. W. (1978). *The World Economy: History and Prospect*. Austin, TX: University of Texas Press.

Royle, T. (1999). *Crimea: The Great Crimean War, 1854–1856*. Boston, MA: Little.

Rubin, E. (1915). *Synsoplevede figure*. Koebenhavn: Gyldendal.

Rudé, G. (1989). *The French Revolution*. London: Weidenfeld and Nicholson.

Rueschemeyer, D., Stephens, E. V., & Stephens, J. D. (1992). *Capitalist Development and Democracy*. Chicago, IL: University of Chicago Press.

Ruhl, M. (1984). Agrarian structure and political stability in Honduras. *Journal of Interamerican Studies and World Affairs* 26: 33–68.

Sabel, C. (1994). Flexible specialisation and the re-emergence of regional economies. In: A. Amin (Ed.), *Post-Fordism: A Reader*. Cambridge, MA: Blackwell; pp. 101–156.

Sachs, I. (1976). *The Discovery of the third World*. Cambridge, MA: MIT Press.

Sahillioglu, H. (1983). The role of international monetary and metal movements in Ottoman monetary history, 1300–1750. In: J. F. Richards (Ed.), *Precious Metals in the Later Medieval and Early Modern World*. Durham, NC: Carolina Academic Press; pp. 269–304.

*Said,* E. (1977). *Orientalism.* London: Penguin.
Said, E. (1993). *Culture and Imperialism.* London: Chatto & Windus.
Sanderson, S. K. (1994). The transition from feudalism to capitalism: The theoretical significance of the Japanese case. *Review* 17(1): 15–55.
Sanderson, S. K. (1995). *Civilizations and World Systems: Studying World-Historical Change.* New York: Sage.
Sarkar, S. (1989). *Modern India 1885–1947.* Hong Kong: MacMillan Press.
Sarton, G. (1957). *Six Wings: Men of Science in the Renaissance.* Bloomington, IN: Indiana University Press.
Sassen, S. (1994). *Cities in a World Economy.* Thousand Oaks, CA: Pine Forge Press.
Sassen, S. (1997). Cities in the global economy. *International Journal of Urban Sciences* 1(1): 11–31.
Sassen, S. (2001). *The Global City: New York, London, Tokyo,* 2nd edn [1st edn 1991]. Princeton, NJ: Princeton University Press.
Sassen, S. (2003). Globalization or denationalization? *Review of International Political Economy* 10(1): 1–22.
Sassen, S. (2007). *A Sociology of Globalization.* London: W.W. Norton.
Sassoon, A. S. (1987). *Gramsci's Politics,* 2nd edn. Minneapolis, MA: University of Minnesota Press.
Sayer, A. (1992). *Methods in Social Science: A Realist Approach,* 2nd edn. London: Routledge.
Schlager, N. (Ed.). (2003). *St. James Encyclopedia of Labor History Worldwide. Major Events in Labor History and Their Impact,* Vol. 2. Detroit, MI: St. James Press/Gale Group/Thomson Learning.
Schmidt, G. (1986). *The Politics and Economics of Appeasement: British Foreign Policy in the 1930s.* London: Berg.
Schneider, J. (1977). Was there a pre-capitalist world-system? *Peasant Studies* 6: 20–28.
Schneider, W. (1963). *Babylon is Everywhere. The City as Man's Fate.* New York: McGraw-Hill.
Schonfield, A. (1965). *Modern Capitalism.* London: Oxford University Press.
Schuman, F. (1942). *Europe on the Eve: The Crises of Diplomacy, 1933–1939.* New York: Alfred A. Knopf.
Schumpeter, J. A. (1976 [1950]). *Capitalism, Socialism and Democracy.* London: Routledge.
Schwartz, H. (1994). *States versus Markets.* Basingstoke: Palgrave/MacMillan.
Sée, H. (1942). *Histoire Économique de la France II: Les Temps modernes, 1789–1914.* Paris: Colin.

Seers, D. (1979). The birth, life, and death of development economics. *Development and Change* 10(4): 707–719.

Sella, D. (1977). The World System and Its Dangers. *Peasant Studies* 6: 29–31.

Sen, A. (1981). Development: Which way now? *Economic Journal* 93: 372, 745–762.

Sen, A. K. (2000). Capital, labour and the state: Eastern and Western India, 1918–1939. *Economic and Political Weekly* 35(28/29): 2564–2568.

Senghaas, D. (1985). *The European Experience: A Historical Critique of Development Theory*. Dover, NH: Berg.

Sherratt, A. (2000). Envisioning global change: A long-term perspective. In: R. A. Denemark, J. Friedman, B. K. Gills, & G. Modelski (Eds.), *World System History: The Social Science of Long-Term Change*. London: Routledge.

Silver, B. J., & Slater, E. (1999). The social origins of world hegemonies. In: G. Arrighi & B. J. Silver (Eds.), *Chaos and Governance in the Modern World System*. Minneapolis, MN: University of Minnesota Press.

Silver, B. J. (2003). *Forces of Labor: Workers' Movements and Globalization Since 1870*. Cambridge: Cambridge University Press.

Simon, D. (2009). From the holocaust to development: Reflections of surviving development pioneers. *Third World Quarterly* 30(5): 849–884.

Simpson, C. (1994). *The Science of Coercion: Communication Research and Psychological Warfare 1945–1960*. New York: Oxford University Press.

Simpson, C. (1999). *Universities and Empire*. New York: The New Press.

Sklair, L., & Robbins, P.T. (2002). Global capitalism and major corporations from the Third World. *Third World Quarterly* 23(1): 81–100.

Slack, P. (1988). *Poverty and Policy in Tudor and Stuart England*. London, Longmans.

Smith, A. (1976 [1776]). In: R. H. Campbell, A. S. Skinner, & W. B. Todd (Eds.), *An Inquiry into the Nature and Causes of the Wealth of Nations*, 2 vols. Oxford: Clarendon.

Smith, D. M. (1971). *Victor Emmanuel, Cavour, and the Risorgimento*. London: Oxford University Press.

Smith, W. C. (1989). *Authoritarianism and the Crisis of the Argentine Political Economy*. Stanford, CT: Stanford University Press.

So, A. Y. (1990). *Social Change and Development*. Newbury Park, CA: Sage.

Soboul, A. (1962). *Précis de l'histoire de la révolution française, 1789–1799*. Paris: Éditions Sociales.

Sohn-Rethel, A. (1978). *Intellectual and Manual Labour*. London: Macmillan.

Sombart, W. (1902). *Der Moderne Kapitalismus*. Berlin: Duncker & Humblot.

Souza, G. B. (1986). *The Survival of Empire: Portuguese Trade and Society in China and the South China Sea, 1630–1754*. Cambridge: Cambridge University Press.

Springborg, R. (1993). The Arab bourgeoisie: a revisionist interpretation. *Arab Studies Quarterly* 15: 13–39.

Steensgard, N. (1990). The seventeenth century crisis and the unity of Eurasian history, *Modern Asian Studies* 24(4): 683–697.

de Ste. Croix, G. E. M. (1981). *The Class Struggle in the Ancient Greek World*. Ithaca, NY: Cornell University Press.

Stern, S. J. (1988). Feudalism, capitalism, and the world-system in the perspective of Latin America and the Caribbean. *American Historical Review* 93: 829–897.

Stoler, A. L. (1989). Rethinking colonial categories: European communities and the boundaries of rule. *Comparative Studies in Society and History* 31(1): 134–161.

Stone, L. (1972). *The Causes of the English Revolution, 1529–1642*. London: Routledge and Kegan Paul.

Stone, L. (1981). The results of the English revolutions of the seventeenth century. In: J. G. A. Pocock (Ed.), *Three British Revolutions: 1641, 1688, 1776*. Princeton, NJ: Princeton University Press.

Stone, N. (1983). *Europe Transformed, 1878–1919*. London: Allen and Unwin.

Strachey, J. (1959). *The End of Empire*. New York: Praeger.

Strange, S. (1994). *States and Markets*, 2nd edn. London: Pinter.

Streeten, P. (1983). Development dichotomies. *World Development* 11(10): 875–889.

Strikwerda, K. (1993). The troubled origins of European economic integration: International iron and steel migration in the era of World War I. *American Historical Review* 98: 1106–1129.

Subrahmanyam, S. (1997). Connected histories: Notes towards a reconfiguration of early modern Eurasia. *Modern Asian Studies* 31(3): 735–762.

Sunkel, O. (1973). Transnational capitalism and national disintegration in Latin America. *Social and Economic Studies* 22: 132–176.

Supple, B. (1973). The state and the industrial revolution: 1700–1914. In: C. Cipolla (Ed.), *The Fontana Economic History of Europe*. London: Collins-Fontana.

Sweezy, P. M. (1970 [1942]). *The Theory of Capitalist Development*. New York: Monthly Review Press.

Sweezy, P. (1976). A critique. In: P. Sweezy, M. Dobb, & C. Hill (Eds.), *The Transition from Feudalism to Capitalism*. London: Verso; pp. 33–56.

Sweezy, P. (1982). Core, periphery, and the crisis of the system. In: H. Alavi & T. Shanin, (Eds.), *Introduction to the Sociology of Developing Societies*. New York: Monthly Review Press; pp. 210–217.

Sweezy, P., Dobb, M., & Hill, C. (Eds.) (1976). *The Transition from Feudalism to Capitalism*. London: Verso.

Swyngedouw, E.(1997). Neither global nor local: 'Glocalization' and the politics of scale. In: K. Cox (Ed.), *Spaces of Globalization: Reasserting the Power of the Local*. New York/London: Guilford/Longman; pp. 137–166.

Taborsky, E. (1961). *Communism in Czechoslovakia*. Princeton, NJ: Princeton University.

Taithe, B. (2001). *Citizenship and Wars: France in Turmoil, 1870–1871*. London: Routledge.

Tampke, J. (1981). Bismarck's social legislation: A genuine breakthrough? In: W. J. Mommsen (Ed.), *The Emergence of the Welfare State in Britain and Germany, 1850–1950*. London: Croom Helm; pp. 71–83.

Tan, T. Y. (2007). Port cities and hinterlands: A comparative study of Singapore and Calcutta. *Political Geography* 26: 851–865.

Taylor, P. J. (2000). World cities and territorial states under conditions of contemporary globalization. *Political Geography* 19(1): 5–32.

Taylor, P. J. (2003). *World City Network: a global analysis*. London: Routledge.

Temin, P. (2004). The labor market of the early Roman Empire. *Journal of Interdisciplinary History* 34(4): 513–538.

Terlouw, K. (2009). Four Centuries of Translocal Development in Three German Peripheries along the Dutch Border. Paper presented at International Development Studies Seminar on Translocal Development in Zeist, Department of Human Geography and Planning, Utrecht University, Netherlands, 30 January.

Thane, P. (1998). Histories of the welfare state. In: W. Lamont (Ed.), *Historical Controversies and Historians*. London: UCL Press.

Thane, P. (1990). Government and society in England and Wales, 1750–1914. *The Cambridge Social History of Britain, 1750–1950*, Vol. 3: *Social Agencies and Institutions*. Cambridge: Cambridge University Press; pp. 1–62.

Theisenhusen, W. C. (1980). Current development patterns and agrarian policy in Latin America. In: I. Volgyes, R. E. Lonsdale, & W. P. Avery (Eds.), *The Process of Rural Transformation: Eastern Europe, Latin America and Australia*. New York: Pergamon Press; pp. 128–139.

Thompson, E. P. (1975). Standards and experiences. In: A. J. Taylor (Ed.), *The Standard of Living in Britain in the Industrial Revolution*. London: Methuen.

Thompson, W. (2004). Introduction: International, 1800–2000. In: N. Schlager (Ed.), *St. James Encyclopedia of Labor History Worldwide*. London: St. James Press; pp. ix–xv.

Thompson, W. R. (1999). The military superiority thesis and the ascendancy of western Eurasia in the world system. *Journal of World History* 10(1): 143–178.

Tilly, C. (1983). Flows of capital and forms of industry in Europe, 1500–1900. *Theory and Society* 12(2): 123–142.

Tilly, C. (1984). *Big Structures, Large Processes, Huge Comparisons*. New York: Russell Sage Foundation.

Tilly, C. (1990). *Coercion, Capital and European States, AD 990–1990*. Oxford: Blackwell.

Tilly, C. (1992). *Coercion, Capital, and the European States, AD 990–1990*, revised edn. Oxford: Basil Blackwell.

Tilly, C. (1994). Entanglements of European cities and states. In: C. Tilly & W. P. Blockmans (Eds.), *Cities and the Rise of States in Europe A.D. 1000 to 1800*. Boulder, CO: Westview; pp. 1–27.

Tilly, C., Tilly, L., & Tilly, R.T. (1975). *The Rebellious Century: 1830–1930*. Cambridge, MA: Harvard University Press

Tipton, F. (1976). *Regional Variations in the Economic Development of Germany During the Nineteenth Century*. Middletown, CN: Wesleyan University Press.

Tipton, F. B., & Aldrich, R. (1987a). *An Economic and Social History of Europe, 1890–1939*. Baltimore: Johns Hopkins University Press.

Tipton, F. B., & Aldritch, R. (1987b). *An Economic and Social History of Europe, From 1939 to the Present*. Baltimore: Johns Hopkins University Press.

Tismeneanu, V. (1989). Democracy, what democracy? *East European Reporter* 4(2).

de Tocqueville, A. (1955). *The Old Regime and the French Revolution*. Garden City, NY: Doubleday.

de Tocqueville, A. (1978). *Souvenirs*. Paris: Gallimard.

Toye, J. (1987). *Dilemmas of Development: Reflections on the Counter-Revolution in Development Theory and Policy*. Oxford: Basil Blackwell.

Trebilcock, C. (1981). *Industrialization of the Continental Powers 1780–1914*. London: Longmans.

Tribe, K. (1981). *Genealogies of Capitalism*. London: Macmillan.

Trumpboar, J. (Ed.). (1989). *How Harvard Rules*. Boston, MA: South End Press.

Uliassi, P. (1971). Government-sponsored research on international and foreign affairs. In: I. L. Horowitz (Ed.), *The Use and Abuse of Social Science*. New Brunswick, NJ: Transaction; pp. 309–342.

UNESCO (2011). *Arab Youth: Civic Engagement and Economic Participation.* Beirut: UNESCO Regional Bureau for Education in the Arab States.

Unger, C. R. (2011). The United States, decolonization, and the education of third world elites. In: J. Düllfer & M. Frey (Eds.), *Elites and Decolonization in the Twentieth Century.* Basingstoke: Palgrave Macmillan; pp. 241–261.

United Nations, Department of Economic and Social Affairs. (1956). *Economic Survey of Latin America.* New York: United Nations.

United Nations, Economic Commission for Asia and the Far East (1950). *Economic Survey of Asia and the Far East.* New York: United Nations.

US Department of Agriculture (1951). *Agricultural Geography of Europe and the Near East.* Washington DC: US Department of Agriculture.

Vatter, S. (1994). Militant journeyman in nineteenth century Damascus: Implications for the Middle Eastern labor history agenda. In: Z. Lockman (Ed.), *Workers and Working Classes in the Middle East: Struggles, Histories, Historiographies.* Albany, NY: State University of New York Press; pp. 1–20.

Vaughan, M. (1991). *Curing Their Ills: Colonial Power and African Illness.* Stanford, CA: Stanford University Press.

De Vries, J. (1976). *The Economy of Europe in an Age of Crisis, 1600–1750.* London: Cambridge University Press.

Wallerstein, I. (1974). *The Modern World System*, Vol. I. New York: Academic Press.

Wallerstein, I. (1990). The French Revolution as a world-historical event. In: F. Fehér (Ed.), *The French Revolution and the Birth of Modernity.* Berkeley, CA: University of California Press; pp. 117–130.

Wallerstein, I. (1991). *Unthinking Social Science: The Limits of Nineteenth-Century Paradigms.* Cambridge: Polity Press.

Wallerstein, I. (1997). *Historical Capitalism.* 2nd edn. London: W. W. Norton.

Wallerstein, I. (2006). The curve of American power. *New Left Review* 40: 77–94.

Warbury, G. R (1981). British rule in the Nile Valley, 1882–1956, and Robinson's theory of collaboration. *Asian and African Studies* 15: 287–322.

Ward, B. (1977). The home of man. In: J. Abu-Lughod & R. Hay, Jr. (Eds.), *Third World Urbanization.* London: Methuen; pp. 54–58.

Warner, M. (1979). *The Crack in the Teacup.* New York: Houghton Mifflin/Clarion Books.

Warriner, D. (1948). *Land and Poverty in the Middle East.* London: Institute of International Affairs.

Washbrook, D. (1998). The global history of 'modernity': A response to a reply. *Journal of the Economic and Social History of the Orient* 41(3): 295–311.

Watts, M. (2001). 1968 and all that. *Progress in Human Geography* 25: 157–188.

Weber, E. (1975). *Peasants into Frenchmen: The Modernization of Rural France, 1870–1914*. Stanford, CA: Stanford University Press.

Weber, M. (1927). *General Economic History*. New York: Greenberg.

Weber, M. (1978). *Economy and Society*, 2 vols (G. Roth & C. Wittich (Eds.)). Berkeley, CA: University of California Press.

Wehler, H. U. (1969). *Bismarck Und Der Imperialismus*. Cologne: Kiepenheuer.

Weiner, M. J. (1981). *English Culture and the Decline of the Industrial Spirit, 1850–1980*. Cambridge: Cambridge University Press.

Wertheimer, M. S. (1924). *The Pan-German League, 1890–1914*. New York: Columbia University Press.

Wesseling, H. L. (1997). *Imperialism and Colonialism*. Westport, CT: Greenwood Press.

Wilkinson, E. P. (1980). *Studies in Chinese Price History*. New York: Garland.

Williamson, J. G. (1965). Regional inequality and the process of national development: A description of the patterns. *Economic and Cultural Change* 13(4): 3–44.

Williamson, T. (2002). *The Transformation of Rural England: Farming and the Landscape, 1700–1870*. Exeter: University of Exeter Press.

Wills, J., Jr. (1993). Review article: Maritime Asia, 1500–1800: The interactive emergence of European domination. *The American Historical Review* 98(1): 83–105.

Wills, J. E., Jr. (2001). *1688: A Global History*. New York: Norton.

Wink, A. (1990). *Al-Hind*, Vol. I. Leiden: E. G. Brill.

Wise, M. L. (1983). *Agrarian Reform in El Salvador: Process and Progress*. Report prepared for the United States Agency for International Development, San Salvador, El Salvador.

Wolf, E. (1982). *Europe and the People without History*. Berkeley, CA: University of California Press.

Wong, R. B. (2003). Integrating China into world economic history. *The Journal of Asian Studies*. An electronic publication of the Association for Asian Studies. Available at: http://www.asian-studies.org/publications/JAS.htm (accessed 12 December 2012).

Wood, E. M. (1999). *The Origins of Capitalism*. New York: Monthly Review Press.

World Bank. (1998). *World Development Indicators 1998*. Available at: http://www-wds.worldbank.org/external/default/WDSContentServer/IW3P/IB/1998/03/01/000009265_3980624090709/Rendered/PDF/multi0page.pdf (accessed 12 December 2012).

World Bank. (1999). *World Development Report 1999*. New York: Oxford University Press.

Wrigley, C. J. (1990). *Lloyd George and the Challenge of Labour*. Hemel Hempstead.

Yeoh, B. S. A. (1999). Global/globalizing cities. *Progress in Human Geography* 23: 607–616.

Young, R. (2001). *Postcolonialism: An Historical Introduction*. Oxford: Blackwell.

Zilliacus, K. (1946). *Mirror of the Past: A History of Secret Diplomacy*. New York: A. A. Wyn.

Zöllner, D. (1982). Germany. In: P. A. Köhler & Hans F. Zacher (Eds.), *The Evolution of Social Insurance, 1881–1981: Studies of Germany, France, Great Britain, Austria and Switzerland*. London: Frances Pinter; pp. 1–92.

# Index